MW01617004

FILMMAKERS SERIES
edited by
Anthony Slide

Cheer up Jerry!
Good luck!
As ever —
Stan Laurel
'62

Ready When You Are,

Mr. Coppola, Mr. Spielberg, Mr. Crowe

Jerry Ziesmer

with an introduction by
Cameron Crowe

Filmmakers Series, No. 69

The Scarecrow Press, Inc.
Lanham, Maryland, and London

SCARECROW PRESS, INC.

Published in the United States of America
by Scarecrow Press, Inc.
A wholly owned subsidiary of
The Rowman & Littlefield Publishing Group, Inc.
4501 Forbes Boulevard, Suite 200, Lanham, Maryland 20706
www.scarecrowpress.com

PO Box 317
Oxford
OX2 9RU, UK

Copyright © 2000 by Jerry Ziesmer
First paperback edition 2003

British Library Cataloguing in Publication Information Available

Library of Congress Cataloguing-in-Publication Data Available

0-8108-4964-X (pbk : alk. paper)

Manufactured in the United States of America.

For Suzanne, she was there at the beginning.

To Francis, Steven, Cameron, and so many more—
I've always been just a kid from Milwaukee
who came to town to help make some
motion pictures. Thank you all for sharing in my
journey and for showing me the way.

Contents

Acknowledgments

I want to thank Francis Coppola for allowing me to share the journey of *Apocalypse Now*. I'm grateful to Steven Spielberg for sharing his early years and to John Huston for sharing his latter years. I'm indebted to Sydney Pollack for beginning my career with *The Way We Were* and to Cameron Crowe for my last film, *Jerry Maguire*, and for writing the introduction to this book.

I wouldn't have had a career if it hadn't been for my assistants, to whom I owe my professional life: Larry Franco, Chris Soldo, Bryan Denegal, Vicki Jackson LeMay, Michael McCloud Thompson, and my special Ziggy, Sig Frohlich.

I'm grateful to the Directors Guild and its Assistant Director Training Program for giving this boy from Milwaukee the opportunity to enter the motion picture industry.

I want to thank the Academy of Motion Picture Arts and Sciences for giving me a professional home and assuring that my education in the art of the cinema will never end.

Three longtime friends added their talents to this manuscript through their prodding and editing: Russ Lunday, Eric Stoltz, and Charles Ziarko. The book wouldn't have been published without their help.

I want to acknowledge my three children—Jillian of the Bunky Club, Tim, our jazz guitarist, and Chris, my beloved tadpole, who first asked me to write the book because he never tired of his dad's stories—for having the strength to accept both the joys and the loneliness of being the children of a filmmaker.

Finally, my thanks go to my wife, Suzanne, who shared the sun and the rain with me, and now shares the memories.

Introduction

by Cameron Crowe

Once a year, viewers worldwide gather around their television sets and watch that glorious tribute the film industry pays to itself. By the end of Oscar night, a handful of emotional writers and directors and stars have blinked back tears as they stared into the spotlight and thanked God, their parents, even their makeup artists. Few ever think to acknowledge the individual who gasses up the engine of moviemaking . . . partially because the job is by nature invisible. Even the job title is suspiciously low-key. But no movie has ever been made, or made well, without the character who toils just outside the spotlight. Hell, he *arranged* for the spotlight, hired the spotlight operator, and even made sure it was trained correctly on the stars. But as a director of three movies, I can now peel back the veil and speak the truth. There would be nothing on movie screens, no teary-eyed Oscar winners, no finished films, good or bad, without the assistant director. And in that world, I have been fortunate enough to work with the best.

Jerry Ziesmer has just been embarrassed by what I've written.

Quietly and with singular good humor, Ziesmer is the King of all assistant directors. On a good night he might tell a classic story or two, but unlike many others, he is a keeper of secrets. Until now. And most powerfully, even after the front-row seat he has held for some of the great films of our time, Ziesmer is a man who understands what it is to be a fan. This book is no cushy tell-all from high atop show-biz hill. It's a love letter to that most precarious art form—cinema.

I was twenty-nine, nervous out of my mind, when I first heard Jerry Ziesmer's name. My first shot at feature directing, *Say Anything . . . ,* would soon begin filming. I had gotten a good break in securing the

xiv   *Ready When You Are*

great cinematographer Laszlo Kovacs to shoot the movie, and I quickly
asked him for a suggestion on hiring an assistant director. Who had impressed him? Kovacs came back with three names. The first one was
Ziesmer, of course. He had graced many sterling pictures, but there was
a palpable myth surrounding his powerful helming of *Apocalypse Now*.
The other two candidates, said Kovacs, were the guys you called if you
couldn't get Ziesmer. In short, I was learning about the two categories
of assistant director: Jerry Ziesmer, and Not Jerry Ziesmer.

"Can we get Jerry?"

The question loomed larger with each passing day. I soon received
another Ziesmerian recommendation from Eric Stoltz, a friend since
he'd first appeared in *Fast Times at Ridgemont High*. In a move that
hasn't happened before or since in the history of Hollywood, Stoltz had
put his own exploding acting career on hold to serve as a low-level production assistant on Ziesmer's then most recent effort, a film by Peter
Bogdanovich. For two months Stoltz had been bringing coffee to other
actors, carrying a production walkie-talkie, and "working with Jerry" as
part of the assistant director team. Poised and ready to dial Ziesmer's
number, I now had no idea what to expect. The world's greatest assistant director was starting to sound like a cross between Martin Luther
King, Jr., and James Bond. "Oh, and something else you should know
about Jerry," Stoltz added cryptically. "He appears in *Apocalypse Now*.
He only has one line, but you'll remember it."

"Which line?"

"Terminate with extreme prejudice."

Ziesmer was all business on the phone. Send the script, he said, and
he would come in for a meeting. I did, and he did. By this time in his
career, with films like *Apocalypse Now* still ringing in his ears, Ziesmer
had become more selective. He was all business, but the twinkle was unmistakable. A true love of movies, the *making* of movies, was quite obviously still in his blood. He quizzed me on the way I like to shoot. I
promptly inflated a bag of wind on my directing methods, but I had no
experience, no real methods, just dreams. Grinning respectfully, a little
slyly, he listened. He knew. He soon came aboard *Say Anything . . .* , in
part because it was a small film, but largely because it was shooting in
town. Ziesmer is a family patriot, dedicated to his brood, and staying
near them in Los Angeles was a big draw. The values and soul of a movie
are as important to him as the participants, and he liked the script. It
probably didn't hurt that I was a neophyte who so clearly needed him.
Plus, I begged a lot.

Our work sessions were invaluable. We discussed the rhythm of a movie. How a director should pace himself. How a director stays on schedule. The choreography involved in staying sharp during the long, long hours. Previous to these sessions with Jerry Ziesmer, the advice I'd gotten from other directors had been of the glib two-sentence variety. You know the kind—"Directing is about clean socks and good coffee!" Bullshit. Suddenly, here was the truth about the job. It was an intense, mathematical, physical, and creative horse race. A job requiring unwavering vigilance, utter psychological warfare, and impossible belief in yourself. You will not sleep. You will dream the movie. And sometimes, even after you've made it through all those minefields, the movie will *still* suck.

Before long, Ziesmer had alchemized *Say Anything . . .* into a shooting schedule. Based on our conversations about each scene, after considering logistics and actor availabilities, my movie had become a six-paneled notebook in Jerry's hands. Ziesmer was extra careful to arrange the first two weeks of shooting so that the studio could soon see a few flashy scenes in dailies and also be pacified that their director would pull the job off. Soon he had named each scene with a phrase like "Lloyd will die for her," and that is how we would refer to the pieces of our filmic puzzle. Jerry had quickly become as invested in the film as I was. Assistant directing, I was learning, was a dizzying task of scheduling and problem solving, with more egos to placate than a big-city mayor (which, come to think of it, is close to the acting role I gave Ziesmer on the next movie). But Ziesmer was also interested in what a film *said,* and his own human values became part of the film's spirit, too. Together we attacked the never easy job of turning people and words and script pages into a film that, for better or worse, would live longer than either of us.

There is a reason that studio production "suits" are respectful of Jerry, almost begrudgingly so. For a studio, hiring Ziesmer to AD means they'll get their world-class movie. Most likely it will be on schedule and under budget. But they won't be able to push the director around easily. Ziesmer is an assistant director in the truest sense of the word. As I would soon find out on *Say Anything . . .*, there was much that was unpredictable about the whole process. But I could always bet on one thing—the guy alongside me in the trenches was *my guy.*

Ziesmer first brought his wife Suzanne and son Chris into the crew. Then, like a wily coach with a couple of Super Bowl rings at home in the drawer, he artfully added the perfect mix of personality and ability to support me. And even though he was a bigger star than most of the actors, Stoltz came aboard again as a production assistant. It is testimony to Stoltz's loyalty, or at least his love of the inexplicable, that for the next six weeks he patrolled the set with one hand always on the walkie-talkie and brought coffee to actors like John Cusack and Lili Taylor. The spirit of the crew was invaluable. Suddenly my first movie set was about people, family, and even on the toughest nights of shooting there was one more thing I could count on—the unwavering and radiant support of Suzanne Ziesmer. She and Jerry had been high school sweethearts. They still are, quietly disappearing together side by side at the end of each night of filming.

On the set of *Say Anything . . .* , Jerry and I communicated with a discreet set of unspoken signals. With a quiet nod, or a shake of the head, we stayed in touch. An unpredictable actor, a scene not quite falling together . . . where a less skilled assistant director might have let anxiety rule the atmosphere, or made himself a hero, Ziesmer diffused the toughest situations with a dry joke or a calm human solution whispered in my ear. He also joined me in the constant monitoring of the storytelling. Was the good guy becoming too good? The bad guy not bad enough? We finished the film under budget and, remarkably, on time. Oh, and that's also Ziesmer playing a lawyer, bartering for the future of James Court (John Mahoney) toward the end of the movie. It's a nice little scene, and in it you get a real glimpse of Ziesmer's comedic style. It's dry, baby.

"Can we get Jerry?"

The big question returned as I finished the script of my second film, *Singles.* Jerry and I had kept in communication throughout the writing process, and now came the issue of him pulling up stakes and traveling to Seattle, where the film was set. Although Ziesmer had grown even more selective of characters and sequences, and we would be working with a number of inexperienced actors, he listened quietly as I grandly said this movie would be easy. He knew better, of course, and let me know it with his trademark wolfish silence.

Now adding his daughter Jillian to the crew mix, Jerry and I shot for several months in Seattle during the very explosion of that city's now-famous music scene. Filming the club and concert sequences, I was able to glimpse a bit of Ziesmer's myth-shrouded *Apocalypse* mode. It wasn't the Philippines, but it *was* the jungle of Seattle rock, and it was a sight to behold his cheerful wrangling of hundreds of newly pierced and rowdy concertgoers. There was Jerry, shepherding Alice in Chains and

Soundgarden and Pearl Jam through their first experiences on film. Eddie Vedder, then a painfully shy newcomer, quickly bonded with Ziesmer. Their on-set conversations helped Jerry understand the life course of his son Tim, who is now a full-time musician. And Eddie was able to witness big-time professionalism, performed with skill and heart.

Eric Stoltz returned again, this time for an acting cameo. There are few things in life you can depend on, and one of them is Ziesmer's hilariously biting relationship with Stoltz. The two of them throw more barbs at one another than a couple of cranky vaudeville comedians. It is the exception, not the norm. While Ziesmer is loved by actors—he is one—he refreshingly does not try to be their pal. Invariably, they court *him*, but Ziesmer mostly keeps a respectful distance. In calling actors to the set, he asks that the "artists" be brought in. I've yet to see the actor who does not shimmer with pride at the description.

In the middle nineties, Jerry Ziesmer retired. In our conversations it was clear he was finally enjoying an uninterrupted family life with Suzanne and the kids, mentoring others, but mostly living a quieter life atop L.A.'s Mulholland Drive. I was finishing my new script, *Jerry Maguire*, and it wasn't hard to glimpse the big question returning.

"Can we get Jerry?"

Thankfully, I found his retirement to be of the fluid, Frank Sinatra variety. He was still in his prime, uninterested in work for the sake of work, but there was no mistaking the twinkle that remained. We were shooting in town this time, and I knew that would help me in my quest to lure Ziesmer back onto the floor. But *Jerry Maguire* was different from our previous movies—much bigger, with greater responsibilities. Tom Cruise was still mulling over his involvement in the project when I met with Jerry and Suzanne. In tribute to the music that was then a big part of the script, jazz was playing on Ziesmer's home stereo when I arrived. For close to two hours we discussed the care and handling of a huge star. Also, the budget of this movie would be close to three times the size of *Singles*. Once again, I told him it would be easy. Once again, he listened with a potent silence. He knew I needed him, and this time *man, I really did.* He accepted the job. As had now become my norm, Jerry Ziesmer was the first person hired on *Jerry Maguire*.

The filming went on for months, with a nervous studio often peering over our shoulders. This was a long way from *Say Anything* . . . . The final budget was more than fifty million dollars, and the movie was filled with delicate acting moments. Plus, with Tom Cruise now signed

on, this was a film far different from the others. I was no longer the
most important person on the set. If a problem arose with Cruise, the
world's most popular film actor, certainly Cruise would remain and I
would be gone. Again, my unspoken communication with Ziesmer
kept me on track. And, thankfully, Tom Cruise was as deeply invested
in the project as Jerry and me. He loved the script, loved each scene, and
quickly noticed that no creative stone would be unturned by us. This
was a victory of scheduling, as well as directing. As Cruise said
throughout the filming, it was "the best experience I've ever had on a
movie." Never did he glimpse the dark side of the heavy load Jerry and
I were shouldering. There were many emotionally complicated scenes,
difficult to act on film, and I began to run slightly over schedule. More
than a few times, I walked swiftly past a gaggle of worried "suits,"
leaving Ziesmer to protect me while I kept my eye on the ball . . . the
creative vision of the movie.

Leaving the set of *Jerry Maguire* one afternoon, I overheard Jerry
soothing the anxiety of an inexperienced moneyman. "This is how it always works on the great ones," he said calmly. I will never forget it. He
had said those words loud enough for me to hear them too, simulta-
neously inspiring me and silencing the worried man in front of him.
That is why he is the King.

The movie turned out to be my greatest success as a director. And
somewhere along the way of our most difficult cinematic adventure, I
had truly fallen in love with the job. In the months that followed, we
returned to our respective corners to write. Me, a script. Jerry, this book.
His voice and style run through every page. The story of his remarkable
journey is as inspiring as it is a ground-zero glimpse of real movie-
making. And there is no greater compliment you can pay a writer than
to say his book sounds like *him*. This book is pure Ziesmer.

There are magical performances in *Jerry Maguire*, and Jerry Ziesmer's
own is on display after Cuba Gooding, Jr., as Rod Tidwell, has been
knocked out on *Monday Night Football*. There is Jerry, playing the team
trainer, yelling into the wounded warrior's face. "Can you feel your legs,
Rod?" It is one of my greatest delights that when Rod Tidwell comes
back to life, the first face he sees is Jerry Ziesmer's. It is a metaphor for
the relationship between a director and his assistant director, or at least
mine. More than a few times, I've blinked back to life only to see the
face of Ziesmer cheering me on. And like Tidwell, he has allowed me to
dance. I didn't used to be a dancer, but I am now, thanks to Jerry. I hope
you cherish this book as much as I do.

Tom Cruise and *Jerry Maguire*

Tom Cruise kissed my wife. It wasn't anything Nicole Kidman or I had to worry about, because before Tom Cruise was born, Suzanne and I had graduated from Rufus King High School in Milwaukee, Wisconsin, class of 1957. It was Tom's last day on *Jerry Maguire*, and Suzanne wanted a photo with TC. The kiss was something a little extra.

We had just finished filming the scene of the Roy Firestone Show with Cuba Gooding, Jr., Regina King, and Renee Zellweger on Stage 8 at the old M-G-M lot, which was then Sony Studios. The crew was moving about two blocks east down the studio's Main Street to the Sydney Poitier Building for Tom Cruise's last shot in *Jerry Maguire*. It was 11:00 on Friday night, and I knew Tom was flying to Europe on Saturday to publicize *Mission: Impossible*. He didn't have to worry about flight schedules; he owned the airplane.

"How long before you're ready?" Tom asked me, as he started out the stage door.

"About a half hour," I said.

Tom didn't believe me and neither did his assistant, Michael Doven; they knew assistant directors were optimistic animals by nature. It would probably be at least an hour.

"We'll be in the Blue Bird. Give us a warning," Tom said, and off they went.

The Blue Bird was Tom's motor home. It was a communication center and penthouse with phones, a TV satellite dish, a full kitchen, living room, bedroom, and bath. It wasn't a home on wheels; it was an estate on wheels. During *Jerry Maguire* I tried never to talk to TC in the Blue Bird because it was like being summoned to the Oval Office; you were in awe. As soon as you entered you knew you were in the presence of a world-class superstar whose pictures make nearly a billion dollars a year. That's billion, with a *B*.

I was Cameron Crowe's assistant director on *Jerry Maguire*, as I had been on his other two films. Suzanne worked with me as a production assistant. Most production assistants were young people looking for an entry-level position in the movie business, but for Suzanne it was different. We had one of those storybook romances people love to hear about. Tom had me tell him our story twice during *Jerry Maguire*:

Suzanne and I had been high school sweethearts, even into college, but then had parted and married other people. My first wife and I had gotten married for all the wrong reasons. The happy marriage lasted one year, but the denial of the inevitable divorce lasted for another fifteen years and three children, Chris, Tim, and Jillian.

During those years Suzanne had been teaching fifth and sixth grades at Huntley School in Appleton, Wisconsin. Suzanne's husband had died, and my marriage had ended in divorce. I realized that I needed a lot of help in raising my three children, and she never had children of her own. I decided to take a chance and gave her a call. That was sixteen years ago, and we're still together.

I don't think I entered the Blue Bird more than two or three times during the movie. If Tom wanted a small favor, like to come in an hour later in the morning because he wanted to take his kids to school, he would talk to me on the sound stage. One day about half way through our shooting schedule, Michael Doven asked me to talk with Tom in the Blue Bird.

As I stepped near the door, Tom's driver opened it and smiled at me. I tried to read his face as I entered, but I couldn't.

"Hi, Jer! Come in! Look, is there anything you'd like? Juice? Tea?" Tom offered.

Tom was a bit over the top, too friendly. Michael Doven was the only other person there. I knew the two of them were up to something. Having been an assistant director for thirty years, I can sense when a superstar is about to pounce.

"Sit down. How're you doing?" Tom continued, and gave me the big Tom Cruise smile.

He didn't have to say another word. There's no signal to any assistant director that is clearer than when a superstar asks about your well-being.

The red lights and whistles were going off in my head. I assumed a defensive mental attitude and waited.

"What's the matter?" Tom said, as he and Michael laughed.

Fish would never get caught if they kept their mouths shut, and that's a big part of my philosophy for an assistant director around the really big movie stars.

"Don't you want to sit down?" Tom laughed.

I learned a long time ago to take it all standing up. If they're going to try to rock you, it's best to be on your feet.

"OK, OK," Tom began. "I hate it that you don't trust me!" He and Michael laughed and rocked back and forth in their huge, comfortable club chairs.

I smiled and waited.

"Nic and the kids are in New York, and I want to fly there this weekend to see them," Tom said.

I was a father of three and had been a junior high school teacher, so I knew there was more coming. I kept my mouth shut.

"I'd like to leave at three on Friday afternoon so I could have dinner with my wife and kids in New York Friday night," Tom said. It had finally all come out.

What a character I had sitting in the club chair in front of me. He was smiling at daddy, teacher, and assistant director all at the same time. He wanted to leave three or four hours early on Friday afternoon. How many times have I seen that same big smile for the same reason from actors like Robert Redford, Mel Gibson, and Robert DeNiro and actresses like Barbra Streisand, Michelle Pfeiffer, and Diane Keaton? I'm not even going to think about the old times when I saw the smiles of Robert Mitchum, Rita Hayworth, and John Huston. I go back a ways.

They all wanted something they probably shouldn't have, and they wanted the assistant director's permission to pull it off. Oh, they all had the power, clout, and guts to just do it on their own, but if they got the assistant director to give his permission, it'd be simpler, more fun, and somehow legal in their minds.

Tom had been wonderful on *Jerry Maguire*. He was punctual in the morning, came out of his dressing room as soon as he was called to the set, and his performance was everything Cameron Crowe wanted in *Jerry Maguire*, super sports agent. Except for one practical joke he pulled in the spring, he was being a model superstar.

For Tom to leave four hours early on a Friday could have been a major problem, but we were filming in Dorothy's House on Stage 21 at the studio, and there were a lot of short scenes with Dorothy and her sister to do without him. I didn't think it would be a problem. I'd talk to Cameron, but I knew we'd make it work, and we did. We might have needed a favor from Tom before the end of the picture. I tried never to say no to Tom Cruise.

There was only one person who consistently said no! to Tom and got away with it every time—his three-year-old son. It was his favorite word.
"Do you want something to eat?" Tom asked.
"No!" was his son's determined reply.
"Do you want something to drink?" Tom asked.
"No!"
"Do you want to go to the moon?"
"No!"
"Do you want to go to Philadelphia?"
"No!"
Soon Tom would be doubled over with laughter at his three-year-old son. He and Nic enjoyed their kids. They were good parents, spent all the time they could with their kids. Tom and Nic tried to take turns doing movies so that one of them would always be with their children. It wasn't easy.

I remember my daughter Jillian was also three years old when Suzanne and I married in December 1982. She alone took a lot of attention, and there was also Tim, age eight, our sports buddy, and Chris, our poet, twelve.

Tim's T-ball team went undefeated at Balboa Park; we never missed a game. Chris had memorized all of the dialogue in *Apocalypse Now*; his questions about the movie never stopped. Jillian and Suzanne were inseparable doing girl things.

Both raising children and making movies demanded a lot of your time. Sometimes you had to choose.

Tom Cruise's practical joke took place in the very early spring when we were filming in the large SMI set, the sports agents' complex. We had more than one hundred extras dressed and groomed to be the mod 1997 sports agents. On the day in question, we were beginning to film the scene of *Jerry Maguire* leaving the SMI office after he was fired.

Michael Doven always radioed to me when he and Tom arrived at the studio, but I hadn't heard from him that morning. I wasn't concerned, because Tom was always prompt.

"Jerry, come in. This is Michael Doven," my walkie-talkie called.

"Yes, Mr. Doven," I answered.

"Jerry, there's a problem. I'd like to talk to you and Cameron privately," Michael continued.

We never had problems with Mr. Doven or Tom.

"What do you mean, Mr. Doven?" I asked, realizing that I was talking on a walkie-talkie and many ears were listening.

"There's a problem. Tom isn't with me," Michael said.

"What?" I was rocked, but not panicked.

"Tom isn't with me. We have a serious personal problem. I have to talk to you and Cameron," Michael said. "I'll come to the set."

"Cameron!" I shouted to him across the SMI Office set. I moved Cameron aside and told what I knew.

"Cameron, look, there might be a problem with Tom," I began. "He isn't here. He has some personal problems."

Cameron looked at me, and the panic set into both of us. Personal problem? Family problem? Separation? Divorce? Oh, my God! Tom and Nic are going to get a divorce!

"What can we do?" Cameron wondered.

I got back on the walkie-talkie.

"Suzanne, go to channel two," I said, to try and get some privacy. "Suzanne? Check to see if Tom is with Michael in his car."

"I can see the car and Michael, but Tom isn't there," she answered.

What are we going to film without Tom? He's in every scene!

Michael Doven hurried onto the sound stage and found Cameron and me huddled together.

"Michael," I said, "please tell us! What's happened? Is it Nic, the kids?"

"It's too personal. Tom's not able to work today, maybe not this week," Michael answered, and his eyes were moist.

Cameron was in shock, and I was entering the lows of manic depression. We had such a wonderful film, so happy, so full of life and now this tragedy that would tear apart the whole production.

I felt Michael Doven was about to collapse in tears. Cameron and I looked at one another, helpless and alone. What could be done?

Suddenly a figure ran onto the set screaming, "April Fools! April Fools!" Of course it was Tom Cruise. He sprinted around the set laughing and yelling and enjoying the fright he had put Cameron and me through. I glanced at Mr. Doven who was smiling and pointing at Tom as if to say, "He planned it all." I nodded and waited for our superstar to stop romping around the set and go to makeup.

• • •

The *Jerry Maguire* crew made their move down to the Sydney Poitier Building and up to the second-floor landing. We were going to use the staircase of that building as the set for the Miami Hotel staircase in *Jerry Maguire*. Tom would come racing down the back stairs with his mission statement on his way to the copy shop. Last shot in the picture for Tom.

The young production assistants were getting the champagne ready in the second-floor hallway. I could hear them on the walkie-talkie telling Suzanne not to wash her face where Tom Cruise had kissed her. Suzanne was back in the production trailer parked near Stage 8. Besides being mom to the other production assistants and the cast and crew, Suzanne took care of the company's communications, walkie-talkies, phones, fax machine, and computers. She was my eyes and ears around the perimeter of the movie company, while I stood at the camera in the center of the storm.

Suzanne told me of the sicknesses, family problems, gripes, and anxieties of the cast and crew. It was very valuable information if you knew your leading actress was fighting with her boyfriend or the key grip's child was ill. If you knew their problems in advance you'd be able to drop the right word or phrase to them at the right time. It all helped to keep the cast and crew happy and able to do their best work.

The main job of an assistant director is to build an environment on the set that allows the actors and director to create and the cameraman and crews to work efficiently. I schedule the movie, I see that the right actors are there for each scene with the right crew and equipment. I am totally committed to helping the director get his or her vision of the script onto the screen.

Each director has different needs. The way I assisted Cameron Crowe was far different from how I assisted Francis Coppola, Steven Spielberg, Brian De Palma, or John Huston. On the two films I did with Steven Spielberg, my primary task was as a logistics manager. For Brian De Palma on *Scarface* I had to be a referee, and for John Huston on Annie I had to be a very attentive son. But with Francis on *Apocalypse Now* it was so much more; we were travelers on a journey within ourselves, an odyssey. That's what made that film so special.

For some directors the assistant director has to be part writer, for others part producer, or casting director, or psychiatrist, or father confessor, but the assistant director is always committed to aiding the director in getting his vision of the film up on the screen. He is the one who assists the director, but he is never the director.

That worked for me. I never wanted to direct, but I wanted to share in making fine motion pictures. I knew I could never be the general, but I could be one hell of a good soldier for him. That's all I ever wanted.

I walked up the back staircase of the Sydney Poitier Building. The crew was lighting; everyone knew it was Tom's last shot. Cameron Crowe was up at the video monitor on the second floor.

I felt it was close enough for Tom's first warning.

"Mr. Doven?" I said into my walkie-talkie. I called him "Mr. Doven." It was a carryover from teaching. The "Mr." got me what I wanted from some of my more challenging students at the junior high and helped me at the studios, too.

"Yes, Jerry," Michael answered.

"Thirty-minute warning, please," I said.

"Thank you. Thirty minutes," Michael repeated.

Everyone on the crew who wasn't already tuned to the production channel on the walkie-talkies, heard me say "thirty minutes." Everyone realized we were very close to the champagne and good-byes.

I made my way up the stairs past the camera and stood near Cameron. I was twenty-five years older than he, but we were a good team. Eric Stoltz, a mutual friend, introduced us when Cameron was going to direct his first picture, *Say Anything* . . . .

When the cameraman started to light the area close to the camera, I knew he was almost ready.

"Mr. Doven?" I radioed.

"Yes, Jerry," he answered.

"Fifteen minutes, please," I said.

"Fifteen," he answered.

I looked at Cameron. We'd almost made it through our third film together. I'd never done more than three movies with any one director. After I got my career established, I wanted to work with different directors. It was more challenging. Now at the end of my career, it was comfortable working with Cameron. He was a young and talented writer who had gotten his chance to direct on *Say Anything* . . . after he had written *Fast Times at Ridgemont High* and *The Wild Life*. I enjoyed

working with a young director before the pressures of Hollywood
formulas could dull his enthusiasm and fresh ideas.

He and his wife, Nancy Wilson, brought the world of Seattle rock
and roll, Pearl Jam, Heart, and *Rolling Stone Magazine* into our lives,
while Suzanne and I contributed our years of film experience to them.
I remembered when I used to be the youngest member of the crew; now
at fifty-seven, I was the oldest. The cast and crew liked my stories of
working with Marlon Brando and Francis Coppola on *Apocalypse Now*.

I always wore blue denim clothes to work on *Jerry Maguire*. Blue
denim pants, a denim shirt, and sandals; that was my uniform. On my
birthday, I arrived on Stage 21 and everyone in the company had come
to work in blue denim clothes and sandals.

"Five minutes, Mr. Doven," I radioed.

"Five, Jerry," Michael said. He would be giving the airplane pilots
their departure time. Tom would want to fly early to be rested for the
publicity tour for *Mission: Impossible*.

Cameron was feeling the emotion of the moment. The last shot.
Tom leaving after all these months. When the filming was completed,
Cameron had the pressure of the postproduction period ahead of him.
Jerry Maguire had to open nationwide on December 13.

"Ready when you are, Mr. Doven," I said into the walkie-talkie. The
crew tensed.

"On our way," Michael answered. I imagined that Tom was already
out of the Blue Bird, into his golf cart, and that Michael Doven was
running to get on before Tom took it out down Main Street to the
Poitier Building.

Cameron and I exchanged a look. We had talked *Jerry Maguire* for
over a year, and we'd been preparing and filming it for another nine
months. We'd communicated each night and morning by e-mail. I liked
e-mail because it was quick, private, and Cameron communicated so
well. We'd talk of scenes for the next day, problems we each had, our
fears of upcoming scenes, personalities in the company, and just friend
and family stuff. I'd try to tell Cameron my experiences from the past;
I hoped that would somehow help him. There are a lot of pressures on
a director. *Jerry Maguire* was only Cameron's third film, and the first
with a bona fide superstar.

· · ·

"Let's go, Ziesmer!" Tom yelled, as he ran up the first flight of stairs to the camera and a quick talk with Cameron. Tom and Cuba Gooding had a race up all the stairs of the L.A. Coliseum when we were filming a night scene there. Tom won, but not by much.

"What am I doing?" Tom asked. The propmaster gave him a copy of the mission statement.

"You just run past the camera," Cameron said. "That's all," and he laughed.

"Let's go! Let's do it!" Tom said and ran up to the third floor.

Cameron got back to the monitor. The camera guys were ready. I looked around at the crew, then I glanced again at Cameron. He nodded.

"Ready, Tom!" I shouted.

"Go!" came his reply.

"Roll camera," I said.

The boom man yelled, "Speed!"

Cameron took a half-beat and then shouted, "Action, Tom!"

Tom shot down the stairs and past the camera. There was a pause; no one said a word.

The camera operator signaled to me that the shot was good. No one moved.

Cameron glanced at me, and I nodded that the shot was good for camera.

"Is that it?" Cameron shouted.

Tom grinned, and we all waited.

"Is it over?" Cameron shouted. He looked at me and nodded.

"That's a wrap!" I said, and the crew exploded. It was over.

I always felt two things when a picture was completed. The first was a heavy weight coming off my shoulders, and the second was tears sneaking out of my eyes. After thirty years and all those pictures, the tears still began. I never knew why, not exactly. Even after the months in the Philippines with Francis on *Apocalypse Now*, and all we went through with the typhoon and Marlon Brando, the tears came after our last shot. Maybe I knew our journeys had only just begun.

The champagne was poured, and Tom held his glass high into the air.

"This has been the greatest experience of my life! You all are the very best! I've enjoyed working with you so much!" Tom shouted a toast to everyone.

The cheers and laughter greeted him.

Cameron was next to toast us all.

"You've all been the greatest crew! I couldn't have done it without you!"

More laughter and screams, shouts and applause.

The other members of the crew from the trucks and dressing rooms had gotten the word we have finished and were running up the stairs to join in the champagne and yelling.

I watched the crew enjoying their praise and drinking their champagne.

"Suzanne?" I radioed.

"Yes?" she returned.

"We've wrapped. Want some champagne?" I asked.

"I'm collecting walkie-talkies," she replied.

"I'll catch you at the production trailer," I said.

"OK," she answered.

I knew she would want to get things wrapped up as soon as we had finished filming. The younger production assistants were shouting and laughing, but Suzanne and I would have a quiet celebration at our home, just the two of us.

I said quick good-byes to Cameron, Tom, and everyone else, then I headed down the stairs and left the Poitier Building and walked to the studio's Main Street. Suzanne's production trailer was almost two blocks away.

I glanced back toward where Main Street began. That's where the old East Gate of M-G-M was. Some of it's still there, but it's not used. The new gate is now a block farther east on the other side of the Thalberg Building. Years ago Ken Hollywood used to be the guard at the old East Gate of M-G-M.

Ken Hollywood was the first one in the morning to greet all the big names: Clark Gable, Spencer Tracy, Katharine Hepburn, John Barrymore—all of the big stars. Ken would get their day started right, no matter what their night might have been like.

I could have used Ken's help with Marlon Brando and Francis Coppola on *Apocalypse Now*. Most movies are about a good story, but with *Apocalypse Now* the best story was about making the movie. Marlon was one of the finest actors I'd ever known. His acting was so pure and simple; there were few like him, but I worked with another. It was a long time ago.

It Began in Milwaukee

I stood in the cold and slush outside the Fred Miller Theatre on Oakland Avenue in Milwaukee. The play rehearsal had ended a few minutes earlier, and I was outside waiting for my ride. It was only a small role, but it didn't matter to me.

It was 1957, and for three weeks at the Fred Miller Theatre I'd be acting with Ethel Waters in The Member of the Wedding. *Only five years before, Fred Zinnemann had directed her in the film version of* The Member of the Wedding *with Julie Harris, and three years before that she'd been nominated for an Oscar for* Pinky, *directed by Elia Kazan.*

In rehearsal she didn't act the part of Bernice; she was Bernice. I'd never experienced acting like hers. She was her role. Somehow she was Ethel Waters and at the same time she became Bernice on the stage. Her performance was so good, so much better than anything I'd ever experienced or had dreamed I could experience.

When I came on stage in the third act, after Ethel Waters sang His Eye Is on the Sparrow *and she was sitting in her chair with Frankie and the packing cases were all around her, her performance was as pure and simple as anything I've ever known. It was life itself.*

"Well, Greek God Barney!" Ethel Waters said to me as she left the theatre and stood under the marquee. That's what she called me in the play—Greek God Barney.

I smiled, but I was too afraid to speak to her.

"Who're you waiting on?" she asked.

I knew a car came every day after rehearsal to pick her up.

"My girlfriend's going to pick me up," I answered, as I looked for Suzanne's car. She drove her dad's pink-and-white Buick.

"Thought so," she said, and laughed. "Where you two going to go?"

"Get a cheeseburger at Shorty's, I guess," I said.

"Where's that?" she asked.

"Over on Villard Avenue. It's kind of a hangout, you know, hamburgers and malts," I answered, and looked for Suzanne again. "The kids from Custer and Rufus King high schools go there."

When I turned back toward Ethel Waters, she was staring at me and smiling like we were friends, and we were talking together like we always did at that time of day.

"Well, that will be nice," she said.

I knew it was my turn to speak. I smiled and tried to get the right words together.

"It's all so good," I said. "You and the play and everything."

She listened with her soft smile.

"You're so real on stage. The play's so perfect," I continued.

"It doesn't happen often," she said, and laughed gently.

She was in her sixties then and a large woman. I'd seen pictures of her as a singer and dancer at the Cotton Club and places like that. She'd changed completely. Now she was older, much larger, and she moved and talked slower than most people. I thought it probably was because of her size and because she'd probably said the same things before.

"When a play like this one comes along, when it's your play, you got to grab on," she said, and laughed again. "Remember that."

I smiled, but I was seventeen and thinking of Suzanne and cheeseburgers and how we'd go on and do great plays for the rest of our lives, maybe half with Ethel Waters and the other half with Helen Hayes and a couple with both of them. Wouldn't that be something?

I could always dream, talk, and listen all at the same time. I didn't think many people could do that.

We stood outside the theatre in the cold with the slush around our shoes and talked about acting on Broadway (the theatres were old), eating cheeseburgers (probably the best food ever), filming in Hollywood (everything moved so slowly), and putting catsup and sugar on French fries (she'd try that tonight), until her ride came and took Ethel Waters back to her hotel.

She loved the catsup and sugar on her French fries, and for three weeks I loved being in her play and walking past the packing cases at the beginning of the third act, seeing Bernice sitting in her chair and watching her smiling back at me.

It was 1961. John Kennedy was inaugurated as our thirty-fifth president. He increased our military presence in Vietnam and founded the Peace Corps. The Berlin Wall was constructed separating East and West Berlin. Alan Shepard made the first U.S. space flight.

In April, I packed my old VW bug with all my earthly possessions, said good-bye to my dad and mom, and set out from Milwaukee for Hollywood.

I really only knew two people in Hollywood, Richard Benjamin and Paula Prentiss. They had graduated from Northwestern University the year before me. As soon as I got to San Bernardino, I got out my map and found their address and headed for it, 141 South Elm Drive in Beverly Hills. I parked my VW bug outside the eight-unit apartment building and knocked on their door. "Here I am!"

I got a roommate, John Hanek, and we shared a back apartment in the same building as Paula and Dick. Got myself an agent, Herman Zimmermann, who had an office on Sunset Boulevard! I enrolled as a graduate student in the theatre department at UCLA. I was granted a 2-S draft deferment, and I got a job as a postal clerk at the Beverly Hills post office. I was an actor in Hollywood, and I loved it.

I finally got a small part in the TV pilot of *The Lieutenant*, starring Gary Lockwood. We were filming at the M-G-M lot, so I drove up to the East Gate, ready to launch my acting career.

"Who are we now?" Ken Hollywood, the studio guard, asked me.

"I'm playing a part in *The Lieutenant* and . . ." I began.

"Well, Lieutenant, why don't you turn that bug around and go park at the lot across the street," Ken said with a smile.

I looked back over my shoulder, trying to see where he meant.

"Oh, across the street?" I asked.

"That's right, Sonny," Ken said, and went back to really important work.

I parked my VW and walked back to Ken, and he directed me to follow M-G-M's Main Street west about a block to a long yellow building on the left that held the TV wardrobe department. They'd take care of me. I thanked Ken and hurried on my way, anxious once again to begin my acting career.

That afternoon when I was through, I walked past Ken.

"See you, Sonny," Ken said, and smiled.

"See you," I answered, and hurried to my VW. I had to get to my job at the Beverly Hills post office as soon as I could.

I stood on Main Street near Ken Hollywood's gate and listened to the *Jerry Maguire* celebration. Then I turned and walked toward Stage 8 and Suzanne's production trailer.

I had done a lot of TV shows as an actor right on the M-G-M lot. I always played the young street tough or soldier. That's all I ever did. I was a parish tough in Gene Kelly's TV series *Going My Way,* and I was a young soldier in Jim Nabors' *Gomer Pyle* show. I did *My Three Sons* with Fred MacMurray, *Sam Benedict* with Edmond O'Brien and Claude Rains, *Eleventh Hour,* and *The Red Skelton Show,* but my acting career was mainly sorting mail at the Beverly Hills post office and going on a lot of interviews for roles I didn't get.

Once I went on an interview for the old *Jack Benny Show.* There were four parts and three actors trying out. When I didn't get selected, I started to get the message.

I had found Stan Laurel's address while working at the Beverly Hills post office. I thought UCLA might accept a master's thesis on Stan Laurel and his comedy, if I could get to him. It was easier than I thought.

I found Stan Laurel's phone number in the Santa Monica phone book, and I called him.

"Hello," came Stan Laurel's familiar voice.

"Mr. Laurel?" I asked.

"Yes, who is this?" Stan asked.

I was so frightened. I was actually talking to Stan Laurel of the world-famous comedy team of Laurel and Hardy. How many of their films had I seen?

"Ah . . . this is Jerry Ziesmer. You don't know me, but . . ." I said, and I didn't know how to go on.

"Yes, Jerry, what is it you want?" Stan asked.

"I'd like to meet and talk about your comedy theories and things," I stammered.

Stan laughed. "All right, Jerry, but I don't think anyone can talk about comedy, really."

Did he say "All right"? "Mr. Laurel, when and where would be good for you? I go to UCLA," I began.

"Well, Jerry, perhaps you could come by some afternoon. I'm at the Oceanna Apartment Hotel in Santa Monica, number 280," Stan said in his so-familiar voice. "Maybe Tuesday, Jerry?"

"Tuesday! Great!" I was so excited.

"About 2:00 P.M.?" he asked.

"Tuesday at 2 P.M. I'll be there," I said.

I was there and on time. Stan Laurel said we couldn't talk about comedy, and he didn't think he had any comedy film techniques, but we spent the next two years talking about them. Stan could hardly walk, but his mind was as sharp as ever. His eyes gleamed as we went over his career and his "tricks."

"How did you get that attitude for your character of being back on his heels?" I asked Stan.

He laughed and laughed. Finally he answered.

"Jerry, it was quite simple actually. I cut off the heels of my shoes, so I was back on my heels!" Stan said, and his body rocked with his famous laugh.

Years later I attended Stan's funeral at Forest Lawn Mortuary above Warner Brothers. The little chapel was filled with mourners. Very softly in the background I began to hear the theme music from so many Laurel and Hardy films, The Waltz of the Cuckoos. Slowly the mourners became aware of the music, and as one or another of the Laurel and Hardy films came into their minds, they smiled, then chuckled, and finally laughed. Stan would have been so happy. Even at his funeral, he left them laughing.

In 1964 I married Mary Kate Denny, a young actress I had met at UCLA. I found that an occasional check as an actor plus my post office salary didn't quite stretch far enough, so I took a teaching position at John Adams Junior High School in Santa Monica. I taught English and American literature and journalism. I loved it and the kids, but it was Santa Monica, and I had wanted Hollywood.

One day I saw a notice in *Variety* about the Directors Guild Assistant Director Training Program. I applied, took the longest test I'd ever taken, and then endured an oral interview with movie industry executives. Finally I was accepted into the Directors Guild Assistant Director Training Program. I had to make a decision.

I drove west down Pico Boulevard toward Santa Monica. I had driven to John Adams Junior High School for nearly two school years, but that day in the middle of June of 1967 would be replayed in my mind for the next thirty years.

I parked on Pearl Street and walked up the steps to the main office, got my mail, and entered my classroom. As always there were a few students waiting. They came from south Santa Monica, less affluent, some surfers, some flower children, various races and religions, a few gangs, some dope, but all basically good kids.

I'd decided to wait and talk with my fourth period class about the opportunity that had come so unexpectedly into my life. We seemed to have developed a special relationship over the school year.

Teachers live for that moment when one of their students discovers a new area of knowledge. When a lamp seems to light up behind their eyes as they read Keats, or Hemingway, or Dylan Thomas for the first time. That's how it was with many in my fourth period class.

They entered full of energy and noise like every other day. I leaned back on my desk and waited for them to settle and get into their seats.

"Something's come up. I have to make a decision," I began. "I'd like to talk to you about it."

They were full of questions and curiosity, but I waited for them to quiet down again.

I told them of my love for teaching. How I hoped to add some bit of knowledge to each of them during the year. That was very important to me.

Then I told them that I'd been accepted into the assistant director training program, an opportunity to participate in the making of motion pictures. That was what I'd wanted to do before I began teaching.

"Do you mean you might not be coming back to teach next year?"

"I guess that's what we're talking about," I said.

"Well, what is it that you want to do?"

"Do what you want to do."

"I want to contribute," I said, as openly as I could put it.

"You do now! Why would you want to leave John Adams?"

"You do that here."

One of the quieter students raised his hand. He sat in the second row near the back.

"Mr. Ziesmer, there are thirty-five students in this class," he began. "How many classes do you teach?"

There were eight periods in a school day, but fifth period was lunch for everyone, and each teacher had one free period.

"I have six classes," I answered.

"Then you contribute to two hundred ten students in a year," he continued.

"That's a lot!" someone added.

Everyone wanted to comment on the numbers and whether that would matter.

"And who do those people contribute to? That's important, too."

"But movies reach millions!" the self-proclaimed class leader added. His dad owned a car agency on Santa Monica Boulevard.

"How many are any good?" his friend countered, who was always late with his homework. "How many movies are worth anything?"

"How do you know if you'll be able to contribute anything to a movie?"

"Why take a chance? You make a difference here."

"What if all you can do is stupid films? You'll contribute to millions and millions of people seeing stupid films!"

"Think what you'll be missing at John Adams," someone said, and the class laughed.

It went on until nearly the very end of fourth period, when the quiet boy in the back of the second row raised his hand to speak again.

He was a good student. He had some problems with expressing himself in English; his family came from Korea. His sister was also at John Adams, but in the seventh grade. I had met both his parents during the semester.

"Mr. Ziesmer, I think you should leave because I believe that's what you want most, but *you must try to only do the very best movies.*" His voice was a pure tone, and the words echoed deep within me throughout my career.

The class was still.

I've always had a hard time letting go, but eight days later when the school year ended, I knew I'd taught my last class at John Adams Junior High School.

• • •

I wanted to be in film. I hoped the assistant director training program was my chance.

The training program lasted four hundred working days. Both the Directors Guild and the Motion Picture Producers Association got jobs for everyone in the program as a trainee on movies and television series.

My first assignment as a trainee was on the TV series *Lassie*. I had no idea what I was supposed to do, and since it was only the third year of the training program, no one else had any idea what I was to do either. I hung around and watched, tried to help if I saw anything I could do. That was about it.

After *Lassie* the training program sent me to Universal Studios, and I worked on all of their TV series. I now did everything and was always on the run. I saw that the actors were in makeup in the morning. I got them their breakfast. I got them to the set. I showed them their dressing rooms. I worked from 6:00 A.M. to 9:00 P.M., five days a week. All the trainees did—Alan Rudolph, Walter Hill, every one of us.

Finally the trainee program mercifully took me from Universal and sent me to Twentieth Century Fox where I trained on part of *The Boston Strangler* with Tony Curtis. The difference between the long hours and rapid pace of television and the more careful approach to filming in features convinced me that I wanted to do features when my training program ended.

It was 1968, and Martin Luther King, Jr., and Robert Kennedy had been assassinated. The U.S. troop strength in Vietnam reached 500,000. That summer antiwar demonstrators clashed with police in Chicago at the Democratic Convention.

Twentieth Century Fox assigned me to *Hello, Dolly!* with Gene Kelly directing. My life was improving.

Hello, Dolly!

The production manager was Francisco "Chico" Day. Chico was to play a most important role in my assistant director training. He was the younger brother of the popular actor Gilbert Roland.

"Look, keed," Chico said. He always called me "Keed," never "Kid." Chico had been the assistant director for Cecil B. DeMille for years and also for Marlon Brando on *One-Eyed Jacks*. Either of those two was a full career for any assistant director. Chico Day was one of the most knowledgeable and respected assistant directors in Hollywood. I couldn't have had a better mentor.

"What is it, Chico?" I asked. We were in his office on the third floor of the administration building at Fox. We were just beginning to shoot *Hello, Dolly!*

"You go down to the stage. You get yourself six feet from the camera, and you stay there all day! That's the only place you'll learn anything! All right, keed?" Chico said.

"All right, Chico," I answered. I was thrilled to be doing something besides answering the stage phone and getting coffee and lunches for people, which is what I had been doing.

"Remember! Six feet from the camera! No further!" Chico ordered. "Now get out of here!"

I left Chico's office and walked down to the Harmonia Gardens set on a double sound stage at the south end of Twentieth Century Fox, right near Pico Boulevard. Harry Stradling was the cameraman, and as soon as I got on the sound stage I could hear him calling out instructions to his gaffer.

"No! The big one! Light it! Yeah! More!" Harry Stradling shouted. I liked him immediately because he was a perfectionist and comical at the same time. All the electricity went out on the whole stage one day, and while all the electricians were panicked, Harry kept shouting that it was all a little fuse somewhere. He did all of Barbra Streisand's early movies. He was a wonderful artist, and Barbra learned a lot from Harry Stradling about the camera and how to light Ms. Streisand.

They were lighting for Barbra Streisand's entrance into the Harmonia Gardens, a turn-of-the-century New York City restaurant set that had been designed by John DeCuir, one of Hollywood's top production designers. The restaurant consisted of many levels, all with tables and private booths. There were magnificent chandeliers, mirrors, long red drapes, and wonderful stained and etched glass panels. All of the wardrobe had been designed by Irene Sharaff, who did *Cleopatra*. Every detail of every dress was authentic. The extras looked as if they were dressed in classic museum wardrobe pieces.

It was a huge, moving crane shot that took Barbra and Walter Matthau into the Harmonia Gardens, past Louis Armstrong who was singing *Hello, Dolly!* and around the whole restaurant to their table. Michael Kidd, the choreographer, was working with the dancers doing food-and-drinks serving during the shot. They were like Olympic acrobats as they danced through the set. I had never seen anything like this, ever.

I saw a camera on a large crane, so I stood six feet from it and prepared myself to learn about assistant directing.

"Hey, pardner! How you doing, keed?" Chico said, as he stood next to me and watched the crew lighting the big entrance shot.

"Hi, Chico," I said, keeping my eyes on the dancers, Harry Stradling, and everything else that was going on. There must have been fifty electricians, thirty grips, probably twenty dancers, all the other crew, and then the extras. *Hello, Dolly!* was the biggest show I had ever seen.

"Pardner?" Chico, said as he put his arm around me, "Someday you'll be in charge of pictures bigger than this. You'd better pay attention and listen. Listen!" Chico shook me back and forth with his arm around my shoulders.

"Not me, Chico. Won't happen," I laughed. "I could never be in charge of all this."

"Keed, someday this'll be a little picture to you," Chico said.

I laughed.

Everyone said some pleasant greeting to Chico as they passed us. He knew them all by name. Their affection and respect for him was obvious in their words and smiles.

"Are you going to listen?" Chico asked. "To every one of them?"

"Yes, I'll listen," I said.

"With what, keed. With what are you going to listen?" Chico asked.

"With my ears. I'll listen with my ears!" I replied.

"No, keed. With your heart. Listen with your heart," Chico Day said to me. "Listen to all these people with your heart."

He roughed up my shoulders again and left me standing next to the camera.

The Directors Guild building is on Sunset Boulevard in Hollywood. On the first Wednesday of every month at 8 P.M. the Assistant Director/Unit Production Manager Council meets in the board room on the sixth floor.

It was 1983, fifteen years after Hello, Dolly! *I hadn't seen Chico since that movie. He had been a council member for twenty years, but this was the first time I had been elected. I sat down at the long conference table not really knowing what to do. When I looked up Chico had sat down next to me.*

"Hi, keed," Chico said as he put his arm around me. "You still listening with your heart?" He whispered and looked at me with his wise, smiling eyes.

I had a great time watching Barbra Streisand and Walter Matthau make their entrance past Louis Armstrong as he sang *Hello, Dolly!* Barbra was interested in every aspect of filming. She was so full of life. Ray Stark, one of the producers of Barbra's first movie, *Funny Girl*, had given her a dressing room trailer and had it done in Victorian decor. We put it on the sound stage with trees and grass around it. Barbra Streisand was a major superstar, and she was in her twenties. Gene Kelly and Michael Kidd, two of the greatest dancers and choreographers, answered all my questions. Gene Kelly and I'd been close friends on his TV series, and working with him on *Hello, Dolly!* made our friendship all the better. Harry Stradling got used to my constant whys. He would begin each answer to my questions with an angry, "Why do you want to know that?" Then he'd explain the answer to me until I finally understood.

• • •

I knew as I stood on the set of the Harmonia Gardens and saw all
the lights, dancers, actors, and crew, that I wanted my life's work to be
in the film industry, but I didn't want to make just any movie. I wanted
to work on the best motion pictures.

It was July 1969 when I finally got my four hundred days and
graduated from the training program. I was finally a second assistant director member of the Directors Guild of America. To make it all official
I had to go into the DGA office and sign some papers. While I was
there, my first day out of the training program, Otto Preminger called
and screamed over the phone at the DGA representative that he needed
an assistant director in Boston immediately!

The DGA representative held his hand over the phone.

"Jerry, you want a job?" he asked. "It's yours if you want it."

Otto Preminger had the reputation of being the loudest, meanest director in the guild. He had directed *Exodus, Anatomy of a Murder*, and
Porgy and Bess—three fantastic films.

"He's doing *Tell Me That You Love Me, Junie Moon* out in Boston. Big
picture," the DGA rep whispered. "Liza Minnelli? *The Sterile Cuckoo*?
The cameraman is Boris Kaufman." I could still hear Otto Preminger
screaming over the phone.

Boris Kaufman had been the cameraman on *The Fugitive Kind,
Splendor in the Grass, Twelve Angry Men*. He was Elia Kazan's cameraman on the early Marlon Brando films. Oh, man! I was so excited! I
wondered why there weren't assistant directors lined up around the
block to do this film.

I could still hear Otto Preminger screaming over the phone.

This was what I wanted, an important film with important people.

"OK! Yeah, I'll do it!" I said. I was full of confidence, and I thought
I was ready for anything.

But I wasn't quite ready for Mr. Otto Preminger.

Tell Me That You Love Me, Junie Moon

On the morning I signed my membership papers at the DGA, I was on an afternoon plane as a second assistant director headed for Boston and Otto Preminger's new film. I arrived in Boston after dark. A film company driver met me, but by the time I got to the hotel, the production office was closed. All I received at the hotel desk was my room key, a copy of the script, and tomorrow's call sheet.

I was down in the hotel lobby at 7:00 A.M., and I began to look for assistant director types. When the crew got into the vans, I did too. I thought that maybe they were already out on location, or perhaps they rode out with Mr. Preminger in his car.

We got to the location, and I continued to look for the first assistant director, or the production manager, or maybe some of the other assistant directors. There didn't seem to be any around, but neither was Otto Preminger. They were probably all together.

I stood within six feet of the camera and waited. Soon a very slight man in his early seventies with glasses and a friendly smile also stood about six feet from the camera. He could have been a college professor or even a watchmaker.

"Boris," a camera assistant approached the man, "you want a fifty on the camera?"

"Yes, that would be fine," he answered.

"Ahh," I began, "are you Boris Kaufman?" I asked.

"Yes," he said and smiled.

"I'm Jerry Ziesmer. I just finished the DGA training program. I arrived last night." I ran everything together.

Boris smiled, "You're the new assistant director."

"Yes, I am," I said proudly. After four hundred days, yes, I was an assistant director. Damn right.

"Good," Boris said, and started to work with the camera.

"Where's the first assistant director?" I asked, "What's his name?"

"He left. They all left," Boris told me. "You're it."

I wanted to run. My head began to spin. Did he say "I'm it"? There's no one else?

"Boris!" I heard a loud Prussian scream, and when I turned around there he was—Otto Preminger. He was totally bald. His face and eyes looked mean and sadistic. Later I was told that his two pet poodles ran and hid from him whenever he entered a room, which was exactly what I wanted to do right then. Preminger charged toward the camera to talk to Boris Kaufman, and I was standing right next to Boris.

"Who are you?" Preminger screamed at me.

I just stared at this huge Prussian cavalry officer, this sadistic dueling master, who stood shouting in front of me.

Boris answered quite calmly, "This is the new assistant director, Jerry Ziesmer, Otto."

"Who?" Otto screamed.

Boris turned and looked at me.

I glanced at Boris. "I'm Jerry Ziesmer, Mr. Preminger. I'm new and . . . ."

"I know you're new!" Preminger screamed, and I thought I would faint. I had never seen anyone like Otto Preminger. I had barely met him, and he was standing less than three feet from me and screaming at me.

"He's the new assistant director, Otto," Boris repeated.

Preminger looked at me as if I had already proven myself to be totally incompetent.

"Now, Otto, what do you have in mind for the first shot?" Boris asked, and distracted Otto from me.

Otto laid out the first shot that included Liza Minnelli and Ken Howard. It sounded pretty simple. I left Boris at the camera and hurried to find the makeup trailer to be sure Liza Minnelli and Ken Howard were getting ready and they knew what scene we were doing.

"What happened to the other assistant directors?" I wondered.

I found Liza in the makeup trailer with Charlie Schwan, an old M-G-M makeup artist that had made up Liza's mother, Judy Garland. Charlie was putting an involved scar makeup on Liza's face. I tried to introduce myself, but I said "Lisa" instead of "Liza," and Ms. Minnelli curtly corrected me. I must have been traumatized from her rebuke because I had trouble with her name ever after that first reprimand.

It was 1962, and I was a young actor filming the Going My Way *TV series. We were doing an exterior shot at Revue, which would become Universal Studios. Gene Kelly was sitting in his cast chair, and I was standing next to him as we went over some lines. A black limousine pulled up and stopped about twenty feet from us, and the driver opened the back door. The figure in the back seat was a tiny little woman.*

Gene Kelly smiled and got up.

"Jerry," Gene Kelly called to me. He motioned for me to follow him to the limo.

He was blocking my view of the woman as I approached the car. When he turned to introduce me, I realized the lady was Judy Garland.

Gene did the introductions, and I smiled and said the right things. In a minute the back door was closed and the limo moved off.

Gene and I glanced at each other on the way back to his chair.

"She's not feeling so good," he said, as if it were an explanation.

I nodded as if I knew, but I didn't.

Liza Minnelli had a scruffy looking mutt at her feet as she sat in the makeup chair. I leaned down to pet the creature, just being friendly and natural.

"Look out!" Liza yelled, and Charlie jumped to one side as the mutt leaped at me. Liza got him calmed down and back underneath her chair.

"Don't ever do that again!" Liza said.

She didn't have to tell me that twice.

"I was in Rome," Liza began. "It was late at night, and I was walking along the Via Venito. That dog came up to me, and I just brought him back to the States with me. Nasty dog," Liza said, and laughed.

Somehow I got through the day, running the set and chasing the actors, but the next day was the big test. The new location was at the intersection of First and Walnut.

We all seemed to have left the hotel at the same time. I was in the crew bus with Boris and his gaffer, Joe Edesa. Otto had driven off in his car about the same time we did. The crew bus was at the intersection of First and Walnut. After a half hour of waiting for Mr. Preminger and the camera equipment trucks to arrive, I got out of the bus and rechecked the street signs: First and Walnut. There could be no mistake—or could there?

At 11 A.M., four hours after leaving the hotel, a movie company car sped up to the crew bus, stopped, and the driver captain came running to us.

"You're at the wrong First and Walnut! There's First and Walnut and First and Walnut!" he shouted. "Otto's gone crazy! Get back in the bus and follow me!"

I sank back into my seat on the bus. The crew bus had somehow gotten to the wrong location, and we had lost a half day of filming. I felt Preminger would kill me. I was dead. Ruined.

There wasn't a sound on the crew bus as we drove to the correct First and Walnut. As we approached I could see Otto storming and waving his arms into the air. I couldn't hear his shouting, but I could imagine what he was going to be saying to me.

"Jerry," Joe Edesa spoke to me, "listen to me."

"What?" I asked. I was shaking.

"When the bus stops, go right at him," Joe said.

"Jerry, charge him! Run right to him and scream at him!" Boris Kaufman said.

"What?" I couldn't believe what they were saying.

"Attack him!" Boris said, and Joe agreed.

I felt I had nothing to lose; he was going to kill me anyway.

The crew bus came to a stop, and when the doors opened I shot off the bus at full gallop. I charged across the parking space toward Otto Preminger. I screamed and shouted and waved my arms in the air and headed right toward him like an angry tornado!

I didn't know what I was saying, but I was loud and animated. When I could focus, I was about ten feet from Otto and closing fast. Suddenly he threw his arms up in the air and backed away from me.

"Don't, Jerry! Please!" He pleaded. "I'm sorry! Don't, please! It's all my fault!"

Otto had both hands in front of him as he begged my forgiveness, and he told me what an arrogant asshole he could be and that he was sorry and couldn't we just have an early crew lunch and he'd make up the time we lost this afternoon? Please?

Talk about an easy show! *Tell Me That You Love Me, Junie Moon* was one of the easiest shows I ever did. The director loved me, and after a while I grew to like him, too. Otto still did the shouting and I did the running, but we were a team. We enjoyed working with each other.

The Great White Hope

We were filming our final two weeks of *Tell Me That You Love Me, Junie Moon* in San Diego, when I received a phone call from the production department at Twentieth Century Fox. They asked if I would be interested in interviewing for a second assistant job on their film *The Great White Hope*. I wondered why out of all the members in the Directors Guild they had decided to call me.

The day I got back to Los Angeles, I had a 10:00 A.M. appointment to see Saul Wurtzel, a respected unit manager. I drove over to Twentieth Century Fox and entered the Pico Boulevard gate. As I turned north and drove up the main street of Fox, I saw the cobblestone streets that were made for *Hello, Dolly!* The studio's time card office had been turned into the ticket office for an elevated streetcar we had on *Dolly*. The park we had built for the film was still on the southeast side of the studio. We had covered the whole east side of the administration building at Fox with false building fronts depicting New York City. There was the large entrance for Harmonia Gardens where Barbra Striesand and Walter Matthau first entered the restaurant, the New York library facade, the front of Grand Central Station; all of *Hello, Dolly!* Street was still there.

I had a strange feeling being back on the *Hello, Dolly!* Street. I remembered Gene Kelly, Barbra, Walter Matthau, all the dancers and extras. Chico Day was gone from his third-floor office, but the street remained. I wanted to be back there, herding extras for Gene Kelly and learning more from Chico and Harry Stradling. I wasn't ready to be out on my own. Now when I looked around for an assistant director, I realized it was me. Life was less complicated back then.

I walked into the studio's production building, an old wood-faced building just west of the administration building. I knocked on the open door and looked into Saul Wurtzel's office.

"Hi, I'm Jerry Ziesmer. I was supposed to see Mr. Wurtzel at ten," I said.

"Come on in. You're in the right place. Sit down. I'm Saul Wurtzel. This is Tim Zinnemann. He's the first AD."

Saul Wurtzel was a wizened old production manager who had been at Twentieth Century Fox for years. All of the old production managers wore suits and ties to the studio. Tim Zinnemann was the son of the famous movie director Fred Zinnemann. He was quiet and thoughtful and the best creative assistant director I ever knew.

"Hi, glad to meet you," I said. It was my first interview. I didn't know what I was supposed to do or say. I just sat down and waited.

"What have you been doing?" Tim asked.

"I was with Otto Preminger on his film for a few weeks," I said, and waited.

"What about before that?" Saul asked, and leaned forward, staring at me.

"Well, I was in the training program. I worked on *Hello, Dolly!* I finished in July," I said, and looked back at them.

"You know Chico Day?" Saul asked trying to draw conversation out of me.

"Yeah, he really taught me a lot," I volunteered.

"Chico said you were OK on *Dolly*," Saul said.

"He's great," I answered, and went back to looking at them.

"This is a picture called *The Great White Hope*. It's a boxing picture. OK? The story of Jack Johnson. OK? Martin Ritt's the director," Saul began.

I knew that Martin Ritt had directed Paul Newman in *Hud, Hombre,* and *The Long Hot Summer*. Paul Newman was one of my favorite actors. During a spring break at Northwestern University, I went to New York City and saw Paul Newman and Geraldine Page on Broadway in *Sweet Bird of Youth*. I had to stand at the back of the theatre for all three acts, but I didn't care. After the play I relived all the Newman and Page scenes in my mind as I walked across town to the Five Spot Cafe and stood for the second night in a row to hear

Thelonious Monk play. Monk's and Newman's performances were both so simple and so good.

"He is? Martin Ritt's directing?" I stammered out.

"Yes, he is. Have you worked with him?" Tim asked.

"No, but . . . ," I said. "I mean he's done so much, so many great pictures and all." I had a problem speaking when I got excited.

"How's your paperwork?" Saul asked.

"Good, I guess," I answered. Part of the work of an assistant director was to do the call sheets and production reports that kept the record of the production.

"You like working with extras?" Tim asked.

"I do, yeah," I answered. "I like that. Better than the paperwork."

There was a long pause. Tim and Saul looked at one another then back to me. I looked at them and tried to think if there was anything I should say, wishing I hadn't hinted that I didn't like paperwork.

"Would you like to do *The Great White Hope*?" Tim asked.

"Yes!" I said. Was he kidding? Martin Ritt!

"OK, you're on," Saul said, and extended his hand and laughed at the naive assistant director sitting in front of him. "Chico said you didn't talk much!"

I shook Saul's hand and then Tim's. I laughed, but I wasn't able to breathe.

"Glad to have you on board," Tim said, and smiled. "I hated the paperwork, too."

I must have been a sight. I laughed and nearly choked. I was so happy.

"Oh, wow! I mean, this is great!" I tried to say.

They all laughed.

"Do you have any questions?" Saul asked.

"I don't know." I tried to clear my head.

"You start Monday. OK?" Tim asked.

"Oh, great," I answered as best I could. I was so excited. I was afraid I was going to start shouting with joy right in Saul Wurtzel's office.

"Oh, Jerry, before you go. Don't you want to know where we'll be filming?" Saul asked, and leaned toward me.

Tim turned and faced me.

"We begin in Globe, Arizona. Then we come back to the studio and the stages for a couple of months," Saul began.

"Great!" I said.

"Then we finish up the last two months in London and Spain," Saul added.

I froze. I was in shock. Was I going to London? Spain? To do a movie?

"So, Jerry, figure you'll be spending December in London and then January and most of February in Spain. OK?" Saul asked.

"Oh, sure." I tried to sound casual and controlled. Me? Jerry Ziesmer from Milwaukee, Wisconsin, was going to London and Spain to film a movie! Oh, my God!

I had only been out of the United States twice. The first time was in the early 1950s when my mom and dad took me fishing for walleyed pike up in Ontario, Canada, outside a little town called Beardsmore. The second time was in 1962 when Suzanne came out to visit and we went to Tijuana. I got sick and we had to leave. That was the extent of my foreign travel.

The filming for *The Great White Hope* began in Globe, Arizona, with all the exteriors for the boxing matches. Tim Zinnemann designed some most unique crane shots for Marty Ritt to use to introduce the town and the excitement of the day. Tim had me running around for blocks, setting background people, horses, buggies, and animals of all kinds. I always thought Tim would be a great director; he had such a strong visual sense for the story.

I admired both Tim and his dad, but they did have an unusual relationship. It seemed that when Tim was in high school, he had to work to earn the money to buy his first car. One day his dad said to Tim that he would sell him one of his cars. Tim jumped at the deal, only to learn later that the car was only worth half of what he had paid his dad for it.

The film company had taken over the town of Globe and turned it into a turn-of-the-century town. The streets were covered with dirt; all the light poles and parking meters were removed, and telegraph poles replaced them. John DeCuir was the production designer, and he was a stickler for detail. Every one of the posters and billboards had to be accurate. He dressed as if he were a white hunter in Africa. He wore bush jackets, scarfs, boots, and a khaki hat. He could have played Bwana of the Jungle.

Irene Sharaff was the costume designer, and she kept me hopping, correcting the wardrobe of the extras; everything had to be perfect for her. She always dressed as if she were the matador for the third corrida of the afternoon. She wore black pants with a wide sash and a blouse top, but with a bolero-style hat.

Both John DeCuir and Irene Sharaff had been on *Hello, Dolly!*, so I knew they were perfectionists, but I wasn't quite ready for how perfectionistic they could be. Irene Sharaff had sixteen Academy Award nominations, and John DeCuir had been nominated eleven times. They each had received Oscars for *Cleopatra* and *The King and I*. John also got an Oscar for *Hello, Dolly!*, and Irene Sharaff received one for *An American in Paris*.

Bernie Guffey, the cameraman, was the only elite member of the crew who was relaxed. He looked like a working cameraman, with his comfortable jacket and slacks. There was no pretense with Bernie; he was dressed to do his job and to be comfortable. Even he had five Academy nominations and had won awards for *From Here to Eternity* and for *Bonnie and Clyde*. What I liked best about Bernie was that with all his awards and honors, he used a Kodak Instamatic camera for his personal snapshots. He told me it was a lot easier.

Tim left for London a week before the rest of us so he could check out the locations before we all got there. Saul Wurtzel and I stayed with the shooting company on a sound stage at Fox. Saul made all the travel plans while I ran the Tijuana Barn set with Marty Ritt and helped him any way I could.

"Jerry, when the company gets to the airport, the wardrobe department is going to have seven hampers for you to check through to London as your personal baggage. OK?" Saul Wurtzel asked.

"Sure, Saul, no problem," I said. They could have asked anything. All I knew was that this guy from Milwaukee was going to Europe to work on a film. That's all that mattered to me. My wife was four months pregnant with our first child, but we packed the baby books and a list of doctors in London and Spain. We were going to Europe.

On the day of our flight to London, we all met at LAX and were waiting to board the plane. Everyone was excited about going to Europe. An announcement came over the public address system for John, our stillman, to come to any white telephone. What could that call be? We all looked at John as he waited to board the plane with the rest of us.

"Don't answer the page!" Triandos, our big dolly grip, said. His brother was a major league catcher, and they both drank a lot of beer.

To save money they once bought a whole railroad car full of beer at a special low price. None of it went to waste.

"John, don't answer the phone," Triandos repeated.

Everyone laughed, but John looked at the white phone and wondered who would be calling him. He walked over and picked up the phone. Big mistake. The studio had changed their mind and decided not to send a stillman to Europe. John turned and looked at us all.

"I'm not going," he muttered, and just turned and walked out of the airport.

Ever since that day, I never answer phone pages in an airport. Never.

"Sir! Are all those hampers yours?" a British customs official asked me at the London airport.

"Ah, yes," I said. I hadn't ever seen the wardrobe hampers before, and I had no idea what they contained. Saul had asked me to check them through as my luggage.

"Could we have a little look-see?" he asked.

I undid the straps and proceeded to open seven hampers filled with long underwear.

"Expecting a chill, sir?" he asked me.

There must have been one hundred pairs of long underwear! What could I say? Could they deport me? Not let me into England? Did he think I was actually smuggling long underwear into England? All of our crew was standing around watching me but were afraid to say anything to help me.

"Ah, I just like to stay warm, you know," I answered. I had flown over the Atlantic and gotten this close to filming in Europe, and now I felt I was going to be sent back to Los Angeles. At least I had glimpsed England when the plane landed.

Just as the customs guard was bearing down on me, Saul Wurtzel and the captain of the British Customs came striding over to me.

"That's enough now, William," the captain said to the customs officer. "Good boy there. Let's move them right along now. No time to spare, William," the captain said.

Saul smiled at me and helped me and William re-do the hampers.

The hardest thing for me to believe as the car drove me to the hotel was that outside of the car's windows was London, England. I couldn't believe I was there. I looked at all the traffic driving on the wrong side of the street, and then I saw a double-decker bus! I saw my first London taxi! We drove past Buckingham Palace! I was in London and working on a film. I wished Ken Hollywood, the gate guard from M-G-M, could see me now.

After we took our bags up to our hotel rooms, we met for a location scout. Being in London, most of us were clothes and style conscious, but not Marty Ritt. We picked him up at the Dorchester Hotel. He was wearing a jumpsuit, the only clothes I ever saw him wear. Marty had been an athlete and had actually coached girls' basketball for a living at one time, but now he was overweight. His round face was ready for the big grin and laughter; he liked to have a good time. What I enjoyed most about Marty was his intellect. I enjoyed listening to the conversations he had on politics, art, government, and philosophy with the actors. He was also a very astute student of the racehorses, and his ability to pick winners was legendary.

We drove through London looking at our locations. I saw all kinds of famous places, including the Piccadilly Circus where we were going to film the next Sunday.

We seemed to be looking for a white building. Saul showed John DeCuir and Martin Ritt all kinds of white buildings. Finally he showed John one he liked, a perfect white building, except for one small thing. It was the wrong white! John DeCuir insisted that he would have to paint the whole building the correct color of white. Oh, my God! Paint an entire white building because it's the wrong color of white!

That next Sunday morning we were filming in Piccadilly Circus. John DeCuir and the art department had changed the whole area over to the early 1900s. All of the TV antennas and neon signs were gone, and in their place were the horse-drawn vehicles of the period. Hundreds of extras in Irene Sharaff's wardrobe paraded through the area. James Earl Jones, as Jack Johnson, was in a horse carriage with Jane Alexander, Joel Fluellen, and Lou Gilbert.

The company was under severe time constraints. We only had permission to film there Sunday until noon. We were moving as quickly as we could before we had to give up Piccadilly Circus. I was setting and cueing the extras, keeping the onlookers back, and getting whatever Tim needed. Suddenly I saw a little man move past the line of onlookers and start into the set. He was dressed like an English gentleman, in a tailored suit with topcoat and umbrella.

"Hey!" I yelled. "Please don't go in there! We're doing a movie here!"

I shouted and moved quickly to him. I gently took him by the arm and led him back to the waiting crowd.

"Look, you can't just walk through there," I said. "If you want to get to the other side, just go around, OK?"

The little man just looked at me, turned and walked off. I hoped I hadn't hurt his feelings, but we were doing a picture here.

"Jerry, did you notice where Fred Zinnemann went?" Bernie Guffey asked me.

"Who?" I asked.

"Fred Zinnemann. He was the director on *From Here to Eternity*. He's just a little man, was here just a minute ago," Bernie continued. "He directed *A Man for All Seasons* and *High Noon*, too."

"A little man?" I said, and the fear began to mount.

"Yes, he's Tim's dad. You know, Fred Zinnemann, one of the greatest film directors we've ever had," Bernie continued to look. "Oh, there he is with Tim. Come here, I want to introduce you."

I looked, and it was the same little man I had asked to leave the set. I followed behind Bernie, wanting to disappear down a hole somewhere. In one blunder I had insulted a top film director and the father of my boss.

Bernie and Fred Zinnemann greeted each other, then Bernie turned to me.

"Jerry, I want you to meet one of the finest directors I've ever known, Fred Zinnemann. Fred, this is Jerry Ziesmer, your son's assistant."

I froze. Tim was standing right there. Fred Zinnemann looked at me.

"Oh, Jerry and I know each other," Mr. Zinnemann began. "He showed me how to keep a movie set clear."

"Oh, really?" Bernie Guffey said, and looked at me. "You've worked together?"

"You know my dad?" Tim asked.

"Ahhh," I said.

"Great to see you again, Jerry. How've you been?" Mr. Zinnemann said, and smiled at me.

"Just great, sir," I said, as I recovered, "Just great. Thank you."

It was more than twenty years later when I saw Fred Zinnemann again. One evening the Academy of Motion Picture Arts and Sciences was honoring him with a retrospective of his films, and Mr. Zinnemann was presenting the Academy with the personal script that he used when he directed High Noon.

> *Suzanne and I attended because two of Mr. Zinnemann's films,*
> Day of the Jackal *and* Julia, *are a couple of my favorite films. When
> the retrospective ended, I greeted Tim, but I was sure Mr. Zinnemann
> would not remember me from one day twenty years ago in Piccadilly
> Circus, so Suzanne and I started to leave.*
> *"Hello," said a small voice behind me.*
> *I nearly didn't look back, but I did.*
> *Mr. Zinnemann smiled at me and said, "I hope you realize I
> haven't walked through any of your sets lately."*

My wife and I spent Christmas Eve at the main cathedral in
Barcelona, Spain. It was a midnight service lit by thousands of candles.

*In 1970, Ohio guardsmen killed four Kent State students during an
antiwar rally; President Nixon sent U.S. troops into Cambodia to
combat the Khymer Rouge; the Apollo 13 mission escaped near
disaster; Jimi Hendrix died of a drug overdose; and the Beatles dis-
banded.*

All of the Americans were staying at the Ritz Hotel in the center of
Barcelona. It was very nice, with all of the hotel staff dressed in tuxedos.
We learned to order paella from room service. That was important since
the restaurants didn't begin to serve dinner until 9:00 P.M. If we wanted
to eat earlier and not in our rooms, we had to go to a drugstore
luncheon counter, and there we could only get a sandwich.

One evening after filming, I had to drop a call sheet off to James Earl
Jones at his hotel room. He opened the door wrapped in a bathrobe.
When it was only the two of us, I always called him "Champion"
because he played the heavyweight boxing champion in our film.
"Champion, here's the call for tomorrow, 7 A.M. leaving," I said.
"Thank you," he answered in his deep voice, and then looked at me
and smiled big. "Have you ever seen a sunken tub?" he asked. "A real
one?"
"A what?" I said.
"Come in here," he smiled, and he pointed into his bathroom.
We both had a lot of the Midwest in us. He was from Michigan, and

I was from Wisconsin. We stood together looking at that sunken tub and just laughed.

When I would get back to the Ritz after work, I would relax in a huge mirrored barroom. Here we would order San Miguel beer and the best roasted potato chips you can imagine. All of us would be in our work clothes and all of the waiters would be in their tuxes, but with white perspiration stains under their jackets' armpits. It said something about Spain in 1970.

Joel Fluellen, the actor who played Jack Johnson's trainer Tick in the film, and I had become friends during the filming and would often sit in the Ritz Hotel's lounge at night, or walk outside and talk. Joel had trouble and pain in walking, so we'd move slowly around the block. He must have been about sixty. He was nearly twice my age. His voice was very melodic, as if he had been part of a musical group at one time. Joel had a long history in show business. He liked talking about it, and I liked listening to him.

We must have been quite a sight ambling along the sidewalks of Barcelona late at night. Joel shuffling along and laughing in his baritone tones, while I stepped around and gleefully added to our current topic of conversation. A lot of our laughter came at the expense of James Earl Jones as we tried to make him say good morning three times to each of us in one morning. James Earl Jones never remembered saying good morning to us. We had gotten him up to as many as six *Good mornings* to each of us before Joel collapsed in laughter and gave our whole game away.

It was a Sunday afternoon, and we had ventured a few blocks from the hotel to the city's plaza. It was nearly a square block in area. There were fountains and statues, some patches of grass, and other areas of crushed rock. The people walked or sat in the plaza on long metal benches, and the cars drove on the outside. It was like an oasis right in the middle of Barcelona.

It was the first time we had walked in the plaza. We walked mostly at night, and we usually stayed closer to the hotel, not for protection or out of fear, but because we didn't have as much time as we did that Sunday afternoon. Sometimes Joel would get tired and, even at our slow pace, would need to catch his breath. We sat down on one of the long metal benches. While Joel was getting a chance to rest, a man came up to us with tiny paper tickets and asked us for money to pay for our sitting on the bench.

Joel threw one of his short but intense fits of anger, but he soon calmed down, and we paid the man the sitting fee and got our tickets.

"I'm sitting here the whole hour!" Joel laughed, as he looked at his ticket. I noted that the tickets were marked and we couldn't change spots; we had to sit right where we were. We fell back into enjoying our time together. Neither of us spoke for quite some time, which wasn't unusual for us.

"Jerry, I'm free here. I'm a black man and I'm free," Joel said. "I don't want to live if I'm not free. You hear me?"

It was the very first time we had ever mentioned race. I had to open different windows in my brain to get myself oriented before I could answer my friend.

"Los Angeles is my home, but I'm not free there," Joel said.

Our whole film, *The Great White Hope*, was about racism in America, yet Joel and I had never discussed it. The topic never came up. We talked about how silly James Earl Jones, Jane Alexander, and Joel looked in the film when they tried to do a vaudeville skit about *Uncle Tom's Cabin*, but we never talked about race or racial prejudice.

"I'm sorry," he said, and he turned away from me.

We sat there silently for a long time.

Finally Joel looked again at his ticket.

"We got to sit here another forty minutes! See if you can find that man and get some of our money back! I'm ready to go back to the hotel!" Joel said, as he tried to regenerate our good times.

I laughed and joined in his game, but words said can never be taken back, not really. I never forgot what Joel had said to me.

On one of our final nights in Barcelona in February 1970, the United States Embassy officials, and the members of the Spanish Government, the local dignitaries from Barcelona and Madrid honored Martin Ritt, as the director of our film, at a special farewell dinner held at the Ritz Hotel in Barcelona.

All of us from the film were there: James Earl Jones and the cast, Bernie Guffey and the crew. We thought it would be a very festive evening, and indeed that's how it started.

The farewell banquet began with the warm speeches from the Spanish government officials, and then our U.S. Embassy representative added his congratulatory words. They both paid tribute to our film, the artists involved, the crews, and especially Martin Ritt, the director. We appreciated their words and enjoyed the food and sangria.

We all applauded politely as Marty came up to the podium to speak. He was dressed in a very nice jumpsuit, but it was a jumpsuit, not a dress suit or even a jacket. Irene Scharaff had even offered to design a jumpsuit for him that he could wear as a tux.

Marty waited until the banquet room was quiet. He then turned toward the representatives from the U.S. Embassy and very quietly began to speak. He thanked them for their tribute to him as a creative artist, but he reminded them that he had been blacklisted for ten years because of the House Un-American Activities Committee hearings. He reminded the representatives of the United States government of the years of employment and creative work that he and others like him had lost in the motion picture and theatrical world because of the blacklisting practices of his government and the entertainment industries.

"For ten years I was not a free man in my own country!" Marty said, in one of the most heartfelt speeches I'd ever heard.

Joel and I exchanged a look. No one was moving or saying a thing. I was glad we had all eaten first because when Marty stopped talking, I knew this party was over.

It wasn't until two years later, when I was preparing the Hollywood blacklisting scenes in The Way We Were, *that Marty Ritt's speech and fervor about freedom made me comprehend the personal tragedies of that era.*

But it was twenty years later in 1990, that Joel's words from that day in the plaza about his freedom came crashing back through my brain. Joel Fluellen, still living in Los Angeles, had taken a pistol and put a bullet through his head.

When *The Great White Hope* ended, my wife and I flew to Rome and did the European adventure that we couldn't afford after college. We stayed in an inexpensive little hotel in the Republic Plaza. The room was tiny and dingy, but we didn't care. We were actually in Roma. I said "ciao" as often during the day as I could, and I bought six Italian neckties at a little shop across the street from the Trevi Fountain.

Each morning we'd walk up to the Via Veneto and have a cappuccino outside at the Café Paris. We'd read the *Herald Tribune* and then wander over Rome until it was time for lunch at the Piccolo Mondo Restaurant, a hangout for the Italian movie industry. I would order a large portion of pasta with lots of red wine. I wished someone would ask me what picture I had just finished, but no one ever did. It wasn't quite la dolce vita, but one afternoon I was sure I saw Fellini.

I was young Hemingway and regal Fitzgerald, Keats and Shelly, and all the other exciting authors and poets that I had taught to my classes at John Adams Junior High School. The best thing of all was that within three months, we'd have a baby.

We left Rome and took a train to Florence. We walked from the railroad station to the Arno River, looking for a small hotel near the Ponte Vecchio. We spent three days enjoying that city's art and history. I was in love with Europe. It was old and solid, secure, and un-changing—everything our life wasn't.

I wanted to get back to Hollywood and continue to do the best pictures with important directors and meaningful scripts in romantic locations for the rest of my life, but that isn't what happened.

On April 30, we became the proud parents of our first child, Christopher. Our life became full of the new baby, new duties, and a new way of living.

I spent the next two years doing very forgettable movies in unro-mantic places like Wheeling, West Virginia; Sonora, California; and Durango, Mexico. Nothing else was offered to me. With a new baby, I had to take whatever picture I could get.

My assistant directing career, which had started by working on quality pictures with important directors, was now going nowhere. I didn't know how to get my career back where I wanted it. I felt I was losing control over my future.

I worked with Cliff Robertson on a rodeo film he directed called *J. W. Coop*, which had Geraldine Page playing his mother and Cristina Ferrare playing his love interest.

I did two movies that McLaglen directed: *Something Big* with Dean Martin and Brian Keith, which was done in Mexico, and a Jimmy Stewart film done in West Virginia. Dean Martin had sent my family a refrigerator, a Westinghouse Golden Harvest, for our new home in West Los Angeles.

I was away from my family for more than two months on each film. When I returned, everything seemed different. The house had changed. Chris had grown. My wife and I weren't the same people we had been. Was it the early '70s, or was it both of us?

It was 1970, and I was filming Fool's Parade on a sound stage at the old Columbia Studios on the corner of Gower and Sunset Boulevard. It wasn't the kind of movie I wanted to do, but I had to bring home a paycheck.

It was lunchtime and the electricians had turned off most of the lights on the sound stage. Just a couple of work lights remained on. You could see to walk, but it was too dark to read. Those crew members who wanted to read the newspaper or trade papers sat at the makeup tables where the bright lights were.

He didn't sit there.

For more than thirty years he'd been a top movie star. He never seemed to change. Maybe that's what made him so special.

He got out of his movie wardrobe and into his own clothes at the beginning of every lunch hour. He wore work clothes, the kind you'd expect to see on the owner of a feed store somewhere in the Midwest, not on a Hollywood star.

He'd leave his dressing room carrying an old fashioned lunch pail, the kind my father used to carry to work at the Milwaukee post office. The lunch pail was black with a rounded top. When he opened it there was a thermos bottle securely clamped inside the top. The sandwich and fruit were in the base of the lunch pail.

He'd enter the sound stage and find an area off by himself. Most often he'd sit on a wooden platform and dangle his long legs off the edge as he explored the lunch his wife had prepared for him. She packed his lunch every day we shot in Los Angeles—one sandwich, fruit, and, in the thermos, her lemonade.

He could've been a grip or an electrician sitting on the platform eating his sandwich, except that his lunch had been packed early that morning at his home on Roxbury Drive, north of Sunset Boulevard in Beverly Hills. That's in the high rent district, even for Beverly Hills.

I sat near him as I caught up on my paperwork under a work light. Once we talked of my new son, Chris. Another time I mentioned that I had known his son from acting on The Lieutenant; he had been a photographer on the series. Nearly every day toward the end of the lunch hour, after he had finished his sandwich and fruit, he'd turn to me.

"My wife makes the best lemonade there is," he'd say to me. "Want some?"

It was 1985, fifteen years later. I liked to take Roxbury Drive as a shortcut to get back onto Benedict Canyon when I was driving north through Beverly Hills toward Mulholland.

One afternoon I was coming up Roxbury from Sunset Boulevard when I saw two big red dogs running down the sidewalk and a tall old guy chasing them. It had to be him.

I drove ahead of the dogs, parked, and stood in the sidewalk as the three creatures approached.

"Now, whoa! Wait there, you!" he was saying, as he moved as fast as he could. His two dogs stopped where I stood, with their tails wagging and their tongues hanging out of their mouths.

He was in the same work clothes he had worn during the lunches on Fool's Parade, but with a floppy fisherman's hat on his head. He got the two leashes onto his dogs as I stood guard.

"I want to thank you," he drawled. "I don't know if I ever would've caught these two," he laughed.

He was older, but nothing else had changed. He had the same voice and famous mannerisms. I guessed that the really great ones don't change.

He was puffing a bit, but smiling down at his dogs and me.

"Would you like something cool to drink? My wife makes the best lemonade there is," Jimmy Stewart said, as he pointed at his home. "Want some?"

Lost Horizon

"He can't meet Ross Hunter looking like that!" Shel Schrager, the first AD, yelled to Ray Gosnell, the unit manager, as they both stared at me.

Columbia Studios had called me to interview for the second assistant director job on the re-make of *Lost Horizon*, which I hoped would bring me back to working on meaningful pictures.

"He's just a second AD!" Ray Gosnell said. "You can't expect him to be in a suit and tie!"

My wardrobe had never been a problem. I've always dressed for comfort, which meant I wore Levi's and tennis shoes, even when I was a teacher.

"You want to introduce him to Ross Hunter?" Shel Schrager continued. "He isn't even wearing a jacket!"

I knew Ross Hunter had produced *Airport*, but he was primarily known for doing fluffy romantic comedies with beautiful people like Doris Day and Rock Hudson in *Pillow Talk* or Debbie Reynolds in *Tammy and the Bachelor*.

Ray, Shel, and I were ushered into Mr. Hunter's office. Ross Hunter and his associate producer and longtime friend, Jacques Mapes, were standing behind a huge desk. Both of them were dressed in very expensive casual clothes—loafers, tailored slacks, the best shirts, and exclusive sweaters from some shop in the Beverly Hills Hotel. I guessed they were each wearing more than a month's salary for me. His office was immaculate in shiny glass and a reddish wood. The chairs looked like antiques. I stood away from them and nearer the club chairs in case he'd ask us to sit down. Maybe we should have waited until I had at least a sports jacket.

"Well, what have we here?" Ross Hunter asked, as he looked at me.

"Mr. Hunter, this is Jerry Ziesmer. We'd like to hire him as our, your, second AD," Ray offered.

"Really! Look, Jacques," Ross Hunter said, and the two of them smiled at me.

"Jerry, is it?" he asked, and looked directly at me.

"Yes," I answered.

"Did you hear, Jacques?" Ross Hunter asked. "He's perfect. Isn't he, Jacques?"

"I should think so," Jacques added.

Shel mumbled something, and Ray started to usher me out.

"Jerry! Do you have any questions for us?" Ross Hunter asked.

I looked at Shel and Ray, and I knew they wanted to get me out as soon as possible, but I thought I should say something.

"Who's going to be in the movie?" I asked.

"Jesus Christ!" Shel exploded, as he felt I had politically overstepped my bounds.

"No! But don't I wish he was!" Ross Hunter shouted, as he and Jacques screamed in laughter.

In Hollywood you never know who your best friends will be. Twelve years after Lost Horizon, *Shel Schrager would be head of production for Columbia Studios and would nominate me for membership in the Academy of Motion Picture Arts and Sciences.*

Ray Gosnell and his wife, along with Suzanne and me, would be members of the foreign film jury for the Academy. We've seen more than four hundred foreign films together in the last fifteen years and still counting.

Lost Horizon *was the last motion picture Ross Hunter ever produced. He was buried near the graves of Helen Hayes and Marilyn Monroe in a small cemetery behind the Avco Movie Theatre in West Los Angeles.*

Lost Horizon had one of the most talented crews ever assembled. We could have had a crew bowling party and used their Oscar statutes for bowling pins.

Charles Jarrott was the director who had done *Anne of a Thousand Days* and *Mary, Queen of Scots*, both critically acclaimed.

The cameraman, Robert Surtees, had been nominated fifteen times and had received Oscars for *King Solomon's Mines*, *The Bad and the Beautiful*, and *Ben Hur*.

Preston Ames, the production designer, had gotten Oscars for *An American in Paris* and *Gigi*, as well as nominations for *Lust for Life* and *Airport*.

Burt Bacharach, the composer, had received an Oscar for *Butch Cassidy and the Sundance Kid* in his five Academy nominations.

Jean Louis, the costume designer, received fourteen nominations and an Oscar for *The Solid Gold Cadillac*.

Hermes Pan, the Oscar-winning choreographer from all the Fred Astaire and Ginger Rogers films, was called in for our dance sequences.

We also had a distinguished cast headed by Peter Finch and Liv Ullmann, both of whom were major international stars, as well as Charles Boyer, John Gielgud, Michael York, Bobby Van, George Kennedy, and Sally Kellerman.

We had a proven hit script. It was a very successful movie made in 1937 with Ronald Coleman and Jane Wyatt. How could it miss?

The Fox Ranch off Malibu Canyon Road had been planted in wildflowers to bloom exactly when we wished to film our exterior scenes. Our sets on the backlot were magnificent, a re-do of the castle for *Camelot*. Every detail of set dressing, down to having real flowers in every vase on the huge sets, was done no matter what the cost. The hills in *The Sound of Music* were nothing compared to the acres of blooming wildflowers covering our hills in Malibu Canyon.

We filmed on the very summit of Mount Hood in Oregon. We all dressed in Himalayan snowsuits, rode huge tractors up the mountain, then hiked the rest of the way. We used helicopters to get our camera equipment to the top. Then we recreated that same location in Bronson Canyon right below the famous Hollywood sign for the blizzards in the movie. We used plastic snow and wind machines, with forty people throwing plastic snow into the air and fifteen huge airplane ritters to simulate a mighty blizzard.

All during the production, the cast and crew were invited to studio showings to see portions of our film. Each sequence we saw was wonderful. It had all the color, music, dancing, and excitement of *The Sound of Music*. In fact we thought we had a bigger hit, much bigger.

When the final cast and crew wrap party was given, it was held on our most beautiful temple set on a sound stage at the Burbank studio. All of us were there, and it was luxurious and wonderful, with real flowers, gourmet foods, wines, and live music. It was exciting and glamorous, and we all felt we were part of one of the great films ever to have been made in Hollywood. We congratulated each other again and again, all evening long.

Six months later we all received our engraved invitations to the special cast and crew showing of *Lost Horizon* at the Regent Theatre on Broxton Avenue in Westwood. I got there early to assure myself of a center seat to view what I was sure would be one of my career's shining achievements.

We were all giddy before the showing. We greeted each other and laughed. We all believed we had a big hit, maybe the biggest and best ever.

I said hello to Robert Surtees. We'd become friends. He had children older than me, but we had grown close while making *Lost Horizon*. During the filming he'd bring a paper bag and eat the lunch his wife had made for him, and I would spend my lunchtime relaxing near the camera. We got to talking about all his films, his wife, and how much he enjoyed living in Carmel. He was an accomplished still photographer, and when I told him my story about Bernie Guffey using a Kodak Instamatic, I thought he was going to die laughing.

Most of the cast was there. I think all of the crew was. When the theatre lights dimmed, we all sat down and *Lost Horizon* began.

Two hours later, when the lights came up, no one moved. We were in shock. We had seen the parts of the movie, and they had been wonderful. The singing and dancing at the Fox Ranch, the love scenes and songs at night on the backlot in Burbank were so romantic. What happened? *Lost Horizon* was not simply lost—it was terrible.

I sat in my seat and stared at the blank screen. It was as if we had seen another movie. The parts were so wonderful, but the whole movie didn't work. How was that possible? All of our work and the long hours were for this?

I don't remember walking up the aisle and out of the Regent Theatre, but I stood with Robert Surtees at the curb in front of the theatre. I was near tears; I had wanted so much for *Lost Horizon* to be the great picture that would turn my career around, that would make studios want to call me to work on their top films. It wasn't a great movie; it was bad. In fact, it was very bad. It was the kind of movie you didn't even mention you had done.

I couldn't go back to making pictures that from the first day of shooting had no chance of being important. I hadn't left teaching to do mediocre films.

Robert Surtees had been where I was that night many times in his career. He was a big man, sort of a cross between a calm farmer and a friendly hardware store man. He put his arm around my shoulders.

"What's the matter? Disappointed?" he asked.

I felt so empty.

"This happens, Jerry. You have to learn to take it," he said.

"How could it?" I questioned. "Everything was so wonderful when we were making it."

"No one can tell how good the movie is until the whole picture is up on the screen," he stated, and gave me a couple of gentle shoulder pats.

"All those nights! The hours we spent. The top of Mount Hood!" I argued. "We've been filming this for months and months!"

"I know," he said, and hung on to me.

"Don't you feel cheated?" I asked.

"Would have been nice," he said, "but it wasn't one of the good ones, was it?" And he smiled down at me.

My eyes welled up with tears.

"Drive up to Carmel this weekend. There's a little cottage place in town called the Blue Bird. Stay there for two days and look out at the sea and walk on the beach. Then come on back and take your time looking for your next film. Don't just look for a paycheck, or you'll never find the films you want to do."

I nodded that I understood, but I was feeling so much pain.

Robert Surtees turned me toward him, and I looked up into his old, worn cameraman's face. He smiled down at the young assistant director. "There'll be others for you, and I hope I'm the cameraman," he said.

I did drive up to Carmel that weekend, and I stayed in the Blue Bird cottage and looked out at the rocks and surf and walked the shore for two days. The pain was still there, but what I had gained was the knowledge that others felt as deeply as I did and that they understood.

Monday morning I drove back down the coast toward Los Angeles. It wasn't until I passed Morro Bay and the Hearst Castle that I got my sense of humor back.

Stan Laurel had told me of William Randolph Hearst's parties where he would have all kinds of expensive gifts suspended in a net high over his guests' heads; then at his signal the net would be opened and all the gifts would come crashing to the floor. The famous guests from Winston Churchill to Douglas Fairbanks and Charlie Chaplin would grab and struggle for the gifts as Mr. Hearst and Marion Davies stood on a balcony above and laughed at all of them. Stan said he never once joined in the scramble for the gifts, but he was always invited back to every party Hearst gave, and a lot of other people weren't.

I wasn't sure why Stan Laurel had told me that story, but about an hour later when I turned off Pacific Coast Highway and headed east on Sunset Boulevard toward Hollywood, I thought I understood.

The Way We Were

It was 1972, and I was desperately looking for an assistant director job on a top motion picture. I knew that I wanted to spend my career working on the very best movies, even if that meant I had to starve once in a while between films. The trouble was that I hadn't made enough contacts to keep myself working steadily on top features, and I couldn't take just any film job because I wanted to stay available if a top picture came along. It came down to this: If I really wanted to work on the best films, I had to sit by the phone and wait for them to call.

Columbia Studios had always produced some of each year's top movies, so I was pleased when their production executive, John Veitch, called me to begin work on one of their new features.

John Veitch had a long career in film production. He had been the first assistant director for George Stevens on *The Greatest Story Ever Told*, among many other films. His honesty and class behavior throughout his long career were a constant reminder that you could be human and compassionate and also be a success in Hollywood. It's still true.

My first day on the job I read the script, and I knew that the film was not the motion picture I wanted. I felt the story was strained and only seemed to generate needless violence. After finally getting a job, now I had to tell John Veitch, the most honorable man in Hollywood, that I didn't want the job because the film wasn't really good. I wished I hadn't been born so stubborn.

I knocked and walked into his office and sat down with the script in my hands. John was sitting at his desk concentrating on some papers.

"Hey, Jerry, how are you?" He smiled only glancing at me. "What did you think of the script?"

I just stared at him. I was afraid to speak. I felt my young career was about to slip away.

"Did you read it?"

I nodded.

"Well, what do you think?" and he put down his papers and looked at me. He was still smiling.

"I'm sorry, but it's just not right for me," I said.

He did not blink. His smile vanished, but he kept staring at me. It seemed like forever before he said, "Why not? What's the matter with it?"

"It's too violent without any purpose. There's no meaning to it. I don't want to work on it." I was so frightened.

He got up from behind his desk, walked to his office door, and quietly closed it. I just looked down toward my shoes wishing this never had happened.

"Are you telling me you're quitting because you don't like the script?"

I couldn't move.

"Why do you care? You're just the assistant director." He was very quiet and very direct.

"Because I only want to work on the best pictures."

"Not every picture you make is going to be a 'best' picture. You have to make some of these once in a while." We stared at each other. John had been a war hero on Iwo Jima. His life and career were everything I wanted mine to be.

"You have another picture to work on?" he asked, as he searched my face.

"No, I don't," I answered. I wish I had, that would've given me an excuse.

"I'm sorry," I said, "I just can't do this picture." I started to get up.

"Wait a minute. Let me tell you something." He was very quiet. "You want a career in this business, you take the first job you're offered and you do it. When it's over you take the next job that's offered to you. You understand? That's the way it is." He never raised his voice and he stared dead into my eyes. "Sometimes you do a good film and sometimes you don't."

"I'm really sorry," I said. I started to go again.

"Sit down, Jerry. We do a lot of films at Columbia, you know that?"

"I know." I felt my career was about to go up in smoke. Why was I doing this?

"Why should I call you for our top pictures if you won't do this one for us?" he said, as he pointed at the script I had in my hands.

"I guess because I care. I don't know. I'm sorry, but I can't do this."

I got to my feet, put the script on his desk, and walked out of his office. I fully expected never to get a call from Columbia Studios again. I felt awful.

It was about three weeks later that John Veitch called me.

"Got a script for you to read. A little thing Sydney Pollack is doing . . . *The Way We Were* . . . with Barbra Streisand and Robert Redford. Mentioned you to Sydney. Told him if you *cared* about the script you'd meet with him on Friday at ten. OK?"

"Yeah!" I was so excited. First to get another call from John Veitch, and then to get a chance to work with Sydney Pollack, Streisand, and Redford. "When can I get the script?"

I read Arthur Laurent's script that night, and I was in love with the story. I wanted desperately to work on *The Way We Were*. Now all I had to do was get the job.

When I first saw Sydney Pollack he was sitting behind his desk looking over some costume sketches for *The Way We Were*. He was dressed casually in jeans, a sport shirt, corduroy jacket with leather patches at the elbows, and tennis shoes. His office was covered with the tools of the director preparing a film: Script research papers and photographs were on every horizontal surface, except on the large coffee table where a scale model of New York City's El Morocco nightclub was displayed. Posters from his previous films *This Property Condemned* and *Jeremiah Johnson* were on the walls. From the look of his office, Sydney Pollack was a hard-working director who was going to be fully prepared to shoot his film. I liked him at once.

The door to his office was open, so I knocked on the door frame.

"I'm Jerry Ziesmer. I just came over to . . ."

"Hi, yeah . . . someone said you were going to come by. Sydney Pollack." He rose and came around his desk as we shook hands.

"Sit down," he said, as he moved to a little sitting area with a sofa and a couple of chairs around a large coffee table. His work was everywhere.

"Thanks," I said. We moved some drawings off chairs and onto the table.

"You read the script?" he asked.

"Yeah, it's sensational. I love it. I mean . . ." I wanted the interview to go so well, but I just couldn't talk. "It's really a great script. I mean really!"

He nodded. "Tell me about yourself?"

"Well, I grew up in Milwaukee. Went to Northwestern University, studied theatre."

"Oh, yeah? With Alvina Krause?"

"Right." I loved that he knew my theatre mentor. "I used to live in the basement of her home."

"You're kidding!" he laughed.

"Did a lot of summer stock."

"Where about?" he asked.

"Ahh, well, Miss Krause had her summer theatre in Eagles Mere, Pennsylvania, and then I did summer stock in Rhinelander and Oconomowoc, Wisconsin."

"I was at the Neighborhood Playhouse," Sydney said. "Used to be Sandy Meisner's assistant."

"You're kidding!" I said in turn. I felt very comfortable with him.

"No, I've only been out here a few years," he added.

"Me, too. Got my masters at UCLA. Then the DGA training program. Been an assistant director for three years."

He smiled and nodded. "Good. Great. You've worked with Howard Koch, Jr.?"

"Sure, he's great," I said. Howard was a good assistant director and friend.

Sydney stared at me, then looked down at the model.

"You did say you *cared* for the script?" he asked with a smile.

"Yeah, a lot. . . . It's great. I really care a lot."

"Veitch thought you might."

I didn't know what to say next, and he just smiled and looked at me. There was a long pause, and then he started to gently nod his head up and down.

Finally he said, "I'd like you to do *The Way We Were* with me."

The next thing I remembered was being in my car and screaming for joy.

John Veitch had the office next door to Cameron Crowe on the third floor of the Poitier Building at Sony Studios when we were doing Jerry Maguire. *John was producing the heart-warming film* Fly Away

Home. *He was still the dapper gentleman who nearly twenty-five years earlier understood the feelings of one very young assistant director.*

My office was just a tiny nook, hardly an office at all. I didn't care. I was working on *The Way We Were* with Sydney Pollack, Barbra Streisand, and Robert Redford, along with one of Hollywood's top producers, Ray Stark. Nothing could have been better.

The first time on the picture I had any contact with Barbra Streisand or Robert Redford was during the wardrobe and makeup tests. The costume designer, Dorothy Jeakins, had spent months selecting the clothes for each scene to give Barbra and Robert the "right look." I did not want to miss a thing.

After six hours everyone was tense, everyone but Robert Redford. He was a young Greek god with blond hair and tanned skin. Redford was the true man's man combined with the classic good looks of a movie matinee idol. Sydney, Dorothy Jeakins, and others huddled around Redford as he stood in his white Navy uniform for the El Morocco nightclub scene. I listened to every word.

"Is the jacket too tight?" asked Sydney's brother, Bernie, who was our set wardrobe man.

"Looks great!" Sydney said, and added, "How does it feel? How do *you* feel?"

Redford stared at everyone and slowly chewed his gum.

"Color's a good white," Harry Stradling, Jr., our cameraman, added. His father had been the cameraman on *Hello, Dolly!*

"Should we take it out a bit here?" Bernie suggested.

"Why? It's perfect!" Dorothy exclaimed.

"What do you think? How does it feel to *you*, Bob?" Sydney asked.

Barbra Streisand entered the sound stage. She was a star and behaved like one. Marty, her manager, was always with her. Barbra had a very quick, questioning mind. She learned quickly and never forgot a thing. Although she had done only a few movies, she was well versed in every aspect of filmmaking. She knew and understood the camera and the use of lighting and lenses as well as the most experienced cameraman. She was a perfectionist who would never be satisfied until her performance was the very best it could be. Barbra immediately joined the discussion.

"Are those medals right?" she said, pointing to the naval decorations on Redford's uniform. "What's this one for? The red and blue. No, this one."

Bernie knew them all. Talk about pressure.

"That's the good conduct. This one's the . . ."

"What color's the set in the El Morocco?" Barbra asks. "What am I wearing? The blue? With the white and the hat?"

Dorothy Jeakins joined the discussion.

"Yes, Barbra, the blue with white and your hat, purse, and gloves."

Redford just stared at everyone and slowly chewed his gum.

"I go to the El Morocco, my apartment, do I wear it anywhere else?" Barbra asks.

Bernie adds, "In the cab. You and Hubbell go with . . ."

"I know the cab!" Barbra was going again. "When we meet again, what do I wear?"

Sydney tried to redirect the conversation, "Now Bob's uniform . . ."

"What?" Barbra asked. "What do I wear when we meet again? Not the darker blue?"

"No, Barbra," Dorothy said, "You're in your work outfit from the radio studio."

"Could I have changed? I don't want to wear the same thing the whole picture!"

"What do we think of Bob's uniform?" Sydney asked.

Barbra moved off with Dorothy, Harry Stradling, and Marty, her manager, leaving Bernie, Redford, and Sydney. Sydney and his brother stared at Redford in his uniform.

"How is it for *you*, Bob?" Sydney asked gravely. I leaned forward to capture every word.

"Guys, it's fine," Redford said quickly. "A uniform's a uniform, OK?"

Bernie tried to add a little something, but Redford continued, "Come on, I've got to get out of here, OK? What's next?"

Barbra quickly came back to the group. "Your first uniform is dress white, but the second has to be tan because it's spring and . . ."

Redford just stared at the ceiling of the sound stage and slowly chewed his gum.

The first major scene in *The Way We Were* took place in 1945 at New York's El Morocco nightclub. The El Morocco was a set built on a sound stage at Columbia Studios. Barbra Streisand played Katie Morosky, a supporter of left-wing causes who also worked for the Armed Forces Radio. Robert Redford played Hubbell Gardiner, an officer in the U.S. Navy who also wrote novels. When Katie first saw him, Hubbell was sitting on a bar stool while sound asleep. They had not seen each other since their college graduation dance in 1937.

Two days prior to filming this scene, we held a major interview for the screen extras we would need to fill the El Morocco set. There were about two hundred extras from Central Casting for us to select the one hundred we'd need.

"Look! Just be patient!" I was shouting. "This is for at least four day's work, if you're selected!"

The two hundred extras were inside an empty sound stage. They'd arrived at ten in the morning for an interview call check, five dollars in 1972, and a chance to work with Barbra Streisand and Robert Redford.

I was doing my best to get them informed and organized before Sydney Pollack, Dorothy Jeakins, the choreographer, and the makeup and hair departments arrived.

"Jerry!" an extra shouted, "What days does it film?"

"We'll begin Monday for at least . . ."

"Monday! I'm at Universal through Wednesday! A bunch of us are. Central Casting knows that."

I tried for calm. "Look, how many of you are at Universal next week?"

About fifteen hands went up as extras asked, "What's Central doing?" "Didn't they know?" "Did you tell them?"

"No one said when you're filming!" an extra explained.

They'd get their five dollars for the interview, but I'd screwed up. I never told Central what days we'd need the extras.

"OK, OK. All of you working at Universal can leave. I'm sorry. We'll catch you later on this one."

"Jerry, if you'd tell Carl at Central what days you're going to film . . ."

"Thanks, Bruce," I said, hoping that no studio exec would hear of my blunder. It's a young AD's mistake, but it cost the company fifteen SEG interview checks at five dollars each. The extras liked me for the most part, so I knew none of them would say a thing.

The extras in 1972 were all members of the Screen Extras Guild, and working as extras on motion pictures and television was all they did. Their guild limited the number of their members, so any assistant director who worked even a couple of years got to know most of the Screen Extras Guild's membership. Since this was a Columbia Studios film, Central Casting had sent all of this studio's favorite extras to our interview. To become a *favorite* meant that you were a member of the immediate family of a Columbia Studio executive, were a friend or relative of the casting agents at Central Casting, or were known by the film's producer, director, actors, production manager, or assistant directors.

I began again, "Now those of you left . . . look. The name of the film is *The Way We Were* with Barbra Streisand and Robert Redford. We're filming on the lot, Stage 16, Monday through at least next Thursday. The set's a nightclub, the El Morocco in New York City . . . 1945."

"Jerry, you need dancers, huh?" Eddie asked as he went into one of his dance routines. Eddie was from vaudeville days, a tap dancer, and he loved the "dancer calls." He was in his seventies, but he made every dance call.

"Right, Eddie. Now listen. We need about one hundred people—dancers, waiters, servicemen, dates . . . ," I continued.

"What about fittings?" Cheryl asked. She'd been an extra at this studio since before the war and knew more about what was happening at Columbia than the president.

"If you're selected . . . ," I continued. "The women will have their fittings today and Friday morning. The men will have to go through hair today and get haircuts if necessary this afternoon or Friday morning, then your fittings."

Half the men have their hands in the air.

"Jerry! Haircuts! How can you cut our hair? We got westerns to do maybe twice or three times a week! We can't cut our hair!"

"Hang on!" I explained. "If you don't want to cut your hair you can't be selected for a serviceman, that's all. There are other roles."

They calmed down a bit.

"You can still be a nightclub patron," I added.

Every show it's the same thing. You can't blame the men about the haircuts because they get a lot of their work on western television shows, and they have to have long hair.

"Now listen up! For all the dancers selected today . . . Friday afternoon at two, our choreographer will be on Stage 12 to work with you on the 1940s dancing." I thought I had covered it all just as Sydney entered the stage. Immediately all of the extras got on their best behavior.

"Mr. Pollack, do you remember me? I was in *Property Condemned?*" an elderly woman asked.

Sydney smiled, "Yeah, sure . . . I remember . . ."

Everyone around the woman gave her a bit more status since Sydney Pollack remembered working with her.

"Please form a line so we can take a look at you," I said.

All of the extras lined up and looked at the reviewing group. Sydney was a bit embarrassed and stood back while he looked at the group of extras. The wardrobe people looked for women who would fit into their available 1940s wardrobe. The hairdressers were counting the number of men who would have to get a haircut.

I was very pleased when Jonathon Bruener was chosen by Sydney to be one of the El Morocco waiters, because he was a real waiter at the Scandia Restaurant on Sunset Boulevard. Jonathon always made the background action in restaurants look great, and he knew how to serve properly, set the table correctly, and told all of the other waiter extras what to do.

I needed people like Jonathon to make me look good as an assistant director. So when Jonathon motioned to me, I walked over to him while the wardrobe ladies were discussing fashions with Sydney.

"Jerry, I want you to meet my friend," Jonathon began. "This is Siggy, Siggy Frohlich. Siggy, Jerry Ziesmer."

"Hi, how are you, Ziggy?"

"It's *Siggy* not . . . ," Jonathon added.

"Beau-tee-ful, Jerry, beau-tee-ful," Siggy said.

I made a mental note to add him to the list of *favorite* extras because of Jonathon.

"Nice meeting you," and I started back toward Sydney.

"Wait, Jerry." Jonathon stopped me. "Siggy is special. Listen, that little problem you had today with the fifteen interview checks. . . . Siggy would've caught that for you. You have to do two hundred vouchers for today's interview. . . . Siggy would take care of that, too."

I looked at Siggy. He was about sixty years old and as short as Mickey Rooney—and for good reason: Siggy had been the stand-in for Mickey Rooney during all of the great M-G-M films with Mickey and Judy Garland.

"You take care of the extra calls to Central Casting and do the vouchers, Ziggy?" I asked.

"Jerry, it's *Siggy*," Jonathon said.

"I'll take care of all the calls and vouchers for you every day," he answered. "And I stand in, too."

Sounded great to me. I hated paperwork, and I knew I could learn a lot from him.

"OK, Ziggy, you're on."

"Beau-tee-ful!" Ziggy said.

"Congratulations, *Ziggy*," Jonathon said.

Ziggy not only got his new name that day, but Ziggy and I became a team for the next twenty years until his *early* retirement at the age of eighty-three.

For as long as I could remember, Ziggy lived in Culver City on the east side of Motor Avenue about three blocks north of the old M-G-M Studios. It was there that Ziggy was the stand-in and longtime friend of Mickey Rooney and the rest of that studio's stars during the golden years of M-G-M.

I remember going to Ziggy's apartment after he finally retired to pick him up for Saturday lunches at my home or at one of his favorite Chinese restaurants. I'd come in and sit for a minute while Ziggy got his things together for our afternoon outing.

On the walls of his apartment were clippings from the M-G-M Studios magazine showing Ziggy in his army uniform when he left M-G-M to serve in World War II. There were more articles from the magazine when he was welcomed back in 1946. There were the 8 × 10 photos of Ziggy with Mickey and Judy Garland, of Ziggy at the racetracks with Clark Gable, Spencer Tracy, and the other M-G-M stars. I saw pictures of Ziggy and Mickey at the Flamingo and Stardust Hotels in Las Vegas. There was a photo from The Way We Were *and one of us from* Annie.

One of my favorite times with Ziggy was when I brought him to our home and he sat with Suzanne, our kids, and me as we showed the video tape of The Wizard of Oz *and Ziggy told us nonstop stories. He told of playing the role of the Captain of the Flying Monkeys, and how the wires hurt him, and how long it took to get through makeup. He told of Judy Garland and the fun involved in making pictures back then. That was 1939, the year I was born.*

He only got to the racetrack maybe once a year now, and he got to Las Vegas even less. He spent a lot of time in his apartment among all those pictures and clippings.

Terry Leonard, my old friend and stunt coordinator from Apocalypse Now, *said that at the end of your career the only things that mattered were memories, friends, and 8 × 10s. Ziggy had them all.*

One day during a lunch break, I followed Sydney Pollack onto Stage 16, the El Morocco set. It was the day before shooting, and the set dressers and drapery crew were doing the final adjustments. Sydney

walked from the entrance of the club to the reservation stand, then he
slowly moved toward the bar. I wondered how often Sydney reviewed
the scene using the scale model of the El Morocco in his office.

"Sydney," a prop person called to him, "we're going to have drinks at
the bar and tables. What do you think of a cigarette girl? You know with
the tray?"

"Yeah, OK," Sydney answered, but he was still deciding on the
blocking for the re-meeting scene between Streisand and Redford.

I stayed back and watched him. He worked so much by himself.
Sydney was a very quiet person. I never heard him raise his voice. He
walked back to the club's reservation stand and then back toward the
bar. He repositioned a bar stool; I knew that'd be where Redford would
be sitting. Sydney was checking the camera angles, then he saw me.
"Jerry, what are you doing?" he said, as he chuckled.

"Just checking the set. Fitting the extras today. Just want to make sure
we've enough," I answered. "Hundred should do it, don't you think?"

"Yeah, it'll be fine. Jer, keep the bar area filled with a bit older folks,
you know?"

"Older?"

"Yeah, put the 'young beauties' in the back, over in the dining area;
keep the folks around Barbra and Bob . . . well, you know . . . a little
plainer. Put the 'prom queens' in the back."

"Got it," I said. I learned something new every day.

Three weeks ago this was just an empty sound stage, and now it's the
interior of New York City's El Morocco, circa 1945. Sydney looked at
the lamps, all from the 1940s. I picked up an El Morocco matchbox
from the bar, exact replica of the original. We laughed, enjoying the
quality of the detail in the set dressing. Everything was so perfect.
Stephen Grimes was our production designer, and he was the best.

"How many days do we shoot here?" Sydney asked.

"About four, maybe five," I answered, and we both laughed.

What work, what craftsmanship, and for only four days of shooting.
Of course, we never thought *The Way We Were* would still be enjoyed
twenty-five years later.

"Looks just like the photos, everything!" I said.

"Wait until all the people are in," Sydney chuckled.

It was 6:00 A.M. when I arrived at the studio for the first day of
shooting in the El Morocco set. Ziggy was already there to check in the

5:00 and 5:30 female extras. The earliest women had to begin their hair and makeup at that ungodly hour if we were to get them all ready and on the set by 9:00. Even by staggering the women's calls, it'd be hard to get fifty women extras through hair, makeup, dressed, and to the set by nine. They all had to love show business to be there at that hour.

"Ziggy, how're we doing?" I asked, as I nursed my coffee and cigarette.

Ziggy was passing out the extras' vouchers and getting the women to begin either makeup or hair right after they finished their coffee and doughnuts.

"Beau-tee-ful, Jerry," Ziggy answered. "Anne, after the doughnut, right to hair, OK? They're using you in the first shot. Might be a silent bit."

What a diplomat he was.

"Ziggy! I need Laura to do my hair. She knows my hair!" Number one "prom queen" shouted.

He knew everyone and could handle every emergency.

"That's who's going to do it. Now go to makeup first."

I checked with the makeup and hair crews, then with wardrobe, but Ziggy had it all under control. It was "beau-tee-ful," as Ziggy would say.

I wondered if he'd done the same things on Mickey Rooney's pictures thirty years ago, or on *The Wizard of Oz*. He probably got to M-G-M early and pushed Judy Garland, the Wicked Witch, and all the other flying monkeys through hair and makeup. That was my Ziggy.

The El Morocco scene demonstrated Sydney Pollack's talent as a storyteller. The written scene was nothing. Katie Morosky came into the nightclub and discovered Hubbell Gardiner passed out, sitting upright on a bar stool. They hadn't seen each other since college graduation. Sydney directed with simplicity. He let us share in his storytelling by simply showing Katie's face as she gazed at Hubbell. We make our own discovery of her feelings. Simplicity was not simple to achieve. Sydney worked hard to gain the trust of the actors, especially Barbra.

He began with a rehearsal period prior to the picture. Many of the rehearsals were nothing more than discussions with Barbra or Redford in Sydney's office. We also used an empty sound stage to tape out the floor plan of the El Morocco. The art department then dressed the floor plan with furniture similar to what would be in the nightclub when we actually filmed. Sydney then rehearsed the El Morocco scene with Barbra and Redford. He would say one thing to the actors and then he'd wait while they, mainly Barbra, would talk-laugh-talk, and then finally move back to the scene. That's the way she had to work; it took time.

Redford could be given direction, and he'd act on it immediately. Barbra got the direction from Sydney and then would have to chew on it while she'd talk of other things, like wardrobe or the set dressing or the lines. But finally she'd come back to the point where the direction had been given, and the rehearsal could continue.

It'd go something like this:

Sydney said, "OK, look . . . Bob's sitting in the El Morocco on a bar stool . . . totally zonked. Bob, try the stool . . . about the center of the bar . . . totally out of it . . . OK. Barbra, you're over here . . . you've just entered . . . OK? Now just stand . . ."

Barbra interrupted, "Over there? Way over there? Is this where the entrance rope is? Why don't I just go to him? How many people are here? Why don't I say something?"

Redford said, "I'm on the bar stool," and he obediently went and sat on his bar stool.

Sydney continued, "The place is packed. You haven't seen him in all this time. You . . . you just look at him . . . see? You don't speak."

Barbra asked, "Why?" She paced. "I'm in my blue-and-white dress with my purse and hat." She faced Redford, "I'd go over to him! " She laughed. "I would! I'd say . . ."

Sydney interrupted gently, "Not yet . . . just trust me . . . you just look at him. . . . It's Hubbell . . . see? From college . . . OK? The grad-uation dance, OK? It's been eight years."

"I don't see why . . . look I'm here . . . I go over to him. . . ." Barbra worked it out. "I go!"

"No, too soon," slowly and quietly Sydney began to explain. "You bought his book. . . . You've read it ten times. . . ."

Barbra looked at Redford, then at Sydney, everyone could tell something was beginning to come to the surface within her. "OK, wait! So I begin back here . . . I see him. . . . OK, so what's next?"

Sydney took a deep breath, and the rehearsal continued.

"I'm still here, right?" Bob asked, still sitting on the bar stool.

"You're asleep!" Barbra laughed. "Sydney, does he look at me? I've my purse, right?"

"No, you just look at him . . . don't move . . . just look at him . . . OK? You hold your purse."

"Why can't he look at me once?" she laughed. "One little look . . ." She laughed some more.

"Because he's passed out . . . zonked . . . OK? You just stand there and look at him. OK? And all you do is remember . . . OK?" Sydney said as carefully as you might pour nitroglycerine.

There was a moment, then Barbra said, "I look at him."

"Right . . . the last time you saw him . . . ," Sydney began.

"The graduation dance, I know," Barbra added quickly. "So I stand here and remember."

"Good," Sydney replied. "That's it. Trust me."

"That's it?" Barbra asked.

"That's all there is." Sydney said.

"I just sit here," Redford confirmed, "I'm asleep."

"Right!" Barbra made it hers. "You sit there 'zonked.' I come in, see you after eight years. I remember the graduation dance. . . . I just stand here and watch you and remember!" Barbra laughed. "That's it! It's so simple!" she said, as though she knew it all the time.

Sydney just smiled, another battle won.

Following the 1945 El Morocco scene, the movie goes into a flashback to 1937 and Katie's and Hubbell's last year at Union College outside of Schenectady, New York. That meant the whole film company, cast, crew, and equipment, traveled from Hollywood to a small, sleepy university town that had never been used to film a major motion picture.

As one of the assistant directors, I helped to organize the travel plans for all of the cast and crew. The crew had loaded what special equipment they'd need into the airline cargo pods that were flown to Schenectady. Crew equipment that could be rented in New York City was driven up to Union College. I contacted all of the actors and crew and gave them their airline tickets and their hotel arrangements. While the crew could get themselves to the airport, I arranged to have a car and studio driver pick up the actors at their homes and take them personally to the airport. I took no chances with the cast.

It was hard to pack for that location because we were filming in September during the daytime, when the temperature was very warm, but we were also filming all night in October, when it was very cold. I also had to pack clothes in case of rain. If I had to stand out all night in the rain, I wanted to be dressed for it. Though it looked like massive over-packing, I had to bring clothes for every possible weather condition. I also had to consider that we were filming six days a week, which meant I had to have enough clothes to go six full days before I had a chance to do the laundry.

An assistant director didn't make enough money to have the hotel do his laundry, nor did he have enough stature to have the wardrobe department do it for him.

I arrived early at the Los Angeles airport to check in the cast and crew as they arrived for our flight. The camera crew brought a lot of their equipment on the plane with them as extra baggage because they wanted to take no chances with their camera and lenses.

Both Streisand and Redford flew earlier on other flights, so I didn't have to worry about them. Each of them flew with a longtime friend who also did their makeup, hair, or wardrobe for them. I was glad, because looking after seventy members of a Hollywood film crew was all I could deal with.

Somehow we all got to the airport, checked our baggage, and got seated on the plane. Before the plane took off I carefully checked the first class section to be sure that Sydney Pollack and our producer and our other actors were comfortable. Then I went back into the coach section and checked off each member of the crew as I called their name.

"Dan, are you here?" I said, looking for our key makeup person.

"May I see you a moment, Jerry?" Dan said, as he motioned to me from his aisle seat halfway back in coach.

I walked back to him because he looked as though he wanted to tell me a secret. I bent down to listen.

"Why am I here?" he whispered. "When I am *with* Barbra, I always fly first class. No coach, never in coach."

"Dan, look, all of the crew flies coach . . . ," I began to explain.

"I am not crew!" Dan still whispered, but with a bit of intensity.

"Jerry!" Helen, our hairdresser, leaned over Dan and joined our whispered conversation. "We are *with* Barbra. It does not matter if she is *on* the plane or not! We are *with* her, and we should be *in* first class!" Helen whispered, though a tiny bit strained.

"We're not cattle, you know!" Dan said. He could get emotional at times. "We create beauty, for God's sake. We don't just hammer nails!"

I gestured for Dan to stay calm and to keep his voice down. All I needed was to have the grips and electricians hear Dan and then I'd have my hands full of ego-injured Hollywood crew members.

"Jerry." It was Helen again. "Do you have any concept of what Dan and I do? Really? Do you?"

I knelt in the aisle and got as close to Dan and Helen as I could get.

"Look, you two are very important to Barbra and to the picture, I know that."

"No! . . . You! . . . Don't!" And with that Helen turned and put her hand to her face and began to cry.

"Are you happy?" Dan asked.

"Helen . . . ," I began. I could sense other crew members were becoming curious. "Helen, why can't we simply work this out? This isn't a big deal . . . ," I whispered.

With that, Helen sobbed louder, and all the passengers within four rows of us turned around to listen.

"Why did you say that?" Dan asked indignantly. "Don't you have any idea what we go through?"

"No, he doesn't!" roared Helen at full voice. "How could he!" she screamed. "He's just an assistant director!!!"

The whole crew had heard. I was totally embarrassed. Then I felt a person in the aisle next to me, and I looked up to see Sydney Pollack.

"Excuse me, Jerry," Sydney began. "I need to talk to Dan and Helen for a moment."

I rose from my crouched position in the aisle and moved a row back as Sydney crouched where I had been.

"Helen, do you remember in the tests the way you did Barbra for the college scenes with the curls and . . . ," Sydney said.

"Yes, Barbra wanted . . . you know . . . the look . . . ," Helen interrupted.

"I know, but you had it perfect. Do you remember?" Sydney continued.

Dan jumped right in, "You know, Helen. You did the tiny curls, little ones in front, then pulled them down. . . ."

"Oh!" Helen laughed. "That! That look, yes. It was perfect, wasn't it?"

"It was," Sydney added. "Can you begin with that when we first see Katie . . . ?"

"Of course she can!" Dan volunteered.

"Yes . . . yes . . . I believe I could." Helen thought out every word.

"Good," Sydney said. "You two are the greatest!" And he gave them the Pollack chuckle as he rose. "You OK, Jerry?"

"Aahhh," I hesitated.

"Oh, he's just perfect, Sydney. We love him!" Helen warbled.

"Perfect!" chimed in Dan, as he smiled with all his teeth showing.

Sydney looked at me, smiled, then turned and walked back to first class.

I looked down at Helen and Dan, but they were deeply involved in Barbra's look that Sydney just adored.

Our crew from *The Way We Were* arrived in upstate New York without incident. They got checked into their hotel, received their meal money for the week, and unpacked for the three-week location. I went directly to our production office in the hotel and began to help organize the next day's filming.

On the call sheet for the next day I wrote out the scene numbers we were to film, along with the leaving times for all the cast and crew. After I posted a call sheet in the hotel lobby, I also put one under each person's door. I took no chances of anyone missing their call. Though the majority of our crew left the hotel at 7:00 A.M., I had to be outside the hotel to load out the actresses and the makeup, hair, and wardrobe crews at 6:00.

We were filming with a hundred extras who were hired from the student body of the local college. None of them had ever appeared in a movie, let alone a film with Robert Redford and Barbra Streisand. Each morning the girls would arrive at 6:30 to get into the 1937 wardrobe and hairstyles. The first day or two it was fun for everyone, and I had no problems getting the young coeds ready for filming. Then on the third day I found that the girls preferred to look 1972 sensational for Robert Redford rather than 1937 sensational for our film.

"Jerry," Jean, a local coed, began. "Wouldn't it be OK for me to wear these shorts instead of this old long dress? . . . please?"

"It'd be more comfortable," Iris, a second coed, added. She also was wearing shorts.

I could see the beginning of a conspiracy.

"Look . . . what the problem is . . . the college scene for the movie is supposed to be 1937. . . ."

"But that's so old!" Jean interrupted.

"Ah, well, it is, but . . . ," I tried to explain.

"Jerry, look. No one will know if a couple of girls . . . ," Jean began.

"A few girls," another coed, Susan, quickly added.

". . . wore shorts or not!" Jean continued.

"Jerry, listen to this," Jean began. "Back in 1937 at this college were a few forward-thinking girls, who. . . ."

"Were ahead of their time and . . . ," added Susan.

"Wore shorts!" Iris happily concluded. All three cheered happily.

"OK, Jerry? OK?"

I took a deep breath and very carefully began.

"How do you think that'd make Robert Redford feel? And Barbra?"

"What do you mean?" Jean asked in wonder.

Redford was a key word, a buzzword, if you will. I am sure if the local hamburger restaurant had come out with a Robert Redford hamburger the line of coeds would've been around the block.

"Jerry, what do you mean?" Iris stared at me, and Susan moved closer to hear.

"He has feelings, too, you know," I said, and moved away.

Feelings was another buzzword. The girls quickly stopped me.

"Jerry, what? What are Mr. Redford's feelings?" Jean stared at me. The others waited upon my every word.

"Do you think you're the only ones who want to be comfortable, who want to look good? Think of Robert once in a while!" I said, as if they'd thought of everything else but Redford since the movie company came to town.

"What? . . . Jerry . . . ?" Susan began.

"Tell us," Iris begged.

Jean was tearing up. "Feelings? What're Bobby's feelings?"

"It's just that . . . 'Bobby' . . . needs your help, that's all," I said, as though it was one of the world's great secrets. The girls were in a trance. "It's difficult for him, you know. Performing, acting . . . for all of you, when you're . . . not exactly . . . helping him." I just floated it out there like fly casting for bluegills on a Wisconsin lake.

"Oh. . . . How can we help?" "What does he need?" "What, Jerry, what?" They all struck the bait at once.

"Well, what would really help him," I said, "would be for all of you to *act* for him like Bobby *acts* for you. . . . *Act* like you all are in college with Bobby back in 1937, you know?" I set the hook. "Bobby's in college. You're in college. Bobby's dressed for his part. You all are dressed for yours. . . ."

"Is that what he needs? What he wants?" Jean asked.

I searched the eyes of each of the girls as I began to reel them in.

"Yes. Yes it is. Make things easier for him. Could you do that for him? For Bobby?" I asked solemnly.

They nodded in agreement. "For Bobby."

To establish the college we used a very wide shot showing Redford jogging through the beautiful campus; the camera followed Redford as he passed Barbra who was handing out political leaflets. It seemed like an easy shot.

My job as an assistant director was to set the background action, to place the extras so as to simulate an active campus.

"Look, everyone! Give me your attention!" I shouted to the two hundred extras.

They'd watched Redford and Barbra rehearse the scene, and the extras were all excited not only at seeing the two stars, but also at being in the movie with them.

"Hello! Can you all hear me?" I finally got everyone's attention. "You saw the rehearsal. This is a very vital scene in our picture. Redford comes running through and goes past Barbra . . . OK?"

There was a lot of laughter and excitement from the extras, and I should've sensed trouble was coming.

"Now what we have to do . . . is to make the college campus look real and busy. You're on your way to and from classes, OK? You're walking with your friend, OK?"

Everyone seemed to understand exactly what I was saying. I felt great.

"OK, now all of you spread out all over the campus grounds, and let's see what you look like. OK . . . just spread out!"

There was no "spread out." What happened was that all the girls stood on the path they knew Redford would be using because they wanted to be near Bobby and also in the movie. The rest of the extras stood where Barbra would pass out her leaflets. It was a total mess. It looked exactly like what it was, a lot of extras standing around waiting for two superstars. It certainly did not look like what we needed for the movie, an active college campus. Now what could I do?

As I began to enter assistant director hell, I saw Redford and Sydney waving to me. I left the extras and ran over to them.

"Jerry, look," Redford said, grinning, "I can't run through that." He pointed at the crowd along his path. He smiled, shook his head slightly, and gave me the "Redford chuckle," which always meant "Jer, have you screwed up," though he never said a word.

Sydney offered the answer: "Ask them to separate, Jer. It doesn't look right."

"Yeah," Redford added, still grinning, "It isn't right, Jer."

I stared at Redford and Sydney, then I ran back to the extras standing along Redford's path.

"If you're not in the front for this first shot, I promise you'll be seen in a later shot. Help me! Please!" I begged. I tried to manually move extras toward other areas of the campus grounds. "Please! Look, you've got to make me look good here! Spread out!" Few, if any, extras moved.

"Jerry!" Sydney shouted to me and waved. I saw Redford enjoying my problem with the extras. I left the extras and ran back to Sydney and Robert.

"What is it?" I asked out of breath.

"They're not moving, Jer," Redford commented, as he grinned and looked at me. "How can I run? What're you going to do?"

"Just ask them to move back," Sydney suggested.

"That's it," Redford affirmed. "Did you ask them, Jer?"

I stared back at Redford, then I ran back to the extras, determined to get them to move.

I begged and pleaded, "Please move back! Spread out! Swing your arms so you don't touch the person next to you! Please! Help me!" I ran among them desperate to get them to move.

Finally some felt sorry for me, and they reluctantly moved off to the background, giving up their moment in time of being seen next to Robert Redford as he jogged past Barbra Streisand in the opening of *The Way We Were.*

It was like that for every scene at the college. If I had extras for a classroom, they all wanted to sit next to Barbra or Redford. If there was a scene with our stars walking down the street, all of the extras wanted to walk down the same side of the street.

About the fourth day with the extras, I noticed that more and more of them were dressing and fixing their hair exactly like Barbra and Redford. On some days of filming I felt I had six or seven clones of our stars.

One of the key scenes during the college sequence was Barbra's speech at the political rally. Her political activist cohort was played by James Woods. He was a very studious actor, always working on his role. I felt like he never wanted to waste a minute. If he was on the set and waiting for the camera to be ready, he wanted to rehearse with Barbra or to talk with Sydney about the scene. At the political rally, James Woods was near Barbra while Redford stood with Brad Dillman and Lois Chiles in the crowd, listening to Barbra's speech.

Barbra as Katie Morosky exhorted the college crowd to support the Soviet Union against Franco's Spain. In the movie the crowd was supposed to be opposed to Katie's speech until near the end. When we began to film, Barbra had the crowd with her from the very beginning. Whatever she said in her political speech, they loved. It was only Redford and the actors with him that were not cheering for Katie.

Sydney called me over to him.

"Jerry, the extras . . . ," he began. "You have to . . . No one is supposed to be for Katie, and they're all with her from the beginning! Do something!"

The extras loved Barbra, and they felt they needed to help her. Barbra wasn't an easily approachable star; she was shy and did not mingle. She stayed in her dressing room until called to the set and then did her work and returned to her dressing room. The extras admired Barbra's intense work ethic and the quality of her performance. When Barbra was acting in the classroom scene or the political speech, everyone saw a working actress struggling through rehearsals and trying every avenue of performance before capturing what was best. They struggled with her and rooted her on to her final victory. They felt they were a part of her labors. Not so with Redford.

Robert Redford seemed above it all. Like his character in our film, everything seemed too easy for him.

Barbra would arrive in the morning two hours before our shooting call. She would spend hours getting into makeup and hair, studying the scene, and talking with Sydney.

Robert Redford would arrive barely ten minutes before he was due on the set. When Redford arrived he was tanned, handsome, well groomed, charming, and basically ready to perform. He didn't ask for rehearsals or talks with Sydney Pollack. He got out of his car, went into his dressing room for five minutes of makeup and then two minutes to get into his wardrobe, and he was ready. The Redford smile came with him. Nearly every day it was the same.

I would be waiting for his car to arrive. As soon as he stepped out I was there.

"Bob, look. . . . Today we're shooting . . ."

"Good morning, Jer," Redford intoned, letting me know I was not culturally correct to speak business prior to wishing one good morning.

"Good morning, Bob. Sorry. We're filming . . . ," I continued, ever the intense AD.

"I'll be ready. Catch you later." And he was inside his dressing room and closing the door.

• • •

In contrast, Barbra arrived hours earlier and looked for me as soon as her car door was opened.

"Jer!" Barbra began.

"I'm right here, Barbra." I usually had to help carry some package or box from her car to her dressing room.

"What's first?" she asked.

"Political speech is up today," I said. "You'll be on the platform and . . ."

"On the platform? Where's the set? Is Sydney here?" she asked at once.

"The set's on the grounds near the statue. Sydney isn't here yet. And . . ."

"The platform . . . why am I on the platform? Shouldn't I make an entrance, you know? Where's Sydney? Have him see me, please," she continued.

"Sure, OK, I'll do that," I answered.

"Jerry, let me know when Robert arrives, will you? If you see props, send them to me, and set dressing, and I have to talk with Sydney."

"OK, I'll do it for you." We were at her dressing room. I placed the package I was carrying for her on her table and moved out.

"Jerry! I need Sydney, props, and set dressing right away, please." Her dressing room door closed, and I had my "Barbra list" for the morning.

Eventually Barbra would get her wish, and Sydney and Redford would join her for a discussion of the scene. Usually this would happen on the set after the other actors and the crew had been asked to take a break and leave them in private.

Being one of the ADs I was left on guard to ensure that no one wandered back onto the set. Those private discussions would go something like this:

Barbra would begin. "The political rally . . . shouldn't I make an entrance?"

Sydney answered, "You're on the dais, the platform . . ."

"Why?" Barbra interrupted.

"You're a scheduled speaker," Sydney continued.

"I think I should make an entrance. I'm on the ground, and my name is called, and I make an entrance up the steps to the podium!" Barbra fought.

"Barbra, there's no time. We have to get to your speech. That's what's important!" Sydney was working.

"No entrance? The speech, huh?" Barbra asked. "What do you think, Robert?"

"Well, yeah . . . uh-huh," Redford said.

"The speech, Barbra, that's where it's at. Can't you see?" Sydney was trying hard.

"OK, no entrance. But where am I sitting? Not there!" Barbra went on.

"Yes, on the dais. Here on the platform. You're introduced, and you walk to the podium!" Sydney was good with her.

Barbra was doubtful. "What do you think, Robert? Sitting here or where? Platform?"

"Yeah . . . sure, good," Redford said.

"Where's Robert?" Barbra asked.

Sydney pointed to the grounds. "He's standing down there watching you."

"You're there?" Barbra said to Redford.

Redford looked at the grounds. "Sure," he stated.

"You're happy there? Why aren't you on the dais? Or over here, closer?" Barbra asked.

Sydney jumped right in, "He's with Brad and Lois. Watching you. Listening to your speech!"

"Is that right?" Barbra suddenly asked Redford.

Redford was caught not paying attention. He had no idea what'd been said, but he took time to nod his head slowly as though he were in deep thought. Finally, as though he were contemplating the answer to a mathematical equation, he affirmed, "Yeah, that's right. It works."

Sydney said, "See, Barbra, it all works!" He gave her the Sydney Pollack chuckle, which signified that all was right with the world.

Barbra looked at him, then turned to Redford and said with great sincerity, "Thanks, Robert . . . really, thank you. You're wonderful."

Sydney smiled and also turned toward him.

Redford gave them his "Isn't life always this easy?" look. He let the moment play, then breathed in heavily and said, "Want to try the scene?"

Then without Barbra or Sydney able to see him, Redford gave me an impatient look that said, "Come on, Jer! You're the AD, let's get things moving!"

• • •

About a week later we were filming all night on one of the college town's streets. We had removed all of the modern signs, TV antennas, and anything else that said "1972," and we replaced them with our vintage 1930s cars, lamp posts, and billboards.

In our film it was supposed to be a warm spring evening around midnight, a week before graduation. The streets were nearly deserted. Hubbell was sitting alone, sipping a beer at a sidewalk table. Katie had worked late at the local newspaper office and was walking home, when Hubbell called to her.

In front of the camera the town was supposed to be deserted, but there were three hundred excited movie fans standing in the street on a cold September night just to see Barbra Streisand and Robert Redford.

It was made my responsibility to keep the three hundred fans not only out of our shots, but totally quiet and motionless during our filming. I found out from the cameraman what area of the street wouldn't be in the first shot. Now I knew where to place the spectators, but how to move three hundred excited fans? It was one of me and three hundred of them. I knew nothing was going to work for me unless they wanted it to work. Here I was, a young, inexperienced assistant director in upstate New York on a movie location with Barbra Streisand and Robert Redford and three hundred excited movie fans that I had to keep under control. I looked over the crowd.

There were the families with kids of all ages, then there were the dates and the groups of young guys and young girls, then the older fans with their beer cans and coffee, even some senior citizens. It was cold and would get colder as the night went on. They had no place to sit and keep warm while they waited. The three hundred fans stared at the movie crew as they went about their work lighting the first shot. It was pretty evident that the time had come for me to move the fans just to allow the crew space to do their work.

I was very frightened that they wouldn't do what I asked. Why should they? It was their town, their street. Who'd I think I was asking them to move out of our shot, to be quiet, to stand still? They lived here. We were the outsiders from Hollywood. We needed them; they didn't need us.

"What are you scared of?" came a gruff voice from behind me. It was Jack Solomon, a grizzled sound mixer who had been around since *Citizen Kane.*

"What?" I was startled and felt vulnerable, off guard.

"Move 'em!" Jack barked.

"I will!" I shot back.

"Then do it!" No bluffing with Jack Solomon. He had seen it all.

I looked at him and then at the crowd spread all over the street. I took a step forward.

"Come here!" Jack ordered. "Where you goin'?"

"I'm going to ask the crowd to move behind the camera."

"No, you're not! Didn't they teach you anything in that training program? You go out there and talk about their weather, their town, their kids, be *country* with them and be yourself. When they're all with you . . . all your friends, you tell them what's happening and why. Then you mention how it'd be nice if they joined you over behind the camera! And remember to say *please!*"

I stared at Jack. He'd received enough Oscars to use them as doorstops for every door to his house, and that's exactly what he did with them. I felt I'd nothing to lose; I had no other idea how to move three hundred excited fans.

I slowly walked to the center of the cold, damp street.

I glanced back at Jack, took a deep breath and . . . "Good evening!" I said, projecting my voice as if I were back in Northwestern University's huge theatre. "I'm Jerry Ziesmer, one of the assistant directors. I just want to thank you-all for having us here in your town tonight! You've got the clearest weather I've found since I left Wisconsin. Are the nights always like this?"

Most of the spectators just looked at me, but then one said, "This time of year we always get the clear nights."

"Is that so?" What do I say next? I glanced back at Jack. He gave me a nod, but I was on my own now.

"Where you from in Wisconsin?" another fan asked.

"Milwaukee," I answered.

"You been to Green Bay? I got a cousin went to school up there," another said.

"You like the Packers?" a boy asked, and everyone laughed.

"When are Barbra and Robert coming out?" someone asked.

"About another twenty minutes or so. I'm real sorry you-all have to stand out here in the cold," I said.

"Oh, that's OK. It's not your fault, Jerry," a voice said, and half the spectators laughed, and so did I.

It didn't take much longer before I was explaining the ins and outs of filming to my new friends.

"Now the reason I have to ask you-all to be quiet when we film is because we're recording sound, what the actors are saying, Robert Redford and Barbra Streisand," I said as a tiny gasp went up at the mention of their names.

I could see the fans nodding and accepting the rules. "And if I ask you-all to stand still during a shot it's 'cause if you-all moved it'd distract one of the actors, OK?" I saw more heads nodding and more smiles from nearly everyone.

I began to feel that old Jack knew a lot more about how to make a motion picture than just being the sound mixer. Here came the big test; would they move from where they were with a good view of our scene and stand behind the camera where we needed them to be?

"I wonder if you-all would, please, do me a favor. And I hate to ask you-all 'cause this is your town and we're just guests here, but . . ."

"What do you need, Jerry?" a voice called out.

"How can we help you?" another asked.

"Well," I said, "when we get ready to film . . . would you-all be so kind as to step back here behind the camera where I'll be? I sure would appreciate your cooperation."

"Hell, yes!" a voice called out, and we all laughed.

"You want us there now, Jerry?" another asked.

"Well, yeah, if you-all wouldn't mind," I began. "The crew needs the room to . . ."

"They need us behind their camera over there!" someone shouted, and they all began to move.

"Well, I really want to thank you-all," I said, as I watched the crowd move behind the camera.

I was so proud. I looked around at the film crew to get their praise and recognition for my success, and then I saw Jack motioning for me to come over to him.

"Jack, thanks! Look at them! How'd I do?" I proudly asked him.

"Pretty good, but you got a bit too *country*, I think," Jack said privately.

"What do you mean?" I questioned.

"Jerry, in Wisconsin, you know, they don't say *you-all* all the time. That's more Texas style," Jack said. "Talk about the cows and cheese instead. Try mooing once in a while! That's more Wisconsin!"

Jack Solomon became one of my best friends.

When the lighting was completed, I brought Redford and Barbra from their dressing rooms to our set. As the three hundred fans got sight of our two superstars, they started to cheer and wave. Barbra self-consciously waved back and smiled. Redford just nodded to the crowd and then turned to Sydney.

"What's this?" Redford asked, obviously referring to the crowd.

"They've been real good," Sydney said. "I think they'll do anything Jerry wants."

Barbra gave us her look of one who has seen it all, "Oh, sure! Right, Sydney."

Redford had me right where he wanted me. "Jer, you're going to keep them all quiet. Right? 'Cause we can't do the scene if they talk, right? You're going to keep them quiet?"

"Look, Robert," I began.

Sydney tried to help me, "He's going to do the best he can. He's doing great with them!"

"Sure, Sydney." Barbra still had on her look.

"It's your ass, you know?" Redford was grinning at me. He loved to get me stuck in the most challenging situations.

"Let's just try it," Sydney suggested. He was always the diplomat.

"Let's go, Jer," Barbra said, as she went down the street to her starting place.

Redford just turned his back and laughed as he went to his position at the outside table. "Sure, Jer, sure."

I walked to the crowd. "Please!" I began. "This is one of the very special scenes in our picture! Please be absolutely quiet, and please, don't move!"

I could hear Redford's low chuckles behind me.

"I'm ready down here, Jer, you know!" Barbra yelled from down the street.

"Waiting on you, Jer," Redford added.

I gave the crowd one more shot, "Please be totally quiet! Help me out, please! Ready when you are," I called to Sydney.

The crowd was quiet as Sydney called, "Action!" Barbra came slowly up the street and Redford called to her. The crowd remained silent.

Barbra came to him, and they played their scene. The crowd didn't make a sound. When Sydney yelled "Cut!" the crew and the crowd broke out in applause. The scene had worked beautifully.

"Thank you!" I shouted to the fans, "You're wonderful! Thank you for being so quiet!"

The crowd clapped for themselves and laughed.

Barbra, Redford, and Sydney then met at the outside table to discuss what could be improved for the next take. I walked toward them, keeping my distance because I knew that the scene was smoking and I didn't want to disturb a thing. A couple of more takes to give Sydney some choices when he'd be in the editing room and then we'd go into the closer coverage of the scene.

"Jer!" It was Redford calling and motioning to me. I cautiously walked over to them.

"What?" I asked.

"They're too quiet," he said. "The people are too quiet! What've you done?"

"Yeah," Barbra added, "Shouldn't they move a bit or something? It's like being in a tomb, you know?"

"Can't you get it right, Jer?" Redford asked, as he and Barbra giggled together. "There's a difference between quiet and dead, Jer!"

Barbra laughed as she shouted to the crowd, "You don't have to be dead, you know!"

The crowd laughed and waved as Barbra and Redford began to get back into position for take two.

I had started back when a lady in the crowd called to me, "Jerry?" I walked over to her.

"See that building across the street from the bar? Is that you?"

I looked where she was pointing, and there on the front of a building our art department had painted a sign in huge letters *J. Ziesmer Optician*.

"Yeah, that's me," I said slowly, as I saw the sign for the first time.

As more of the crowd became aware of the sign and began to point at it, Redford called to me and I ran over to him.

"Jer, did you do that?" Redford asked as he glanced at the sign. "You did! You painted that sign!" Redford chuckled, but I was already running back to the crowd.

The graduation dance was the scene all of the extras had waited to film. We'd spent days fitting our college girls and boys into the beautiful gowns and tuxedos of the 1930s. We'd hired choreographers to teach them to dance in the '30s style. The graduation dance was the final scene in the college flashback sequence. Everyone was excited with the clothes, the hairstyles, the dancing, and the chance that Barbra Streisand might actually serve them a glass of fruit punch or that Robert Redford might actually dance with them.

I wanted to reward the most deserving extras with those parts, but only one girl was scripted to dance with Redford. I'd an idea to reward more of the extras, but it required Redford's total cooperation. I felt my best chance to make my idea work was not to tell Redford anything until the day we were to film the dance.

Finally the big day came. Our excited extras in their gowns and tuxedos anxiously awaited the filming to begin. I brought all of them into the beautifully decorated gymnasium. Then I went to Redford's dressing room, knocked on the door and politely entered.

"Good morning," I carefully began. "How are you this morning?"

"Finally!" he laughed. "Finally you don't start with business!"

I smiled for all I was worth.

"I am fine. How are you, Jer?"

"Good. I'm good," I said, and then I just looked at him. I was afraid to go on.

"What is it you want, Jer?" he grinned.

"I . . *we* . . . need to have you dance with a few of the girls so we can choose a dancing partner for you. The opening shot, you know?" I waited.

He studied me. "Have Sydney choose one."

I stared at him. Finally I said, "Sydney has to see you dancing with them to choose." My words just hung there.

Redford looked at me, and I knew he smelled deception, but I just stared back at him.

"You want me to go in there and dance with a couple of the girls, right?" he questioned.

"Right. That's it. Ten or twelve should do it. An audition, you know," I answered as nonchalantly as I could, and then I started to leave.

"Good morning, Jer!" Redford laughed. "Ten or twelve?" he asked feigning disbelief.

I stopped at his door. "Right. OK? You coming?" I asked.

The moment of truth was there. I stared at him; he stared back. He got up slowly as he studied me. I smiled as charmingly as I could.

"Good morning, Jer!" he laughed again.

Perhaps he suspected my deception, but we left his dressing room and walked to the gymnasium and the "audition."

As soon as Redford walked onto the set you could feel the excitement and anticipation of our female extras. While Redford talked with Sydney, I got the music playback operator all ready to cue the dance music, and then I asked all of the dancers to make a large circle.

"What we want to do here is audition girls to be the dancing partner for Robert Redford!" I shouted.

The extras sighed, groaned, covered their faces, and did everything but pass out.

I continued, "Now form a large circle. I'll ask Robert to be inside the circle. Then when I call out a girl's name, she'll enter the circle and dance with Robert Redford."

There were more sighs, groans, tiny screams, and hands to their faces. I glanced over at Redford and Sydney. They'd heard me but were casually involved in their own conversation, not giving me their total attention. Would Redford go through with my audition?

"Everyone ready?" I asked.

I could hear a few muffled screams, looks up to heaven, eyes tearing, hands clasped together in prayer. I glanced at Redford and Sydney who appeared to be totally unaware of what was happening around them.

I was scared the audition might not work.

"OK, cue the music!" I shouted.

The playback operator started our music tape, and the dance music filled the set. I glanced at Redford, who was still talking with Sydney. He looked like he was ignoring me, the extras, and the music.

"OK, I'm going to read the first contestant's name for Hubbell's dancing partner!"

I glanced again at Redford, and this time he was staring at me, then at the circle of extras. When he glanced at me again I shouted, "Janice Pitman!" and I pointed to the circle.

As Janice entered the circle, Mr. Robert Redford, superstar, walked charmingly to her, took her hand, and they began to dance. There were cheers and laughter and it was wonderful.

After less than a minute I called, "Virginia Marcello!" Redford escorted Janice toward the edge of the circle as Virginia entered and began her turn to dance with Robert Redford.

The cheers and yells from the extras could be heard over the music as each new name was called. As about the sixth or seventh dance partner began to dance with Redford, I noticed that some of the other cast and the crew were dancing with the other girls. James Woods danced. Brad Dillman danced. Then there was a bit of excitement on the edge of the circle, and Barbra came onto the set and watched the dancing.

One brave tuxedoed extra, a lot braver than I could ever be, asked Barbra Streisand to dance. I held my breath as I watched her. She hesitated a second, then smiled and began dancing with him. It was a magical moment.

• • •

The college flashback ended as Hubbell walked away after dancing with Katie.

"See ya, Katie," Hubbell said.

The camera stayed on Katie's face as she watched Hubbell leave.

"Good-bye, Hubbell," Katie said quietly.

Sydney's storytelling was so simple and so effective. There was no other action, dialogue, or additional shots needed; Katie's look told the story—she was deeply in love.

For an assistant director, filming love scenes can be very difficult. In *The Way We Were* the first two love scenes between Hubbell and Katie took place in her New York apartment, which was a set on a sound stage in Hollywood. Though there never was any nudity, great precautions were taken to secure the set and the sound stage.

Both Barbra and Redford wanted total privacy for the love scenes, and Sydney insisted upon it. Sydney made a point of the importance in keeping our stars comfortable and at ease. Nothing must inhibit their performances. The night before filming, the grips put up long black cloth around the set to block out the view of any person who might be tempted to peek.

That morning, extra studio guards were stationed on every door to the sound stage to challenge anyone who wished to enter. *The Way We Were* was a totally closed set. It didn't matter if the visitor was the head of the studio—no one came on the sound stage! Of course, the responsibility to enforce the total privacy fell to me, the lowly assistant director. I was the lowest on the totem pole. I made the least money, had the least prestige, and had the least amount of job security. Who better to tell the "suits" that they couldn't come on the stage?

"Excuse me, sir," the guard would say, as he stopped two men in suits as they attempted to breeze onto the stage.

"This is a closed set today. May I help you, please?" the guard asked.

The suits would try to go right by the guard, but he was well trained.

"Excuse me. No one enters the set today. No visitors."

Of course, they said they were Barbra's or Redford's agents, or from publicity, or from the producer's office, or ran the studio.

If they insisted on coming onto the sound stage, the guard would send for me, and I'd do my best to get them to leave without anyone losing face.

"Hello, how are you? Can I help you?" I began as politely as possible.

"We're just going to say a quick hello to Barbra and then we'll be gone," one of the suits would inform me. "We're from her agency," the other added. "So if you don't mind, son . . ."

At that point I'd recall Chico Day, my wise old mentor from *Hello, Dolly!* and what he taught me to reply in that situation.

"Absolutely! Just need your business cards, gentlemen," I would say. "Barbra wants absolutely no visitors, but I'll show your business cards to her, and I'm sure she'll be real glad to see you!"

When I held out my hand for their cards, you'd be surprised how many "suits" suddenly remembered something they had to do and quickly left the sound stage.

The first love scene began when Katie brought Hubbell back to her apartment after finding him drunk at the El Morocco nightclub. Hubbell staggered into her apartment, and as Katie straightened her living room, he passed out on her bed. There was only one line of dialogue in the whole love scene. Katie's whole subtext of her love for Hubbell, of her admiration for his writing talent, of her dream for their life together was crystallized in that scene. Sydney relied on the simplicity of Barbra's performance to create one of the most memorable love scenes ever filmed.

The second love scene also took place in New York City. Hubbell couldn't find a hotel room in New York, so he called Katie to accept her offer to let him use her apartment's couch.

We began filming the exterior portion of the love scene on location in New York City on the street outside Katie's apartment building. On her way from work Katie stopped to buy groceries to prepare a special dinner for Hubbell. While Katie was shopping she saw Hubbell as he came out of her apartment building and started off down the street. She called to him and explained all the dinner preparations she'd already made for him and that he must have dinner with her.

It appeared to be a relatively easy scene to film, but it wasn't. The primary problem was that we were filming on a New York City street in 1972, but in our film it had to be 1945. The most obvious problem that we had to solve was to remove all of the television antennas along the street. Then we had to get access to all the store windows so they displayed 1945 merchandise and prices. From the city we received permission to not only control the traffic on the street, but also to eliminate all of the parking. We couldn't have a 1970s car on Katie's 1945 street. Next we had to control any modern-day pedestrians so they would not be in our shots, and we had to replace them with our screen extras in their 1945 wardrobe and hairstyles. In order to create a 1945 look for Katie's street, we had to have the total cooperation of the merchants, the neighbors, and the local government.

To achieve their cooperation, the movie company's location managers, months before we were to film, went door to door to sign each neighbor to a location agreement. Each neighbor and business was paid relative to the inconvenience and loss of business they would incur to them during the days of filming. After the location manager had signed up the complete neighborhood, he joined with the local businesses and political leaders of the community to petition the city for all necessary permits.

A week before filming, the set dressing crew was on the street, removing the modern traffic lights and replacing them with the 1945 variety. All television antennas were removed. The storefronts were restocked with goods and prices from the '40s. Signs were added to show the 1945 political leaders and the nation's dedication to the war effort.

On the day of filming, our crew began arriving at 7:00 A.M. Hours earlier the transportation department had been parking the 1940s cars and trucks on Katie's street. The production van and crew trucks with all the film equipment were parked as close to the street as possible without being in any shot.

After I'd gotten Barbra and Redford to rehearsal with Sydney and then back into makeup and hair, I turned my attention to the extras.

One of my jobs as an assistant director on *The Way We Were* was to decide on the number and type of extras for each location or set. During my preproduction time, I met with the art department and looked at actual period photographs of similar streets and locations. From these photos I'd be able to get an accurate idea of the number of people I'd need and the mix of ages, sex, race, and occupations. I'd actually count the people in the photographs to determine how many sailors, soldiers, police, young women, old men, etc., were on a street similar to Katie's in the 1945 research photographs. Then I compiled a list of the numbers and types of extras for her street, and I'd pass this information to the screen extras casting agency, our wardrobe department, the prop department, and our makeup and hair departments. Every effort was made to give *The Way We Were* the authentic look of the period.

While Sydney rehearsed with Barbra and Redford, I looked for every opportunity to have the extras enhance the scene. I noticed if Barbra needed a salesperson to wait on her when she bought flowers or the steaks for her dinner. I noticed if Redford was going to be hurrying down the street and if he'd be helped by an extra moving slowly across his path. When our cameraman and Sydney set the camera angles for the first shot, I looked through the camera to get the exact sidelines so that I knew what portion of the street was seen and what the principal actors would be doing. I then gathered the screen extras together and began to set the background action.

I took all of the extras onto Katie's street, and I told them about the scene we were to film and how that scene fit into the whole movie. I then gave each extra or group of extras a bit of story that told them why they were on the street and what they wanted. The actors get this information from reading the script, but extras get their information from the assistant director. I tried to treat each extra as an actor. I gave them their motivation along with a reminder of what it must have been like to be in New York City in 1945 during World War II.

After the first full rehearsal, it was evident that most of our extras were matching the rhythm and attitudes of our actors. If Barbra was hurrying to buy all her groceries, then the extras had a tendency to be hurrying, too. A clever trick I learned a long time ago to control the speed of extras is to announce to them that all of them born on an even-numbered day should move very slowly during the scene. That announcement should reduce the number of speeding extras by 50 percent. If Sydney would request a further reduction in the speeding extras, I'd make a second announcement that those born on the odd days of the first half of the month should also move very slowly. That reduced the speeding extras by another half so that 25 percent of the extras were hurrying and 75 percent were moving slowly. I often used this *birthday* technique to direct screen extras to change their attitudes from all happy to a portion less happy, or to control the actual number of extras moving in a shot. If Sydney said that he'd like 10 percent fewer extras moving in the shot, I'd announce that those born on the first, second, and third days of the month shouldn't walk during the scene. The possibilities are endless.

Following the Katie's street portion of the second love scene, it was a month later on a sound stage in Hollywood that the love scene continued inside Katie's apartment. Matching the appearance of the actors from the exterior street to the interior set was the job of the script supervisor. Careful notations and photos were made to detail exactly what Barbra was carrying. What was Redford wearing, and what was in his left hand, his right? Every detail was noted to give the illusion that the street scene occurred seconds before the apartment scene, when in reality a month and three thousand miles had intervened.

Barbra and Redford had to get back into their attitudes from the street scene. Sydney had the film from the Katie's street portion of the scene to show them. He talked them through what he saw in their performances so they could remember how they felt in New York and match those feelings when we continued the scene in Hollywood. Barbra's hair was exactly as it was a month ago in New York; Redford's jacket and shirt were buttoned identically. Barbra was a total master on being able to know what was a match; Redford wasn't.

The script supervisor reminded Redford what hand he used to carry his package and how his jacket was buttoned. She'd carefully explain exactly how he had to match his action.

"You have the packages in your left arm and hand. Your jacket is unbuttoned, but your tie is done, Robert."

"Left arm? No . . . I had them in my right . . . ," he smiled and challenged at the same time.

The rest of us stood and watched Redford and the script supervisor debate. We knew she was right, but Redford had to be convinced. It was like a dance that must be danced. Finally the photos were shown to Redford, and he hesitantly conceded that she might be right after all.

Redford was a lot of fun for the crew, and we enjoyed him even though he'd put us through every kind of testing during the making of the film. He knew a little about everyone's job, and that was very dangerous.

If Redford had a break between his shots, time on his hands, he could sure get me stirred up. It often went something like this.

"Jer, how long do I have?" he'd ask me very matter-of-factly.

"Hard to tell. Half hour?" I answered cautiously.

"You got two, three hours before you're ready! Come on, Jer!" His fun began.

"No, we don't." I tried not to be drawn into a debate with him.

Redford would now become Mr. Production Person. "Look, Jer, you got all these extras, right? And you've to get Barbra ready, right? You think Harry's going to have the set lit anytime soon, Jer?"

"We'll be ready in a half hour," I said, as I held my ground.

"Why do you say that? You know how long it takes to get ready. Why do you say that?"

He has moved from "How long before they need me?" to questioning my judgment, if not the whole essence of my being.

"What do you want?" I finally asked.

"I just want you to be honest with yourself. That's all, Jer!"

I walked off as I heard him chuckling, "Honesty. OK, Jer?"

Redford was a handful, but we all enjoyed him.

It was a late Friday afternoon in early November. The film company was working on a cold and drafty sound stage. We'd been filming *The Way We Were* for eight weeks, and we were all tired. The hours, the travel, the cold, all added to the weariness we all felt that afternoon.

Harry, our cameraman, was working with his grips and electricians on lighting the next shot in Katie's apartment. Those of us not involved just stood or sat around the sound stage sipping cups of coffee and waiting for the lighting to be completed. It was that time in the making of a film when we'd already heard everyone's favorite stories. There wasn't a lot of conversation. We were a tired group.

About three weeks earlier we'd filmed the El Morocco set on this stage, but now the nightclub's walls were folded and stacked to one side. All of the tables and chairs had been returned. The platform for the band was gone, and only the piano remained.

None of us saw her walk to the piano or heard her begin to play, but slowly we all become aware that Barbra was at the piano playing Marvin Hamlish's music from our film. The sounds were pure tones, simple and beautiful, coming across the cold and dreary sound stage. Barbra was lost in her thoughts, unaware that we were watching her.

All of us listened to her playing, enraptured. Someone started to say something, but Sydney hushed them.

"Shhh! Maybe she's going to sing!" he whispered.

We listened again. Slowly she became aware of the quiet and then of all of us watching her.

"What? What are you looking at?" Barbra asked, with her comic New York brusqueness.

We all laughed and so did she.

I'll never forget Barbra's playing on the sound stage that day. The impact of the pure, simple tones of her music reaffirmed to me why I left teaching to be in film and to make movies like *The Way We Were* with people like Barbra Streisand.

• • •

Barbra Streisand was a perfectionist when it came to her own performance and appearance. She insisted on take after take until Sydney convinced her that she'd done her very best and it was time to go on.

As an assistant director I had one foot in the aesthetic world of the director/actors and the other foot in the commercial world of the producer/studio. One of the hardest concepts for any assistant director to learn is to be ready to sacrifice the shooting schedule to get a shot or scene filmed properly. This can be a source of great anxiety when working with some of our film artists.

They tend to be perfectionists and don't work by schedules. They demand the best quality performance from themselves and those around them, no matter how long it takes. When you hire a Barbra Streisand you're employing an artist who'll give you an electrifying performance, but it'll be on her own terms and in her own time.

No one can determine how long it'll take for her performance to be up to her standards any more than we can determine how long it'll take an artist to paint a picture or to write a novel. Electrifying takes its own time, but it also lasts.

The Way We Were was made more than twenty-five years ago; does anyone care today that we went over our shooting schedule to do it right?

After filming Katie's street, we finished our New York City schedule by filming on the twelfth floor of an apartment building overlooking the East River. The apartment belonged to J. J., Hubbell's old college friend, played by Brad Dillman.

Katie's apartment was selected to be a set in Hollywood so we could take out walls to get the lights in the best position for each shot, but J. J.'s apartment had to be a real location in New York City because we wanted to see the East River traffic and all of the city outside the windows.

The J. J. apartment filming consisted of two party scenes with a lot of beautiful people, but the important action was the tension between Katie and Hubbell over whether his writing should consist of serious novels or Hollywood screenplays.

Our equipment trucks and dressing rooms were parked on the streets all around the apartment building. In the early morning our crew would unload their equipment from their trucks and then have to pack it in the elevators and bring it up twelve floors to our set.

When our actors arrived in the morning they reported to their dressing rooms and the makeup trailer parked along the curb. After I'd check them in and get them started through makeup, I'd get them a walking breakfast—a breakfast they ate while they continued with their hair and makeup. The actresses arrived two hours before our shooting call to get ready for the camera. The actors generally needed about thirty minutes to an hour.

What I liked to do was to have all of the actors and actresses begin to get ready as soon as they arrived. Then when the crew came at 7:00 and had lugged all their equipment up to the set by 8:00, I asked all the actors and actresses to leave the makeup and hair work and come up to the set for a full rehearsal.

Sydney always arrived early and walked around the set, planning where he wanted to place each actor to begin the scene. Nothing can be written in granite until the actors do their rehearsal, but Sydney always had a game plan for filming each scene.

As soon as the actors began to arrive on the set, I asked the crew to stop their work and leave the set. The set then belonged to Sydney for rehearsal with his actors.

The supporting actors, Brad Dillman and Lois Chiles, along with the New York party actors came onto the set first. There was the interest in the various set decorations, the paintings and lamps, but finally they'd settle down and wait for Barbra and Redford to come up to the set. I always tried to call them last to give everyone else a chance to adjust to the set before Barbra and Redford arrived.

Redford walked onto the set, glanced around a bit, then said good morning as the new actors got over the shock of being in the same room with Robert Redford. His eyes would still be going over the set and the new actors as he walked to Sydney. Since I thought Redford and Sydney would be discussing vital issues to the scene, I only once got close enough to listen to their first-of-the-morning conversation.

They just chatted about who they saw last night or where they went to dinner and with whom—nothing about the scene. I looked around the set. As Redford and Sydney were chatting to one side, the rest of our cast and the new actors for the scene were sitting around just waiting for something to happen, and it soon did.

When Barbra entered the set, the new actors tensed and took a deep breath; here was a superstar. Barbra was a New York stage star before she ever came to Hollywood and the New York actors paid her due respect. After quick *good mornings* to all, Barbra joined Redford, while Sydney provided any necessary introductions.

Next was the time set aside for the actors to become familiar with the set. Sydney aquainted the actors to the set as you'd introduce friends to each other. He slowly walked through the living room along with the actors, pointing out the possible seating arrangements, noting where the piano was, showing the views out of the windows, and getting all of the actors comfortable with the set and familiar with the other actors.

Many of the actors were tense or nervous around Barbra and Redford, and being introduced to the set allowed them time to deal with their problems. Invariably there was the new actor or actress who told everyone of his or her latest big role coming up soon, as well as the actor who dropped the names of New York's most famous. Once the set questions were answered and all had a chance to gain their secure position within the group, Sydney would begin his rehearsal.

Sydney Pollack is an actors' director. That means he understands how actors work, how they think. He is an actor. He knows what makes them comfortable, and he senses how to bring his actors to their best performance. Sydney's years as assistant to Sanford Meisner, one of the great acting coaches of our day, taught Sydney about the world of actors.

The first task Sydney wanted to accomplish was to ensure that all of his actors were at ease, secure, and comfortable with their surroundings and with each other. He listened to any problems they might have with their dressing rooms or wardrobe or anything that might distract them from giving Sydney their best performance that day.

When the personal problems were handled, Sydney went on to the character each new actor was playing in the film. Was the character a longtime friend of J. J.'s in the movie? Had they been college friends? What were the characters' feelings toward Katie and Hubbell? Toward Roosevelt? Toward each other?

Soon Sydney was telling of the feelings of the Roosevelt years in New York during 1945. He was building individual characters with unique feelings, not just a crowd at another party scene.

When he felt the actors were ready, he began to place them around the set. He started to block the scene. Usually Redford would be comfortable moving wherever Sydney thought Hubbell should be, but Barbra challenged.

She had to be convinced that Katie was in the right place for the scene and for Katie. Was that where Katie would be? Why? Would she be eating? Drinking? Barbra's questions would go on until she was comfortable with Sydney's blocking of the scene.

Finally Sydney would ask the actors to just read through the scene. "Don't act. Just try the words," Sydney would suggest. "See how it feels." The first time the actors said their lines they were strained and self-conscious. Sydney would try it again, but the next time he changed a bit of his blocking to make the dialogue easier for the actors.

As the attempts increased, Sydney began to mold the scene and set the blocking for the scene; he saw where each actor would be during the scene. When he felt every element was in place, Sydney would ask for the crew to be brought back into the set, and the actors would do a final rehearsal for the crew.

Then the first shot was decided upon, and the actors left the set and returned to getting into their makeup, hair, and wardrobe. Sydney and our cameraman would then go over the various shots that'd be needed to cover the scene and the order in which we would be filming each shot.

Many considerations go into selecting the order of shooting. Generally the master or wide shots are shot first to set the positions of all the actors, set their performances, and capture the establishing shot showing where the scene takes place and all entrances and exits, but the heart of a scene is played in tighter shots.

To make their work easier, the cameraman and his crew prefer to shoot every shot in the same lighting direction before filming in another direction, which would require changing the lighting setup. The labor-and-time saving elements play an important part in the order of shooting, but the most important factor is the actors themselves.

Tom Cruise on *Jerry Maguire* would generally prefer to film his coverage first, whereas Marlon Brando on *Apocalypse Now* seemed to want to do his coverage last. Since the actresses usually begin their day hours before the actors, it's generally better to film their closeups earlier in the day when their makeup and hair is still fresh.

For example, I would never give Barbra an early call, get her into makeup and hair, film the wide master shots and other people's coverage, and then at the end of the day film Barbra's close-ups. Unless there are excellent reasons for doing otherwise, it's generally best to begin the day's work with the master shot to set all aspects of the scene, then to do the close-ups and coverage of the actresses, leaving the close work on the actors until later in the day. I have found that the cameraman and his crew can relight a set much faster than the makeup and hair people can re-do a Barbra Streisand.

• • •

When we finished filming the J. J. apartment interiors, the film company moved back to Hollywood to complete *The Way We Were* using the sets at Columbia Studios and local Los Angeles locations.

I was enjoying the film; it was everything I'd hoped it'd be. I liked Barbra Streisand for her great performances and her work ethic. I enjoyed Robert Redford for his equally talented performances and the everyday challenge of working with him.

Redford was the guy you wanted to have around to talk sports, the outdoors, cars, politics; whatever you wanted to talk about he'd talk, and he was always happy. I felt that he was the perfect next-door neighbor, ready to help in any way he could with whatever you were doing.

However, I was an assistant director whose job it was to get Redford to do things where and when the film company needed him to do them, not necessarily where and when he wanted to do them. That became a problem.

I was standing with Sydney Pollock at 5:30 A.M. across the street from the Beverly Hills Hotel on Sunset Boulevard. We wanted a shot of Redford driving in his movie sportscar coming east on Sunset Boulevard with the dawn sun behind him and then for him to turn north into the Beverly Hills Hotel.

Sydney was there, as were all the crew—but no Mr. Redford.

"Don't worry," Sydney said to me. "He'll be here. He wouldn't do that to me, not show up."

I looked down Sunset Boulevard in both directions for any sign of Redford. There was nothing.

Our cameraman was looking at the eastern sky. Dawn for the world of movies happens in a very few seconds and then photographically it is *day*, and there is no more magical dawn light. The eastern sky was getting hints of light, and still no Redford.

"Let's use his stand-in for a few takes until Redford gets here," Sidney suggested.

I quickly ran to get Redford's stand-in dressed in the proper wardrobe and into Redford's movie sportscar. The crew was ready and we were about to begin filming with the stand-in when there was the screeching of tires and Robert Redford got out of a car and casually walked toward Sydney.

Sydney was very excited, "Get in your sportscar. Hurry! The sun is coming up! We've got to get this shot at dawn!"

The wardrobe people grabbed Redford's shirt and jacket and dressed him right on the street as Redford casually mentioned to Sydney, "No one told me about a dawn shot, Sydney."

Redford looked directly at me.

He shook his head, smiled his grin, shrugged and said, "I'll help you guys out, but no one told me. Honest. You never told me, Jer. Sorry, but you didn't. You know I'd have been here if you had."

I just stared at the ground and the ever-brightening dawn light.

Redford got in the sportscar and drove to his start position. We cued him, and he turned into the Beverly Hills Hotel just as the last of the dawn light was still in the morning sky. We got the shot.

Sydney looked at me when the shot was over.

"Jer, didn't you tell him?" Sydney asked me. "No, you told him. You must have told him. Why else would he know to be here?"

We watched Redford drive the sportscar toward us.

"Why else would he be here, Jer?" Sydney asked again. "Isn't he something?"

Oh, yes, he was something. And there was a lot more to come.

Katie and Hubbell's beach house, where they lived while he worked as a struggling writer, was located in Malibu about thirty miles from Hollywood. The first scene showed Katie unpacking keepsakes from their wedding while Hubbell rewrote his screenplay. It was a wonderful, cozy scene that showed them very much in love. Sydney had designed a wonderful opening shot, but it was a long and complicated lighting setup.

Barbra and Redford were relaxing in their motor homes while they waited for the crew to light the shot. Not only had we gotten them matching motor homes, but we parked them equidistant from the set so that neither star was given preferential treatment.

Redford sent word that he'd like to talk with me in his motor home. I knocked on the door and entered.

"Hi, Jer, sit down. How you doing?" Redford began.

Those words—"How you doing?"—uttered by a superstar requesting information on the personal comfort of a lowly assistant director, were a major danger signal. I sensed red warning lights all around me.

I said to Redford exactly what I told any superstar who asked me about my personal well-being—nothing! I've found that most superstars have two topics of conversation: The first topic, they talk about themselves; the second topic, you talk about them.

"Come on, Jer, what's wrong?" he added, grinning and motioning for me to sit down.

I stood silently and stared at him.

"I need to go for a short walk, Jer, right down the beach," he began.

"Not a chance," I countered, as I started to leave his motor home.

Protocol's unique in the movie business. Even though Redford was a major superstar, protocol dictated that he not leave the studio or location without an assistant director's permission.

"Jer! Come on!" He stopped me at the door. "You're not going to be ready for twenty minutes, you know that."

Our cameraman had told me he'd not be ready for another hour, but I didn't want to take a chance.

"Give me ten minutes, I promise. Ten minutes. I'll be right down the beach, Jer! Come on!" Redford pleaded.

I stared at him sitting there grinning up at me. I wasn't going to make an assistant director mistake. There were only two people in the scene, Redford and Barbra. Nothing could be done without him. But I felt sure that I wouldn't need him for an hour, and he was only asking for ten minutes. Even if he was triple that time late, thirty minutes, I would still be safe and by an additional thirty minutes! Also I knew if I did a favor for him he'd be obligated to me for a favor, which could be very helpful to me. I might need him to come in extra early some day or to rush every time I called him to the set if we were running late at night.

I looked at him, calculated all, and then I said, "OK, go ahead."

"Thanks, Jer," and he left his motor home. It was 10:15 A.M.

True to our cameraman's word, we were ready for Redford at 11:15. Barbra was ready. Sydney was ready. No Redford. I went up the beach. I went down the beach. No Redford.

Sydney demanded an explanation, as did Barbra, as did the crew. I found a large rock near Redford's motor home, and I sat down and waited for him. The rest of the company went to an early lunch.

At 12:47 Redford returned. I just stared at the ground.

"Hi, Jer, how's it going?" he said as he walked past me.

"Where have you been?" I asked.

"What do you mean? You said I could go for ten minutes."

"Right. That was over two and a half hours ago," I stated in measured tones.

"Really? Did you need me?"

I just stared at him.

"Sorry, Jer, what are you mad at? I couldn't help it. Why didn't you tell me? How am I supposed to know you needed me? I'm here! What do you want me to do? You're the assistant director, Jer, you should've done something!" he grinned. Then a chuckle, "When are we back from lunch?" and he entered his motor home.

I vowed he'd never get to me again, but, of course, he did.

Though there never was actual proof, I have always felt Barbra and Redford orchestrated my next superstar encounter. We were still filming at the Malibu beach house. We were doing the scene where Katie tells Hubbell she's pregnant.

It was a difficult scene because it could not be the ordinary "Guess what, I'm pregnant" scene; it had to be very special and unique. The task fell mainly to Barbra, so I wasn't surprised when her hairdresser found me between lighting setups and asked me to see Barbra in her motor home. I expected Barbra to ask me to be sure and clear the set before each take or to make sure it was totally quiet all around the beach house.

I got to her motor home and knocked. She opened the door without saying a word, and I entered. Though her motor home was identical to Redford's, Barbra had hers beautifully decorated, which made the inside of Redford's seem institutional by comparison.

"Jer, how are you?" Barbra began, and again I heard bells and saw red blinking lights of warning. A superstar was asking about my well-being!

"I am fine. How are you?" I was totally on guard, ready for anything.

"Jer, I notice that when you call us, Robert and me, to the set that I seem to get there first, and you know what the wind and salt air and all does to my hair and makeup, right, Jer?"

Whenever Barbra began and ended a sentence with my name I knew there was big trouble for me, because Barbra had thoroughly thought out whatever she was after. Barbra at times reminded me of General Patton and that was one of those times.

"I'm sorry. I'll try and not have that happen in the future," and I quickly turned to leave.

"Jer!" I stopped, still inside her motor home. "Can I make a suggestion?" she asked.

I looked at her, a superstar in her spacious motor home. I was a sweating assistant director without even a chair of my own. I nodded and waited for her words.

"Why don't you call Robert first and then when I see him coming, I'll rush right out to the set, OK?"

A trout would never get caught if it'd keep its mouth closed. I'd worked with Barbra on *Hello, Dolly!* during the time I was an assistant director trainee, and she'd been wonderful to me. She'd also been very prompt and professional on *The Way We Were*. I stared at her. I considered our past relationship, her honesty, her professional integrity, and her reputation as a perfectionist.

Finally I said, "I think that's a good idea. Let's do it. I'll call Redford first, and when you see him leave his motor home, then you leave your motor home and come right to the set."

We both smiled acknowledging our mutual agreement, and I left her motor home and returned to the set.

As soon as I knew that Sydney was ready for Redford and Barbra, I hurried out to Redford's motor home and knocked.

"We're ready for you," I said.

He grinned, nodded, and got ready to come to the set.

As I passed Barbra's trailer on my way back to the set I gave her a thumbs-up sign to signify that I had told Redford to come to the set and that she should watch for him.

She smiled and nodded.

When I got back on the set I smiled and told Sydney they were on their way.

It was a dangerously simple scene. Great care had to be taken not to make it ordinary. We all knew Barbra was going to take her time with every beat of the scene, and we wanted to get on with it.

Just as Sydney's patience was wearing a bit thin waiting for his actors, Redford wandered on to the set.

"Hey, what's happening? Hi, Sydney, what is this?" Redford asked, as he looked around the set in total wonder as though we had changed the beach house into King Tut's tomb.

Many times Redford would enter a set and ask questions as though he was not sure what movie we were doing, let alone what scene. I learned to ignore this.

Redford and Sydney entered into a brief prerehearsal chat as we all waited for Barbra. The crew shifted from one foot to another as they stared at me.

Finally Sydney gave me the *Where's Barbra?* look. I opened the back door to the beach house and looked at her motor home; she was not coming.

Sydney came up behind me. "Where is she?" he asked, as Redford joined us.

"Did you remember to tell her?" Redford added.

I stared at Redford. He was smiling, enjoying every moment of my pain. I looked again at Barbra's motor home. She was not coming. The crew members were watching me as they got closer to hear every word.

"Why did you call me if she wasn't here?" Redford asked.

Sydney nodded and both looked at me for an answer. I said nothing. Then with everyone watching me I walked back to Barbra's motor home and knocked.

She opened the door and smiled at me.

"Ready?" she asked, just Ms. Cooperative Superstar.

I nodded, and she walked with me toward the set.

"What happened?" I asked her. "I thought you were going to come when you saw Redford go to the set?"

"Jer, I didn't see him, honest! Nice weather, huh? How's my hair look? You feeling OK, Jer?" she asked, as she smiled all the way to the set.

Those red warning lights wouldn't leave me alone, and for good reason.

It was about a week later, and we were still filming at the beach house.

"Jer," Sydney implored, "you've got to do something to get Robert and Barbra into the set faster and at the same time!" Sydney was, understandably, stressed.

"I know, Sydney. I'm sorry, but I have a plan," I said.

The next time we needed our two superstars, I knocked on Redford's motor home and told him and then I ran over and knocked on Barbra's door and told her. I then stood and watched both their motor home doors. If one came out and the other didn't, I ran over to the still-occupied motor home and told them the other star was already on their way to the set and to please come right away. That procedure seemed to be working, and Sydney was very pleased.

The next day I continued with the same procedure. I knocked on each motor home. Redford came out first and headed for the set, so I ran over and reknocked on Barbra's door.

"Barbra, he's on his way, OK?" I said.

"Coming, Jer!" she said through the closed door.

Just as I watched Redford enter the beach house, Barbra stepped out of her motor home, and we walked quickly to the set.

When Barbra and I entered the beach house, the crew and Sydney were waiting, but no Redford. I couldn't believe it. I'd seen Redford enter the beach house.

"Where's Bob?" Sydney asked me.

"He came in here," I answered, continuing to look for him.

"Jer, he's not here," Sydney continued. "Do you see him here?"

"Sydney, I swear . . . ," I began.

"Where's Robert?" Barbra asked me, as she stared into my soul.

The crew watched me. They'd not seen Redford. It was a small beach house and obviously Redford was not there. Nor was he outside the beach house.

Sydney stared at me.

Barbra stared at me. "Where is he, Jer?"

I looked at everyone, then I walked out of the beach house to Redford's motor home. As soon as I knocked he swung open the door.

"Hey, Jer, ready?" he asked.

"Yes," I muttered, and we began to walk back to the set. "I saw you enter the beach house before I came with Barbra."

"Right. I know that," he chuckled.

"So how did you get back out to your motor home with me behind you?" I asked as we were entering the beach house.

"I stepped into here," Redford said showing me a closet, "And then when you two walked past, I went back out to my motor home." He grinned at me as we entered the set.

"Never knew, Sydney. Sorry. No one told me!" he announced. He glanced at me with victory in his eyes, but I already had another plan.

The next morning I carefully explained to Sydney that my new idea was perfect; it couldn't fail. I took three walkie-talkies and set them to an isolated channel. I placed one in Barbra's motor home and the second in Redford's, and I kept the third. I asked both Barbra and Redford to please come to the set when they heard me over the walkie-talkies.

The moment arrived when we needed both Barbra and Redford to the set at the same time. Sydney and all the crew watched as I took my walkie-talkie and said, "Barbra, Robert, we're ready for you on the set. Please come out of your motor homes." We all watched. Both motor home doors opened. Out of Barbra's motor home stepped Barbra. Out of Redford's motor home flew his walkie-talkie.

• • •

There was a very gracious moment during the filming of *The Way We Were*. It happened on the week before Thanksgiving when we were filming the Armed Forces Radio Station sequences on a sound stage at Columbia Studios.

Making *The Way We Were* was a long endurance test, a struggle against your aching muscles from standing for hours in the cold outdoors or on the drafty sound stages, your absence from friends and family, your mental and physical weakness from twelve- and fourteen-hour days without a break for months on end. The shooting company was tired and in need of a lift.

As I returned from our lunch break, I saw workmen carefully unloading two hundred frozen turkeys onto our sound stage. They were a simple thank-you gift from our producer Ray Stark to the entire cast and crew of *The Way We Were*. Ray included everyone who helped us, from all the studio guards to the office secretaries in every department at Columbia Studios.

Ray Stark was a feisty little guy, a master showman, and a slick agent turned slicker producer. He had produced Barbra's first movie, *Funny Girl*, and went on to do many of John Huston's movies, including *Reflections in the Golden Eye*, *Night of the Iguana*, and *Fat City*. Once I explained to Ray that we needed a camera operator. The best one was Tommy Laughlin, but he was up in Oregon and didn't want to come out to New York. "Tell him I'll buy him a Mercedes!" Ray yelled. Ray Stark was a piece of work.

"Jerry, you don't know me," a studio secretary said to me, as she glanced at the substantial pile of frozen turkeys, "But I'm Jeannie, I work in accounts, and I got this call that there was a free turkey for me on your stage . . . from Ray Stark? the producer? Is this a joke or something?"

"They're against the wall there, Jeannie. Take your pick," I answered.

Our grips and electricians had chosen their turkeys early and had them in their equipment trucks wrapped in burlap. The wardrobe department had put their turkeys in plastic bags, and the prop department had theirs on ice in their cooler along with the soft drinks.

Three studio guards stood admiring our pile of turkeys.

"We're from the Hollywood Way gate, and . . . Mr. Stark's office called . . . is he serious?"

"Help yourself, fellas," I said, as they happily selected their Thanksgiving turkeys.

Ray Stark could be the most unique, creative producer I've ever encountered, and he could also be the most stubborn, hardheaded, and uncompromising person I knew in the entire film industry. There was only one Ray Stark, and a lot of people were very glad of it, but on that November day in 1972, Ray Stark was our angel from heaven.

A Marx Brothers party motif was chosen for J. J.'s birthday party scene. All of the cast and eighty extras were all dressed as one of the Marx Brothers. Barbra was a wonderful Harpo with a red wig and long coat. Redford and Brad Dillman were both Grouchos with the glasses and mustaches. Redford and all of our Grouchos were doing all of his famous one-liners, while Barbra and the other Harpos were honking and running all over the set. It was a madhouse of Groucho's "That was no lady, that was my wife!", Harpo's honking, and Chico's broken English.

When our Marx Brothers impersonators remembered *Room Service*, and then *A Night at the Opera*, the stage was filled with their imitations. Sydney had his hands full just getting the actors to concentrate on our movie long enough to get a shot.

I kept looking at the stage door because I knew he was coming. We'd sent a car to pick him up at his home on Hillcrest Drive in the Trousdale Estates high above Hollywood.

Finally our stage door opened, and in shuffled the eighty-two-year-old Groucho Marx. Age had slowed down his body, but his mind was still quick and biting. He walked slowly onto the sound stage and moved toward our set.

As soon as the cast and crew got sight of the real Groucho, everyone left the camera and formed a respectful circle around the master of the one-liners. Groucho seemed mystified by all the actors and extras in Marx Brothers costumes, with Groucho glasses, mustaches, and Harpo wigs.

For the time that Groucho Marx was on our stage, Barbra and Redford were just two more excited fans like all the rest of us. The still cameras came out, and everyone wanted their picture taken with Groucho.

The filming not only stopped on our stage, but when the word spread around the studio that Groucho Marx was on our stage, the work stopped on all the other films as well. Soon our stage was crowded with excited directors, actors, grips, electricians, all wanting to get a look at the legendary Groucho Marx.

The people and all their attention became a strain on Groucho. After only thirty minutes he left our stage and returned to his home. The other casts and crews returned to their stages. We slowly got back into our birthday party scene. Barbra and Redford were there as actors, and they were very good that afternoon, but there was a difference. They weren't legends, not yet.

About three-quarters through our shooting schedule we filmed the scenes in *The Way We Were* that involved Katie's political opposition to the House Un-American Activities Committee hearings of 1947, which dealt with the influence of Communists in the Hollywood film industry.

I recalled Marty Ritt's emotional speech at the end of *The Great White Hope* during the farewell banquet in Barcelona. Marty expressed such deep feelings for the loss of creative years suffered by so many artists in our country, including himself. His words were so clear and simple; they broke my heart.

We used the old Jack Warner office on the Warner Brothers lot as the studio office of George Bissinger, the director of Hubbell's script, played by Patrick O'Neal. It was an eerie feeling to be filming the 1947 portion of our script in the actual office of Jack Warner, who played a major role in the House Un-American Activities Committee hearings.

In our script two intellectuals, Paula and Brooks, played by Viveca Lindfors and Murray Hamilton, shared in Katie's fight against the House Un-American Activities Committee hearings and their attempt to control the creative rights of motion picture artists.

If a person went before the committee and refused to answer their questions or refused to give the names of Communists working in Hollywood, then that person risked being blacklisted in the motion picture industry. However, if that person went before the committee and answered their questions and gave the names of possible Communists, then they were allowed to continue their film careers.

Both Katie and Hubbell opposed the actions of the committee, but Hubbell was the pragmatist who believed that Katie's demonstrations wouldn't make any difference. Katie felt she had to demonstrate because of her political and moral principles.

A crisis moment for Hubbell occurred one evening in George Bissinger's home when he and Katie and many other guests were about to watch a screening of a film. Marvin Hamlish, the composer of the music for *The Way We Were*, was cast as a party guest.

As a large painting covering the movie screen was raised in preparation for showing the evening's film, a tear occurs in the painting. A secret microphone, a bug, has been hidden behind the painting. All the guests feared that it was the United States government spying on their movie group, and they scrambled to leave Bissinger's home. Only Hubbell remained, staring at the hidden microphone.

Sydney Pollock ended the scene with a shot of Hubbell illuminated by the flickering images of what was to be that night's movie, an American western.

Hubbell and Katie were caught in the Hollywood dilemma of that day: Do you talk and work, or do you not talk and not work? Your principles or your paycheck?

The political sequence reached its climax at the Union Station location in downtown Los Angeles, where Katie and Bissinger and the others returned from Washington, D.C., by train after demonstrating in front of the House Un-American Activities Committee's hearings.

Hubbell met Katie at the train depot as the crowd jeered the returning political demonstrators. Ziggy played one of the reporters. As the unruly crowd pushed toward Katie, Hubbell engaged in a scuffle with one of the demonstrators. The scuffle between Redford and a stuntman was well rehearsed.

Even though Redford was a fine athlete and he carefully rehearsed the stunt with a well-trained stuntman, any fight directly involving a superstar caused anxiety throughout the film company. The last thing anyone wanted was to have Redford get injured so that we couldn't film with him, and the first thing Redford wanted was to do the whole fight himself without using a stunt double.

Any time a fight or action was dangerous we'd use a stunt double, a trained stuntman made up and dressed to look like the actor, to perform the dangerous shots. Then we'd use the actor for the close-ups. When the scene was cut together the audience believed that it was the actor who had done all the action.

In the Union Station scuffle, the stuntmen showed Redford everything he should do to make the fight look real, while still keeping it safe for all concerned. Action and stunts take time, but it's well spent because the stunts get in the movie, not on the cutting room floor.

• • •

Hollywood film crews would use any excuse for a party, and so it was in late 1972 that I was presented with my Cake of Honor by the cast and crew of *The Way We Were*. I don't remember the reason, but it wasn't much. Probably just an excuse for some cake on a Friday night after shooting. The company also gave me a megaphone with good wishes written all over it from the cast and crew, and the obligatory photograph was taken, both of which are among my treasured possessions. Barbra was wonderful, as always, and gave me three of her record albums nicely autographed.

Redford smiled, shook my hand, and asked, "What exactly do you do, anyway?" We had good times together. His good times were then, and my good times were looking back on it a quarter of a century later.

I'll occasionally see some of the cast and crew from *The Way We Were*. One of Sydney's children and our son Tim attended Crossroads High School, so we would see each other at some of the school functions, and I talked with him on the set of *Annie*.

I've seen Barbra a half dozen times in the intervening twenty-five years. Barbra's and Elliot Gould's son, Jason, attended the same elementary school as our son Chris. Years later both Chris and Jason were actors in Cameron Crowe's film *Say Anything* . . . .

Even after twenty-five years in release, *The Way We Were* is still revered as one of Sydney Pollock's greatest films and as one of the most highly acclaimed movies for both Barbra Streisand and Robert Redford. You don't get many like *The Way We Were* in your career.

I remembered talking with Ethel Waters after a rehearsal of *The Member of the Wedding* in Milwaukee.

"It's all so perfect," I said.

"You don't get many good ones," she explained. "When one comes along, you gotta hang on."

I hung on. *The Way We Were* was one of the best I ever got.

We finished *The Way We Were* in New York City that early spring of 1973. Even the sophisticated New Yorkers turned into lookie-loos when Barbra Streisand and Robert Redford embraced outside the Plaza Hotel. It was not only the last day of filming on *The Way We Were*, it was also my last day as a second assistant director. I was moving up.

The Wrath of God

I had worked with the director Ralph Nelson when I was a trainee on his picture . . . tick . . . tick . . . tick with George Kennedy, James Brown, and Fredric March. Ralph had done four really great movies: *Lilies of the Field* with Sidney Poitier, *Soldier in the Rain* with Steve McQueen, *Charly* with Cliff Robertson, and *Father Goose* with Cary Grant. When Ralph got ready to do *The Wrath of God* in Mexico, he asked me to be his first assistant director. I was thrilled.

Robert Mitchum was the lead actor, and Rita Hayworth, the pinup girl from World War II, was the female lead. It was years since she had starred in *Gilda* and *Miss Sadie Thompson* and Robert Mitchum had done *The Night of the Hunter* and *Not As a Stranger*. They weren't in their prime, but even so, Robert Mitchum and Rita Hayworth were two of the greatest challenges I ever had as an assistant director.

I wanted the excitement of filming outside our country again, and Ralph Nelson had selected locations in Taxco, Guanajuato, Vista Hermosa, Durango, and the stages at Chiarabusco Studios in Mexico City. It all sounded romantic and exactly what I wanted.

The problem was that it wasn't just me. There was my first wife and Chris, not quite two years old. It was fun and romantic for me to be off filming in a foreign land with famous movie stars, but for my family's needs it was best for them to stay in our home in West Los Angeles. We were becoming another filmmaker's family with a dad, a mom, a child, a home, and a film to be made that kept the family apart.

When they did fly down to be with me for the holidays, we managed to have a Christmas tree in our rented home in Guanajuato. Chris kept pointing under the tree and grunting happily as one-year-olds will. On closer examination, we discovered that the home had an infestation of mice nesting under our tree.

When Christmas was over and my family and many of our crew members' families were about to return to their homes in England, New York, or Los Angeles, the movie company rented a private dining room in Guanajuato and held a final good-bye dinner for everybody. It was a bittersweet evening with many families about to be separated, wives, husbands, and children. We still had more than five weeks of filming to do; it was a long time to be apart. The talk and speeches all touched on the lonely life of the filmmakers on location and the sacrifice of their families back at their homes. I was moved by the dignity and caring of the evening, the closeness of the families, and the genuine love for husband, wife, and family.

Ralph Nelson spoke, Robert Mitchum said a few gracious words, and finally the civic leader of Guanajuato gave a moving speech about hospitality and love between peoples. Husbands and wives held hands under the tables. Children hung on Dad and Mom. There were quite a few somber faces and even a tear or two. I thought that was the end of the speeches, but I was wrong. There was one more unannounced speaker.

Rita Hayworth got to her feet and said, "I don't want any of you wives worrying about your husbands. Me and the other ladies of the company will take care of them, just like we did before you came down here! Now go on home and leave us alone!"

Oh, my God! I was frozen. Even Marty Ritt's emotional speech in Barcelona didn't get the stunned reaction that Rita Hayworth's did.

The dining room was totally silent. All stared at Rita Hayworth. Then wives turned toward husbands, and husbands turned toward wives to explain questions not yet asked.

The good-bye dinner was definitely over.

I shouldn't have been surprised. I remembered when we were filming on the backlot at Chiarabusco Studios in Mexico City. The set was the entrance of a mining tunnel, and the action was for Rita Hayworth to walk past a row of packhorses and enter the mine.

The cameraman told me he was ready, so I walked over to the motor home we had for Rita, and I knocked.

"Miss Hayworth? We're ready when you are," I announced through the closed door.

The motor home door swung open, and Rita stood there staring down upon me.

"You tell Ralph Nelson if he wants me to come to the set, he's got to come in here and fuck me!" Rita exclaimed, and slammed the door.

I stood still and looked at the closed door. I made very sure that I had heard what I had heard. I turned and saw Ralph Nelson talking to some crew members about twenty yards from the motor home, and I slowly walked over to him.

"Ralph?" I began.

"Where's Rita? Is she ready?" he asked.

"Ralph, may I talk to you, please?" I asked, and moved about five feet away.

"Sure, Jerry. What is it? Is Rita coming?"

"Not quite," I said.

"What's the problem?" Ralph asked.

"Ralph, I don't know exactly how to say this . . . ," I began.

"Well, what is it? You can tell me."

"Ahhh, Ralph? Rita Hayworth says she won't come out of her dressing room until you go in and fuck her." I let all the words run together.

Ralph Nelson must have been in his late fifties, maybe sixty years old. He stared at me, and a smile came upon his old face. His eyes lit up, and I felt I was looking into the eyes of a World War II soldier who had stared at Rita's photo for months in the mud and rain somewhere in France or the South Pacific.

"Really? She said that?" Ralph said slowly and quietly, as though it was part of a dream from long, long ago.

"Yes, I didn't know what to say . . . ," I began.

"It's all right, Jerry. It's all right," Ralph said, and looked over my shoulder at her motor home. He still had the same wide, dreamy grin on his face.

I had learned when not to speak to directors.

He slowly walked toward the motor home of Rita Hayworth; it was all still a part of a GI's dream from thirty years ago. The only difference was that Ralph was now in his sixties, and Rita Hayworth wasn't far behind.

Both Ralph and Rita came out of her motor home after a bit, and we did film the mining tunnel scene that day. She was quite good in it, actually.

Rita Hayworth had one unusual hotel request. She only wanted to stay in hotel rooms on the ground floor, nothing higher. In all of

Mexico City there were very few hotels with any rooms on the ground floor, but that wasn't her most unusual request.

By contract, all her travel within Mexico had to be by car. We had a company move from Mexico City to Guanajuato. It was all freeway for the 175 miles. Rita Hayworth wouldn't allow the car to be driven more than ten miles an hour for the whole trip, seventeen hours. When her car finally arrived, the driver parked in front of her hotel and ran off. I never saw him again.

Ralph Nelson came out of live television, the days of *Playhouse 90* and *Kraft Theater*. Because of his live television background, Ralph was one of the best prepared directors I have ever seen. However, he wasn't perfect. He enjoyed the bottle, and he had horrible insomnia that would keep him up until the very early morning. Often he would get very little sleep and would be quite groggy and a bit tipsy when we picked him up in the morning.

Ralph had rented a very nice home in Mexico. It was white stucco with two or three fireplaces, one right in his bedroom. Each morning Ralph's car and driver with his script supervisor, Bob Forrest, and me would arrive at Ralph's home. Usually Ralph would still be awake, and he would be waiting for us. Sometimes Bob or I would have to go to the front door and knock, and then Ralph would come staggering out and get into the car. We knew not to talk to him if that was the case.

One morning Ralph was not waiting for us, and he didn't answer our pounding on the door. Finally Bob Forrest found a way to climb up on a wall and got himself onto the roof. He carefully made his way across the roof to where we knew Ralph's bedroom was. When Bob got to the right area of the roof, he moved carefully to the chimney of the bedroom's fireplace.

Taking a deep breath, leaning down the chimney as far as he could, and shouting as loudly as he could, Bob bellowed, "Ralph, it's time! You've got to come now!"

Ralph had only gotten to sleep a scant hour before. He was still half asleep, but he realized there was a voice calling him.

"What?" Ralph said, as he looked around his bedroom trying to find the person who had called him.

Bob leaned even farther down the chimney.

"Ralph, it's time! We have to go now! You don't want to be late!"

Seeing no one in his bedroom and hearing the voice, Ralph Nelson thought he was being called by His Maker.

"What? I can't come now! I'm doing a movie!"

"Ralph, I know that! You must come now! It's time!"

"Can't you wait!" Ralph clutched the bedclothes and stared around his room.

"We've been waiting! You're late now!" Bob screamed down the chimney.

"Please not now! Please, give me a while longer!"

"We can't! It's time for you to go!" Bob insisted.

"I'm not going!" Ralph screamed, and he started to sob as he continued to clutch the bedclothes to himself.

"Ralph! We can't be late! Let's go!" Bob was getting angry.

"Where are you taking me?" Ralph asked.

"Where do you think?" Bob screamed.

Ralph sobbed harder. He was sure he was going to hell.

During all of this I got out of the car and began to pound with all my might on the thick wooden front door. Finally Ralph heard the pounding.

"What's that pounding?" he screamed.

Bob, still on the roof, shouted down the chimney, "That's Jerry, your assistant director. He's trying to take you to location!"

Something clicked in Ralph's mind, and he bolted out of his bed, ran down the hall, flung open the front door and screamed, "Take me to location, Jerry!" as he wrapped his arms around me and wouldn't let go.

I really loved working with Ralph Nelson, but there was one person who gave Ralph some trouble, and that was Robert Mitchum.

We were filming at an old silver-mining town outside of Guanajuato that was called Laluz. At one time it had been a thriving city, but the silver had run out, and most people had moved away years and years ago.

The Wrath of God company took over the whole town. The buildings and streets were perfect for our film, and all of the citizens could be extras in our movie. The only possible problem seemed to be that right on the plaza, near the church where we did most of our filming, was a bar that served home-brewed alcohol and beer.

As soon as Ralph Nelson saw that bar, he decided, because of Mr. Mitchum's reputation, to have the production manager pay the owner of the bar to close, and so he did. About two hours later, I couldn't help but notice that Robert Mitchum was inside the bar enjoying a libation or two.

The production manager had paid to close the bar, but Mr. Mitchum had paid more to re-open it. For all the time we filmed in Laluz, the production manager had to stay on the set with a pocket full of money to be ready to outbid Robert Mitchum, should his throat get dry.

We would leave our hotel in Guanajuato and drive through the hills toward Laluz. It would be very early in the morning. As we got closer to Laluz I would look out of the car windows, and I would see the day laborers and their families walking over the hills to work for our movie company in Laluz. The family would sit and wait all day for the worker to finish, and then they would walk as a family back across the hills to their home. Each worker was paid $2.25 a day for his labors, and we had to pay the caterer almost twice that, $4.25, to feed him lunch.

The cast and crew would forgo their fruit and desserts, beverages, and second helpings, and they would give them to the workers' families, who would happily eat the food, but always stayed around the perimeter of our location.

Though the town of Laluz was close to being a ghost town, there was a beautiful church that had been built during the silver-rush days. It had huge vaulted ceilings, carved statues, and heavy wooden pews. The tile in the floor was a work of art unto itself. With such a church, I wondered why there wasn't a priest there, for there was no religious leader in Laluz.

No one wanted to talk to me about it, but finally one old woman told me the story of the last priest who had been in Laluz. It seemed that the year before, he molested two of the children, and the local people took the priest to the plaza and stoned him to death.

Robert Mitchum was one of the best storytellers I have ever heard. Each morning that we'd film in Laluz, I'd ride out with him in his car, and he would tell me stories from his life and famous people he knew, that type of thing. Most mornings he'd have me laughing so hard I'd be falling on the floor of the car before we left Guanajuato.

Ken Hutchison, a young actor from Britain, would ride with us. Ken was a bit of a wild man, or so he hoped. He tried to keep up with Robert Mitchum in all vices, and he couldn't. I looked upon it like Mitchum had been in the big leagues for forty years and Ken was just a rookie.

This particular morning we literally had to carry Ken from his room to the car. He had been going one-on-one with Robert that evening and finished a distant second. We propped him up in the front seat, and Mitchum and I got in the back, and he began the morning story for me.

He started with a tale about the time he sold his horse ranch in Virginia and told all his hired help that they were included in the sale price. He was sorry, but he had sold them, too.

Ken groaned once and slumped down to the floor next to the driver. Mitchum went right on with his stories.

Seems he and Howard Hughes were friends when Mitchum was a struggling writer in Hollywood before he switched to acting. Howard Hughes would give Mitchum office space and some money to keep himself together.

As the stories continued, the sounds emitted from Ken on the floor of the front seat became more and more sickening. Ken had been with Mitchum the previous evening, and Bob had gotten him back to his room—after they had closed the bar and finished the bottles they had bought from the bar as they left.

We arrived at location and lifted Ken out of the car. Mitchum and I had to literally carry him into the makeup room. The makeup people wouldn't touch Ken until we cleaned him up.

We stripped off his clothes, gave him a sponge bath, poured Listerine down his throat, dressed him in his wardrobe, and held him in the chair while his makeup was applied.

"This ever happen to you?" I asked Mitchum.

"Oh! Hell, yes!" Mitchum barked. "He'll be fine. This isn't anything."

I hurried over to the church where we were setting up to shoot the first scene of the day. Ralph told me he wanted to start with the scene of Ken praying in the pew with all the candles burning around him. It was one of the most moving and tender scenes in the picture.

Praying? Ken couldn't keep his head up. We couldn't keep him awake. I was afraid of what Ralph would do if he realized the condition Ken was in that morning. I tried to talk Ralph into doing another scene without Ken, but his mind was set on doing Ken's scene first.

When the crew was ready, we put Ken in the back of a car and drove him right to the church steps. Then the driver, Mitchum, and I lifted him up the steps and into the church. Ralph saw him and came over.

"Good morning, Ken," Ralph smiled. "How're you?"

Ken was comatose.

"Ahhh," I said, as Ralph gave me a look.

"Best not to talk to him, Ralph," Mitchum began. "Ken's been preparing for this scene all night."

We took Ken to the pew and put him right where the cameraman wanted him, bent forward with his head resting against the pew in front of him. Mitchum and I backed off and left Ken there in front of the camera.

The camera guys had to make a couple of adjustments, and Mitchum gestured again to Ralph that it was best not to talk to Ken before the shot. I know I heard Ken snoring; I know it.

Mitchum gestured for me to go on with my job and leave Ken as he was. I got everyone quiet. The crew was ready. I glanced at Ralph who was respectfully awaiting Ken's performance. Mitchum nodded to me, and I rolled the cameras. "Ready when you are, Ralph."

Ralph whispered, "Action!" Nothing happened. We all waited. I was about to turn to Mitchum, when I heard a sob from the depths of the human soul. I looked in front of the camera and saw that Ken had raised his head off the pew in front of him and tears were pouring down his face. He groaned again and began a soliloquy to God and man.

I don't know what all he said. It was a hell of a lot more than was written in the script. When Ken sobbed the last time and returned his head to the pew in front of him, I looked around and Ralph was in tears. The crew was deeply moved, and most of them couldn't speak English. I was choked up, and Mitchum was smiling the biggest Robert Mitchum smile I have ever seen.

"Cut," Ralph whimpered, and then broke into his own sobbing. Mitchum led the applause and everyone joined in.

"Jerry!" Mitchum shouted over the clapping. "Ken's emotionally drained. Help me get him out of here."

I grabbed one side of Ken and Robert grabbed the other. We lifted him up and carried him down the aisle. Ralph followed us.

"That was beautiful!" Ralph sobbed. "That was the most beautiful scene I've ever seen. The fire! The feeling!"

We struggled to get him down the front steps of the church and toward the car.

"Ken," Ralph continued, "thank you! Thank you!"

"Yeah, well, he's had it. Exhausted," Mitchum said, as we got him into the car. "Send him back to the hotel. Right, Ralph?"

"Oh, yes. Ken, just rest. Really!" Ralph still had tears on his face.

We watched the car turn and take Ken Hutchison out of Laluz and back to the hotel in Guanajuato.

Mitchum turned to Ralph and me, "You guys want a little pick-me-up? I've got a little something in my bag do you guys some good!"

One morning we were again about to leave the hotel for Laluz. Ken wasn't working that day, so it was just Mitchum and me. I sat in the car and waited. Soon Mitchum came out of our hotel carrying a whole baking pan full of brownies.

"Want one? I made them myself," Mitchum offered as he approached the car.

I may be from Milwaukee, but I knew enough not to eat a brownie made by Robert Mitchum!

"What is that?" I said.

"What?" He smiled as he got into the backseat of the car with his baking pan.

"What? That pan of brownies!"

"I made a little something for the company," Mitchum laughed.

"Please, put that in the front seat," I said.

Mitchum laughed, but he put the baking pan in the front seat and we rode out to location.

I didn't really think too much more about Mitchum's homemade brownies. I was busy moving the company, getting actors through makeup, and taking care of Ralph.

About an hour later I saw Mitchum standing next to Ralph, who was about to eat a Mitchum brownie. "Don't eat that!" I screamed.

"Jerry," Ralph began, "Robert's made these marvelous-looking . . ."

"Don't eat that, Ralph. Put that down," I said, and I looked at Mitchum.

"It's only a brownie, for God's sake," Mitchum laughed.

Now Ralph was on a first-name basis with Jack Daniel's, but he had never met Ms. Marijuana, and this was no time for the first time. I stared at Bob.

"All right, all right," Mitchum said, and moved off with his brownies.

Ralph was mystified. "Was there something wrong with the brownies, Jerry?"

I assumed the crew was better versed, but about an hour later the men's wardrobe helpers came to me. It seemed that our head wardrobe man had eaten one of the brownies and had been staring into his button drawer without moving for a half hour.

I quickly got the word around the company for no one to touch another one of Mr. Mitchum's brownies.

At lunchtime I was sitting by myself on a low wall that ran along the cobblestone street of the plaza. I was just relaxing and enjoying the quiet and the beauty of Laluz, when someone sat next to me. It was Robert Mitchum.

"Don't give any of those brownies to Ralph, " I said.

"I'm not," Robert said. "Here," and he handed me a brownie.

"I'm not taking that!" I said to him. "Are you crazy?"

"OK, just a half," he said. "Just take the edge off a bit."

"No," I said, and Robert ate a half of the brownie.

"See?" he said.

"I don't want any," I said.

He took the remaining half brownie and broke that into two parts. "Go ahead," Mitchum offered.

I looked down at the tiny quarter of a brownie. I had been to UCLA in the '60s. What could a quarter of a brownie do?

Mitchum ate one of the two quarters that was left.

"See?" he said. Mitchum had eaten three-quarters of the brownie.

I stared at him and then down at the very small quarter of a brownie that was left.

The next thing I knew it was more than an hour later, and I was still sitting on the low wall. But now I was staring at the multicolored, iridescent cobblestones sparkling in the yellow afternoon light, and I watched as the prop man walked past me for the fourth time doing the exact same things each time. I was so stoned!

"Longest lunch hour I've ever had," Mitchum grinned. "Well, let's get back to work," and he helped me to my feet, and we moved toward the church. "I got the actors going through makeup for you," Mitchum added, with his laugh, "and the crew's lighting a shot in the church."

I nodded and made my way over the still-iridescent cobblestones with dancing yellow light toward the church for the afternoon's work as the prop man passed me for the fifth time, still doing exactly the same things. I was still so stoned.

When *The Wrath of God* was over, I returned to my family. Our second son, Tim, was born during the season and a half that I worked on the *Kung Fu* television series and some movies of the week. He brought some laughter back into the marriage, but it didn't last.

• • •

*There wouldn't be many people in the movie theatre. It was a
weekday afternoon in August 1988. Normally Suzanne and I would
want to see a good comedy with a full audience to enjoy all of their
laughter, but somehow seeing this one had slipped by us. The Avco
Theatre would be cool inside. It would be a nice way to spend an
afternoon together.*

*We drove south on the San Diego Freeway and got off on the
Wilshire Boulevard East exit. We passed Westwood Boulevard, and I
turned into the alley west of the Avco Theatre. We parked in the lot
they shared with the tiny cemetery where Marilyn Monroe is buried.
We had our choice of places; no tourists today.*

*Suzanne and I smiled at one another as we walked down the aisle
of the huge theatre. We were the only ones there. We were about to see
the best comedy of the year, and we were in an empty theatre. We
decided on a row toward the front and moved into the center. Soon
the lights dimmed and* A Fish Called Wanda *began.*

*We held hands as we laughed at the characters and situations in
the film, but soon we could hear that we were no longer alone. There
was another source of laughter, a man's and a woman's, coming from
twenty rows behind us.*

*All four of us enjoyed the movie, and our combined laughter
echoed in the cavernous theatre. After laughing for nearly two hours
together and being the only people in the theatre, we had somehow
formed a bond.*

*They were sitting closer to the back of the theatre, so when the
lights came up, they reached the lobby before we did. The other couple
laughed at something they remembered in the movie as Suzanne and
I walked toward them.*

*As they turned toward us I realized with whom we had shared the
pleasant afternoon.*

She excused herself, and went into the ladies' room.

*"She's not feeling so well," he said to us, and smiled his famous grin.
All the tears were held behind his eyes, and nothing was coming out.*

*Suzanne and I smiled. I had worked briefly with her a couple of
years ago on the comedy* It Came from Hollywood. *She was so alive
back then, and so frail now. We looked at him as if maybe there was
something Suzanne or I could do to help.*

*"Don't worry," he said. "We'll be fine." He smiled again, and I was
the one holding back the tears.*

I nodded. Suzanne squeezed my hand, and we began to leave.

When she left the ladies' room and rejoined him, we heard their laughter begin again.

Gilda Radner and Gene Wilder were good at laughing together.

Harry and Walter Go to New York

My career could have been lost in the television series and movie-of-the-week syndrome, but the same production executive from Columbia Studios called me again in the summer of 1975. This time they had a picture called *Harry and Walter Go to New York*, with Mark Rydell directing.

Mark was a hot director. He had done *The Reivers* with Steve McQueen, *The Cowboys* with John Wayne, and *Cinderella Liberty* with James Caan and Marsha Mason. He came from the world of theatre and acting. He was a longtime friend of Sydney Pollack's, dating back to their days at the Neighborhood Playhouse with Sandy Meisner.

Mark and I hit it off at once. We became a good team on *Harry and Walter Go to New York* and also worked together eight years later on *The River* with Mel Gibson and Sissy Spacek.

Mark Rydell was an excellent actors' director, a lot like Sydney Pollack was on *The Way We Were*. He worked with James Caan and Elliott Gould, our Harry and Walter, to hold down the broad comic characters the two actors had created. Mark let the comic events in the story propel the movie, not only the characters.

We had a talented cast. Diane Keaton was the love interest. Michael Caine was the heavy, and Charles Durning, Jack Gilford, and Burt Young were the comic characters.

Theoni Aldredge was the costume designer. She had done *The Great Gatsby and Network*. She was so regal, like Irene Sharaff. There was one major difference, however, and Theoni and I kept it to ourselves.

Back in 1958 and 1959, Alaska and Hawaii became our forty-ninth and fiftieth states. Nikita Khrushchev and Fidel Castro came to power. Leonard Bernstein became the New York Philharmonic's conductor, and Pelé led Brazil to the World Cup. At the Tower Ranch Summer

Theatre in Rhinelander, Wisconsin, Theoni was the costume designer for the theatre. Her husband, Tom Aldredge, the Broadway actor from *Passion* and *On Golden Pond*, was the leading man, and I was the juvenile actor in the summer stock company.

Why Theoni and I didn't mention our summer theatre connection was that during those summers she would design, build, and wardrobe the whole production of a play like *Teahouse of the August Moon* for under five hundred dollars. On *Harry and Walter* the ruffle on Diane Keaton's skirt was more than that.

The best thing that happened to me on *Harry and Walter Go to New York* was that I began working with Larry Franco. Ziggy was still with me, but we needed a second assistant director, and Larry was the man.

Larry Franco was an enthusiastic, energized piece of work. From the moment I met him, I knew he'd run through a wall for me and when he got to the other side, he'd ask, "What's next?" His voice had a natural laugh in it, so that when he talked he could laugh along at the same time.

He was shorter than I and heftier. He could have been a hockey goalie or a baseball catcher. He had a round face and a body to match. He was the most *unstoppable* human I have ever known.

Larry had worked as an extra while he was going to college. It had taken him three tries to get accepted into the DGA training program; nothing would stop him. This guy was my kind of assistant, plus he and Ziggy liked each other immediately.

Larry had married Kurt Russell's sister. Larry and Kurt had played a couple of seasons of minor league baseball up in Portland, Oregon. Kurt's dad, Bing Russell, owned the Portland team. Bing had been a Hollywood stuntman. Kurt and I'd worked together on a Jimmy Stewart film, *Fools' Parade*, in Wheeling, West Virginia. Everything and everyone seemed to fit. As Ziggy said, "It's Beau-tee-ful!"

Harry and Walter Go to New York began filming in Mansfield, Ohio, at the all-male prison. The inmates were in for all kinds of crimes, from murder to marijuana possession. The prisoners were some tough folks, and we were using them as our movie extras.

Our crew was nearly all male, except for one of our camera assistants. She was a very attractive young lady and an excellent camera assistant. I'd assumed that she wouldn't work inside the prison but would load film outside the prison walls in the camera truck.

The first day inside the prison we were in a cell block setting up the camera on the third-floor metal corridor that ran outside twenty cells on one side, with a three-floor drop-off on the other. Everything seemed to be working fine, until I saw her. She had put on a large trench coat, the kind Harpo Marx wore, and she had placed above her upper lip a large black mustache.

There were inmates walking freely down our corridor, past our crew. The cell doors were open. There were no extra guards around. Did she really believe that silly disguise would fool those male prisoners?

"What are you doing? Are you crazy?" I whispered to her, making sure none of the prisoners could hear me.

"I'm doing my job," she answered, in the lowest-pitched voice she could utter.

Oh, my God. I imagined prison riots, mass rape. I imagined the Ohio government authorities kicking us out of the prison and the state, closing down the movie.

"How could you do this?" I asked. "How did you get past the guards? They searched me!"

"I just walked through carrying some camera cases." She continued to use that ridiculous low-pitched whisper.

Prisoners were walking past us on the corridor all the time. I was terrified. Had their confinement made them forget what a female looked like? I was sure not.

"I've got to get you out of here," I whispered. I couldn't take my eyes off her mustache.

"Let me do my job," she said, as she tried to pick up a heavy camera case.

"If they find out you're a girl, there'll be a riot!" I whispered. "Don't you understand?"

She struggled with the heavy camera case, just as a huge, tattooed prisoner started past us.

"Can I help you with that, ma'am?" he asked.

Did he say *"ma'am"*?

"Thanks," she answered, in her bass voice.

He moved the heavy case for her, then walked on down the corridor to his cell without giving any indication of anything being unusual up on the third-floor corridor that day.

In the prison cell block, there was an area behind each row of cells that contained the plumbing pipes and electrical cables. There was a metal grid in that area for the maintenance workers to walk on. In our film, Harry and Walter were to begin their escape from prison by running down the metal grid. As they ran, they were supposed to pass a number of rats that lived in the area behind the cells, but as soon as James Caan and Elliott Gould started to run, the rats we had placed on the grid scattered before we could get the shot.

The prop man had brought cages and cages of rats, but we kept losing them. We needed something to keep the rats on the grid. We tried food, candy, cheese, but they would flee before we could get James Caan and Elliott Gould running near them.

I noticed what looked like a crew union meeting down the cell block corridor. There was some discussion, gesturing, and then it broke up.

"What's happening?" I asked the prop man. "What about the rats?"

"Just be five minutes," he said.

"What're you going to do?" I asked. "How're you going to keep the rats from running?"

"Just give me five minutes."

A few minutes later I saw some of the crew members join the prop man, but when I walked toward them everyone quickly separated.

"What's going on?" I asked the prop man.

"Get everyone ready, Jer," he said. "Those rats aren't moving!"

I got Mark Rydell and the crew ready to film. James Caan and Elliott Gould walked down the grid and turned toward the camera; they were ready on their start mark. I looked for the prop man. He walked past me and placed seven rats on the grid, then walked behind me.

"Go, Jer," he whispered.

"Roll camera," I said, as I watched the rats nibbling and calmly looking around.

Mark called, "Action!"

James Caan and Elliott Gould came running down the grid, and those rats didn't move. They hardly noticed Harry and Walter running past them. The shot was everything Mark Rydell wanted. We did the shot again with the same rats, and they still didn't move.

"What did you do?" I asked the prop man. "That was fantastic!"

"Found something they liked," he answered.

I looked at the rats still not moving.

"What're they eating?" I asked.

"Marijuana," he answered.

Oh, my God! I went blank. Marijuana!

"You brought marijuana into a prison!" I could hardly control myself.

"Shh! Don't say a word," he said, and went to gather up the rats.

There were a lot of drugs on the film sets of Hollywood during the '70s, and I lost many friends because of their drug abuse. The young camera assistant who wore the Harpo Marx trench coat and mustache was one. A few years later she turned on the water in a bathtub, eased herself down into the soothing water, and slit her wrists. I've shed a lot of tears during my years of making movies.

Though it was a Columbia Studios film, we rented the old *Dolly* street at Fox to use for the New York streets in *Harry and Walter*. That was the third time I had filmed on the *Dolly* street. First, of course, was *Hello, Dolly!*, then on *The Great White Hope* we used it for Chicago's Rush Street.

We were filming a day scene with James Caan and Elliott Gould running across the *Dolly* street, now changed back to being New York City. Chris, my five-year-old, was one of the newspaper boys on the *Dolly* street that day. It was his first time to be in the movies. Ziggy watched over Chris and showed him how to sell his newspapers.

The crew was preparing the shot. Larry and I had the extras working, when I noticed someone tucked down between the cast chairs. It was Barbra Streisand.

Of course, she was Elliott Gould's wife, but to see Barbra Streisand hiding, not wanting to be noticed, that was unique.

"Barbra?" I said. "I didn't see you."

"You didn't?" she answered, still crouched between two cast chairs.

"Are you OK?" I asked, ever the assistant director.

"Sure. I'm just visiting. You didn't notice me?" she asked, obviously pleased.

I looked at her hiding between the chairs like my two-year-old son Tim would do if he were playing some child's game. That wasn't the Barbra I knew from *Hello, Dolly!* or *The Way We Were*. Was it that she wasn't the star that day, but Elliott was? Maybe she didn't want to detract from him and James Caan? But then why was she there at all? Whatever the reason, Barbra was happy that day; she was childish, giggly, and very happy.

Before *Harry and Walter* was over, Paramount Studios called me to interview for their big action movie, *Black Sunday*, to be directed by John Frankenheimer. Mark Rydell and Columbia must have given me

a good report, because why else would Paramount consider me? I'd
never even done an action film, nothing close to one.

Robert Evans was the head of Paramount. His big claim to fame was
that as an actor he played the role of the matador in the Ernest Hemingway film *The Sun Also Rises*, and Ava Gardner fell in love with him.
Robert Evans kept the attitude and swagger of the matador as he
worked his way up the producing ladder until he became head of
Paramount. His most famous achievement was producing *Love Story*
and then marrying the female lead, Ali McGraw.

I drove over to Paramount during my lunch hour on *Harry and
Walter*. I was worried about getting all the way back to Columbia in an
hour, but Larry, Ziggy, and I needed another picture, and *Black Sunday*
could be it.

I found the production office and knocked. They were waiting for
me. There was a Paramount production executive, Lin Parsons, Jr., John
Frankenheimer, and his producer, Robert Rosen.

John Frankenheimer, like Ralph Nelson, came out of live television
and the *Playhouse 90* series, but John had also directed *The Manchurian
Candidate*, *The Birdman of Alcatraz*, and *The French Connection II*. He
fit my criteria as an important director.

John was a very tall man, given to excited speech and hand movements.
He spoke only French to his secretary, which for a kid from Milwaukee
was very cool. John dressed in casual clothes, but tailored casual. His
passions were gourmet cooking and deep-sea fishing all around the world.

Robert Rosen was even more tailored casual than John. Bob looked
like the country club set, or the group at the old Polo Lounge in the
Beverly Hills Hotel—casual and cute, but able to run up the big tabs
and leave the bigger tips. I usually have an aversion to producers, but
Bob Rosen was one of the finest I have ever known. He was totally dedicated to the film project and to John Frankenheimer.

Lin Parsons, Jr., made the introductions, and I sat down. I knew Lin
from my days as a trainee; he was smiling at me and friendly, so I
thought he might be on my side. Bob Rosen was happy and smiling and
watching John Frankenheimer, so I figured if Frankenheimer liked me,
I had the job.

"Tell us what you've been doing, Jerry," Lin said.

"Well, I've been filming *Harry and Walter* with Mark Rydell for a
while, and I did *The Wrath of God* with Ralph Nelson in Mexico before
that . . . ," I began.

"Ralph Nelson? You worked with Ralph Nelson? On what? *The Wrath of God*? When? Did he do that in Mexico?" John Frankenheimer exploded in a burst of questions, but he was smiling at me.

"Yes. He's great," I said. "We had a great time. Good movie, too."

"Sensational movie! Sensational! With Ralph!" John got so excited at times. "You've got to tell me everything, and about Ralph."

I nodded and smiled. I didn't know what to say.

"What else have you done?" Lin asked.

"What else? What else? He's done Ralph's picture! Mark's picture! Who cares?" Frankenheimer was going. "He's done more than you have!"

Everyone, including Lin Parsons was laughing.

I sensed that the interview was going well. I glanced at Rosen and he smiled at me.

"When do you finish *Harry and Walter*?" Lin asked.

"Who the hell cares! We don't start filming until January, for Christ's sake!" John said, and he looked to Bob Rosen for help.

"There's no problem with Columbia's movie," Rosen added calmly to Lin Parsons. "I've checked their dates."

Coming to me! I thought. *This job's coming to me, Larry, and Ziggy!*

"Good! Done! He's hired. Agreed?" John checked the executive and Bob. "Jerry? . . . what's your last name? " Frankenheimer asked.

"Ziesmer," Rosen added. "Two hundred fifty dollars above scale, OK? Do you have your second?"

"Of course he does. You're both on! You like to fish?" John asked.

I heard Bob Rosen say I'd make an extra $250 a week in salary, that Larry was hired too, but had John Frankenheimer asked if this Wisconsin boy liked to fish? I thought I had died and gone to heaven.

Black Sunday

Larry and I flew to Miami right after the Christmas holidays; Ziggy would join us as soon as we moved back to Hollywood. A movie driver met us at the airport and took us to the *Black Sunday* production office at a Holiday Inn beside a freeway. Not the greatest of neighborhoods, I thought, but it's *location* not vacation. We'd make the best of it.

Bob Rosen was in the production office to greet us.

"Hey, guys, how was your trip?" he asked.

"Great," Larry answered.

"OK," I said.

"You guys seen your place yet?" Bob asked.

Place, I heard, not *room* as in hotel room.

"No, we haven't. We came right in from the airport," I answered.

"Oh, hell, you've got to see your place. Then come back and we'll talk!" Bob said. "You're both at the same condo building; thought that way you could ride back and forth together. Here are the keys to your car. It's right downstairs; you probably passed it when you walked into the hotel."

Larry just stared at Bob and the car keys. I thought he was going to burst. We had never been treated like this.

I tried to stay cool, even when I heard *condo building* and *your car.*

We got out of the production office, got a map, and put our luggage in the car. Larry drove as I navigated.

Larry and I had our own condos in one of the most prestigious areas of Miami. We were both on the fifteenth floor and had views of all Miami.

"Oh, Jer!" Larry exclaimed, as he saw the view.

"Man, beats Mansfield, Ohio," I said, as I checked through the full kitchen with washer and dryer, all the pans and dishes. The living room

119

was huge and wrapped in floor-to-ceiling windows that looked out on the whole city.

"Oh, Jer!" Larry was about to burst. "It doesn't get better than this!"

The next morning I met Larry in front of our building, and we drove back to the production office. We had a big production meeting at ten with John Frankenheimer, Bob Rosen, and most of the crew. The subject: How to film during the actual Super Bowl.

In *Black Sunday*, a terrorist had supposedly stolen the Goodyear blimp, loaded it with explosives, and was going to explode it during the Super Bowl. I had never been an assistant director on any film like that. I was flying by the seat of my Wisconsin pants.

We all entered a large conference room and sat down. Bob Rosen introduced himself and then we each had to introduce ourselves around the table. Our cameraman was John Alonzo, who came from the world of the handheld camera; he was a good one. The rest of the crew looked solid and experienced. I felt good. Only Larry and I had never done anything like this movie. We sat next to each other as Rosen continued.

"Well, we all know why we're here. January 18, the Super Bowl, that's the big day," Bob began. "Now, we have permission to film during the first half of the actual game. That's perfect for our story; because our movie ends before the half."

I thought of the condo, the car. Now we're going to be filming at Super Bowl X. Larry was right. Nothing could be better or bigger than this.

"We can't be near the field, and they won't help us in any way, but we can get the wide shots that establish the Super Bowl," Bob continued. "We'll have to get all the scenes with Robert Shaw, our entrance of the president of the United States, and the other acting scenes, and the fan panic scenes on the days after the Super Bowl when we have our extras in the Orange Bowl."

Everything was going fine, but I raised my hand.

"Bob," I said, "Why don't we try filming some of the acting scenes during the actual game?"

Larry and everyone turned and looked at me.

Bob laughed and so did the crew. He and Frankenheimer exchanged a look.

"Well, Jerry, maybe you'd like to come up with a plan for how we could shoot at the Super Bowl game?"

Larry shot me a panicked look, but I had taught junior high school, and I could bluff with the best of them.

"OK, I'll get it to you tomorrow morning," I said, as easily as though Bob had asked me to stop and get bagels for tomorrow's meeting. Frankenheimer stared at me, then at Rosen. Larry looked at me and smiled. He knew we could do it, somehow. Maybe I had made an inexperienced assistant director's mistake, but my words were out there. I felt I either had to make good on my words or eat them.

The rest of the day was taken up with paperwork and new pages for the script. That night Larry and I got together and started to work out a plan on how to film the acting scenes from *Black Sunday* during the Super Bowl game with every scene completed by the end of the first half. We were up most of the night.

The next day we all took a trip out to Miami's Orange Bowl, the stadium for the Super Bowl game. John Frankenheimer took us around and showed us all the areas he wanted to film with the actors when we had our paid extras. He was still planning on only doing the wide establishing shots during the actual Super Bowl. It was like they had all forgotten what I had said about shooting acting scenes during the real game. I guessed they were just writing it off to an inexperienced AD. I wondered if I shouldn't just forget it, too.

John, Bob Rosen, John Alonzo, Larry, and I got into the basket of a huge crane, and we were lifted high over the Orange Bowl. Frankenheimer was going to pick some high angles for the establishing shots.

I looked down at the stadium and then at the freeways and all of Miami outside the Orange Bowl. What a view! This was great.

"What are you looking at? Have any ideas?" Frankenheimer asked.

I looked again at the freeways running near the stadium.

"John, what we could do is have a photo double driving the car and trailer waiting down on the freeway with a radio. When the game is on this end of the field, I could cue them, the camera could follow the car and trailer, and then continue the pan all the way into the Super Bowl." I had never said words like that before. I don't know how those words got into and then came out of my mouth.

"What!" Frankenheimer exclaimed. "You think we can do that? That'd knock all of Paramount on their asses!"

Everyone looked at me.

"Absolutely, and after the pan, you see the whole Super Bowl with the actual game going on. Why not zoom in and I'll have Larry with Robert Shaw on the sidelines, he'll cue the actors, and you can continue the shot with Shaw running along the sidelines. Film some acting scenes with the real Super Bowl game."

The crane basket rocked with John's excitement.

"Are you kidding? Are you . . . you think we can do that?"

"It can be done," Alonzo said. "It'd be a great shot! It'd be unbelievable to tie it all together!"

"I'd have to get permission, but, hell, let's go for it!" Rosen said.

"Are you serious?" Frankenheimer kept saying to me as the crane lowered us to the ground. "You think we can do that? Do you?"

"Hell, yes!" Larry affirmed. "It's a piece of cake!"

"Sounds great," Rosen said. "Now tell me how're you going to get the eighty-six thousand people in the stadium to stand up on your cue for the entrance of our president?"

Rosen and Frankenheimer laughed, enjoying their banter as we all began to walk off the football field.

"How you going to do that? Have eighty-six thousand people stand up on your cue?" Frankenheimer asked again, and laughed with the others as we all continued to walk.

I looked at Larry and he smiled at me. We had worked that one out last night.

"That's a simple one," I said.

"How?" they all asked and laughed, expecting Larry and me to stumble back down to earth.

"We'll have our president enter when everyone stands up for the national anthem," I said.

"Right!" Larry shouted. "the national anthem! You gotta stand up!"

Everyone else stopped, but Larry and I just kept right on walking.

The next day we passed out copies of the shooting plan that Larry and I had done for filming at the Super Bowl. We had included every possible acting scene in the script. We included all the tie-up shots that Frankenheimer wanted, and we added everything else Larry and I could think of.

We would have multi cameras all capturing crowd reactions, the game, the sidelines, but John Alonzo, Frankenheimer, and I would be dealing with the principal actors and filming the dialogue scenes.

Robert Rosen went to the NFL and the Orange Bowl officials and explained the plan of shooting and got their permission. He also got permission to have Robert Shaw run along the sidelines during the game and for us to be warned just before they would begin playing the national anthem. He'd have to stay up in the press box with a walkie-talkie to me during the filming in case the Super Bowl officials wanted to cancel our filming.

• • •

When Super Bowl Sunday arrived, the butterflies were cascading around my stomach. Robert Evans, the head of Paramount, had come out to watch the game and our filming progress. Robert Evans was the Cary Grant of the studio executive club in the way he dressed, swaggered, and talked. I always felt that he was just playing another matador, this one as head of Paramount Studios.

Larry was hyped, as I knew he would be. We arrived at the Orange Bowl and got all the crew ready, with their various cameramen. Each mini-unit had its own responsibilities before the game and would then cover the actual game as soon as it started.

Outside the Orange Bowl were thousands of fans. The traffic was snarled hours before the kickoff. The Super Bowl was the biggest sports event of the year. The media trucks and vans with their huge antennas and satellite systems were ringed around the open end of the stadium. Pittsburgh was on the press box side of the field, and Dallas was across the way. Media people, the NFL press corps, all the representatives of the league and the teams were everywhere. Everyone was a VIP and had to be handled carefully. The NFL commissioner's office could pull our permission to film during the Super Bowl anytime they wanted.

Larry was dressed in a sport coat and slacks, and so was I. We were supposed to be FBI men in the movie. Larry went off with Robert Shaw and a walkie-talkie so we could talk to and cue him.

It was hard just to move from one area to another because of all the people. I had planned the shooting to begin in the closed end of the stadium and then move around on the Dallas side, ending at the open end where the huge crane was for our most important shot.

John Frankenheimer and John Alonzo began to get shots of Robert Shaw with the crowd as he looked for the terrorists. I stayed on the radio to cue Larry and to move us around the stadium.

Other mini-units had set up for the arrival of each team at the stadium, the lines of fans coming inside, and everything anyone could think of that said Super Bowl.

John Alonzo with a handheld camera was an artist. He had come out of the world of film documentaries, and he was using that style of filming at the Super Bowl. All the mini-units moved to their game positions before the kickoff, but Alonzo, Frankenheimer, and I were free to film everything we could get with the actors.

"Jerry?" It was Bob Rosen on the walkie-talkie.

"Yes, Bob?" I answered.

"Just a reminder, the national anthem will be in ten minutes," Bob said.

We got the mini-units in position, and then we moved down to the seats on the Pittsburgh side of the field we had selected for our president. We had doubles for each possible candidate winning, but we were betting that a Georgia governor named Carter would be the winner.

We got our "Jimmy Carter" ready and the cameras in position, and waited.

"Jer?" Rosen radioed.

"Yes, Bob?" I answered.

"Sixty seconds," he said.

I looked at my watch, got the crews ready, and rolled all the cameras over my walkie-talkie.

Frankenheimer yelled "Action!" as the national anthem began, and our "Jimmy Carter" walked down the aisle as eighty-six thousand people stood up.

"Looked great!" came the words from each camera over the radio. Larry and I had pulled that one off, but the car and trailer going past the stadium on the freeway with Robert Shaw's run during the actual Super Bowl, that was the big money shot for the movie. That would say to the world that *Black Sunday* was real, that it had all happened during Super Bowl X.

"Bob?" I asked over the radio.

"Yup." He answered as if he were totally calm, but I knew Rosen was as excited as I was.

"When can we do Robert Shaw's run on the sidelines?"

There was a long pause.

"Whenever you want, Jer," came Rosen's answer, but I could imagine his stomach was churning.

Larry got with Robert Shaw on the Dallas Cowboy sidelines and put him up in the stands.

The main camera was up on the huge crane high above the Orange Bowl. It would be panning the car and trailer along the freeway, continue the pan to the Super Bowl game, then zoom in to Robert Shaw jumping out of the stands and running along the sidelines.

Everything was ready. The car and trailer had a radio and was warned and ready. Larry was next to Robert Shaw. I had walkie-talkies with each camera. I wanted this shot.

Frankenheimer and I were in the huge crane with the main camera high above the stadium. Oh, baby, if we could pull this one off! Anything could have ruined the shot. A congested freeway, even a slow-moving freeway, would ruin the timing. If anyone stopped Shaw, the shot would be ruined. Also, the football had to be on the near side of the field for us to see the players.

"Bob, I'm ready," I radioed to Rosen. The teams were on the near thirty-yard line.

"Ready when you are," was his quiet reply.

I took a deep breath and set it off.

"Roll all cameras!" I said into the radio. I was just a kid from Milwaukee; how did I get here?

"Stand by, Larry! Stand by, car!"

I checked with the camera operator on the crane.

"You ready?"

"Yeah."

"Cue the car. Go, car!" I shouted into the radio. There was a break in the freeway traffic, and our car and trailer got up to a good speed.

"Stand by, Larry."

The car and trailer moved down the freeway in the direction of the Orange Bowl. Our camera panned with the car and when the Orange Bowl came into his frame, he continued the pan into the stadium, seeing eighty-six thousand people and Super Bowl X.

"Now," the operator said to me.

"Larry! Send him!" I cued. "Send Shaw!"

Larry did, and Robert Shaw ran along the Dallas sideline.

As soon as we saw Shaw running, the camera assistant began his long, slow zoom into the actor.

"Perfect!" our camera operator said.

The other cameras reported they had all gotten the shot as well.

"Was good, Bob. We got it!" I said to Rosen.

"They'll be on their asses all over Paramount!" Frankenheimer kept shouting and laughing at the same time. "No one in Hollywood will believe it!"

We got down from the crane just as the first half ended. Robert Evans and Frankenheimer took off for the phones to let Hollywood know what had been done at the Super Bowl.

Larry and I spent the second half watching the Super Bowl, and my first NFL game ever, by sitting an inch from the field on the Pittsburgh sideline. We were two excited young ADs who, with a lot of help, had begun to make a name for themselves at Super Bowl X.

Apocalypse Now: Part One

Ziggy handed me the phone. We were on a sound stage at Paramount Studios filming rear-projection shots of the Goodyear blimp approaching the Super Bowl for *Black Sunday.* It was our last week on the picture.

"Hello? I can hardly hear you!" I shouted into the stage phone.

"Jerry Ziesmer? Are you an assistant director?" The voice shouted back.

"Yes?" I covered my other ear so I could hear better.

"Are you available for about six weeks?"

"What do you have?" I shouted. This was a terrible connection, I thought.

"We're filming a Vietnam War story, and we need an assistant director for the war stuff," the voice told me.

"Oh, yeah? Six weeks, huh? Where you filming?" I asked. I thought this could be a nice filler between pictures for me, Ziggy, and Larry Franco, my second assistant.

"We're over here outside of Manila. In the Philippines!" he shouted.

"The Philippines!" I thought they might be filming in Pasadena at the Desconso Gardens jungle area, or maybe a couple of miles outside Los Angeles in Newhall, but I was not ready for the Philippines. "What's the name of your film?"

"Apocalypse Now," he said. "Heard of it?"

"Apocalypse Now!" I shouted.

Ziggy mouthed, "Beau-tee-ful!"

"Right," the voice said. "Francis Ford Coppola's directing."

"Coppola! Francis Coppola?" I respected him more than any other director in the world. I would have worked with him if he wanted to film the phone book. Francis Coppola! He had done *The Godfather,* and he wrote *Patton!*

"Yes. Do you think you might be interested?" he asked.

"Sure! I mean . . . yes!" I was almost too excited to speak.

"Take it, Jer!" Ziggy whispered. "Coppola! Beau-tee-ful!"

I nodded and patted Ziggy.

"What kind of salary you need, Jerry? Only six weeks, you know."

"Salary? Only six weeks, well. . . ." I tried to speak, but I couldn't think. Assistant directors don't make the big money like actors, directors, and producers. We have to negotiate our salary for each film or else accept Directors Guild scale. I was numb; I didn't know what to say.

Just then Bob Rosen, the producer of *Black Sunday*, tapped me on the shoulder. He had obviously heard my shouted phone conversation. He took out a little pad of paper and wrote down the amount he thought I should ask in salary.

I looked at the number Bob had written, then I stared at him and then at Ziggy. Both nodded, and I said the number into the phone.

There was a long pause, and I was about to laugh and say that I had meant that amount as a joke and that I was just grateful to be offered a chance to work with Francis Coppola and I would work for whatever they wanted.

"That's fine, Jerry. Agreed. When can you be here?" The voice said.

I stared at Bob Rosen, who was beaming and scribbling again. This time it was a living allowance. I read the figure and said it into the phone. Ziggy held his breath.

"You got it. When can you be here? You have to get your shots . . . ," he shouted.

Bob scribbled again: *Four first class round-trip tickets to Manila every six weeks.*

I held my hand over the phone's mouthpiece, "Bob, it's only a six week shoot." I whispered.

Bob tapped the paper adamantly.

"Go for it." Ziggy urged.

"Oh, another thing," I began. "Could I have four first class round-trip tickets every six weeks?" I asked.

"Jerry," the voice shouted back, "you're only going to be here six weeks!"

"Right." I was ready to forget the airline tickets, but Bob had something else he had to say. I held my hand over the mouthpiece.

"It won't cost them anything if they only film six weeks. So why not?" Bob whispered.

"He's right," Ziggy added.

"Ahhh, if you're only filming six weeks, what does it matter?" I asked.
"You want four first class round trips every six weeks? OK? When can you be here?" the voice asked again.

"And my second assistant, Larry Franco . . . ," I began. Bob had already written out Larry's wages and deal. I read them off.

"OK, OK. Jerry, when can you and Larry be out here?"

"Larry? He'll leave in two days. I'll be there on Monday," I said.

"Our L.A. office will be in touch with you for flights, passports, visas, shots, OK?" the voice said.

"Yeah. Great," I said. Rosen was smiling like a producer who has negotiated every last nickel out of the other side.

"See you in Manila on Monday," said the voice, and hung up.

I just stood there with the phone in my hand. "Ziggy, we're doin' *Apocalypse Now*. Go get yourself a passport!"

"Jerry?" It was Bob Rosen. "Shouldn't you tell Larry he's going to the Philippines the day after tomorrow?"

"Larry!" I shouted, as I saw my assistant across the sound stage. "Guess what?"

It was Friday, three days later, that Larry called me transoceanic from the Philippines to our sound stage at Paramount.

"Larry! Hey, man, how's it going?" I shouted into the phone. Ziggy was standing right next to me.

"It's OK. When you gonna be here?" he asked.

"Man, I'll fly Sunday! Be to you Monday afternoon with the time change and date change and all. How's it going?" I asked again. "You all right? How are the hotels? Where are you anyway?"

"We're shooting in Baler *[bah-LAIR]*. It's on the coast."

"Bel Air?" I laughed; this was great!

"No, Baler! It's on the east coast of Luzon. Jer, it's gonna be fine," Larry said. "Just get out here."

"What do you mean? Larry . . ."

"It'll be fine, man. It's a piece of cake. You're the right one for this film, Jer. I'll see you Monday, right?" Larry continued.

"Right, Larry. I'll be there in the afternoon. I'm the right one, huh? Six weeks! Vacation, huh?" I laughed out loud at our good fortune. "Man, did we fall into this one. Ziggy'll ride a water buffalo! How lucky can you get, right? Piece of cake!"

"Right, but Ziggy should sit this one out; trust me. See you on Monday, Jer," Larry said, and hung up.

It was the early spring of 1976. The Vietnam War had been officially over for only a year, Gerald Ford had become president when Richard Nixon had resigned a year and a half earlier, Chinese leader Mao Tse-tung died, black student protesters in South Africa were massacred in Soweto, and the unknown Sylvester Stallone wrote and starred in and the year's top picture Rocky.

I was flying on Philippine Airlines from Los Angeles to Manila. My first class round-trip ticket was nearly $1,500! "Four first class round-trip tickets every six weeks!" Rosen was so crazy; I'd never be there over six weeks. Never. I laughed to myself.

I'm uncomfortable on airplanes, and this was the longest flight I had ever been on. Fortunately, I had asked the *Apocalypse Now* production office if there was anything I could read on the flight that might help me to understand the film project, since there didn't seem to be a current shooting script available in Los Angeles. They suggested I read Joseph Conrad's *Heart of Darkness*; the movie was based on his book. It was a very thin book; how difficult could filming *Apocalypse Now* be? Be back home within six weeks; that's what they told me, and I had no reason to doubt them. Six weeks in the Philippines would be like a vacation, a very highly paid vacation for me and Larry. We deserved it.

We had done Mark Rydell's *Harry and Walter Go to New York* and then immediately went into John Frankenheimer's *Black Sunday*. They weren't exactly easy pictures; we had paid our dues.

I dreamed of exploring a different culture, eating exotic food, staying in quaint hotels. I couldn't exactly grasp what the Philippines meant: water buffalo and thatched huts? How bad could it be? And it was for only six weeks. I wondered why Larry didn't think Ziggy should come to the Philippines; must be the heat. I'd love to see Ziggy on the back of a water buffalo! He was going with Howard Koch, Jr., on a film at M-G-M, Ziggy's old home studio. Howard said he had recommended me for *Apocalypse Now*. I'd send him a postcard of thanks as soon as I got to Baler. I'd send another thank you to Bob Rosen.

Heart of Darkness by Joseph Conrad is a simple story, very short. I read it before I was halfway to Manila. No wonder I would only be there six weeks; there wasn't much to it. A guy gets on a boat and goes up a river to see another guy in the jungle. The jungle guy, Kurtz, has gone a bit whacko and the river guy, Marlowe, takes him out. Larry's right; this *Apocalypse Now* will be a piece of cake, but I'm going to miss Ziggy.

The jet circled and I saw the Philippines for the first time. I had never been farther west of California than Hawaii. I looked out for the first time on Southeast Asia. There was the lush vegetation in every hue of green. I saw thousands of coconut palms, then the rice paddies covered with water that reflected the clouds back up to the plane. There were soft, moisture-laden clouds around the mountains. Long rivers moved slowly through the lush valleys. Then there were the dirt roads leading to small towns, then freeways, and finally Manila itself. What a huge city! I was used to seeing Los Angeles from the air, but Manila seemed to dwarf L.A. The plane dipped again, straightened, and began its approach. I waited for the wheels to touch down; that meant I was really in the Philippines! I was the first assistant director for Francis Ford Coppola on *Apocalypse Now*! I couldn't wait.

The line to get off the plane moved slowly. We had been on board for over fifteen hours with only a short stop in Honolulu to refuel. Outside the plane we all got into transport buses that took us to the customs area; military guards armed with Uzis rode with us. I looked for a small sign saying *Apocalypse Now* or maybe *Ziesmer* held by someone who would be driving me to Larry in Baler. I guessed they would be waiting for me after the customs area.

I passed through customs, but I still didn't see any *Apocalypse Now* sign. I picked up my luggage and just followed the crowd as I searched for the all-important sign. Soon I found myself outside the terminal, and still there was no sign, no greeting, nothing! The heat and humidity were overpowering. I had flown from Los Angeles to the Philippines to be the first assistant director for Francis Coppola, and no one met me at the airport. I sat down on the curb next to the short white curved metal fence with my suitcases around me and I waited.

The military presence was everywhere. I had never experienced armed guards with their automatic weapons at the ready. I was a long way from a sound stage at Paramount Studios. I hoped Larry was really all right. An hour went by, and no one came up to me, no sign, no greeting, nothing. I couldn't believe it. Taxi drivers kept waving to me, but I had no idea where I was to go. Where was everyone?

I looked through the papers from the Los Angeles production office for any help. Finally I found an address and phone number for an office in Manila, but how did I make a phone call? I didn't have any Filipino money, and I had no idea how to use their phones.

"Can I help you, sir?" an elderly taxi driver was looking down on me.

"What happened is . . . I'm supposed to be picked up. I'm doing *Apocalypse Now*, a movie."

"*Apocalypse!*" he shouted. "I drove Mr. Coppola! Come! I know where their offices are. I take you right away!"

He didn't have a sign, but he did speak English, so we got my luggage into his taxi, and off we went through the streets of Manila looking for *Apocalypse Now*.

Manila's international airport was next to the Philippine Village Hotel and a large shopping area of beautiful shops and roadways. Everything looked so clean and fresh.

"I drive Mr. Coppola. Very nice. Wife, too; very nice. You know Mrs. Coppola?"

"No, I never met either of them," I answered, as I tried to take in all the sights.

The taxi soon turned onto roads that were pitted and without curbs. It must have rained that morning because puddles stretched across the road. Jeepneys, a taxi-van combination with a silver horse for a hood ornament, brightly colored paint, gold fringe, and religious decorations began to race with their full load of passengers. My taxi driver smiled and waved as we sped along. He seemed to know half the drivers in Manila.

"You from Hollywood?"

"Yes," I answered. "West Los Angeles, actually."

"You know Dustin Hoffman?"

In the intersections, street vendors were selling single cigarettes, bags of peanuts, oranges, perfumed herbs strung into necklaces, religious medals, and comic books. Jeepneys were everywhere.

"No, I don't."

"Muhammad Ali?" he asked, grinning at me in the rearview mirror.

"Ahh, no," I admitted. I had met Ali at a child's birthday party in a McDonald's in Los Angeles, but I didn't think that counted.

"We have a whole plaza named for Mr. Muhammad Ali," the driver announced proudly.

As we drove further into Manila, the city changed from the beautiful and clean area around the airport and the Philippine Village Hotel to the poor and shabby areas that make up most of Manila. Posters showing pictures of Ferdinand Marcos and his wife Imelda, the president and first lady of the Philippines, were everywhere.

"Do you know Joe Frazier?" he asked.

Our lane of traffic was stopped by the blue-uniformed traffic police. There seemed to be no reason, but then suddenly an army truck filled with Philippine soldiers dressed in their khakis zoomed through the intersection. Though the soldiers looked very young to me, they were grim faced and each held an automatic weapon. My taxi driver said nothing until the military truck passed.

"Joe Frazier is very nice man. You know Al Pacino?"

The taxi then turned, and we were on a beautiful tree-shaded avenue in the Makati area of Manila that could've been Wilshire Boulevard in Beverly Hills. Businessmen in their suits got out of Mercedes and Cadillacs. Women in the current fashions from Tokyo, Paris, or Hong Kong shopped with their children. Every shop and office building seemed to have its own armed security guard. There were no street vendors, puddles, or debris; it was like suddenly being in another world.

I was explaining to him what an assistant director did when the taxi stopped in front of a Goodyear factory sign. All I could see were warehouses and industrial metal shops.

"Over here, Jerry." The driver and I had become well aquainted. He took me around the side to the rear of the compound. He pointed proudly at a metal door, and at last there was a sign that clearly read *Apocalypse Now*.

I paid Anjo, my taxi driver, with U.S. currency that he readily accepted.

I gathered my luggage and entered the door. Nothing seemed to be happening, and there was no one there. What was going on? I settled my luggage into a corner of what must have been a waiting room, and I began to explore. I could find no one. Finally I resorted to shouting, "Hello! Anyone here?" I wandered through other doors. "Hello! Can anyone help me?" Nothing. "*Apocalypse Now?*" I shouted. Then down a long corridor a door opened and a man came toward me.

"Hello. Who are you?" he asked.

"Look, I'm Jerry Ziesmer and I just . . . ," I began.

"Jerry? Hey, I'm Gray Frederickson! I'm producing *Apocalypse Now*; I talked with you on the phone in L.A.!"

"Ahh, OK, you're Gray Frederickson," I said. "Look I . . . no one met me at the airport. I mean . . . "

"I'm sorry. We just . . . so much going on, you know?" he answered, as he gestured to the vacant offices. "Where are your things? Let me get you a hotel room, relax, get yourself together, and in a couple of days we'll go up to the set in Baler. How are you feeling?" he asked.

"Gray, look, I'm an assistant director. Larry Franco, my second assistant, is already up at the set. I really want to get up there, wherever it is, and as soon as possible." I wished I had paid more attention when I read *Heart of Darkness*; maybe this was all a part of it.

"Sure, sure. Well, let's get out of here then." Gray entered an empty office and called someone on the phone. "Need to get up to Baler. Yeah, right away. I got the assistant director for Francis right here. Half hour, OK?"

Another person walked slowly toward me smiling and nodding. He wore white cotton gloves; he had to be a driver. Anjo had worn that same type of gloves.

"Jimmy," Gray said to the driver, "get the black Mazda Crown out front for an airport run right away and get Jerry's luggage, too."

Things seemed to be moving. I had promised Larry I would be on the set Monday afternoon, and I wanted desperately to be there.

Jimmy drove us back toward the airport, but turned into the private section. A large plane that could easily seat twenty to thirty passengers was waiting for us. Jimmy drove onto the runway and right to the plane. He loaded my luggage on board with the help of the two pilots, as four armed military guards watched us. Gray saw me looking at the guards.

"The Philippines," he said. "You'll get used to it."

I looked around for other passengers, but Gray and I were it. We had the whole plane to ourselves!

"Francis is expecting you. Man, you can't imagine what has been happening! I mean, no organization, you know?" Gray began, as the plane lifted off. "I can't understand it."

"Really?" I watched Manila slip away as we followed the eastern coast of the Philippines north into vast agricultural areas, then jungle, and finally after about a half hour, a jungle clearing where the pilot expertly put down our plane on what looked like a homemade runway.

There were four other planes parked there. Gray saw me looking at them.

"The *Apocalypse Now* air force," he laughed. "Great if you want to get away for the weekend."

I grabbed my luggage as Gray motioned for me to get in a waiting Jet Ranger helicopter.

"No runway in Baler!" Gray shouted.

I took all the luggage I could get into the helicopter; the rest would go to Baler by jeep. I hoped.

The whooshing of the helicopter blades got stronger, and we lifted off and headed north for the film set, Larry Franco, Francis Ford Coppola, and Marlon Brando.

When we were up, Gray turned to me and shouted in my ear, "You want to put down and get a little lunch first? I know a great seafood restaurant! We're too late to eat with the company." He checked his watch and shrugged his shoulders.

I smiled "No, thanks" to Gray and turned to look out the copter's window. What had I gotten into? What did Larry mean "It was a piece of cake"?

The helicopter circled and came in over the Pacific Ocean and then Baler Bay. The water was every shade of tropical blue, no whitecaps, but a gentle surf. I could see a lazy village with thatched huts, bamboo bridges over quiet lagoons, a few outrigger canoes, and the deep-colored jungle vegetation.

Our helicopter set down on the beach. It was a beautiful sight, but I saw nothing happening, no activity. Crew types were standing around leaning on their equipment or lying in the sand. Locals were everywhere just lounging, waiting for orders, or sleeping. Extras by the hundreds were in groups just sitting in the hot sun. I stepped out of the helicopter and looked for Larry.

He came from about a hundred yards away, running and waving at me with his big smile showing through his red beard.

"Jer! You're here! You made it!" he shouted.

"Look, Jerry," Gray shouted over the helicopter noise, "I'll take your luggage into Baler for you. Leave it in your rooms. I'm going to get something to eat. Catch you later." The helicopter started to shake, and as Gray sat in the copilot seat, it took off, sending sand over everything within thirty feet, including me.

I watched Larry run up, and I had to smile. "Larry!" I barely recognized him. He was stripped to the waist, with the residue of sweat and sand covering his body. He had only been here two days, but already he was well sunburned. He had put white ointment all over his nose and with his reddish beard, red face, and hairy potbelly, he looked like a Christmas troll.

"How you doin', Jer?" Larry asked, brimming with excitement.

"Larry, what's going on?" I asked, as I looked around at about five hundred inactive bodies trying to find comfort from the hot sun.

"Can't film! Helicopters didn't come," he said.

"Film something without them," I countered.

"No one wants to tell Francis they're not coming," Larry answered.

"Larry, it's 3:00 P.M., right?" I asked. "Who's running things?"

"Well, as I understand it, Francis got real frustrated about two weeks ago and told his producers to go get the top assistant director in the world, like the guy who did *Lawrence of Arabia*! So they did, but that movie was made fifteen years ago, and when the assistant director came out here he was over seventy years old, and the heat damn near killed him!" Larry laughed as he fought to get me to understand.

Larry continued, "Instead of an old man, Francis then wanted a young guy who did big Hollywood pictures with lots of extras. Well, we just did *Black Sunday* at the Super Bowl with eighty-six thousand extras, right? So they called you!"

I had to take a beat, so I just waited for Larry to stop laughing. I looked at him and then at five hundred lounging bodies in the afternoon sun on a remote beach somewhere in the Philippines.

"Larry, where's the piece of cake?"

"Oh, Jer, are you kidding? We can do this! This is perfect for us!" Larry could get excited.

"Where's Francis Coppola?" I asked. "Marlon Brando?"

"Over in that hut, over there," Larry said, as he pointed to a small thatched hut on stilts about thirty yards away. "Marlon isn't here yet."

I took one more look around and then started to walk toward the hut. I knew I didn't have to stay in the Philippines. I knew Larry and I could get out of here on the next plane and be back working in Hollywood on another picture next week. I kept walking.

Finally I stood next to the hut, and I put my hand on the ladder leading up to the door. There was still time. I could turn back. I glanced at Larry thirty yards away; he was watching my every move. I could hear a typewriter tap-tapping in the hut; that had to be Francis Coppola. I stood at the ladder and looked up to the door.

I missed working on the two *Godfather*s. I did work the Academy Awards show the years that Marlon Brando was awarded the Oscar for *Godfather* and the Indian girl gave his acceptance speech and again when Francis received the Oscar for *Godfather II*, but that didn't count. I wanted to work on a film with them, to be there during the creation.

I felt Francis Coppola was the greatest film director of our time and that Marlon Brando was the best film actor in the world. To work with people like Francis Coppola and Marlon Brando was the whole reason I wanted to do film in the first place.

I looked again at Larry, then at the sand and dirt already caked to my sweaty arms. The tap-tapping of the typewriter continued. I took a deep breath and climbed up the bamboo ladder.

Francis turned from his typing. He had a full beard and was wearing dark glasses even inside the hut. A khaki baseball-style cap was on his head. He wore tan shorts with a well-worn, loose-fitting cotton T-shirt that advertised a San Francisco rock group and dark socks that came only about six inches above his shoes.

"I'm Jerry Ziesmer," I said. "I'm your new assistant director."

"Great. Come in," Francis began. There wasn't much room in the hut, just a tiny desk, chair, and a couple of pillows on the floor, so I stayed on the ladder. "They told me you were coming out. Welcome," he added. We stared at each other for a moment.

"Look . . . I heard you're not getting any helicopters today. Is there something else we can film?" I asked. "I don't have a script, but . . ."

"No helicopters? Really?" he replied, "No one told me." He looked at me as though that answered everything. It was after lunch, nearly 3:00 P.M., and the company hadn't done a shot all day.

"Right. Why don't we find something else to shoot, without helicopters?" I suggested, always the assistant director.

"OK. Why not? No one told me, Jerry," Francis said, as he got up and followed me down the ladder. "No one tells me these things," he continued.

We gathered Vittorio Storaro, the cameraman, and his crew, all from Italy. I knew Vittorio's work from the Bernardo Bertolucci films, especially *Last Tango in Paris*, but Vittorio was an interesting choice for cameraman because he was primarily known for his lighting of interiors, and *Apocalypse Now* was an exterior picture.

Vittorio Storaro looked and carried himself like an Italian aristocrat. Even on the beach he was properly dressed, never dusty or dirty. It always appeared to me that Vittorio did not sweat. His hair and facial features were Roman and dignified, classic, and reflecting a culture extending back thousands of years. He had a regal bearing about him; he wasn't quite a star, but he certainly was a star in the making.

Francis introduced me to the rest of the crew, as Larry got the cast going back to makeup. Francis then showed us some shots we could get without helicopters. The crew seemed happy to be doing something. I watched everyone working to set the camera and moving lights and building a dolly track. Italians or Americans, everyone did basically the same things to make a picture. Like boiling an egg, it's done the same around the world. I glanced at Larry running back and forth getting the actors ready and letting them know what we would be filming. I saw Francis showing Vittorio some handwritten script pages as they talked about the next shot.

"Jerry!" Francis was calling to me. "Next shot we'll do is Marty Sheen in this same setup, OK?"

"Sounds good to me. One shot after another, just like D. W. Griffith," I quipped.

Francis smiled, but he had to translate and then explain everything I had said about D. W. Griffith to Vittorio and his Italian crew. The Italians just stared at me. I guess it didn't translate too well.

"Jer!" Larry proudly shouted. He pointed at the actors all made up and waiting.

I nodded to Larry, then I glanced at Francis and Vittorio. They were working with the film crew, Francis at the camera wheels setting the shot for composition and story content and then Vittorio working his magic with lighting, lenses, and filters.

"Ready when you are, Francis," I said, and our journey began.

We lost the light at about 5:30, and I called a wrap for the day and got Francis and Vittorio to discuss the next day's shooting. We all followed Francis about a hundred yards down the beach. When he was opposite the tiny village he turned, and with his back to the Pacific Ocean he started to describe the action of the helicopter attack on Village II.

"Vittorio, look, over here is where Kilgore's helicopter comes down." Francis stood on the beach about twenty feet from the ocean. Vittorio and all of us were watching him. "Now is it better for the helicopter to be turned so that Kilgore gets out toward the camera? Dick?" Francis yelled for Dick White, our Vietnam pilot expert. "Dick, look, could Kilgore's helicopter come straight in, with all the other ships . . . Jerry, how many you think we'll have tomorrow?"

I had no idea, but I glanced at Larry, and he gave me two thumbs up. "All we can get, Francis. We asked for everything, all they've got," I said.

"OK. Dick," Francis continued, "can Kilgore's ship come in with all the others, the Wagner playing, the formation, and then Kilgore's ship lands here so Duvall comes out toward the camera?"

"Yeah," Dick said, "unless there's a hell of a wind." Dick White was one great helicopter pilot, both in and out of Vietnam.

"OK. Jerry, no wind tomorrow!" Francis said. That's an assistant director joke, as if I could control the wind. Francis early in his career was an assistant director type for Roger Corman on a number of low-budget films, and he occasionally would hit me with an old assistant director one-liner.

"Duvall comes out of the chopper to about here." Francis walked the sand for us. "OK? Now Marty and Sam come up from there. They came around the chopper, see?" Francis continued, and everyone watched. "Now, Vittorio, the scene is about the surfing, you know?" Francis was never sure that Vittorio knew the scene.

"Yes, Francis, of course," Vittorio said.

"The surfing scene occurs about here and then Duvall does his 'napalm speech,' probably over here. Now it's Duvall, so we never know, but we hope he is over here," Francis said, as he showed us where Duvall could be standing. "OK, Vittorio? How is that for you?" Francis asked.

"Sure, Francis. Whatever you want we do," Vittorio answered. "This is very good." Vittorio's Italian accent and his ability to speak and understand English vacillated greatly depending on audience and circumstances.

Francis was pleased. "OK. Effects, for the explosions . . ." Francis began.

"Francis, what we got for you is this," said Joe Lombardi, who with A. D. Flowers was in charge of special effects. "We got rocket explosions in the sand and the water, all you want. We got your napalm in the hills with twelve thousand gallons of gasoline! We got your colored smoke grenades, every color you want, Vittorio."

"Oh, thank you, Joe," Vittorio said with real feeling, as though Joe Lombardi had brought van Gogh a special yellow paint.

"Twelve thousand gallons, wow. OK. So, what else? Oh, yeah. Jerry, you got to do a real safety thing with the helicopters and all the people . . . and . . . is there anything else?" Francis asked.

We all looked around and nodded, and the meeting started to break up. Sounded easy. Tomorrow we would begin our filming with Robert Duvall's helicopter actually touching down and Willard (Martin Sheen), Capt. Kilgore (Robert Duvall), and Lance (Sam Bottoms) deciding whether to surf or fight.

After Francis talked all of us through the first shot, Vittorio suggested a remarkable shot that required his Italian crew to build a dolly track actually secured onto the ocean floor.

"Francis, maybe you would want . . . What we could do for you is . . ." Vittorio spoke and gestured out into the rising tide. "For you we build a dolly track . . . The camera moves . . .You see beach and sand, then village! What you think, Francis?" Vittorio asked.

You didn't have to have three Academy Awards like Francis to know Vittorio had described a sensational shot.

"Wow, Vittorio, you could do that?" Francis was grasping the idea for the shot, a dolly shot on the ocean.

"Sure, Francis. Yes, for you." Vittorio said, "You think you'd like?"

I looked around the crew and then at Francis; how the hell were they going to build a dolly track in the ocean?

"Vittorio, yes! That would be great!" Francis said.

I still remember the end of my first day on Apocalypse Now *as I stood on the beach at Baler Bay and listened to the plans of Francis and Vittorio. I had no way of knowing then that I had already begun two simultaneous journeys. One journey consisted of those experiences we all shared in making one of the finest films of our time. The second journey was deeply personal, forcing me to accept the dark side of the human soul and to begin my struggle across the abyss of Death. My second journey would take me to a small West Los Angeles cemetery, past the crypts of Marilyn Monroe and Helen Hayes to a fresh grave, and then to a glamorous Hollywood premiere twenty years after I stood on the beach at Baler.*

I waited for Larry to tie up the loose ends on the set, making sure everyone knew the 7:00 A.M. call for the next day, and then we set off across the sand toward a large lagoon. The whole cast and crew seemed to be walking in the same direction. At the edge of the lagoon were about seven bancas, large canoelike boats that held about eight people. The cast and crew would wait their turn and then enter the bancas for a ride across the lagoon on the first leg of the nightly trip to their rooms in Baler.

On the other side of the lagoon, jeepneys were waiting to take them over jungle roads to Baler. I noticed that Francis and Vittorio didn't get in the banca line. They stood to one side, and soon the Jet Ranger helicopter landed. They ducked under the rotating blades, and scurried aboard.

I pointed at the departing helicopter, "Larry, where are Francis and Vittorio going?"

"It's almost 6:30, Jer. They go back to Manila each night. That's the latest they can leave because of the dark," Larry informed me, as we entered our banca.

We have canoes in Wisconsin, so I knew to only step and sit in the center of the banca. Tippy things, those bancas; most of us would learn how tippy firsthand. One day after filming, Martin Sheen was bare-chested as he sat in a banca. Somehow it tipped and Marty fell into the water. We all laughed, until Marty came back up to the surface and we saw ten dark purple blood leeches already attached to Marty's back and chest.

It was about a fifteen-minute jeepney ride through the jungle on a machete-constructed roadway to Baler. The road was full of potholes and puddles with eight-foot tropical branches cut and laid across the worst holes to give the jeepneys some traction.

Even as late as 6:30 it was still hot and sticky; I had never felt such heavy, moist air. Just being in it sapped your strength; your clothes seemed to drink the moisture right out of the air. Soon they were wringing wet, and you hadn't even moved. Everyone in the jeepney was drenched in sweat with dust and sand caked onto their legs and arms; most had a variety of insect bites on their necks and faces, along with the bright red sunburn you get in this part of the world by the glare of hot sun off the ocean and the white sand. Most people wore shorts and either T-shirts or no shirts, a cotton cloth that was continually soaked in ice water and then tied around the neck, and some kind of head covering. They looked like a crew of pirates.

Among the twelve people in our jeepney I could hear Tagalog, the native tongue of the Philippines, Italian, something that sounded like Vietnamese, Australian English, Dutch English, and good old United States of America English. Just like in the Vietnam War, nobody understood everyone.

Larry turned to me and said for the first time (of what would be 246 times), "Jer, you know what I could go for now?" He had to shout over the noise of the jeepney. "A McDonald's Big Mac, and a Quarter Pounder with cheese, a Filet-O-Fish, a large order of fries, and a chocolate shake!" He laughed, and all the other jeepney passengers laughed with him. I really didn't understand the humor until we sat down to dinner that night.

As our jeepney took us farther from the lagoon, I began to see more huts on stilts just placed randomly in the jungle. Then the huts seemed to be grouped. This was the outskirts of Baler.

The main street of Baler, and there was only one, stretched for about three blocks. In the center of town the houses were still raised off the ground, but the construction was wood and plaster and the corrugated tin that was used for roofing and siding all over Southeast Asia. The most unusual building material used in Baler was for flooring; beautiful thick mahogany was in nearly every home and office. Not only was it cheap and plentiful, it was nearly indestructible.

The Baler community building and schoolhouse appeared to be the most important building in town. It was directly across the street from a low plaster-and-wood building that the film company had rented for their production offices.

The jeepney stopped in front of the production offices, and Larry took me inside while the rest of the jeepney passengers dispersed to their accommodations. There was no real hotel, motel, or rooming house of any kind. The film company had rented houses and other rooms in private homes for all the film workers. The overflow had to be housed in the thatched huts I had seen coming into Baler. The normal population of Baler had swelled with the film company adding their crew and support helpers of 350 plus another 750 extras with their support help. Added to those figures were the wives, children, and girlfriends of the workers, and you had a total influx of over 1,350 brought into the small town of Baler.

Larry introduced me to Leon Chooluck, the production manager, and he showed me around the offices, introducing me to those in charge of accounting, those in charge of helicopters, those in charge of extras, those in charge of catering. The size and scope of this picture was mind-blowing. The crew lunch, those who were served food by our company caterer, totaled 550 a day; this was in addition to the 750 extras that were fed and housed by the company.

I listened to everyone, and I looked at all their plans and budgets, but my head was swimming with the thought that *Apocalypse Now* had its own air force of four private planes and one Jet Ranger helicopter just for the use of the company personnel. I had to accept that *Apocalypse Now* was a gigantic production on the scale of *Cleopatra* or *The Ten Commandments*. In Baler I was witnessing its mere infancy, and infants grow bigger very quickly. And where was Marlon Brando, and when would he begin on *Apocalypse Now*?

Finally, Larry and I left the production office, and he took me across the unpaved street to the schoolhouse, where a caterer had been hired to feed the cast and crew; there were no restaurants in Baler. There wasn't really much of anything in Baler.

There were wooden planks over what looked like a drainage ditch between the street and the school.

"Don't look down," Larry said, as we stepped across the planks and entered the school yard.

"Why?" I asked, as I glanced into the ditch. Larry didn't have to say more. The ditch was used as a sewage removal receptacle for the school and for the caterer's garbage disposal.

I followed Larry to a cafeteria-style line where we got trays, utensils, and approached the area of entrees. Larry was ahead of me and took some of this and some of that, none of which I recognized.

"What is that stuff?" I asked him, pointing at a stewlike substance he had on his plate.

"You don't see many dogs around here, do you?" Larry laughed and moved down the line. One of Larry's best traits was his immediate assimilation of native humor.

I took some bread, a roll, and a plate of pasta covered in a dark red sauce with the distinct flavor of pineapple.

Larry had found a spot at one of the long eating tables, and I sat across from him. He ate with a gusto that I am sure was to impress me both to the gourmet values of the meal as well as to the beauty of Baler itself and the sheer joy of our present employment.

Larry was just finishing his tan rice with black specks, when the strings of light bulbs surrounding the eating area flickered and then went out. Then suddenly on the large white wall that made up part of the school yard, a film projector's light beamed and a movie began, obviously the night's entertainment. The problem of sound for the movie was solved very simply; there wasn't any. The films were obscure silent movies from the 1920s.

I looked around at the audience made up of the native children of Baler as well as some of the film workers who had been here a week or two too long. With an early call in the morning, I suggested to Larry that he show me our living arrangements or we would never wake up in the morning.

"We're going to wake up, Jer, don't worry about that," Larry said, as we recrossed the Baler outdoor sewer system. I followed him down the main street to what he assured me were the best living accommodations available. "We were very lucky, Jer," Larry assured me.

I followed Larry in the dark for about a block. Then we came to a home with an open garage area below and what looked like an adequate living area for the two of us above. We climbed the outdoor stairs and entered what would be called a two-bedroom apartment with one bath, a small living area with a solid mahogany floor, and a tiny kitchen with a hot plate and an icebox the size of a two-drawer file cabinet. After seeing the rest of Baler, I didn't think that this two-bedroom apartment for us was that terrible.

Just then Allan Levine and his assistant, Teddy, climbed the stairs and entered. I was very pleased to see Allan, as he was a wonderful prop man; I had worked with him on *The Boston Strangler*. There would be no trouble with props; Allan's presence assured me of that. I didn't know Teddy, but anyone Allan wanted was great with me.

We all were lounging in the living room area when Allan said, "Teddy's going shopping tomorrow at daybreak."

Larry and Teddy smiled and nodded.

Allan laughed, "Need to do a little shopping."

More laughter from Allan, Teddy, and Larry. I felt totally left out. Assistant propmen went shopping nearly every day. So what?

"How long you going for, Teddy?" Larry asked and laughed at the same time.

"Five days," Teddy said, as Larry and Allan nearly fell on the floor laughing.

I stared at the three and finally asked, "Five days! Where you going?"

Allan jumped right in with the answer, "He gets one of the planes in the *Apocalypse Now* air force with a private pilot and flies first to Hong Kong for a day and a half, then Bangkok for a day, Singapore for a day and a half, then Bali, and back here!"

Larry, Allan and Teddy were laughing and pointing at me.

I had to get used to the size of this production.

When Allan and Teddy said goodnight, instead of going out the door and back down the stairs, they went into one of the two bedrooms and closed the door. I shot a look to Larry, but before I could utter a word he said, "Our room's big, Jer. You can have the best bed."

It wasn't really a big room. There were two single beds, one nightstand, a bare bulb hanging from the ceiling, and a solid mahogany floor. At least it couldn't get any worse.

I entered the bathroom, and I couldn't find the shower. I saw where the shower drain was in the floor, so I looked straight up from the drain and saw a large wooden barrel with a rope on one side. I just stared at the contraption.

"Jerry," Allan Levine entered with instructions, "what you have to do is pull on the rope just easy, let the water get on you, soap quickly, then pull the rope again to rinse. Got it?"

I had myself all ready. I stood under the barrel and pulled the rope. What hit me was the coldest water I have ever known. I lathered in a second, shivering and chattering, then I pulled the rope and was hit by another sample of cold Baler water.

As I entered our bedroom Larry clued me in. "Jer, the barrel is filled in the morning. All day long the sun heats the water. The first two showers are fine, but after that the barrel is refilled with cold water. It isn't reheated by the sun until the next afternoon." Another part of my Baler education.

Larry Franco was a master of adjusting to his surroundings. When Larry was in boot camp in the army, he made up his bed perfectly . . . once. He never slept in the bed again; he slept on the floor of his barracks for the next six weeks so his bed would always stay perfect.

All of my luggage was in the room. I thought that was a major miracle. I was going through my suitcases looking for my alarm clock, but I couldn't find it.

"What you looking for, Jer?" Larry asked.

"My alarm clock! We have an early call," I answered.

"Don't worry. You'll be up about 5:00, no problem," Larry said, as he turned over to go to sleep.

"Did you set your alarm, Larry?"

"Don't need it. Good night, Jer, trust me," and Larry was snoring.

I trusted him and fell asleep.

It was exactly 5:10 that I heard the first piercing shriek and high-pitched scream of terror that seemed to be coming from directly beneath our bedroom. I shot out of bed and ran for the door. The shrieks continued with more screaming, then snorting and pawing, screams, panting . . . I was ready to save the victim of whatever was happening, when Allan casually exited the other bedroom, wished me a good morning, and entered the bathroom. Larry was up, yawning and calmly pulling on his clothes. Teddy wandered out into the living area and began his morning exercise of touching his toes three times without bending his knees. Throughout this, the terrified shrieking and high-pitched screams continued and no one else seemingly heard or paid any attention.

"Larry! What the hell is going on?" I demanded.

"Our Baler alarm clock, Jer," Larry explained. "The caterer slaughters the pigs underneath us every morning about this time; pork chops for lunch, and we never oversleep!"

Good morning, *Apocalypse Now!*

Julius, the Filipino houseboy assigned to us, arrived just as we were about to leave for breakfast at the school yard. He was about twelve years old, and his primary duties were to do the daily shopping for each of us, buy a chunk of ice and put it into the icebox, tidy up the rooms, and then spend the rest of the day polishing the mahogany floors by standing on a half coconut shell, the cut portion on the floor. Then like an ice-skater with one skate, Julius would propel himself back and forth across the wooden floors for hours at a time, cleaning and polishing as he went.

Larry and Allan gave Julius their grocery orders for the day. This might include shaving supplies, but it always included a six-pack of San Miguel beer and a bag of garlic peanuts. I had an electric razor, so I only needed the San Miguel and the garlic peanuts, which came to about two dollars a day in U.S. money. If that was all the money the crew could spend a day, they were going to be saving a lot of living allowance money.

As Larry and I walked down the stairs to the street, I glanced at the area underneath our bedroom, but the caterers were already hosing the remains into the drainage ditch at the front of our house. We stepped over the ditch and headed for breakfast at the school yard.

I recognized scrambled eggs, a roll, and coffee, so I stuck to that. Larry dished the daily special onto his plate and told me again about not seeing many dogs in Baler, as he laughed his way to a table.

Village II Scene

The jeepneys took us to the edge of the lagoon, and the bancas took us across to the beach. I had told Larry to get a walkie-talkie for himself and one for me, then to get all the extras organized and ready. I looked for Vittorio and his crew. On my first full day as the first assistant director on *Apocalypse Now* I wanted to get the company off and running.

I found the Italian crew around their closed trucks, having their morning coffee and waiting for Vittorio to arrive with Francis in the Jet Ranger helicopter from Manila. After we had greeted each other in Italian and English and laughed at my Italian and their English and discussed the morning weather, I politely asked Alfredo Marchetti, Vittorio's key grip, "Alfredo, do you think it would be possible to begin laying the dolly track in the ocean while we waited for Vittorio and Francis?" I might as well have said something derogatory about their mothers.

Alfredo stared at me. Enrico Umetelli, the camera operator, and Luciano Galli, the lighting gaffer, stopped their morning conversations and moved closer to me. The whole Italian crew put down their coffees and became still. No one had to tell me I had stepped on holy ground, but they did.

Enrico, who spoke the best English, struggled to make me understand as Alfredo, with lowered head, shook his index finger at me, and Luciano, who resembled a lion with a full mane of hair, just stared into the heavens and sucked in his lower lip.

"Jerry," Enrico began, "no. We can do nothing without Vittorio."

"No, no, no," Alfredo said gently, but as though it was the truth of the ages.

"Impossible," stated Luciano, still gazing for God's help in dealing with this ignorant first assistant director from the United States.

The other Italians were now gathered around, asking for translations and muttering to each other.

"How?" Alfredo reasoned, "Where? No!"

"Not possible," Luciano added.

"Jerry, Vittorio must be here to tell," Enrico felt he had said it all.

I stared at the Italian crew, realizing that we were on an isolated beach in the Philippines, approximately a third of the way around the world from Italy and also a third of the way around the world from the United States. We each had to adapt to differences in each other's culture, language, etc. It took me less than a millisecond to know that I was the one who was going to do the adapting.

When Francis and Vittorio arrived, we greeted each other, and I immediately got Vittorio together with his crew. He showed Alfredo exactly where to put the dolly track in the ocean, the very same place Vittorio had shown all of us the afternoon before. As the Italian crew began to plan and build the dolly track, I got Francis and Vittorio to rehearse with Robert Duvall, Martin Sheen, and Sam Bottoms, while we waited for the arrival of the Huey helicopters from the Philippine military. This was the helicopter attack on the surfing beach called Village II, so I had asked for as many Hueys as the Philippine air force could send us—thirty, forty, whatever I could get. This was the biggest action sequence in our film. Francis wanted the Hueys to come out of the dawn sky with Wagner's *Ride of the Valkyries* blaring from huge speakers attached to the lead helicopter. It would be awesome.

I didn't know it until days later, but there were fewer than twenty Hueys in the whole Philippine air force, and their pilots never knew until that very morning whether they would be playing *Apocalypse Now* with us in the north at Baler or fighting with actual guerrillas on the island of Mindanao.

Larry stood beside me as we watched the cast rehearsal. From the camera angles we would see not only the beach where Duvall's Huey would land, but across a lagoon to a second beach and most of Village II. It was a huge area that had to be filled with our 750 extras, divided among villagers, Viet Cong, and American military, plus village animals. Then we had to see the results of rockets shot from the helicopters hitting the village, causing fires and smoke, as well as the results of rockets hitting the lagoon and the beaches themselves.

I had always been taught to cast real extras. If you need waiters, cast real waiters. If you need blackjack dealers, cast real blackjack dealers, etc. On *Apocalypse Now* this same theory was followed. The extras we cast as South Vietnamese villagers were actual South Vietnamese refugees from placement camps around the Philippines. The extras playing the roles of the Viet Cong and North Vietnamese regulars were also cast from the masses of refugees from North Vietnam housed in these same camps. When Larry and I got to know the Vietnamese extras better, I asked them what determined whether they wanted to be South Vietnamese villagers or Viet Cong extras in our film. "Easy," they told me, "just like in real war. All depends on who has best rice!" All of the refugees laughed and smiled at us, but I knew they were telling the truth.

The American soldiers and pilots were selected from the thousands of U.S. citizens who chose to stay in Southeast Asia after the Vietnam War. Many were on medical discharge, but most didn't want to leave the beaches and coconut groves of Southeast Asia. They took their military money and existed in the little villages along the South China Sea coast north of Manila. It was absolutely true that a lot of the American expatriates didn't want the Vietnam War to end, and with *Apocalypse Now* they saw a chance to relive the highs they found during the war.

The biggest single problem I had in staging the Vietnam War action for *Apocalypse Now* was to keep control of the U.S. expatriates who were cast as our U.S. soldiers. Whenever the Hueys hovered and the simulated bombs and rocket fire began, many of them were back in the manic depression that was the Vietnam War. They had such joy and abandonment during the scene, as though they were tasting some exotic narcotic only available to the men who had also run in the jungles of Vietnam, and such terrible lows when it was all over.

At 11:00 A.M. we still hadn't gotten a shot. I kept looking toward the southern sky for the Hueys, but I didn't see any. It was about a half-hour flight from the air force installation to Baler, but if there was any action in Mindanao, we wouldn't get the Hueys that day.

The job of the assistant director was to keep the company moving forward. I had Francis rehearsing with his actors, but once they were ready, I needed the Hueys to film the scene.

I walked over to where the Italians were building the dolly track in the ocean.

"Alfredo, how long before you're ready?" I shouted to our key grip.

"Soon, Jerry! Very soon, don't worry!" he shouted back to me.

I checked the southern sky, but there were no Hueys.

Larry went across the lagoon and began to set the extras on the far beach and the village. I began to set the extras on the near beach, where Duvall's Huey would touch down and the scene with Willard and Lance would play. Joe Lombardi and A. D. Flowers, the two special effects men, went over the action of my extras with me. Terry Leonard, our stunt coordinator, rehearsed the soldiers in helicopter safety and showed them where the explosive charges were set in the sand and water. I kept looking into the southern sky, but no Hueys. When I caught Alfredo's eye, he waved and smiled, signaling that they were coming along fine.

I guess it was a good morning. We didn't film, but Larry and I got all of the 750 extras set and rehearsed, and we worked out all the special effects. Francis had rehearsed with his actors; they were ready. All we needed were the Hueys. Just before lunch I got a radio communication from our production office in Baler that there would be no Hueys today but that tomorrow looked good.

I looked over to the dolly track and the army of Filipinos working to build it under the direction of the Italian crew. It looked like it was coming along, but the tide appeared to be coming along also. When we arrived that morning, the tide was out and the grips stood out of the water as they worked, but now the tide was rising.

"Alfredo!" I shouted. "The tide! Coming in!"

"Jerry! No problem!" Alfredo shouted back. All the Italians were smiling as they worked knee-deep in the ocean; I felt secure. Sort of.

"Alfredo! I'm going to call lunch! We'll film the dolly shot after lunch, OK?" I called out to him.

"Good!" he answered, and the Italians moved to the beach and toward lunch. You didn't have to call them twice.

I radioed "Lunch!" to everyone and started to the caterers' tents near the lagoon where the bancas deposited us.

Larry met me in the catering line, and I told him we would be ready for the dolly shot just after lunch and to get all the extras ready for that shot as soon as lunch was over.

Our daily lunch on the beach at Baler was for hundreds of extras and crew plus perhaps sixty visitors that could consist of international press, local dignitaries, and military officers from Manila. On one day we thought we were having Ferdinand and Imelda Marcos as guests for lunch, but I guessed that the local guerrillas were a bit too close to risk an appearance by the nation's president and first lady.

One day during lunch we actually had a live round of ammunition fall onto our Village II set and explode in the sand—the local guerrillas just reminding us that they were up in the hills and weren't going to go away, not for *Apocalypse Now*, nor for Ferdinand Marcos.

The caterers had set up four huge tents similar to circus tents for our cast and crew. We would line up, pick up our trays, plates, and plastic utensils, then continue along banquet-style tables where the caterers' helpers would serve your choice of foods from huge pans. The lunches would consist of an entree, usually a choice of fish, meat, or a pasta, at least two vegetables and, of course, rice, followed by bread, rolls, and butter. Finally there was a table with desserts, usually flan or custard and a cake. After the cafeteria line, you would carry your tray to other long tables where chairs were set up. Of course, there were not enough chairs for the hundreds being served, so it was expected of those eating first to finish and get up from the tables so those who came later in the line would have a place to sit.

It would be dishonest of me to say that the food was gourmet; it wasn't. I tried to remind everyone that we were filming on a remote beach in Southeast Asia with an international crew and a multicultural group of extras from every region of the Asian continent as well as the varied islands of the South Pacific, Australia, and New Zealand. It would be impossible for the caterers to please all; that they pleased none was disturbing to me, but having a common enemy became useful as the weeks passed. All the foodstuffs had to be flown from Manila to a jungle runway and then transported by jeep to Baler and by banca to the cooking tent.

One day I had to run to the extras' lunch tent because the sticky rice was not of proper quality for the Vietnamese, and I had a full-scale rebellion on my hands. I learned most painfully that the varied cultures and nationalities of Southeast Asia have differing tastes when it comes to rice. I successfully solved nearly all dietary disputes by offering to double their daily ration of Coca-Cola. The Coke plant was right in Manila. We always seemed to have a lot of it, and every culture liked it.

Though our official lunch break was a half hour, it took nearly two hours to get the crew fed and back to work.

As soon as I walked back onto the beach, I checked the rising tide. I found Alfredo, but he assured me there was no problem. Larry had all the extras ready and in place. Francis and Vittorio had discussed the shot, the speed of the dolly, everything. Now all we needed was to have the crew finish building the dolly track.

I could see the sun beginning to descend in the west behind the hill of coconut palms. I implored the Italians to hurry. I begged. I pleaded. "Alfredo! Look at the sun! Hurry!" I shouted. They all seemed to be working, but the tide was rising and the sun was setting!

"There is no problem, Jerry!" Alfredo shouted.

"Don't worry!" Luciano smiled and waved, as well.

Vittorio just pointed to his crew and assured me that all would be fine.

The tide was now lapping the top of the dolly track! The workers were chest-deep in the water. Now they were using small boats instead of walking out on the sand as they had done at low tide.

"Alfredo! The water is so high! How can we get the cameras out there?" I asked.

"Jerry, don't worry!" he shouted back. "We'll walk the cameras out and lift them onto the dolly track!"

"Walk! Look at the tide! We can't walk the cameras out there!" I was getting crazed.

"Not now, but tomorrow! We'll walk the cameras out tomorrow!" Alfredo shouted back and all the Italians nodded in agreement.

"Tomorrow?" I was in cardiac arrest. "Tomorrow?"

"Of course, Jerry," Vittorio calmly replied. "We can't shoot today, but maybe tomorrow. We'll see."

• • •

I stood alone on the beach at Baler after my first full day as the assistant director on *Apocalypse Now* and had to face the fact that even with the largest crew in motion picture making history, we hadn't gotten a shot all day. It wouldn't be the last time that would happen.

The following day we only got two Hueys, so we did Vittorio's dolly shot across the ocean and it was marvelous. The idea to build a dolly track in the ocean was insane, like van Gogh, but the results were art, also like van Gogh. I talked with Vittorio about the concept of the shot.

"Vittorio, the shot may be great, but whose point of view is it? A dolphin? No one can be where you placed your camera," I argued.

"Jerry," Vittorio answered me with the patience of Michaelangelo talking to a workman from the local granite quarry, "the shot *is*. That's all. It exists; that's enough. You see?"

I didn't see, but I tried to see. It was an interesting shot. There was so much for me to learn. We were so different. Vittorio was a true artist from Italy, Rome and Florence, and with the bearing and graciousness of the world of Leonardo da Vinci. I was a sandlot shortstop from midwest America, Milwaukee and Green Bay, and with the simplicity and openness of the world of Norman Rockwell. Somehow the Milwaukee sandlot shortstop and the Florentine cultured artist bonded on *Apocalypse Now*, so that we could work together to create Vittorio's rich cinema tapestry and turn a double play once in a while, too.

The next day we got eight Hueys, and we began filming the attack on Village II. We would have our cameras pointed toward the beach and the small village. Larry had his extras: the South Vietnam villagers, the Viet Cong prisoners, and a couple of North Vietnam regulars, about 700 extras in all, ready for the shot. Terry Leonard got all his stuntmen ready. I loaded the cast—Robert Duvall, Martin Sheen, and Sam Bottoms— into the command helicopter, then I signaled for all of the fifty U.S. Army extras to get into their helicopters. When all the choppers were in the air, the set dressers and propmen covered our beach with the bamboo debris that would fly up when our choppers landed.

Vittorio had his cameras ready. I always checked with his number-one camera operator, Enrico, just to be sure. I radioed to Dick White, the helicopter pilot in the lead ship, and put him on alert to hover in their start position. I checked with Joe Lombardi and A. D. Flowers of special effects to be sure they were ready.

I checked the set to satisfy myself, glanced at Francis, said a quick prayer, and "rolled" the cameras over my walkie-talkie. When the confirmation came through that all six cameras were running, I checked Francis for his nod. I then called "Action!" into my walkie-talkie. Larry sent his extras; the colored smoke, fires and explosions began from special effects; Dick White brought all the choppers over us and then landed Duvall's ship right on its mark. The landing of the Hueys sent a great force of air down toward the beach that allowed the choppers to gently set down, but the force of air sent the bamboo debris and sand from underneath the helicopters up into the chopper's rotor wash and shot it out with a tremendous force at all of us within fifty feet of the Hueys.

The soldiers were out of all their helicopters as Robert Duvall, Marty Sheen, and Sam Bottoms began the scene. As I watched Duvall as Colonel Kilgore pacing the beach, taking off his shirt, and wanting to surf, the sand from the choppers' rotating blades was hitting my face like thousands of sharp needles. All of us behind the cameras were being tortured by the flying grains of sand, and we had nowhere to go.

When Francis called "Cut!" I radioed to stop everything and reload. All of us around the cameras had red and swollen faces from the flying sand. As the special effects crew reloaded, all the extras got back into their start positions, and the cameras got a new supply of film, we searched for something, anything, that would protect us from the flying sand.

The take was not perfect. Vittorio didn't like the yellow-colored smoke from the grenades; we'd try more green. Francis needed another take for the actors. Enrico wasn't happy either.

When it was time for take two, we had all devised some protection against the sand. The Italian grips and camera crew had T-shirts over their heads, goggles on their eyes, and scarfs around their necks. Others tried pulling up their buttoned shirts over their heads and peeking out between the buttons. Those that did not have to watch the shot just turned away and buried their heads in their chest. I held my hands over my face and peered out between my fingers. Francis and Vittorio ducked behind Enrico and his camera.

I had set some extras as Viet Cong prisoners, blindfolded and with their hands tied behind them. Then I had them tied together in a line of eight. For safety, I had a soldier leading them. During one of the takes with the landing helicopters and their deadly blades and the special effects explosions, the soldier who was to guide them fell down, and as he did he let go of the lead rope. The extras were blindfolded and weren't aware they didn't have a leader, so they continued walking forward, right toward the rear blade of a Huey. It would have cut up that line of extras like slicing a sausage. Francis yelled and pointed to the chain of extras blindly stumbling forward, then we both started to run toward them. The Italian grips got to the prisoners first and tackled the front ones. There were less than five feet between the Huey rotor blade and the blindfolded prisoners. I was so frightened; tragedy can be so close. I needed all the people I could get watching over me.

By lunch we had done three complete takes, none perfectly. We would have to do more in the afternoon. As Larry and I stood in the lunch line, I could feel my face was swollen and raw from the sand. I didn't want to smile because of the pain, and around Larry that was hard. I talked with pursed lips, not wanting to move my mouth and face.

The inventiveness of the crew came out after lunch, as they devised cardboard, plastic, wood, and metal protection from the flying sand. Some looked like ghosts with plastic ponchos covering them. Others more imaginative had fashioned their protection out of the caterers' Styrofoam cups, paper plates, and plastic eating utensils. A couple of the crew looked like the Tin Man from *The Wizard of Oz* with their metal suits and helmets of protection. We all did the best we could.

I cranked up the shooting company again. Larry got his extras ready. Special effects were always ready and waiting. The extras near the landing helicopters were suffering as much as the rest of us, but they were ready. I got the helicopters up, and Dick White put them in their starting formation. Vittorio and his cameras were ready. Francis nodded and waved; he was ready. "Please make it the last take," I said silently. I checked the set quickly, "rolled" all the cameras and then called "Action!" over my walkie-talkie.

Minutes later, Vittorio and Francis were excited and waving. We'd finally done it! Even Enrico was gesturing with his thumb up. Duvall was pleased and embraced Francis. The exultation spread to the extras near the choppers and then to Larry and all his people across the lagoon as everyone realized we had finally gotten that shot and we were moving on.

I knew we had only gotten the first shot in the scene, a wide master shot at that, but arms and fists shot into the air as the cast and crew screamed in victory, as pagan warriors must have done over their fallen enemy.

It had taken all day, with a crew of 350, six cameras, and 750 extras, but we'd done it. We'd captured some images on a short piece of film. The shot lasts fewer than six seconds in the movie, but it's the right six seconds. Tomorrow we'd be back struggling to put new images on another piece of film.

The following days were filled with breaking up the master shot. Terry Leonard got his stuntmen, along with A. D. Flower's special effects and Dick White's helicopters, and we filmed the individual stunts and explosions within the attack on Village II.

Francis then concentrated on the coverage of the actors from the time they got out of Duvall's helicopter through the napalm attack and Kilgore's famous line, "I love the smell of napalm in the morning."

I thanked God that we were through filming the Hueys landing. Now all we had to do was to have Kilgore's Huey on the beach and start the blades just moving for each shot; no more showers of sand hitting all of us.

We had to save the point-of-view shot of the actors looking out at the big surf for a second unit shot somewhere where there was good surf; we didn't have it on Baler Bay. That shot was picked up months later somewhere off Hawaii.

We also had to avoid any shot showing the napalm explosion until we knew we would have the jet fighters to simulate the dropping of the napalm bombs and then the special effects explosion of twelve thousand gallons of gasoline. That was a one-shot deal.

The day arrived for the special jets and the napalm run. We got all our extras ready and in place. Terry Leonard had all his stuntmen set. Dick White had his choppers turning, but not in the air. Our actors were standing with Francis behind the cameras.

All that we were told was that at about 10:30 A.M. the jets would make one pass over Baler Bay, turning slightly to their right and then dipping and releasing three mock napalm bombs directly over our trough rigged in the coconut forest behind Village II. Joe Lombardi and A. D. Flowers had poured the twelve thousand gallons of gasoline in the trough and were standing by to ignite it.

That coconut forest was a favorite living area for many of our extras. We had used our security guards to sweep the area, post signs, and were now using huge speakers to warn everyone away from that forest.

"Jerry!" It was Dick White on his chopper's radio. "I just got contact with the jets! They're over Japan!"

"Japan?" I said into my radio. I was a long way from Milwaukee. "How much time do I have, Dick?"

"We're getting up!" he answered. "Get everything ready!"

We had all six cameras prepared to film the napalm explosion, but I had to get them turning before the planes arrived and the gasoline went up. How much time should I allow? There was no take two. We could only have the jets for one pass, and we could never re-do an explosion of twelve thousand gallons of gasoline, never again on that hill—the trees would be gone. This was a one-timer.

"Everyone ready! Places! Larry, get everyone set and ready!" I was shouting into my walkie-talkie. I looked and saw the choppers up in the air and moving toward their start mark over the far beach and Village II. Larry had the extras marching and moving in huge circles so they would always be moving, no matter when the jets came. Terry Leonard had his stuntmen ready.

"We need ten seconds before you'll see the napalm explosion!" Joe Lombardi reminded me.

"Right, Joe," I said. "Ten seconds." I checked the sky.

"Dick?" I was trying to get in contact with Dick White up in his chopper.

"Jerry, I can't hear them on the radio! I've lost them!" Dick said. He had the only air-to-air radio that could monitor the jets' radio.

"Can you see them?" I asked.

"If I see them it's too late!" Dick said. "They'll be to Guam before the cameras are rolling!"

I looked and Francis had the actors in place. Everyone was watching the sky trying to spot the jets.

Joe Lombardi checked again, "Jer, just say 'Go'! Remember, we need a ten-second lag time. Just 'Go'!"

"I'll remember, Joe." I said, looking at the hill and praying everyone had been removed.

Vittorio was watching the sky, then turned to me and smiled. I felt he understood where I was. He'd gotten his people ready. Everyone knew how vital this shot was.

Francis started walking slowly toward me, still watching the sky.

"Jerry!!!!" It was Dick screaming into his radio. "Less than thirty seconds!!!"

I could see nothing in the sky. "Roll film!" I shouted. "Roll all cameras!" There was nothing in the sky—no jets, nothing.

Francis ran back to Enrico's camera.

"Larry! Action! Start them!" I radioed, and the extras began to move in their huge circles.

Dick White had his choppers moving into position and beginning their action.

Robert Duvall was in place and ready. The other actors were set. Sometimes you go on instinct . . . "Action!" I screamed for the actors, and Duvall began his lines.

I glanced into the sky and saw nothing. Said a quick one. Then I shouted to Joe Lombardi, "Go!!! Go!!!" He stared at me for a beat and then gave the order to ignite the gasoline. I started counting off ten seconds in my head.

I still couldn't see any planes. Suddenly there was a streak of light through the sky, the jets dipping down, and a simultaneous explosion in the coconut trees with the rising, turbulent, boiling flames of a napalm attack. There was a tremendous sonic boom, and the jets were long gone, maybe over Guam. We'd never have to do that shot again. It was perfect! Almost.

The extras, cast, and crew were very excited. Dick White was alive with joy and accomplishment over the radio, "Jerry! We got it, man! We got it! Looked real, man!"

Larry was shouting on the walkie-talkie, "Jer! Man, I could feel the heat from the explosion! Was that great?"

We got it all right, but it wasn't perfect, and I had to tell Francis. He was celebrating and reliving the shot with Vittorio, Robert Duvall, Marty, and Enrico. I touched Francis's arm and gestured that I wanted to say something to him in private. He walked five feet away with me.

"What, Jerry? It was perfect! Perfect!" Francis said. He stood staring at me with his hands on his hips and his head tilted slightly to the left.

The assistant director often plays the role of the messenger who brings the bad news. "Francis, I just want you to know something. The jets never dropped their dummy napalm bombs," I said.

"What do you mean?" Francis struggled with my words. He never moved; he just stared at me.

"We see the jets and the whole village, Duvall, the extras, everything, but nothing fell from the jets, no dummy bombs, before the napalm explosion." I said the message as clearly as I could. He had to be told, and I had to tell him.

Francis looked at me, turned and looked at the still smoking hillside, then he said quietly to me, "If they're watching for a couple of falling

bombs with all that going on, we're in trouble." Francis then turned and
went back to the celebrating, and so did I.

It was Saturday, and we had just finished filming the last of the
coverage on Robert Duvall's scene in Village II. For an assistant director,
Robert Duvall is a dream to work with because he's so dedicated to the
picture and his role. I wished he was in more of *Apocalypse Now.*

We shot a bit late, and Francis and Vittorio had to spend the night in
Baler; it got a bit too late to fly to Manila and make it there before dark.

Larry was busy with the extras, and I was just waiting around enjoying the fact that the week was over. We filmed six days and had every
Sunday off. I wondered what people could do in Baler on Sunday; there
didn't seem to be much of anything there.

"Jerry." It was Vittorio. "Can you come to our house tonight for
dinner?" The Italians had one large house in Baler, and that's where they
all stayed, including Vittorio when he couldn't fly back to Manila.

"Dinner? Well, yeah, I guess so. Thanks, Vittorio," I stammered. I
wasn't much on social graces. I knew my job, baseball, fishing, but I
didn't know dinner with the Italians.

"Good, Jerry." Vittorio was the Roman gentleman even on the beach
in Baler. "About eight?"

"Sure, Vittorio, thanks. Yeah, I'll be there," I answered. "Ahhh, can I
bring something?" I discovered some social grace I must have picked up
around a dugout.

Vittorio stared at me, smiled, and said, "What? What, Jerry, could
you bring? This is Baler!" He laughed, and I did too.

"Eight, I'll be there."

I got back to our room and showered as quickly as I could. I was just
finishing getting dressed, when Larry came in.

"Hey, Jer, where you going?" he asked.

"Dinner with the Italians," I answered.

"Oh." Larry looked at me and sat down on his bed. It was obvious
he wasn't invited.

"Just a little dinner. Something, I don't know. Vittorio asked me," I
went on.

"What are you going to bring?" Larry asked.

"Vittorio said I shouldn't bring a thing. I have nothing to bring
anyway," I said.

Larry jumped and ran to the corner of the living room that contained the hot plate and icebox. He returned proudly.

"The hell you haven't! You got this!" he proclaimed, as he held a bottle of Italian red wine vinegar.

There were no lights except on the main street of Baler. I had to stop and ask at least six different people where the Italians lived, but they all knew and pointed me on my way. When I got to the house, I knocked even though the door was partially open. Macro, the Italian camera assistant and also the son of the key grip, answered the door, and I entered. The small house was crowded with all the Italians from the camera, grip, and electric crews. I looked around trying to find Vittorio; I thought that's who I should give the bottle of red wine vinegar to.

"Jerry Z.!" Luciano, the electric gaffer, shouted to me. The Italians were so wonderfully gracious and social off of the set. They all started to greet me and smiled their warm welcome.

"Where's Vittorio?" I asked as I held the bottle.

They pointed to the kitchen and I made my way over to it.

There was Vittorio, tasting the sauce for the pasta. He could have been Marcello Mastroianni, the most Roman of all Romans. Vittorio was dressed in an open shirt with a gold chain, tailored slacks, and loafers. It was like he had just paused in this kitchen long enough to taste the pasta sauce and then he would continue walking along Rome's Via Veneto.

"Jerry, good," Vittorio said. "Nice to see you." Italians are so gracious.

"Here," I said as I handed him the bottle of Italian red wine vinegar. You would have thought I had handed him the last bottle of vino in Italy.

"Alfredo! Mauro!" Vittorio called, as he held up the bottle. "Look, for the salad!" It seemed like the kitchen filled with half the Italian crew admiring my gift. The bottle found its way to Mario, Alfredo's other relative, who was in charge of the salad.

I saw someone who was obviously the chief cook. He was Italian, but I hadn't seen him during the filming. Vittorio saw me looking at him, and he introduced us.

"Jerry, I want you to meet Fabrizio, our extra electrician. Fabrizio, this is Jerry, our assistant director from Hollywood."

We shook hands and smiled, but why did Vittorio have to introduce me to an electrician when we've been filming all week? Why hadn't I met him on the set?

Vittorio saw my confusion, and he took me aside. "Jerry, Fabrizio is our 'extra' electrician, our cook! Do you understand?" Vittorio said and laughed.

"You have an extra electrician. You've brought him all the way from Italy, to be your cook," I said, just to get all straight in my head.

"Yes, Jerry, and wait until you taste the sauce!" Vittorio said, and moved around the kitchen sampling the salad.

The dinner was fantastic, with perfect pasta and sauces, freshly baked Italian bread, salad with Italian red wine vinegar. We all sat around the living room balancing our plates as they chatted, mainly in Italian, with frequent interruptions for laughter and smiles. I couldn't understand much, so I got up after a bit and wandered over to a corner of the room that was set up like a reading area, with a rough chair and large wooden coffee table.

The table had large books of artists' works on it. I glanced around at the happy group and, feeling I wouldn't be missed, I sat down and opened one of the books. Suddenly Vittorio was standing right next to me.

"Jerry, you like art?" he asked.

"Yeah." I felt like he had caught me doing something I shouldn't have. Maybe in Italy you don't look in other people's books in their homes.

"Each movie I do, I study one artist," Vittorio said.

"Really? Why?" I asked.

"After I have read the script, I search for an artist for that film," Vittorio continued. "I look through all the artists until I find the one who 'speaks' that film. Do you understand, Jerry?"

I looked at Vittorio. I felt it was like my moment to be talking with Renoir or maybe Rembrandt. I wasn't going to miss it.

"I don't understand," I said. "Explain it to me."

"Look, Jerry," Vittorio said, as he took out a large volume and put it on the table. "After I read *Apocalypse* I talked with Francis, then I began to think of artists. Who speaks *Apocalypse Now?*"

"I don't know," I admitted; I was way out of my league.

"Paul Gauguin. You know him? Look, Jerry," and Vittorio opened the huge art book and turned to a work by Gauguin. It was Gauguin's allegorical painting *Where Do We Come From? What Are We? Where Are We Going?*

"Jerry, look at the jungle leaves," Vittorio began; the tone of his soft voice seemed to stroke the painting. "See all the greens? Look at just the dark greens. Ah, Jerry, see?" That Gauguin painting shows lush jungle vegetation, animals, birds, and natives; it even shows a Buddha-like statue.

"Look, Jerry, here. See the bright yellow, the red . . . This is the color from Joe Lombardi's smoke grenades, you know?"

Vittorio was trying hard to make me understand. I wasn't sure why.

"See here, the dark greens. Brooding jungle, Jerry. Like in *Apocalypse Now*. See here, the darkness, the danger, the fear? Brooding, you understand?"

"And this speaks of *Apocalypse*?" I asked.

"Yes, the colors . . . Look, Jerry," he continued, as he had gotten some news magazine photos of the Vietnam War. He pointed at the bright-colored smoke grenades against the dark of the jungle vegetation. "Look at the photo, Jerry. Now look at Gauguin. You see? It's the same."

Vittorio smiled, the art master with a street urchin, but he never talked down to me. I always felt Vittorio was totally sincere in communicating his ideas and feelings to me.

"The light! Jerry, see the light?" Vittorio was pointing at the Gauguin work.

"Light?" I asked. I didn't really see any bright sunlight.

"Yes, the light! It's the energy, the life. Life itself. Light! Look, Jerry," my teacher continued, as he stroked the painting showing me the flow of light. "See?"

Suddenly I became aware of silence. I turned quickly, and everyone in the room was listening to Vittorio and me. They smiled as I stared at them, and then Vittorio smiled and patted my shoulder, then everyone laughed and the party continued. I don't know how long the party was suspended for my art lesson. Then I closed the book and sat back in the chair and watched the Italian crew as they enjoyed the night.

I woke up early on my own; our neighborhood slaughterhouse was closed on Sunday. Larry was still asleep. I went into the small living area and sat where I could look out the window at the street below. Across the road there was a small plaster house with jungle plants around it. It had a homemade stick fence, common in Baler, and mainly dirt and a couple of large rocks for a yard. Wasn't much. I watched the family, a mother and father and a little girl about two or three. The mother swept their dirt yard with a long broom she had made out of sticks and a pole. Any debris she swept into the drainage ditch. The father and little girl just seemed to walk around, and then he would sit on a rock for a while and watch her try out her walking skills. He would laugh, and the little girl would squeal with joy.

I had some film company stationary and began to write a letter to my two young sons. Chris had his sixth birthday on the day before I flew for Manila; Tim was two years and four months. I was their father, and I was sitting on a Sunday morning in a jungle village a third of the way around the world from them. My father had worked his whole adult life for the U.S. post office in Milwaukee; I always knew where he was. Chris and Tim had no idea where I was or why; all they knew was that their dad was not home with them that day. There'd be no roughhousing, no baseball catching, no special time in the backyard tree house, no father for them that Sunday morning. What could I say to them?

There was another squeal and laughter, so I put down my pen and looked out the window again. The little girl had peed in the front yard; Chris had done that once.

Larry finally got up, and we walked down to the school house for our breakfast. Very few people were there. I just had coffee and a roll, but Larry had it all, like every other morning. The catering people loved Larry.

The owner of the whole catering company was a Filipino lady in her fifties. She drove a dark Mercedes; the crew nicknamed her the Dragon Lady. Her Mercedes was a symbol to everyone of the huge profits she was making by serving the poor-quality food we ate.

"Larry, what do people do here on their day off?" I asked, as we put up our dishes and walked over the ditch and started along the main street.

"Well, there are really only two things to do," Larry began. "See that?" Larry said, and he pointed to an area off to the side of the street where some young people had set up what looked like one row of a bleacher. The deal was for the crew members to sit in the bleacher seats, and then the enterprising young people would cut their toenails. It was midmorning, but business was already good.

I looked at Larry, "You've got to be kidding. Getting your *toenails cut* is one of the two highlights of our day off?"

Larry stopped walking and turned toward a tiny shop. He motioned to me and we entered.

"Two mango ice creams, please," Larry said.

The owner of the shop scurried around and got two of the smallest ice-cream cones I have ever seen. He smiled and handed them to us. Larry paid and thanked him.

"Flavor of the month?" I asked, as we continued down the street.

"Only flavor," Larry answered.

"OK, so what's the second highlight of our day off?" I asked.

"You're eating it," Larry said.

The next day of shooting we split into two units. Larry and Enrico would get a couple of shots of a helicopter dropping a wooden replica of our patrol boat into the mouth of the river, just like Colonel Kilgore said he would, so Willard's journey up the river could begin. It was simple shooting with a few extras, the helicopter, and Enrico and his camera. Piece of cake.

While Larry and Enrico knocked off those shots, Francis, Vittorio, and I were on one of our real PBRs, river patrol boats, a smaller version of the World War II PT boat. We were filming Marty Sheen (Willard), Albert Hall (Chief), Fred Forrest (Chef), Sam Bottoms (Lance), and Larry Fishburne (Clean) actually beginning their journey to deliver Willard up the river to where Marlon Brando (Captain Kurtz) was living with his followers.

I got our cast and crew aboard and shouted for Francis. As he stepped onto the boat, he said privately to me, "I heard you had dinner Saturday night with the Italians."

"Right," I answered.

"They're courting your favor. Better watch yourself," Francis added, as he moved past me.

I had no idea what Francis meant.

We all were on a small twenty-five-foot boat running up the river; no one could wander off. I was in assistant director heaven. There was so much noise from the boat engine that I didn't have to keep anyone quiet while we filmed. There were no extras, and the crew was down to six people. I had it made in the shade. What a change from the sand, heat, dust, and sweat of all the days filming at Village II with hundreds of crew and extras.

I just laid back, and Francis and the actors rehearsed, while Vittorio set up a shot. Alfredo was the only grip, and Luciano was the only electrician. Nat Boxer was both the boom man and the sound mixer while we were on the boat. Mauro did the focus and reloaded the camera. I sat up above the pilot house on a soft canvas roof with a walkie-talkie in one hand and a bullhorn in the other, in case I had to be heard above the engine noise. My kind of filming.

Jungle trees and plants grew right down to the river's edge; it reminded me of the jungle ride at Disneyland. Occasionally there would be a small clearing with a hut or two and some kids playing or running with their dogs. Once in a while we'd pass a water buffalo at the river's edge with a whole family washing it off; water buffaloes were a valuable commodity to a family. They were like tractors in Wisconsin.

Francis was getting shots of Marty Sheen looking through the papers he had gotten when he accepted his mission to go up the river and kill Colonel Kurtz (Marlon Brando). Vittorio was both cameraman and the camera operator today. Vittorio liked doing both jobs. He loved lighting the scene, but he also liked doing Enrico's job of framing each moment in the scene.

Since Enrico was back with Larry, I thought this was a good time to get some questions answered. When we were turning the boat around to go back and make another run past the same background, Francis and Vittorio were standing right below me so I climbed down.

"Vittorio," I began, "if you like operating the camera so much, why is it you have Enrico as your operator? Why not do it yourself?"

"No, Jerry. Not so good," Vittorio answered.

Francis joined in, "You don't understand about Enrico, Jerry."

"Not so good," Vittorio repeated.

"That's exactly it!" Francis was going. "Enrico looks at the world just a bit different." Francis held his hands out in front of himself and then turned both hands and his head about twenty degrees. "Like this. His looks are unique, different!"

"Exactly, Francis," and Vittorio laughed. "Only Enrico!"

"Right. I want 'different.' Every camera operator is the same, like a machine, a factory. Enrico is unique," Francis said.

I tried to understand. "Is he the best?" I asked.

"Best?" Francis could get excited. "I don't want the best! Best has nothing to do with it!"

"Jerry," my art teacher spoke, "art is meant to be like lightening, never the same."

"Best!" Francis was running with this one. "Do you think any of us would be here if everyone wanted the best? Are you the best assistant director in the world? Am I the best director? Jerry, if I drop dead right now, you get Sydney Lumet to direct this film! Best!?"

I was sorry I opened this up.

"Look." Francis again. "Enrico is a total individual. I'm a total individual. You are. Vittorio is. If you want 'best' go to Sears! If you want individual . . . We're here."

All of us laughed, especially Francis; it was funny and true at the same time. I certainly wasn't the best, but here I was.

Marty Sheen was older and became the adult of this boat crew and of the actors. He was tanned and in good physical shape. His wife, Janet, was up in Baler with him. Their kids were in school back in Malibu and were to join up later. The filmmaker's life seemed to work for Marty's family, but it didn't for mine.   .

I couldn't quite understand why. Why weren't great film projects, exciting personalities, and interesting foreign countries appealing to everyone? I was learning that a lot of people preferred a home with a picket fence, and not in Baler, the Philippines, but in a safe neighborhood in West Los Angeles. I wasn't one of them, but my first wife was. It was a painful lesson for me to learn.

I liked Marty because he was never any problem for me and he kept everyone else in line just by setting an example. Fun was fun, but we had to shoot the movie, too. He worked for me, and I cultivated our relationship.

Albert Hall was the chief of the PBR. He was rock steady as a character in the movie and as a person. I respected Albert's acting talent as much as I did Marty's. Assistant directors love actors who get down to business and do their job; that was Albert. Great performances and great work habits. If I was back teaching I would give him **A** for achievement and **A** for effort.

Frederick Forrest played Chef, the saucier from New Orleans. Fred was well meaning and a fine actor, but not quite grounded. Larry and I had to watch him. He was perfect for Francis and the movie, but as a teacher I would have placed him in the last seat in the first row, away from the windows and any other distraction.

Sam Bottoms was Lance, the California surfer. Well, if Fred had to be watched, Sam had to be *watched!!!!!!!!* You had to have a special person to *watch* Fred and Sam, or you might never see either of them again.

Larry Fishburne played Mr. Clean, the youngest of the crew. Larry was fourteen when we filmed *Apocalypse*. He had his mother and aunt with him in the Philippines. Larry Fishburne was my favorite. Being only fourteen and playing an eighteen-year-old gave an unusual spin to his character. He was just so extra young to be in Vietnam. A lot of the mornings on *Apocalypse*, Larry, this tall, lanky fourteen-year-old, would come up behind me and give me a hug. Fifteen years later I was standing outside of the Los Angeles airport when someone came up behind me and gave me such a hug; I didn't have to turn around to know it was 1976's Larry Fishburne, now encased in the body of one of our most respected actors, Laurence Fishburne.

My walkie-talkie started to bark. It was Larry Franco with Enrico.

"Jer, Larry! Do you read me?"

"Yes, Larry. What is it?" I answered.

"Enrico needs the stop," Larry said. The *stop* means the setting for the lens, the f-stop, the amount of light that needs to come through the lens.

"The stop!" I exclaimed. "Doesn't he have a light meter? Have him take a reading!"

"Jer, Enrico won't shoot unless Vittorio gives him the stop," Larry said.

"We're miles from you; we've been going up river all morning! We can't come back to you and have Vittorio read his meter and give Enrico a stop!" I yelled.

I had attracted the attention of Francis and Vittorio.

"What's wrong?" Francis asked.

"Is it Enrico, Jerry?" Vittorio wondered.

"Look, Larry, just a minute." I put down my walkie-talkie. "Francis, Vittorio, look. . . . We are a long ways from the mouth of the river where Enrico's to film. OK? Now Enrico is saying he won't film unless Vittorio gives the stop. OK? We can't go back!"

"Jerry, please, this is no problem," Vittorio said, as he held out his hand for my walkie-talkie. "Enrico, can you hear me. This is Vittorio!"

In a second I heard, "Yes, Vittorio, this is Enrico. I need a stop, please."

Vittorio then took out his light meter on our PBR, which was at least twenty miles away from where Enrico was filming, and Vittorio read the light meter and gave him the stop. When he was through, Vittorio handed my walkie-talkie back to me.

"Vittorio, how can you possibly give him an f-stop for his shot when you're twenty miles away and don't know where his camera is and where the boat is and where the sun is and . . . ," I questioned.

"Jerry, sometimes f-stops are not so important," he answered, and went to set up our next shot.

Francis looked at me and laughed. I had to smile. Vittorio and Enrico were two unique individuals.

Gambi and the Tiger Scene

Gambi was the name of the tiger. He came from Hollywood with his two trainers. Gambi was a Hollywood tiger; he had done many movies where white hunters or natives jumped and ran screaming from him. He was a veteran.

After Gambi's trans-Pacific plane landed in Manila, he was transferred to a smaller cargo plane to make the flight to our jungle airstrip. He would then be carted by truck to Baler. Gambi's trainers saw no problem in releasing the tiger from his cage once they had him inside the smaller cargo plane. He had been cooped up on the long flight from Hollywood, and it was another hour before the small cargo plane would be taking off because of customs and immigration. They placed Gambi's cage at the rear of the plane, opened the door of the cage, checked his food and water supply like you would do for a traveling puppy, and then they exited the cargo plane, being careful to push down the long lever that secured the cargo door. The two trainers then went about their business, knowing that they had the better part of an hour before their flight.

At this same time, seven wives of the Italian crew recently arrived from Italy were looking for a way to join their husbands in Baler. At the Manila production office for *Apocalypse Now* they were told that there wasn't any vehicle driving north to Baler that day but that a cargo plane was set to fly there within an hour. Elated at their good timing, they took two taxis to the private airport section of Manila's international airport. The only plane in view was the small cargo plane. Not wanting to make a mistake, they asked an airport attendant if the small cargo plane belonged to *Apocalypse Now* and was flying north that morning. The attendant answered that yes the plane did belong to the movie company and yes it was scheduled to fly north within the next half hour.

That's all the Italian wives needed to hear. As soon as the attendant and the airport guards were out of sight, they hurried to the small cargo plane, pushed the lever that secured the cargo door, swung the door open, and began to scurry onto the plane with all of their luggage. Once inside, they discovered it was a cargo plane without seats, but they made themselves as comfortable as possible by moving small crates and boxes to form makeshift airline seats.

Meanwhile, Gambi, who had fallen asleep and was snoozing comfortably, was awakened by all the activity going on inside the plane. Being a curious animal, Gambi left his cage at the rear of the plane, walked quietly between the large crates, and peered at the seven Italian wives arranging the smaller crates to use as airline seats for their flight to be with their husbands.

The wives were very happy and chatted with each other as they moved boxes to the windows and arranged their luggage. They had brought pasta, sausages, wine, and olive oil directly from Italy, and they took care packing their precious imported foodstuffs all around them.

Gambi, interested in the movement of the wives and the noise of their excited talking, walked slowly and silently forward. He was not on a hunt, for he had been fed by his trainers; he was simply curious. Gambi was a veteran of many Hollywood films; he was used to being around humans. As he moved closer to the seven Italian wives, his movement attracted the attention of one of the women.

There was a moment between woman and beast, a split second of "Oh, no! It can't be!" and then the realization—"Oh, yes it is! A TIGER!!!!!"

The seven Italian wives jumped and ran screaming through the plane, trying desperately to get to the cargo door without getting near Gambi. Finally, when Gambi was distracted by the aroma of the Italian sausage the wives had packed, they ran to the cargo door, opened it, and leaped to the runway.

Gambi moved to the open cargo door and watched the Italian wives as they screamed and ran away from the plane. It was nothing Gambi wasn't used to seeing; white hunters, natives, Italian wives, what did it matter? Just another day in the life of Gambi, a Hollywood tiger.

Gambi came to us in Baler to work in a scene with Fred Forrest and Marty Sheen. In the script the PBR was docked on the side of the river for routine maintenance. Chef wanted to go into the jungle and get some mangoes. Willard said he'd go with him for protection, while Lance, Clean, and the Chief would complete the maintenance on the riverboat's engine. Chef and Willard then searched through the jungle, but instead of finding mangoes they found a tiger. The scene ends with Willard and Chef running back to the boat.

Vittorio had broken up the scene into three portions. First he wanted to film all the shots on the boat, leaving the boat, and returning to the boat. All of these shots were to be done on the first day. Then Vittorio wanted to do all of the shots of Chef and Willard moving through the jungle looking for mangoes on the second day. These shots were vitally important to Vittorio; he wanted to work his cinematic artistry to create the jungle of Gauguin. The final section Vittorio wanted to film was the confrontation with the tiger, our Gambi, which would be done on the third day.

Both Francis and I thought Vittorio's plan to film this sequence was fine. We all agreed, and the first day we filmed everything to do with the boat. Vittorio sent his electrical crew and most of his grips out into the jungle to prelight the next day's work: Willard and Chef walking through the jungle.

All during that first day different Italian crew members would come back to Vittorio from having been in the jungle, and they would whisper to Vittorio, receive instructions from him, and then scurry back into the jungle. I was curious as to what was going on, but I had my hands full with the PBR cast and getting the day's work.

After about the sixth messenger ran to Vittorio, spoke to him, received Vittorio's reply, and ran back into the jungle, Francis took me aside.

"Jer, what's going on?" he asked, looking at the departing Italian crew member.

"Just working on prelighting tomorrow's work, I guess," I answered. Francis stared at me. "Then why are they whispering?"

I stared back at him.

Francis laughed, "Why aren't they using their walkie-talkies? Answer me that!"

I looked at Vittorio, then at Francis. "What's he up to?" I asked. Francis had gotten me terrified because I remembered my experience with Vittorio's dolly track in the ocean.

"I don't know, and I'm Italian," Francis said, and moved away.

The shooting on the boat went great. We finished the day's work on time, which is the primary responsibility of the assistant director. I was happy as I called a wrap and the company prepared to go back to Baler.

The next day we arrived out at location, and I had Larry get Marty and Fred Forrest ready to film. I saw Vittorio talking to his crew, so I joined them. Vittorio was speaking in Italian to his whole crew. Everyone was there—even Fabrizio, the cook. The mood of Vittorio's speech to his crew was both like a tense NASA countdown to launch and like a brain surgeon going carefully over every detail just before a very critical operation. Vittorio spoke in Italian, so I couldn't understand a word, but I was impressed anyway. Alfredo, Luciano, Mauro, and everyone were listening with bowed heads, nodding gravely, and glancing back to Vittorio. I wished I understood Italian; it was obviously a moving speech by Vittorio.

Then the fear hit me; I pulled Enrico to one side and whispered to him, "Enrico, did someone die? Someone's wife or family?"

"No, Jerry," Enrico whispered. "Vittorio is just explaining today's work."

Now I was scared. Vittorio never explained the day's work. For the most part Vittorio preferred to wing it, he came out in the morning and lit the scene as he was inspired. He was an improvisational artist, not a calculating brain surgeon. I looked at Enrico, but he had rejoined the circle around Vittorio and had bowed his head.

Soon Vittorio finished, smiled at his crew, and walked casually away. The crew loitered around, not doing much of anything. They certainly were not working feverishly to prepare a shot for Vittorio.

As soon as I saw Francis I got him with Marty and Fred to rehearse. Vittorio joined us, and some of the Italians wandered over to watch. The first little sequence was Willard and Chef looking through the jungle. Francis showed us the first shot, and the actors did their action. Vittorio saw, nodded, and no one moved, not Vittorio or his crew.

"Francis, can we see what happens next, please?" Vittorio asked.

Francis glanced at me, but there wasn't really anything unusual for a cameraman to see what shots were coming next, so Francis moved deeper into the jungle, and he showed the next little sequence of the actors moving farther into the jungle. The actors did the action.

Francis nodded at Vittorio, "That's it, Vittorio."

"Francis, can we see what happens next, please?" Vittorio asked.

Again Francis and I exchanged a glance, but I had worked with cameramen who just liked to know what was coming up.

Francis marched us further into the jungle and showed the next little scene of walking through the jungle. The actors did their thing, and Vittorio again wanted to see more.

This continued until we had marched all through the jungle and had shown Vittorio every shot we had to do that day, twelve shots. I urged Francis, the actors, and especially Vittorio that we did have a lot of work to do, but if we got a running start, an early start, I felt we could get it done. Francis and the actors nodded and went back to get ready;

Vittorio silently walked into a tiny jungle clearing and his entire crew surrounded him.

I looked for Francis; he understood Italian, and I needed to know what Vittorio was talking about. Francis was gone, so I walked over to Vittorio and his crew. As I got close, Vittorio looked at me and stopped speaking Italian.

"Hello, Jerry, how are you today?" he asked.

I want to tell you what I experienced behind my eyes. I saw red warning lights, I heard European-style sirens, I saw red-blue-gold spinning lights. Vittorio had me panicked; what were they up to?

I smiled, nodded, and said I was fine. No one moved; they all just stared at me. I felt embarrassed or out of place, so I turned and walked back toward the jungle area of our first shot.

"We'll begin back down here, right, Vittorio?" I called back.

"Yes, Jerry, of course," Vittorio answered. The whole Italian crew had turned to look at me again. It was about 8:30 A.M.

I stood at the jungle site for our first shot, and I was alone. No one was there. No, Vittorio, no crew, nobody was there.

"Larry!" I called on my walkie-talkie, "Larry, come in."

"Yeah, Jer," Larry answered. He was back near the boat, the actors, and Francis.

I had to be careful, because I never knew who was listening to our walkie-talkie.

"Larry, I'm lonely here."

"Where are you?" he asked.

"I'm at the first location, and there's no one here." I was careful.

"Oh, yeah. Well, I don't see anyone here either," Larry answered.

"What! Where is everyone?" I said.

"Jer, there's no one here. I thought the crew was with you!" Larry answered.

At 10:30 I was still standing at the mark for our first shot. Still no one was here. I had seen some of the Italians moving through the jungle, but no one seemed to be doing anything to get the first shot ready.

"Larry!" I called him again on the walkie-talkie.

"Yeah, Jer."

"Larry, I'm coming down to talk with Francis," I said, and started through the jungle toward the boat.

I found Francis sitting on a fallen log throwing bits of bark into the river. I walked over to him.

"Francis?" I said.

"How are we doing? We ready yet?" he asked. He kept breaking off tiny pieces of bark and throwing them sidearm into the river.

"No, we're not," I said.

"How long you figure?" Francis asked.

"I don't know; I can't find Vittorio or the crew," and I expected Francis to react, but he just sat there and threw bits of bark into the river.

"They're up to something, Jerry. We'll know soon enough. When's lunch?" he asked, as he looked at me for the first time.

"We have to eat at one," I answered, even though I was getting numb and tones were vibrating around my head.

"Good. Call me when it's lunch, OK?" he asked, and he returned to throwing pieces of bark into the river.

I walked slowly away, stunned that I couldn't find the cameraman or the crew and that the director didn't seem concerned.

I walked back up to the location of the first shot, but the only people there were Marty and Fred.

"Still working?" Marty asked, as he looked at the empty jungle.

"Be a bit," I answered.

Fred Forrest was not so kind. "Where the hell is everyone! It's almost lunch!"

"Come on, Fred," Marty said, and led him back down toward the river.

Just before 1:00 P.M. I called lunch over the walkie-talkie, walked down to tell Francis, and had Larry shout that it was lunch all through the jungle.

Amazingly everyone came to the lunch line to get a boxed lunch. All of the Italians were there. Vittorio was there. They were chatting and happy, as though it was just any ordinary day. The boxed lunches were worse than the normal lunches, but the Italians were happy all during the lunch break.

When Larry and I felt that everyone had an ample time for lunch, we called the crew back to work. Everyone stayed seated. Then they got up slowly. Then they walked slowly toward the jungle. I looked toward Francis. He had been an assistant director; maybe he could help me.

Francis always appreciated that I told him exactly why we had a delay. I always did that. I walked toward him, but before I could speak he said, "Jer, I don't know what's going on, and I don't want to know. Let's just go with it."

What the hell did that mean? I started to say something, but Francis held up his hand for me to stop, and he walked back toward his fallen log by the river. It was just after 2:00, and we hadn't gotten a shot, hadn't gotten the camera to the set, hadn't gotten anything, but a box lunch! Tension tears me up inside sometimes.

I walked back up into the jungle and sat down at the exact location for the first shot; no one and nothing was there. I was totally alone. "Let's just go with it" Francis had said, and that was exactly what I was going to do.

At 3:00 I took out my walkie-talkie and called Larry. "What's happening?"

"Nothing," he answered. "You see the crew?"

"No."

"You see Vittorio?" he asked.

"No."

"I'm glad you're here, Jer," he said.

I waited. At 4:00 I called Larry again. He saw no one; I saw no one.

At 4:30 Marty and Fred visited me and then went back down to the river.

At 4:50 a single figure moved through the jungle about one hundred yards from me. I tensed and watched it. The figure would move, stop, raise its arm; move, stop, raise its arm. The figure walked across my view from right to left, then he came slowly toward me. It was Vittorio. He had his light meter in his hand.

I stood up when he was about thirty yards from me and walking slowly toward me, step by step. There wasn't a sound in the jungle. Only me standing and Vittorio walking step by step toward me as he stared at his light meter.

Vittorio came closer. Finally he stood where the camera was to be for the first shot. He stared at his light meter.

"Hello, Jerry, how are you?" he asked, as though we were seated at a Roman cafe having a cup of cappuccino.

I didn't move, breath, or speak. I just stared at him.

Suddenly, as if lightning had hit him, Vittorio began to shout, "Alfredo! Luciano! Mauro! Enrico!"

I looked around me, and the Italian crew came running through the jungle toward us as they shouted, "Here, Vittorio! Here!"

Vittorio turned to me with utter urgency in his eyes, "Jerry, we must film now! Right now! Have Francis and the actors run up here now!" he was shouting at me and at his crew that was running madly around setting cameras, lights, dolly track all at once.

"Larry!" I shouted into the walkie-talkie, "Have Marty and Fred and Francis get up here right away!"

Vittorio grabbed my walkie-talkie from me, "Excuse me, Jerry," Vittorio said graciously to me, but then screamed into my walkie-talkie, "Larry! They must run now! They must run! I only have thirty minutes of light and we must do twelve shots!!!!!"

Thirty minutes of light for twelve shots, I had heard Vittorio say. We had sat doing nothing all day, from seven in the morning until five at night, and he had only thirty minutes of light for all twelve shots?

"Vittorio? What are you doing?" I begged.

Vittorio was like a madman shouting orders to his crew, looking through the camera, checking his light meter.

I looked and saw Francis, Marty, and Fred running through the jungle being chased by Larry Franco.

"Francis! We must go!" Vittorio shouted.

"OK," Francis said, and nodded at me as if to say "Didn't I tell you?"

Vittorio shouted to his crew, moved Marty and Fred into place, put Enrico behind the camera, called to roll the film, shouted "Action!" for the actors, and helped Alfredo move the dolly along its track.

As soon as the shot was over, Vittorio looked at Francis for a split second. Since Francis seemed to like the shot, Vittorio stormed ahead through the jungle toward our second location. The Italian crew ran ahead, not bothering to take the camera off of the dolly, but carrying the whole thing, dolly and camera with lens, through the jungle. Everyone was running and shouting and scurrying. Marty and Fred were in shock, which I thought might work for the scene.

Francis just came plodding along through the jungle, and just as he got to the camera, Vittorio was shouting, "Roll film," then "Action!" and as soon as that shot was completed, he ran wildly ahead to the next shot, with the Italian crew madly in pursuit. Everyone was shouting and running through the jungle. And so was I.

I have never experienced anything like it. We continued to run, then shoot, then run again, then shoot again, until at 5:30 we got our twelfth and final shot of the day.

The crew was lying all over the ground; they were totally exhausted. It had been like a one-mile sprint for them while they carried all of our equipment on their backs.

Marty and Fred were staring at all of us; they could not believe what they had just experienced. Francis was calm. I don't know how he did it. I was exhausted, frightened, and adrenalized all at once.

Vittorio took a deep breath, then walked up to Larry and me. He put his hands on our shoulders and said, "Thank you. The lighting was magnificent!"

I stared at the crew and equipment strewn around us as I watched Vittorio grandly stride through the jungle, once again the cultured Roman artist sauntering along the Via Veneto.

The next morning we all met in a small jungle clearing. This was Gambi's big day. Francis explained the action to Marty Sheen and Fred Forrest while all of us listened.

"Marty? You and Fred are over here," Francis said, pointing to a tiny jungle path leading into the underbrush.

"Here?" Marty said. He pointed at the path, but he looked at the jungle underbrush about fifteen feet from him where Gambi's trainers stood.

"Right," Francis answered. "Now, Fred, you're in front of Marty."

"Where's the tiger, Francis?" Fred asked right up front.

"You don't know where the tiger is," Francis explained; he meant that Chef, Fred's character, didn't know where the tiger was at that moment in the scene.

"Francis, I want to know where the tiger is," Fred Forrest was a wonderful actor, but he wasn't Rambo. He was scared of the tiger, and I didn't blame him.

"The tiger is in the underbrush! You can't see him, OK?" Francis answered. "Now you and Marty hear something and carefully walk toward the underbrush. You don't see anything!"

The trainers were nodding.

Francis continued, "You two inch forward. Slowly. Toward the tiger."

Terry Leonard, our stunt coordinator, who was there to help with Gambi, shouted a cowboy's, "All right!"

"Where's the tiger, Francis? I'm not acting with any damn tiger!" Fred said, and he meant it.

"Did you read the script?" Francis began at him, but Marty jumped in.

"Freddie, come on. Francis. It's OK, Fred," Marty said. He often helped us get Fred Forrest or Sam Bottoms grounded so we could film with them.

"It is?" Fred asked Marty.

"Look, Freddie," Francis began, "Gambi isn't in the shot!"

"He's not?" Fred asked, "Where is he?"

"He's not in this shot!" Francis exclaimed. Marty smiled and moved away. Fred looked at Marty and Francis, then at the trainers.

"OK, Francis, what do I do?" Fred asked.

"You two just walk up to the underbrush! I told you!" Francis was getting a bit frustrated.

"Where's the tiger?" Fred asked.

"He's later!" Francis said, as he walked away.

We all began to get the first shot ready. Vittorio placed the camera where Gambi eventually would be, and we filmed Marty and Freddie sneaking up toward us. Francis called "Cut," and we were discussing the next shot, when suddenly behind the camera there was a snarling sound in the underbrush with dry grass flying through the air, then a tremendous growl, followed by Terry Leonard leaping out of the jungle undergrowth and rushing toward Fred Forrest!

"You asshole! You asshole!" Freddie was shouting and running around the clearing.

A few of the Italians didn't think it was too funny, either. Marty just shook his head slowly from side to side as he prayed for this scene with Freddie and the tiger to be over. Francis laughed a little, and Vittorio, once he understood what had happened, thought it was very funny. I was thinking more along the same lines as Marty.

Freddie was still pacing around the clearing repeating "You asshole! You asshole!" over and over again. Terry was trying to corral him, but he kept erupting into his honking cowboy laughter. I realized that there was no way we were going to get another shot with Freddie for quite some time, so I called lunch.

After lunch Freddie was the calmest actor I have ever seen; you could have lit his toes on fire and he wouldn't have said "Ouch." I don't know why, and I don't want to know why, but we could have shot Freddie putting his head in the tiger's mouth and yelling "Eat me!" if we had wanted to. Some method actors are like that.

Francis and Vittorio covered the scene from every angle. We saw Marty and Freddie walk up in a wide shot, in a medium shot, in close-ups. We saw them from straight on, from the right side, and from the left side. We saw them from a very high angled camera and from a very low angled camera. There was only one thing left to be filmed—Gambi. Gambi had two trainers. The first was a man in his mid-thirties; he was covered with scar tissue on his knees, elbows, and lower arms from various tigers, but he assured us none from Gambi. The second trainer looked like Sheena, Queen of the Jungle; she was in her late twenties and was definitely a match for man or beast.

Francis laid out the shot. "OK, could Gambi be back there in the underbrush?" Francis pointed, and then looked at the male trainer. "And then when you cue him, he leaps out!"

The trainer moved closer to the underbrush. "Can we put a small ramp of plywood in there for Gambi to stand on?" he asked.

"Sure, Francis. We won't see the wood," Vittorio said.

"OK, if we don't see the wood," Francis said. "Gambi just leaps out and runs past the cameras. That's all he has to do." Francis looked at the trainer, who was nodding.

The grips and the trainers went to work and built the plywood ramp for Gambi. It was covered with dirt and leaves to hide the wood from the cameras. The ramp was ready and the cameras were ready. Time to explain the Gambi shot to Fred and Marty.

"Larry," I called into my walkie-talkie, "bring the first team."

Soon Fred and Marty arrived, and Francis carefully explained his shot.

"Now guys, what this is . . . we have two cameras. One is just on the underbrush and Gambi leaping out. The second is over the two of you and seeing Gambi."

"As Gambi leaps out?" Marty asked, staring at Francis and then at me.

"Where am I, Francis?" asked Freddie.

"Well, right here in front of the second camera," answered Francis. "Next to Marty."

"Francis, have you seen Gambi? He's huge!" Marty said softly.

"He won't go anywhere near you. He'll leap off that platform and right past the camera," the male trainer volunteered. Sheena just smiled and nodded in agreement.

"See?" Francis said. "He's trained; he's a trained tiger from Hollywood. He's done more movies than both of us," continued Francis.

"Where are you going to be, Francis?" asked Marty.

The trainer jumped right in. "Everyone should be back at least ten yards!"

"Whoa, wait a minute!" Marty needed to breathe.

"Who's back ten yards, Francis?" Freddie asked; he was coming around.

"Do you want me to put on your clothes and do the shot?" Francis said.

Oh, boy, here we go. I could feel myself sliding into big trouble. Francis as a photo double for Marty Sheen? Francis is twice Marty's size, plus Francis has a full beard and Marty is clean shaven!

"I just want to know what's going on, that's all," Marty said.

"Look, Marty, Freddie, do you want to do the shot or not? Yes or no?"

"Nothing is going to happen," the trainer repeated. "Gambi's like a house cat."

"Then why the hell does everyone have to stand back ten yards?" Marty said.

"Marty, look. I have two shots of Gambi leaping out," Francis said. "One camera, just him. One camera, over you and Freddie. I'd like to have that shot over you and Freddie. I'd like to see the tiger and the two of you in one shot, just one!"

For me as the assistant director, this was one difficult situation. I took the trainers aside. "Is this thing safe with the actors and Gambi?" I asked them.

"Absolutely. No one moves. One of us will be with him; one will be behind the camera with something he wants," the trainer continued.

"Man, look, if there's anything I can do, I mean . . . ," Terry Leonard said.

"Jerry," Vittorio joined our discussion, "I think it's perfectly OK, but I would like to turn on the cameras and everyone go away before the tiger comes."

Everyone nodded that they felt that was OK.

"The fewer distractions the better," the trainer added.

I felt a bit more assured. I moved back to Francis with Marty and Fred.

"OK, so, Marty, you're here," Francis said, as he placed Marty to the camera.

I guessed everyone was fine to do this, but I would check.

"Freddie, a bit closer to Marty. Good," Francis continued.

When Francis moved away to talk with Vittorio, I whispered to Marty and Fred, "You feel good about this?"

"Yeah, I'm all right, Jer. Let's do it," Marty said.

I looked at Freddie. He was just staring at the underbrush where Gambi was to come from.

"I'm here. I'm going to do it!" Fred declared.

I nodded to the camera crew, and Enrico and the camera guys got ready.

I addressed the whole cast and crew, "Look, we're going to bring out the tiger. Now it's very important that you all stay back and stand still. Don't have any food or drink. Don't make any sudden movements. Stay calm!" I said, as my stomach and heart kept changing places inside of me.

I looked, and here came Gambi being led by Sheena with the male trainer behind. They led Gambi around the edge of the crew and brought him to his platform behind the jungle underbrush. Sheena came back to us behind the camera and got two chickens out of their cage. She handed one to Terry Leonard and held one herself.

"Everyone be quiet," I said as softly as I could. "Let me know when I can roll the cameras?" I asked of the male trainer.

A loud growl came from the underbrush, and six of the crew raced back six yards. That's respect.

"You ready?" the trainer asked. "OK, let's try it."

"Roll both cameras," I said, and then stepped back.

As soon as both cameras were running, the camera crews scurried back twenty feet. I looked around at the actors in place, at the crew standing silently, and I nodded to Francis.

"Go ahead. Action," he said.

Terry and Sheena shook the chickens and made little yelps and bird-calls, moos and oinks, but no Gambi. The male trainer was shouting behind the underbrush and making weird animal attack type noises. Nothing, Gambi didn't come out.

"Hold it, " Francis said.

The camera crews ran in to turn off the cameras. Terry and Sheena put down the chickens, and the crew relaxed.

"Do you have Gambi?" I asked.

"Yeah, he's fine," the male trainer shouted. "He just didn't charge out!"

"Right," I said, "so what can we do?"

Sheena and Terry came and joined me. "You wouldn't have a pig would you? Gambi'll leap out if he hears a pig," the trainer said, still with Gambi behind the underbrush.

"Well," and I looked for Allan Levine, the propman. Who gets pigs in the middle of the jungle? "Allan! We need a pig to squeal for Gambi!" I shouted. Allan heard, and he and his men scattered to find a pig.

"What do you want us to do, Francis?" Marty asked.

"They'll get a pig, and we'll do the shot," Francis answered. "He'll hear the pig, leap out past the camera, and we're outta here."

The male trainer brought Gambi back around through the edge of the crew while we waited for Allan and the prop guys to find a pig. He was right; Gambi was like a house cat. The delay was good because everyone settled down, including me.

About twenty minutes later one of Allan's guys came running with a pig; he had bought it from a family a hundred yards down the river.

We seemed to be set. The actors were back in front of the camera. The camera crews were ready. Sheena and Terry were ten yards in back of the cameras with the pig.

"Guys, be careful," I started. I checked the actors and the pig. "Gambi ready?" I asked the trainer.

"Let him hear the pig!" the trainer shouted.

Sheena and Terry pinched and pulled the pig, but the squeals were not very loud.

"He can't hear the pig! You've got to get it closer!" The trainer yelled.

"Give me that pig!" Terry said, and he pulled the pig from Sheena. He took the pig and walked down next to the cameras and sat on the ground, with his legs extended toward the jungle underbrush as he held the pig between them.

I couldn't believe it! "Terry!" I knelt next to him. "What are you doing?"

"Just roll the cameras! That son-of-a-bitch is going to hear this pig!"

"Wait, Terry," I said. "How's this going to work?"

"You roll those cameras, and when I hear 'action' I'll squeeze this little mother and it'll squeal!" Terry was intense, but clearly he was having one great time.

"Yeah, but . . . ," I began.

"When Gambi leaps out, I'll turn and cover the pig. Gambi'll see Sheena and the chickens, and we'll get the shot!" Terry was ready.

"I think it'll work," Sheena volunteered.

"You ready with the pig, yet?" the male trainer with Gambi asked.

"Hell, yes!" Terry shouted.

I wished there was a chapel near by. I looked at Marty and Fred; they seemed perfectly all right. I looked to Francis, who was back a bit farther but ready. The camera crew was set; Sheena held a chicken in each hand.

"OK," I said. "Everyone stand real still! Cameras ready! Gambi ready?"

"Just make that pig squeal!" the trainer shouted.

I looked to Terry, who had that pig held between his legs and was ready to squeeze. "You OK, Terry?" I thought I'd better ask.

"Yes, dammit! Roll the cameras!" he answered. "This pig'll squeal!"

I rolled the cameras, and the camera crew ran back to their safe positions. I glanced around at Terry, the pig, the actors, Sheena, then I nodded to Francis.

"Action," Francis said, and Terry grabbed hold of that pig between his legs and squeezed!

Squeal! You've never heard such squealing!

The underbrush only began to move, and in a tenth of a second before any of us could move, even Terry Leonard, Gambi leaped out, took the squealing pig from between Terry's legs, and bounded back into the jungle!

We were all in total shock. Nothing moved that fast. Terry just stared at his empty hands that a split second ago had held a pig.

"Oh, shit!" the male trainer yelled, as he ran through the jungle after Gambi. Sheena got a large 4 × 8 sheet of grip plywood, hoisted it over her head, and ran into the jungle.

Terry was still sitting with his legs outstretched, staring at his empty hands. "I didn't have time to move! So fast!" Terry kept saying. "You should have seen his eyes!"

Marty and Freddie were through; they had had it. There was no way they were doing anything else that day.

Francis and Vittorio were talking with the camera guys. I walked over to Francis. "Jer, I think we got it. I mean, who knows, but it happened right in front of the lens. I think we got it," Francis said.

I turned to my left because I thought I saw some movement in the jungle. Suddenly I heard Sheena and the male trainer shouting and running toward us! Then I caught a blur of Gambi about twenty feet behind them and coming on fast!

I yelled and ran directly away from the charging tiger. Francis and Vittorio were behind the two cameras with the Italian camera crew. Those crew members farther back just ran toward the river. One of the grips climbed up on a steal grip stand. All the others just scattered; this was an out-and-out panic!

"Did you get the shot?" the male trainer shouted, as he ran near the cameras, grabbed a 4 × 8 sheet of plywood, held it directly in front of him, and charged screaming and yelling directly at the equally charging Gambi.

Sheena had run and grabbed a chicken and was shaking it as she ran behind the charging male trainer.

Gambi, seeing this 4 × 8 sheet of plywood charging him and hearing the god-awful screams and yells, stopped his charge.

The male trainer was holding the sheet of plywood in front of himself and couldn't see where he was going. He ran past Gambi on his left, which left Sheena running directly at Gambi, screaming and holding up a chicken.

Gambi had just had enough of all this and stopped still. So did Sheena, still holding up her chicken.

When the male trainer realized he had run past Gambi, he looked back and saw what was happening between Sheena and Gambi. He then threw down his plywood and moved quickly to Gambi's side.

It was over. Gambi was just Hollywood Gambi again.

I looked around the crew. Francis and Vittorio were looking out from behind the cameras, the Italian grip was still up on the grip stand, Larry Franco was standing fifteen yards away with a big grin on his face, and Terry Leonard was still counting and recounting his ten fingers and his three legs.

Unlikely Miracle Maker

The final location we had to film in Baler was near the mouth of our river. We needed to get shots of our PBR, the river patrol boat, moving up a wide river and first entering jungle vegetation. These shots would be a bridge between our PBR and crew after they left Village II on the Pacific Ocean and prior to their being on the smaller river in the deep jungle. The cameras would be on the shore, and we would film our PBR and actors as they motored past us going upriver.

The cast and crew were very anxious to move out of Baler and into Olongapo, next to the U.S. naval base at Subic Bay on the picturesque South China Sea. Real hotels, restaurants, pizza, Laundromats, clothing stores, hot dogs, hamburgers, French fries, real ice cream with a choice of flavors—all of this awaited them.

We were one day away from making the move. It was a Friday, which seemed perfect. We'd finish shooting today, pack and travel tomorrow, and have Sunday to party in Olongapo! Everyone in the cast and crew was talking about what they were going to do on Sunday in Olongapo.

"Jer, guess what I'm going to do Sunday?" It was Larry Franco, and I already knew. "I'm going to find a McDonald's and order a Big Mac, a Quarter Pounder with cheese, Filet-O-Fish, large fries, and a chocolate shake!"

"Pizza, Baby! They have a Shakey's, and I'm there Sunday!" Terry Leonard was excited.

The Italians were anxious to leave the jungle because more of their wives would be arriving in Olongapo from Rome and bringing more Italian food for them.

Both Francis and Vittorio were looking forward to leaving Baler, Francis because he was finally through with the Hueys and their unpredictable availability from the Philippine air force, and Vittorio because he would be together with his wife Antonia and their three children.

I was tired of sleeping over the town's slaughterhouse, and living on San Miguel beer and bags of garlic peanuts. I wanted a private hotel room with a real shower where the water came out of a pipe and not a bucket. I'd share a large cheese-and-sausage pizza with Terry and maybe a Big Mac with Larry.

Everyone was sky-high. They had made their plans. They had packed. They were all ready to make the move on Saturday. Let the party begin!

Our *Apocalypse Now* air force was transporting 350 people to Olongapo on the day before the company move: wives, children, and girlfriends. No movie production had ever come close to the size of *Apocalypse Now* in terms of personnel.

Part of the reason was economics—not the company's, the crew's. For example: Each member was given $350 a week in living allowance, and they had nowhere to spend the money except to get their toenails clipped every Sunday and have a mango ice-cream cone. Each crew member had amassed a lot of cash. Different crew members adjusted to their affluent financial position in different ways. The Italian grips and electricians hired local Baler natives to carry and lift the heavy equipment. When a dolly track had to be laid, Alfredo would call to his local helpers, and they would come running with the wood, metal track, cribbing, etc. The Italian grip crew would then walk empty-handed to the dolly's location and supervise the laying of the dolly track. No one seemed to find this practice disturbing. If the Italians wanted to hire on their own ten or fifteen locals, who cared? However, the painter from Hollywood took the hiring of locals to the extreme.

In the morning our Hollywood painter would line up his twelve local hires. He had taught each of them one word of English, the color of paint in their bucket. When our painter was called upon to touch up some paint on the set, he would decide what colors he needed to mix, and then he'd shout, "Red! Yellow! Green!" and they'd come running.

But the filming wasn't going smoothly on that Friday. First of all, the crew wasn't focused, but most important, the PBR we were to use was having mechanical problems. We had two identical PBRs, but neither engine was reliable. We had only used the PBRs for a few shots up to this point, but after Baler nearly all of the shooting, until we got to Kurtz's compound, involved the PBRs moving upriver. The boat mechanics were working hard, but the engines were worn out, used, and misused junk from years on the rivers of Vietnam.

I walked over to the boat mechanics. They were checking the engine and talking theories. Finally a PBR Vietnam War relic, Pete Cooper, turned to me. Pete was huge, ugly, and scarred by every weapon used in Vietnam, both in the war and in the alleys. "Jerry, we've got about two to three hours of work here before she'll get up that river. If she ever will. That's the way it is, Jer."

I liked Pete because he was a no-bullshit type of guy. I felt if there was a way to get these PBRs working, pretty or not, Pete was my man.

"What about the second boat?" I asked. We had two in case of trouble.

"We're using parts from her to fix this one," Pete answered.

"Look, will the PBR be able to get upriver in three hours?" I asked.

"I'm not sure. They're both pieces of crap!" he said.

"Do everything you can, Pete. I've got to get these shots today," I said.

Pete went back to work on the PBR's engine, and I walked toward Francis and Vittorio.

"Ziesmer!" Francis called to me. His using *Ziesmer* meant he wasn't happy or thought he wasn't going to be happy soon. "What's happening?" Francis continued. "How long?" I could tell he was sensing problems.

"Probably three hours," I answered. "Pete Cooper's doing everything he can." I had been taught to protect crew members first and foremost.

"Three hours!" Francis exclaimed, "It's noon! Three hours! That's 3:00, and we lose the light at 5:00!"

"Francis, it's possible in two hours to finish," Vittorio said.

"I have to have at least four, maybe five, shots, Vittorio!" Francis added.

"We can do it sure, Francis," Vittorio said.

Francis didn't buy a thing, and he walked slowly into the jungle.

I called lunch and sat near Pete Cooper and the PBR mechanics in case there was anything I could do. I wasn't right on top of them; I sat down about forty feet away, but Pete knew I was there.

When lunch was over, Larry started the cast back through makeup and sent the crew down to me at the river. As soon as I saw that the crew was on its way, I went back to Pete.

"How's it looking?" I asked.

"We'll know more soon; another hour or so," Pete said. No one was smiling.

The crew stood in the jungle clearing looking at the PBR and the mechanics. I walked back to them.

"Jerry, what you think?" asked Alfredo.

Everyone gathered around. "We'll know more in about an hour," I said.

Luciano said, "Jerry, you think the boat she'll be all right?"

Josh Weiner, our still photographer from New York, said, "What happens if we can't film with the PBR today? What then?"

I felt the whole crew lean in to hear my words. "Well, look . . . we have to get these shots."

Our wardrobe man, Leonard, asked, "But here, Jer? Why can't we take these shots to Olongapo?"

"We could do that, Jerry, sure," added Alfredo.

The crew agreed, but only with their hearts.

"I want to get to Olongapo as much as anyone," I said, "but we need a wide river and jungle. It's only here, not Olongapo."

Luciano added quickly, "Our wives left today from Roma, Jerry!"

Mauro agreed. "What are they going to do? We have to go tomorrow!"

"Listen," I said, "the sun sets after five. A lot can happen."

"When are we going to travel if we don't film today? If we film here tomorrow?" asked Josh.

"Come on, guys," I said, "we'll have to stay over and leave Monday, you know that."

Alfredo, Luciano, and the rest of the Italians were visibly upset. Josh and Leonard just bowed their heads.

"Please, Jer," Alfredo said.

"Please," added Luciano.

"Our wives coming to Olongapo. They don't speak English, only Italian!" Mauro said.

"Jerry," Josh began, "you have got to get us out of here tomorrow! You have to!"

"He'll do everything he can," Nat Boxer, the sound man, said to help me out, but he looked like he was going to throw up.

Both Nat and Josh had done the *Godfather* films with Francis. They were incredibly loyal to him, but I could understand how badly they wanted to get out of Baler and not spend another Sunday here.

The crew backed off from me and talked in their little groups and just waited for the mechanics to be finished with the PBR's engine. I moved closer to the boat and just tried to relax. I didn't hear Larry Franco come up behind me.

"Hey, Jer! Am I gonna have a Big Mac or a mango cone Sunday?" he shouted, as he broke out in his big belly laughter. None of the crew laughed.

At about 3:00 the boat's engine turned over, and then died. The whole crew gathered around the PBR. The engine coughed and started again, then died again. Finally it started and kept running. Everyone cheered and you could feel their anxiety dissipate. I called for Larry to get the cast and Francis up to the PBR.

"What do you think, Pete?" I asked.

"They're tired engines, run all over 'Nam! How far does the PBR have to get upriver?" Pete asked.

"Four hundred yards, start to finish," I answered. "Four times will do it."

Pete looked at me, shook his head and walked away; I started to feel ill.

Vittorio and the Italians had the cameras placed and ready. All we needed were a few runbys in this locale with the PBR moving upriver.

Francis, Marty, Freddie, Sam, Albert, and Larry Fishburne came quickly to the boat. Everyone was excited and making plans for traveling tomorrow and making a lot more plans for Sunday in Olongapo.

Francis explained the actors' positions on the boat, what they were supposed to be doing, and Vittorio showed the distance the boat had to be away from the cameras. Everything was ready. I put Larry Franco on the boat with a walkie-talkie and told him to stay out of sight. We pushed the PBR out into the river. The engine took over and brought the PBR downriver about 150 yards to its start position. We had two small Wisconsin fishing-type boats with outboard motors that we used to block any unwelcome river traffic from entering our shot. We got everyone ready and in place. I rolled the cameras, and when Francis called "Action" I radioed for Larry to bring the PBR on.

We all watched. The PBR was hardly moving forward against the river current!

"Larry!" I yelled into the walkie-talkie. "Faster! Get that PBR going!"

"We are!" Larry answered. "This is full throttle! This is all she's got, Pete says!" Everyone around me, Francis, Vittorio, the camera crew, all heard Larry's radio transmission.

"Cut!" said Francis. He threw his cap to the ground and then kicked at the dirt. All of us just stood still. We all felt so badly for Francis. So utterly helpless. We had worked so hard in Baler on Village II, on the Tiger scene, and now this engine failure.

"Larry, call for the other boats to help and bring the PBR back to us," I radioed.

The crew stared at the ground; we felt we were so close and then our victory was seemingly snatched away.

Vittorio came up to me, "Jerry, what can we do? It must go faster!"

"I know, Vittorio, I know," I said. Francis was off by himself about ten or fifteen yards from the river. I walked slowly to him.

"I'm the bad guy, right?" Francis asked me. "If it wasn't for me we'd get out of here tomorrow, right?" We stared at each other. "There's no other jungle with a wide river anywhere else we're filming! Anywhere! Iba! Olongapo! Anywhere!" Francis said.

I've found that sometimes the best thing an assistant director can do is to stand there and listen.

"Jerry, just get me two shots! I have to have two shots! No, one shot, but with two cameras! That's all I ask!" Francis said, and looked down to the river. "There's hardly any current and that boat can't move!" He looked at me. "So, I'm the bad guy, right?"

"We'll get your shot, Francis," I said.

"Sure, but when? Saturday? Monday! Look, it takes two other boats to even move the PBR upriver! I can walk faster!" he said, as he saw the PBR nearing our shore. He moved back into the jungle, and I went down toward the river.

The crew gathered around the PBR and the mechanics. Even the cast listened—they all wanted to get out of Baler as badly as the rest of us. Pete Cooper shook his head.

"There's nothing else we can do. These PBR engines we got are worn out, pieces of crap!"

"What has to be done?" I asked.

"Needs a full overhaul, Jerry. I have to get the engine out, open it up, a complete, total overhaul," Pete answered. "They're worn out! That's it."

The crew stood in silence.

"How long will it take?" I asked.

"If we get the PBRs where we can work on them, back down the river, 'bout twelve to fifteen hours would do it, working nonstop, all night," came Pete's answer. "And providing we have all the parts! Which isn't likely!"

"Look," I started, "we've got to get just one run with that PBR moving upriver in the next hour and a half. Now how do we do it, Pete?"

"There's no way! You'd blow the engine! That'd shut you down good," Pete said.

"How do you blow the engine?" I asked.

"Wait! Also you'd have to film the boat further out in the river, another fifteen feet farther out. Less current and deeper, we can get a better run," he added.

"Great! Whatever it is, do it! Let's go! Blow the mother!" I said.

"I'm not going to be responsible!" Pete said. "You blow that engine, you might have to go to Thailand to get enough parts! You're talking weeks without any PBR!"

"Jerry," Vittorio said sadly, "impossible. If you move the boat away fifteen feet, I have to build a platform in the river for the cameras. There's no time." He looked at the sun.

Suddenly a duet of crazed, shrieking voices were heard two feet from our faces. "What the fuck do you need!!!!! I want to know what the fuck you need!!!!!" It was Josh, the stillman, and Leonard from wardrobe, insanely screaming at me.

I pointed out into the river and screamed back at them, "I need a platform in that river fifteen feet from shore right now or you'll be eating mango ice cream Sunday morning!"

Josh and Leonard turned and picked up a caterer's table, and charged madly toward the river. We all stared at this unlikely pair as they dashed into the river holding the table over their heads, slammed the table into the water, and then pounded on its top as they shouted, "Here's your fucking platform!!!!"

It was electrifying! Energy ran through the crew as they grabbed the cameras and equipment and ran into the river to set up the shot. The grips secured the table as the mechanics hurried to put the PBR engine back in order.

"Help me, Pete," I begged. "I gotta get just one run out of that PBR."

"They're gonna fire our asses!" Pete whispered.

"You scared?" I asked, and smiled at him.

"You are one of the biggest assholes I have ever run into," Pete grinned.

"What are we going to do?" I whispered.

"Mix in helicopter fuel. Did it in Vietnam once." he whispered back.

"Remember, one run!"

"One run," I confirmed. "Did it work, Pete?" I asked. "In Vietnam?"

"Almost," Pete answered, and ran toward our company's fuel supplies.

"Larry," I called on the radio, "get Francis and the cast!"

I glanced around at Enrico and the camera crew wading out into the river to place the cameras on the table. Alfredo and Mauro were standing in the river, bracing the table, with Luciano and his electricians helping. What had I done?

It was seconds later that the cast, Francis, and Larry were running through the jungle and toward the river. The actors scrambled onto the PBR. Francis came over to me just as Pete Cooper ran back onto the PBR, struggling with a couple of five-gallon fuel cans.

"What happened?" Francis asked me. "Is the PBR fixed?"

"Jerry, we must go right away, the light!" Vittorio said. He was in the water waving frantically.

Larry Franco got on board the PBR and took it back downriver toward its start mark. The other two boats were a couple of hundred yards on either side of the camera to hold all river traffic.

"Jerry, is the PBR OK?" Francis asked again. "Is it fixed?"

"Francis, we must go soon!" Vittorio shouted.

Francis nodded his "OK" to Vittorio. "Ziesmer!" Francis said. "Is the PBR fixed?"

"Almost, Francis," I said, as I got my walkie-talkie ready.

The PBR was on its start mark. I looked at the cameras, somehow braced fifteen feet out in the river. "Roll cameras!" I yelled. "Larry, we're rolling, be ready!" I said into the walkie-talkie.

Francis looked toward the river and just did a hand wave toward me for "Action!" not wanting to take his eyes off the PBR even for a second; I radioed to Larry, "Go, Larry! Action! Full throttle! Go, man!"

Everyone watched the PBR. A lot of Italian prayers were being said, along with a Wisconsin one. Nothing seemed to happen at first, but then the PBR sat itself back for a second, let out a whine like a hot dragster, and then she came on!

Francis cheered and screamed, and the whole crew did, too. "Look at that!" Francis screamed. "Look at that!!!!"

As the PBR sped upriver and past the cameras, the camera crew put their thumbs in the air to show that both cameras got good shots. Everyone was shouting and jumping with their arms raised over their heads in final victory.

"Francis, the light is not so good," Vittorio said. "I don't think we can go again." Both Vittorio and I saw the smoke coming from the back of our PBR; that engine had run its last race.

"Who cares!" Francis yelled. "Did you see that! The PBR! That was fantastic! See you all in Olongapo! Have a great Sunday!"

"Wow, Jer!" It was Larry on the walkie-talkie. "Was that a ride!"

"Thank everyone, Larry! Thank Pete! Catch you in Olongapo, man!" and I put my walkie-talkie away and turned to leave.

"I'll find out what you and Pete did, Jerry," Francis said, as he walked past me. "Someone will tell me. I'll find out what you did," he said, as he smiled back at me. Maybe he did and maybe he didn't, but Francis never mentioned it to me again.

It's not like me, but I slept in Saturday morning, moving day. There wasn't any *Apocalypse Now* alarm clock—the caterers were packed and on the road. By the time I got up, the film company's vehicles were out in the streets picking up the luggage from all the rented homes in Baler. Larry was up and packing. Allan and Teddy had already left. It didn't take me long to get my things together. I looked for Julius, the houseboy, but I didn't see him. He could have been helping Allan and Teddy.

I sat in the living room area and looked out the window at the street and the house across the way. The little girl was out watching the activity; I guessed that her mom and dad were working or in the house. I tried to figure what time it was right then in West Los Angeles and what my boys, Tim and Chris, would be doing.

Larry had brought more things than I had, and I helped him get his suitcases down to the street.

"Have you seen Julius?" I asked him. "The houseboy?"

"No, hasn't been here," Larry answered.

Julius never missed a day and was never late a minute; something didn't figure.

The street was busy with the loading of trucks, marking the luggage for different hotels, and getting all the film company's furniture and beds out of the rental units and onto trucks. Everything was going west to Olongapo, all the way across Luzon on the South China Sea. We'd still be a good deal north of Manila but close enough to spend some Sundays there.

I checked the icebox, no ice had been put in. I wondered if Julius was ill. I packed the last couple cans of San Miguel, put in a bag of garlic peanuts (hopefully my last), zipped my suitcase, and carried it down to the street.

Larry was going by some kind of road transportation, but Francis wanted me to fly to Olongapo. I'd be driven to the *Apocalypse Now* jungle airfield and then fly out of there. I guessed that there would be a meeting or location scout after I got to Olongapo. They wouldn't fly me unless they were going to get some work out of me.

I was standing on the street outside of our building, just watching the last of the trucks and cars moving out through the road dust. Larry's vehicle came, an old blue and white bus. I said I'd catch up with him at the Olongapo Hotel that evening. I knew I'd get there first but that I'd probably have some movie work to do.

I looked at the home and family across the road; I mentally said good-bye, though I had never spoken to them.

The open-backed trucks were just finishing loading the beds and mattresses from our place and the other residences nearby, when I saw Julius, our houseboy. He was up the side street about forty feet from me. I started to wave to him.

The two trucks collecting the beds had stopped on the side street because there was a line of about fifteen or twenty young men blocking their path. They were all holding AK-47s, and Julius was with them.

I was the only film company person around. I guessed that everyone else had already gone. My car and driver had arrived, and the driver loaded my suitcase. It was already hot and sticky. He was anxious for me to get inside the car. I watched the line of armed young men. One was talking to the drivers of the trucks and to the workmen who had loaded the mattresses and beds.

Julius was a head or two shorter than the spokesman, but he was also carrying an AK-47. I guessed he wasn't quite twelve years old. If he lived in Los Angeles, he'd be playing Little League.

The workmen and drivers seemed to have had a change of plans. They unloaded the mattresses and beds right in the dusty street, and then backed up their trucks to where I was standing. The guerrillas just stood in the street holding their AK-47s and waited.

I watched Julius for a minute longer, but he never looked at me. The empty trucks turned behind me and drove out of Baler. When their dust settled, I got into my car and the driver closed the door. Julius was still up the street, standing with the others.

I glanced again at the little girl who lived across the road. She was standing with her dad, while her mom swept the dirt yard; the AK-47–carrying guerrillas didn't seem to bother them at all.

I wondered who'd be sleeping on the mattresses tonight.

The car drove forward, and soon I was out of Baler, headed toward a jungle airfield and a flight to a city directly across the South China Sea from Vietnam and Cambodia. And ever closer to working with Marlon Brando, the greatest film actor of our age.

Apocalypse Now: Part Two

The driver wasted no time in getting us out of Baler and headed for the jungle airfield. He was visibly shaken by the guerrilla confrontation he had witnessed and kept glancing in the rearview mirror. I wondered about Julius; he was just a kid. The road took us west, away from the Pacific and into dense jungle vegetation.

I was the last to arrive at the airfield, and the driver took me directly to the large plane. "You going back to Baler?" I asked him.

He smiled at me, "No, I leave for Olongapo. No more Baler." He loaded my baggage onto the plane.

I thanked him and walked up the stairs and into the plane. I wished I was on the bus with Larry, just relaxing and enjoying the laughs and scenery. Leon, the production manager, was on the plane. I knew he would have work for me when we landed.

Leon Chooluck was a scrapper. He was in his fifties, overweight, loud, and always smiling. Leon hadn't stopped sweating from the day he arrived in the Philippines. He rarely wore a regular shirt, and when he did, he never buttoned it; he usually wore an undershirt without sleeves, like my father wore. He had been the production manager on *The Battle of the Bulge*, a World War II epic starring Henry Fonda, and also on *El Cid* with Charlton Heston and Sophia Loren, so he knew how to do big productions in foreign countries.

"Sit down, Jer," Leon said, as I struggled down the aisle with my two small carry-on bags. "Want a window?" he asked. When I hesitated, he got up. I slipped into the window seat, and Leon sat next to me. I was trapped.

"Thanks," I said, as I got my small bags arranged around me.

Neither of us spoke as the plane taxied down the short runway, then turned and accelerated, gaining as much speed as possible before it lifted off the ground and cleared the tops of the coconut trees. After we gained more altitude, we turned and headed west toward Olongapo. As far as I could see there was nothing but jungle, with an occasional small clearing and a nipa hut. Whoever thought Southeast Asia was crowded should fly over Luzon.

"Jer, I want you to know that Francis is very pleased with you and Larry," Leon began.

"That's great," I said. Francis hadn't said anything to me about our work. He asked me if I liked working on action pictures with lots of extras, and I said that I did. That was it. I wasn't the kind of assistant that directors gushed over or took out for dinner and drinks. I did my job and went home; that was it.

"Everything hasn't been too smooth, you know. The Hueys not coming when we needed them; that type of thing," Leon said. "We're through with them now."

"Right," I said. I had no idea where Leon was going with this, so I turned to the window and watched the scenery. Then I remembered that it was Francis who had insisted I fly to Olongapo.

"Jerry, I just want you to know that I'm here," he said. "You tell me what you and Francis need, and I'll get it. Know what I mean? I don't care who's in charge."

I turned back and looked directly at Leon Chooluck, who had been doing huge film productions all over the world since I was in grade school. "What are you telling me, Leon?" I asked.

"I'm telling you that Francis feels more comfortable with you running things," Leon said. "Tell me what you need, and it'll be there. I mean it."

I nodded. In Wisconsin we have a saying: "New brooms sweep cleaner." Maybe I was just Francis's new broom. "Sounds good to me, Leon," I said. Then I turned back to the window and watched the jungle pass by me.

Leon Chooluck was pure quality; he could have gotten his nose bent out of shape, quit, and flown back to the States, leaving me to face certain failure trying to run the massive production of *Apocalypse Now*. Fortunately for me, he didn't.

Our plane circled Olongapo. I saw the U.S. naval base at Subic Bay, with eight warships out in the harbor and its huge airfield that must have been a square mile of concrete. I saw the South China Sea for the first time. Its surf looked calm, not like Malibu or even Baler. When our plane leveled again, I tried to see Vietnam, but it was too far away. Olongapo was a regular city; it joined Subic and the naval base, with its businesses and residential areas spread along the coast.

Our plane turned and headed back to the southeast, away from the airfield. Leon watched me as I realized that we weren't going to land at Subic. "No cooperation, Jer. They won't even let us land at Subic," he said.

"Who won't?" I asked.

"The U.S. government. No cooperation; we're on our own," he said. I searched his face. "Why?" I asked.

"They don't like *Apocalypse Now*," he answered. "That's all."

"It's Joseph Conrad's *Heart of Darkness* set during the Vietnam War," I argued.

"A film about the Vietnam War isn't welcome. It's too soon. Give it another ten years or so," Leon answered, and smiled. He held up his hand to stop my next comment. "We get no cooperation, no equipment, no soldiers, no technical support, nothing. They won't even sell things to us; nothing!" He laughed and continued, "I tried to buy scrap, some burned out Hueys. Asked to hire off-duty personnel as extras. Officially, we're not here; *Apocalypse Now* doesn't exist."

I couldn't believe what Leon was telling me. Francis had received three Oscars; he was a world-famous cinema artist. *Heart of Darkness* by Joseph Conrad was required reading in almost every college freshman English lit. course in our country. It was as if Leon was talking about some other United States of America.

Leon smiled and then laughed; he nodded at me as if to say that my schooling had just begun. I felt like a rookie in spring training camp listening to an old major league veteran. I smiled because Leon smiled, but nothing seemed amusing to me.

Our plane landed at a small airfield, and the company cars were there waiting for us. It was just as I had thought—Leon and I were going to scout every film location in and around Olongapo. Everyone else was going to their hotel to clean up and begin to party. Somehow my baggage would get to the Olongapo Hotel.

Leon and I were ushered to one of the cars. We sat in the backseat, while a local location person sat next to the driver. We passed the naval base, with its huge warships in dry dock, acres upon acres of warehouses, hangars, housing, and the hundreds of naval personnel all clean and sharp. The whole base was ringed with chain-link fence with concertina wire looped on top.

The driver followed the coast, and we came into Olongapo from the south. It was just a city near a huge naval base. It was where the local workers lived and where the military officers had their off-base apartments. The city wasn't pretty, but it was functional, with restaurants, hotels, shopping, and Shakey's Pizza.

Outside Olongapo, the drive along the South China Sea was classic South Sea Islands, with date and coconut palms, sandy beach, and gentle surf. When I looked away from the coast, I saw thatched huts and small villages. Beyond the villages, farther inland, were the rice paddies with the water buffalo and the white egrets, the small birds that accompanied them. I enjoyed looking out over the South China Sea and then back over the acres of rice paddies. It was comforting to be out of the jungle and along a seacoast that was open and peaceful.

Our car drove over a four-lane concrete bridge that spanned a river flowing calmly to the sea. I saw nipa huts grouped along the river's banks, with three generations of families living together. I saw kids running along the river with their dog. The grandparents were caring for the young children, while the parents worked in the rice paddies or fished with their circular nets. Could have been my family's homestead north of Green Bay in Pensaukee, Wisconsin, my grandmother's farm.

The car slowed and then turned left toward the sea. I looked out at a concrete docking area and Pete Cooper with our two PBRs. Less than twenty-four hours before we had been standing on the other side of Luzon, watching a PBR engine bellowing smoke. I got out of the car and waved to Pete.

"Pete!" I called, and I walked to where he was standing on the long concrete dock with his mechanics and our two boats.

"Jer! How the hell are ya?" Pete asked. He was all smiles, so things couldn't be that bad.

"How are the PBRs?" I asked. "How did you get them here so fast?" All the mechanics started to laugh and hold their heads; I figured that was a story that could wait. "Pete, can we film with them Monday?" I asked.

"You're not going to get any more out of them than you did in Baler," Pete started. "These are two worn-out Vietnam veterans ready for the graveyard!" Leon joined us. "Leon knows, Jer," Pete continued.

"We couldn't get the PBRs we wanted," Leon said. "Too much money, too much time. They bought these two, and we're stuck with them," Leon offered. He saw me looking at him. "The PBR adviser before Pete bought them for us. He's no longer here, but the PBRs are," Leon added.

The shots for the next two or three days were all on the moving PBR, with the cast preparing the boat after they first pick up Martin Sheen. We would put the actors on one PBR and film the close-ups from that same boat, but the wide shots we would do from a second boat, hopefully the other PBR.

"We're gonna give it all we got, Jer, but they're Grade A shit, both of them," Pete volunteered. "You wanna do this right? You go film something else, while we get a couple of good-running PBRs!" Pete added. "I don't know how to make a movie, but I know what's gonna run up a river and what's not!"

Leon explained, "To get two PBRs, even one PBR, we're talking four weeks, maybe more. Have to find it, buy it, ship it."

"Sounds like Vietnam," Pete said, and moved off. I left Leon and followed Pete.

"What do you mean, Pete?" I asked. "Sounds like Vietnam?"

"That's how it was in Vietnam. PBRs would break down. No parts, nothing you could do." Pete said. "The shit continues falling!" he shouted, as he walked off. Sometimes the demons from Vietnam still attacked Pete.

Leon wanted to push on with our scout; he was on a schedule, just like every production manager. We had more locations, and he wanted to be back at the hotel in Olongapo before dark. That suited me.

When Pete got himself calmed down, he asked me to stop in at the bar he owned in Olongapo. When I asked for the bar's name and address, everyone laughed. Obviously I didn't need an address, Pete's Bar would do. I said I'd be there Sunday afternoon. I was just happy to see Pete smiling again.

Leon and I got back into the car and drove on to Iba, a small village right on the sea. Some of the actors, including Martin Sheen and his wife, Janet, were staying there. They seemed to have everything they needed, and it was almost an hour closer to the sets than driving from Olongapo. That saved two hours a day; seemed to make sense to have people stay in Iba.

We drove on and saw the Medivac set. There were about fifteen large tents set up along a river, with a long wooden dock for the PBR. The art department had created a military outpost. It's amazing how real they can get with telephone poles, electric wires, vehicles; they even had laundry hanging on a line.

Leon showed me a couple of other places we were going to film with
the PBR, and then we started the long drive back to Olongapo. The
best thing about it was a brilliant orange sunset that stretched up into
the clouds high above the South China Sea.

The Olongapo Hotel was built in a horseshoe shape around a large
swimming pool with gardens of tropical plants and trees. The front of
the hotel was on a small rise that overlooked a business and middle-
income residential area. There was a circular drive, with palms and
coconut trees lining the front of the hotel. The Olongapo Hotel wasn't
fancy, but it was serviceable, and after Baler, it looked very good. Inside
there were high glass windows in the doors around the dining room
facing the front street. The lobby was tiled and had the large, thick
wooden doors used so much in the Philippines. A little bar and cocktail
area was off the lobby, with tables and comfortable, overstuffed booths.
    I could have been in Milwaukee. I walked up the stairs to my room
on the second floor. My luggage was there. The room was fine; it was
clean and fresh smelling. There was a closet and a bureau, so for the first
time in the Philippines, I could unpack my clothes. The shower had hot
water that came out of a pipe, and I had my first real opportunity to
wash the Baler dirt and sand out of my hair. I was beginning to feel
human again.
    Larry arrived after I did; his bus broke down halfway across Luzon,
and they had to switch buses. As soon as he got to Olongapo he asked
about McDonald's, but there wasn't any. Maybe Manila. I'd be sure
Larry and I got to Manila next week on Sunday.
    As soon as Larry had showered, he came knocking on my door, ready
for Shakey's Pizza. We got a cab and found Shakey's. Terry Leonard was
already holding court with Nat Boxer, Josh Weiner, and a few of the
Italians in attendance. As soon as we entered, Terry wanted to know if
we wanted calamari or langostinas on our pizza. He then let out his
honking laughter. We didn't care; it was pizza!
    At the time it tasted as good as my favorite pizza—a large, extra
cheese, sausage and pepperoni from LaBarbera's Pizzeria in West
L.A. The only difference was that at Shakey's in Olongapo there were
langostina and calamari where the pepperoni and sausage would have
been.

    That night, back in my hotel room, I looked at a copy of the John
Milius script of *Apocalypse Now* that Leon had given me. He told me we

weren't really following it too closely. Francis was doing a lot of rewriting as we went along. I was comfortable with that; look for the fastball and be ready for the curve. I had been told Francis liked our work. My hotel room was all right. I could live on Shakey's Pizza. I liked Francis, Vittorio, Leon, and the cast and crew. I felt good.

Pete Cooper was right; I didn't need an address for his bar. When Larry and I got into a taxi at the hotel Sunday afternoon and I mentioned Pete Cooper's bar to the driver, he just drove us straight there. Larry got out of the taxi as I paid the driver, then I got out and we both looked for Pete's bar. The building that stood in front of us was a blackened structure, part decaying bomb shelter and part rusted hull. There must have been a sign at one time, but it was gone, and so was the front door. The only door covering that day was a beaded bamboo curtain. As I entered Pete's bar, I wondered what kept the riffraff out, but when my eyes got use to the darkened interior, I understood. All the riffraff was already inside the bar.

Pete's bar was indestructible only because long ago anything that could have been destroyed, was. I felt we were on the set of Gorky's *Lower Depths* or Samuel Beckett's *Endgame*. The walls and ceiling were painted black; the floor was solid concrete. The furniture was heavy wood tables with a mix of dinette chairs that looked as if they had come from forty different distress sales. Everything was like Pete—strong, solid, and durable; there wasn't one pretty thing in sight.

Pete's clientele consisted of merchant seamen from Asia and Africa, old soldiers and sailors from minor Asian nations, and veterans from the Vietnam War who couldn't find their way back home again. Alcoholism and manic depression seemed to be their common denominator. They were an ugly, rough-hewn, motley collection of the world's outcasts and the forgotten, and that's how they wanted to be. Every customer had a pitcher of beer and a thick glass in front of him. This was a serious drinking establishment.

I was sure that this was the final place, the end of the line. Nothing could be below this. Pete claimed he cleaned his place by hosing it down once a week and flushing the water out the front doorway.

As soon as Pete saw Larry and me, he let out a primal hoop and rushed toward us. His customers greeted us as "Pete's friends from the movie." Larry fit right in, as he always did; he got a pitcher of beer and just joined the crowd. Before Pete greeted me with his big bear hug, I was desperately looking to get out of there. I was a Caucasian, church-going, former junior high school teacher, with a home and family. I didn't think I could find much in common with Pete's customers.

Pete introduced me to everyone as the biggest asshole he had ever met, and then he began the story of our PBR experience the last day in Baler. He impersonated me as being insanely driven to get the PBR up to speed! He told how he mixed helicopter fuel into the PBR, and then he mimed Larry's wide-eyed look when the PBR rocketed up the river! All of us in the bar roared with laughter at the story and Pete's telling it.

From there the Vietnam War stories began, and it was four hours later that Larry and I left Pete's bar. As we got into our taxi, Pete and his friends toasted us from the bar's entrance with animal screams and raised beer pitchers. Not bad for a Presbyterian.

The next day we all made it out to the location near Iba and began filming with our actors on the PBR. It was pretty pitiful; the riverboats were not going to get up any speed for us. Pete did everything he could. We tried towing the PBR, then we tried to hide a smaller boat alongside and help it along, but nothing got any speed out of the PBRs. By the late afternoon, Francis grew more and more despondent. I felt terrible for him. I didn't know what to do.

Bill Graham, the rock-and-roll producer; his group, Alabama, and three genuine Playboy Bunnies were flying into Olongapo that day to be in *Apocalypse Now*. I felt it would be possible to film the Medivac scenes with them and to get the Bunny Show set ready and film those scenes. However, after the Bunny Show there wasn't anything else we could film. We'd have to shut down until we got our new PBRs.

To shut down the company while we acquired another PBR or two was very expensive, and Francis had put up all of his own money to complete the picture. His home and other investments were put up as security for the loans to keep *Apocalypse Now* going. It was a terrible dilemma for the film and for Francis personally. Shutting down for four weeks didn't mean the costs didn't continue. The major portion of the crew and all the cast had to be kept on salary. We had production offices, hotel rooms, and movie-making equipment on rental that had to be carried during any break in our filming. All of those costs continued unless we shut down because of *force majeure*, an act of God. Two broken-down PBRs were not an act of God.

Later that afternoon when the PBR came back to the dock after failing another try at getting any kind of acceleration, Leon Chooluck and Gray Frederickson met us. Francis was very depressed. He walked off the boat and slowly moved down the dock. Finally, he stopped and stood all by himself. I didn't know what to do. I walked over to Gray and Leon.

"We saw you," Leon said. "The PBR can't make it."

"There's nothing there, Leon," I said. "We have to get new boats."

"Where? We've tried to get new PBRs. They're not available!" Gray said.

"We'd have to go to Thailand, Jerry," Leon said. "That's weeks."

"We can't do that!" Gray said.

I watched Francis. He was standing forty feet from us, turned away and looking up the coast toward Iba. All his work on the *Godfathers*, everything he'd saved, everything that he owned was invested in this picture. I wondered if I could have done that—put up everything for a film. The home for my children? Maybe their college education?

"Jerry!" Francis called, still looking out toward Iba.

I looked at Leon and Gray and then walked toward Francis. I circled and stood facing him. I waited and didn't say a word.

"Tell me what to do," he said softly, and never looked up at me.

I took a deep breath. "Film the Medivac with Bill Graham and the bunnies," I said quietly.

"Are they here?" Francis asked, and looked at me.

"Came in today," I answered. "Then do the Bunny Show."

"Can Dean Tavoularis get that set ready?" he asked. "What about extras?"

"Dean'll do it. We'll have to scramble for the extras," I said.

He looked out to the sea. It was starting to blow and getting colder. The cast and crew were standing near the PBRs. "Then what? What do I film next?" Francis asked, and fixed me with his stare.

"We shut down and go buy two new PBRs." I just said it flat and waited.

"Shut down! Are you crazy? We can't shut down!" he fought.

I didn't say another word. What could I add? It was his house and his kids, not mine.

"Do you know what that'll cost me?" he asked. I still didn't say anything; I felt guilty. "You're standing here and telling me to shut down this company and go buy two more PBRs?"

Francis looked out at the sea, glanced back toward the company, and then looked back to me. "We'll film the Medivac scene, then the Bunny Show?" Francis asked. "Then you're saying to shut down the film until we've got two good-running PBRs. Right?"

"Yes," I answered, and waited. I didn't know if Francis would just clobber me and then fire me, or fire me first. He was looking out at the sea toward Iba. Finally he turned and looked back at the cast and crew.

"I'll tell them," Francis said, and he walked back toward the cast and crew.

I stood near Leon and Gray while Francis told everyone what his decision was about the PBRs and the possibility of shutting down the company. Gray and Leon would get together on who would stay on salary in the Philippines and who would be sent back. Then Francis entered the Jet Ranger with Dick White, Vittorio, and Gray, and they took off for Manila.

Pete had gotten a bad weather forecast, and he was securing our boats and naval equipment in a little harbor in Iba. The cast and crew were getting into their cars for the ride back to Olongapo or on to Iba. I saw that Larry was all right, then Leon and I got in his car and drove toward Olongapo. I was feeling very low. I felt somehow that I had failed Francis.

"There's nothing else that could be done," Leon tried to comfort me.

"I know," I answered. Francis was risking everything he had for this film. It haunted me why I couldn't ever do that.

By the time we got to the hotel, it had started to rain and the wind was picking up. I took a shower, met Larry, and we ate in the hotel dining room. We saw Bill Graham with his rock group, Alabama, and the three Playboy Bunnies sitting together in the dining room. About halfway through our meal, one of the dining room's floor-to-ceiling glass doors swung violently open from the wind and driving rain. Two waiters hurried to mop the wet floor.

After all we had been through, a little rain on a dining room floor didn't mean much. Then Leon crossed to our table.

"Kids, I just got a weather report," he said as he stared at us.

"What's it say?" I asked.

"If the weather report is right, we've got a typhoon headed for us!"

"A typhoon!" Larry laughed.

"This could be serious; I mean it," Leon said, and I could see he was worried.

Suddenly the lights went out and then came back on. I could see the rain pounding down outside the window and the wind whipping the palms and plants against the front of the hotel. Leon went to try to call Francis in Manila. Larry and I paid our check and walked out to the hotel's lobby. The driving winds were forcing the rain through the cracks in the door, soaking the floor.

Larry and I looked out the lobby windows. We could see that the rain was being caught by the driving wind and then sent nearly horizontally against the buildings. I'd been in some heavy rain in Wisconsin and California, but this typhoon dwarfed anything I had ever seen. It was as if there were no individual raindrops; it was a constant sheet of water.

Leon came back down into the lobby. "The phones to Manila are down. It's a typhoon! We're in a typhoon!" Leon said, and hurried into the dining room.

"What do we do?" Larry asked.

"Maybe it'll be over by morning," I said.

My hotel room was dry. I checked the windows and tightened their latches. This was an astounding storm. Since the lights had gone off when the electricity was knocked out, the hotel had brought around two candles for each room. I tried the water tap, but there was no pressure. From the sound against my room's window, the typhoon was picking up force. Not many of us slept that night. *Apocalypse Now* indeed.

The next morning I looked out my window, and the rain was worse than the night before. The typhoon's pulsating winds were whipping the coconut trees nearly to the ground. As I watched the typhoon batter Olongapo, I saw pieces of the corrugated tin used for roofing and siding fly through the air like giant kites. Those flying pieces had been the walls or roofs of people's homes. I wondered what had happened to the people. The roadways were flooded, and soon the parked cars were being moved by the rushing water, then turned by the wind and actually propelled down the street. I watched as two men tried walking braced against the typhoon. They were bent nearly double as they struggled against the rain and wind. They tried to huddle against a car, then gave up and moved back with the wind. Why would anyone be out in this weather?

Leon, Larry, and I met in the hotel bar and tried to make sense out of our situation. We had to make sure all of our cast and crew were safe. Leon kept trying to get through to Iba and to Manila, but the phone lines were out in both directions. There was a short-wave radio available at the hotel, and he would continue to try and get through to Iba. What little news we had indicated that the area north of us, which included

Iba, was getting it worse than we were. I had a hard time believing that. Rain could not fall harder than it was falling in Olongapo!

All that day Typhoon Ruby continued to batter Olongapo with its fury. Bill Graham was desperate to communicate with the outside world. He had his rock-and-roll empire to run. The Playboy Bunnies were numb with fright. The crew took turns looking out the windows and reporting the latest example of Typhoon Ruby's strength. The hotel workers prepared food for all of us and stuffed cloth under all the doors to keep the rain out.

That night Larry and I, along with Bill Graham, Terry Leonard, the three bunnies, the members of Alabama, and most of our crew were all sitting in the small hotel bar. There was no water or electricity in Olongapo, so the hotel had placed candles all around the bar for us. Our dinner was primarily tropical fruit, banana chips, and garlic peanuts. We used club soda to brush our teeth. Suddenly we heard a loud pounding on the hotel's front door. The typhoon was still raging, and no one had dared leave the hotel! We cautiously opened the door, and a soaked figure in white pajamas stumbled into the lobby, followed by a second figure. It was Francis! Francis and his driver!

We were all holding candles and trying to lead them into the hotel's bar.

"We made it!" Francis shouted.

"My god, Francis!" Leon could hardly speak.

"Francis, what in hell . . . ," Terry Leonard began.

The driver was coughing, and someone got him to the bar and poured him a drink.

"You can't believe the typhoon!" Francis exclaimed. "Manila's a mess! Flooded. All the roads are closed. We just got out, or we'd never have gotten here!" he continued.

"Is Ellie OK?" Nat Boxer asked.

"Fine! House is flooded a bit, but they're fine!" Francis assured us.

"Why, Francis?" I was finally able to speak. "Why did you come here?"

"Had to. I had to. That's it!" Francis answered. "What's it like in Iba?" he asked.

"Francis, we have no communication with Iba," Leon said. "We have no communication with anyone!"

Once Francis and his driver had changed into dry clothes and everyone was calmed down, it was decided that the next morning we would send out search parties to try and reach the rest of our company in Iba. We knew Martin and Janet Sheen were there, and Freddie, Albert, Sam, and Larry Fishburne with his mom and aunt were scheduled to be staying there but may have gone into Manila before the typhoon hit. We didn't know. Because of the obvious emergency, Leon would ask the U.S. naval base at Subic for help in reaching our people in Iba.

The following morning the rain and wind continued to batter Olongapo. Francis, Leon, Larry, and I got into a company car and started north along the South China Sea toward Iba. The rain and winds pushed the car sideways across the highway as the driver fought to keep our car going forward. The windshield wipers did little to improve our vision of the road ahead.

Debris from the storm littered the highway. Whole huge coconut trees were completely uprooted and lying along the highway. Every low spot in the road was flooded, and we had to drive slowly through the water, being careful not to splash water onto the car's engine.

Halfway to Iba, we came upon the long concrete bridge over the river where I had seen the village of nipa huts. Cars and trucks were stopped on the bridge and we could go no farther. All of us got out of the car and walked forward to see what was causing the delay. About a third of the way across the bridge we saw the problem. Typhoon Ruby had taken out one hundred feet of the concrete bridge's center section. I looked over the edge and saw a rushing, turbulent river, forty feet higher than what I had seen less than two days ago. The nipa huts and the families were gone. I looked to where their rice paddies had been, and all I could see was a huge lake of water with a series of waterfalls spilling into the river. Where were the people, I wondered.

We stared across the missing section of bridge. There wasn't any way motorized traffic would be using this bridge for months, and it was the only highway from Olongapo to Iba. When we learned that the rest of the bridge's foundation was being undercut by the rushing water and there was a real danger of further collapse, we got back into our car and returned to Olongapo.

Most of us had been sitting in our hotel watching Typhoon Ruby through the windows. After driving along the coast, we realized the true extent of the destruction of property and loss of life that occurred to the western coast of the Philippines. We intensified our resolve to reach Iba and find out the condition of our cast and crew.

Late that afternoon we arrived back at our hotel. The wind and rain had seemed to intensify as it got closer to sundown. We held a meeting in the dining room. It was determined that it was impossible to reach Iba by car. All attempts at phone and short-wave communication had failed. Our hopes rested on help from the naval base. While we had tried to get to Iba, Leon had driven through the storm to the naval base at Subic to get their help. He returned to the hotel during the meeting.

Leon reported that the U.S. naval base refused our request for help to reach our people in Iba. I felt as if I had been kicked in the stomach. I felt bitter, disillusioned, helpless, and very frightened for our people in Iba.

Suddenly we heard the unmistakable sound of a landing helicopter! We all rushed to the front door and windows. There, struggling against the wind and rain, was our Jet Ranger with Dick White attempting to land on the top of our hotel. We all ran up the stairs and forced the roof door open.

Dick White was hovering the helicopter, not landing, so he could fight the wind. He threw out ropes and motioned for us to tie down the helicopter while he hovered inches off the roof. We ran out and tied down the Jet Ranger; some of us sat on the skids until Dick shut off the chopper. He then secured the tie-downs, and we all ran out of the rain and back down the stairs to the sanctuary of the bar. Everyone was screaming and yelling at what an amazing thing Dick White had done, flying in this weather.

When we put a beer in Dick's hand, he admitted he had been frightened, but he had gotten word that Francis had set out for Olongapo, and there had been no word from him. Dick White's arrival was exactly what we needed to raise the morale and spirits of our beleaguered group.

It was too dark to attempt to fly to Iba, but plans were made for Dick, Francis, and me to leave at first light. Our plan was to find out the condition of our people in Iba and to evacuate them if necessary. Then we would fly over our sets to see what the damage was.

Francis was sitting by himself at a small table in the bar. He motioned for me to join him. I left Dick, Terry, the bunnies, and Bill Graham at the bar and sat next to Francis.

"It's better than our script," he laughed, as he looked around the candlelit bar. We were in a decimated area of the world, but our folks were celebrating and partying anyway.

"What do you think, Jerry?" he asked. "We'll find out about Iba tomorrow."

"Right," I answered. "Hope they're OK. Get them out if we have to."

"Then what?" he asked. "We're through. There'll be no sets standing."

"Probably not," I answered.

"I thought it was the PBRs that sunk us, but it was Typhoon Ruby." Francis looked down at the tabletop.

"Difference, you know?" I said. "Typhoon is an act of God."

"So what? Some God we got!" Francis smiled.

"Francis, I think your insurance might cover natural disasters," I said.

"No way!" he said. "Insurance to cover this? No way!" he said.

"It's *force majeuer*, an act of God," I said.

Francis stared at me. "You think that? And insurance?" he said.

"Leon!" Francis shouted, as he saw Leon enter the bar.

"Leon, listen. Do you think there's a chance we have insurance for this typhoon?"

Leon looked at the two of us. "We should have," he said. "I'll call Los Angeles as soon as I can."

"Are you guys serious?" Francis was seeing the light. "Do you know what this means?"

"You got to film everything you can before insurance kicks in," Leon warned. "If there is insurance."

"You think we have any sets left?" Francis said. "I'm worried about our people in Iba!"

The next morning I was awakened by the sound of a helicopter leaving. I jumped out of bed, got dressed, and ran to the roof. Francis, Larry, and Dick White had flown off to check Iba! The rain and wind were still strong, but at half the intensity of the last two days. Flying in this type of weather was dangerous even with the best helicopter pilots. I was upset that Larry had gone instead of awakening me.

I went down to the dining room where the hotel staff had prepared a breakfast of tropical fruit and two-day-old rolls. Just as I was about to enter, something caught my eye out at the pool. It was about half of our crew bathing in the center of the pool with shampoo bottles and bars of soap being shared. Around the edges of the pool the other members of the crew were shaving and brushing their teeth.

The bunnies had turned out to be very good sports through all of this and were now in the shallow end of the pool washing each other's hair. Bill Graham was toweling off as he shouted to all who would hear that he had to get to a phone! His rock group always slept at least until afternoon, sometimes until dark, but Bill Graham had a hundred rock groups! Terry and the crew were laughing and splashing each other, throwing the soap and bottles of shampoo across the pool. I continued into the dining room and got breakfast.

About twenty minutes later the helicopter returned. We all ran to the roof, and Francis and Larry shouted their report as Dick White hovered the Jet Ranger.

"The Iba people are fine!" Francis shouted over the helicopter noise. "We didn't put down, but they waved and threw kisses!"

"They're great!" Larry laughed. "Waving!"

"There's two bridges out!" Francis continued. "Forget trucks or cars! Jerry, I want you to come with me and look around at the Medivac set!"

"OK!" I shouted over the engine noise, and then I looked at Larry as we changed places in the chopper. "Why did you go? What if something had happened?" I shouted at him.

"You've got two kids!" he shouted at me and laughed. Francis got back in the helicopter, and I joined him. Dick White was smiling and laughing as he checked us in, looked around the sides of the ship, and took us up.

The rain and wind buffeted the helicopter, but I felt we had seen the worst of the typhoon. Dick brought the ship to the south, and we flew near Subic before he headed north toward Iba. We were the only aircraft in the air. I saw some activity on the ground, some moving cars and a few people, but Olongapo was quiet. There still was no electricity or water in our whole area of western Luzon.

From the air I could see the devastation stretching miles inland from the sea. The rice paddies and farmland were under seawater. The seacoast north of Olongapo looked as if it had moved inland two miles. I looked again at the devastated bridge and the surging river underneath. The raging waters came down the river from the highlands to the east taking everything in their path.

Dick White flew us over what had been the set for the Bunny Show. It was now a pile of broken lumber and twisted metal. The stage was torn apart, and the huge metal light standards were bent to the ground. Filming the Bunny Show anytime soon was impossible. At best, Francis could file an insurance claim for the cost of rebuilding the set.

Francis gestured to me that the set was useless, and Dick brought us around toward Iba. The helicopter shook as we buffeted against the strong wind. I'd be happy to be back on the ground.

We flew over Iba and then headed north for the Medivac set. There was a sea of mud where the art department's set had been. The dock for the PBR was nearly covered with water, and the rains were continuing. The remnants of the Medivac tents were torn down and strewn across the mud. The telephone and electric poles were lying on the ground.

Francis pointed down at the set and shouted, "They had rain and mud in Vietnam! Can we film there?"

I looked out the helicopter's window at the mud and water. How could a company of actors, Playboy Bunnies, and crew film in that? I had to play it through; I motioned for Dick to set us down. He found a low rise behind the Medivac set, and Francis and I got out of the chopper.

Francis wanted to capture a scene in rain and mud for his film. There was no denying that we had the opportunity here. He got very excited at the possibility of having the PBR stationary at the dock and then the cast leaving the boat and discovering Bill Graham and the Playboy Bunnies inside the tents. The story line was that the bunnies' helicopter needed gasoline so they landed at the Medivac camp. A potential trade would be made, extra gasoline from the PBR in exchange for the services of the Playboy Bunnies.

We couldn't walk far because of the mud. We knew the PBR could be gotten to the dock; it didn't have to run. That much would work. The Medivac set would have to be completely re-done. The crew would be knee-deep in mud.

Francis wanted to put wooden sidewalks across the mud. I thought that we would have to walk all of our equipment in from a roadway two hundred yards away. The heaviest equipment we could bring in by boat.

He wanted to film in the rain and mud, and I wanted to give him what he wanted if I could figure out a way of actually making it work. The other issue was that if Francis did have insurance coverage, we would be required to film everything we could before shutting down. Attempting to film in this sea of mud would more than fulfill that obligation.

I told Francis that the company could physically film here but that it would take the art department at least two to three days to put the set back together. I had hoped that in three days the river would drop a few feet and that the natural drainage would decrease the depth of mud. I wanted Dick to follow the river to be sure we could get the PBR to the set, and then I wanted to follow the road all the way south to Iba to be sure we could get trucks close. My plan was to take whatever truck route was needed to go from Olongapo to Iba, even if it meant taking three days and circling the whole island of Luzon.

Francis was happy, but we still had to sell the plan to Leon and the crew—and then we all had to make it work. We'd have to move the company to Iba just for the three or four days to film the Medivac scene. Dick flew the river route back toward Iba, then followed the roadway back north to within a few hundred yards of the set. From the roadway's closest point it would still be a hike through deep mud to our set. All of the actors, bunnies, crew, and equipment would have to walk through the mud to the set. This wasn't going to be fun.

Dick put the helicopter down in a small mud field near Iba, and our cast and crew came out to meet us. They had all the dirt and markings of true savages. Iba had also been without electricity and water, but they did have food because the Dragon Lady and her caterers were there.

While Francis began to tell about the plans to film Medivac, I looked around for housing opportunities. Even with a skeleton crew, we would have to double up in every room, and in some cases triple up. After looking forward to being in Olongapo, I didn't know how the crew would take to that. Of course, after completing the Medivac scenes nearly everyone would be free for weeks while *Apocalypse Now* shut down until our sets could be rebuilt.

The personnel in Iba were in surprisingly good condition and spirits. A lot of that was due to Marty and Janet Sheen. I had heard that during the typhoon they were outside their home giving out rice and other foodstuffs to everyone who was hungry. They had kids, schools, and they made it all work. Somehow they stayed together as a family, and I couldn't.

Francis was eager to get back to Olongapo and tell everyone of the plan to film Medivac before we shut down. We got back into Dick's chopper, and he took us to the Olongapo Hotel roof.

After Francis had met with Leon and the rest of our crew, he and Dick flew back to Manila to get Dean Tavoularis and the art department working on Medivac and to spread the news of our filming during the last stages of the typhoon.

The bad news for the cast and crew at the Olongapo Hotel was that we would be filming in mud and rain, but the good news was that most people had three days off until then. You could say that the party began when Pete Cooper walked into our hotel's lobby.

Leon worked on getting the minimum crew requirements for the Iba filming. Housing space was at a premium. Leon was a magician; he loved a challenge, and he had one here.

The bar was the busiest place in the Olongapo Hotel, as more and more crew members learned that we would be filming in mud and then shutting down. Along the bar and the tables, among the San Miguel and rum drinks, a romantic concept began. Most crew members had been receiving a $350-per-week spending allowance for months and had spent very little, so they were "cash rich." I have no idea where the idea of world travel began, but it tore through the crew like fire through a haystack. Since the film would be shut down for a few weeks, why not just travel around the world a bit before coming back to the Philippines to begin filming again? The film company would give you a round-trip ticket back to the States—or the cash equivalent, and you could make your own travel plans. Everyone was exploring the possibility of traveling to the very ends of the earth, where they had wanted to go all their lives! Call it boredom from Baler, anxiety from the typhoon, or just the realization that if they are already halfway around the world, why not travel on!

"If I go to Tasmania, should I go to Sydney or New Zealand first?" a crew member asked.

"Russia! Hell, if I'm in Athens, I'm sure as hell not going to miss Moscow!" the wardrobe man said.

"Tasmania is an island! Go to New Zealand first, then double back," the answer came. "When do you plan to be in San Sebastian?"

"What's there?" asked wardrobe.

"Did you read Hemingway? The bulls! Pamplona!" a crew member shouted. "I've wanted to see that all my life!"

Suddenly there was the unmistakable sound of Pete Cooper shouting from the pool and Terry Leonard shouting from the roof of the hotel.

"You can do it! Just don't look!" shouted Pete, as he swung his arms wildly and bellowed.

"Clear the pool!" Terry shouted from the edge of the roof. "I'm coming down!"

The cast and crew quickly made their way out of the pool and looked up at Terry perched on the very edge of the roof. He was honking his laughter and waving his hands as though he were swatting away pesky flies. "I'm coming down!" Terry shouted again.

"Clear! Clear! Give him room!" Pete shouted.

Some people were screaming "Don't! Don't jump, Terry!" while others were urging him on: "You can do it!"

I ran out to the pool just in time to see Terry Leonard dive off the roof of our two-story hotel and land in the pool! Everyone cheered. Pete Cooper dived into the water with all his clothes on and helped Terry to the shallow end. The bunnies thought it was all so exciting, and everyone applauded.

Luckily I had taught for a couple of years in a junior high school in Santa Monica, so I could adjust to most any kind of misbehavior. Terry and Pete stretched me a bit that day, but I didn't crack.

"Jerry!" Larry shouted from across the pool, "are you going to Bombay or Nairobi?" He laughed for all he was worth. I took a deep breath, smiled, and kept going on.

The next day we began shuttling people by the Jet Ranger from the Olongapo Hotel roof to Iba. Three of us at a time could get into the chopper with our necessary luggage. Dick White would take off and get us to Iba as soon as he could. Once there, we would unload the helicopter, and Dick would immediately fly back and land on the hotel's roof, ready for more passengers.

The crew's spirits were high, even when they saw their Iba living accommodations. Larry and I shared a room with a bath; we were very lucky. Our room had two single beds and a table and chair. The floor was wet from the rain, and the window to the west was broken by the typhoon and wouldn't close. There was no heat and still no electricity. The rain and wind continued, but it was now just normal rain showers. I was eager to film as soon as we could before the rain stopped. I had told Joe Lombardi and A. D. Flowers that if the rain did stop, they would have to give us artificial rain. Francis wanted the whole Medivac scene in rain. A. D. and Joe didn't have a water truck, but once they got their special effects truck close, they would set up their rain birds and a pump in the river, just in case the rain did stop. I felt I had that potential problem covered.

The Dragon Lady had set up her catering lines out in the rain. That night when we all stood in line to get our food for dinner, the rain filled our plates faster than the caterers could. The people who had soup couldn't eat the soup as fast as the rain refilled their bowls. Iba made Baler look good. It was miserable, but it would only be for three days.

The first day, our wardrobe people were passing out plastic ponchos to everyone; I thought that was great. Our whole crew seemed up to doing this filming, no matter what the circumstances. We had awakened in rain-dripping rooms, ate rain-soaked food, and now waited in the rain to get into vehicles to spend all day working in the rain. I noticed that Francis wasn't down at the caterer with us, so I went up to his room and knocked to be sure he was awake.

"Francis!" I called.

"Jer! Come in!" he answered.

I opened the door, and there was Francis in a large double bed; he was surrounded with pillows. His room was warm and dry, but that wasn't what caught my attention. At the foot of his bed were trays of bacon, scrambled eggs, sausage, toast. He could have fed half the crew with that food. Francis saw me staring at all the food.

"Help yourself," he said. "I didn't ask for any of this."

The Dragon Lady had struck again!

When the crew vehicles got as close to the Medivac set as they could, we all got out and started across two hundred yards of mud to get to the set. It was still raining and the wind was blowing. When you stepped into the mud, your foot sank down into mud just below your knee. Once you had both feet in the mud, you then had the problem of raising one of your feet so you could put it in front of you, once again sinking knee-deep into the mud. You were lucky if you could keep stepping across the mud field. What happened to a lot of us was that our shoe or boot would stay down in the mud and our foot would come out. Soon at least half of us were trudging through the mud field in our stocking feet. The bunnies were carried across the field, as was Nancy, our script supervisor.

Pete Cooper had gotten the PBR into place, but it had taken him twelve hours to make his way down the river. He and his mechanics had to get out of the boat and pull the PBR along whenever there were too much debris or silt in the river.

The Italian crews had gotten their equipment to the set through the mud field. They made platforms for the camera and those crew members who had to stand near it. The electricians strung their cable from their generator at the road all through the mud to our set. Joe Lombardi had the special effects crew ready with their rain birds if the rain ever did stop, which seemed unlikely.

Vittorio and Francis were marvelous working in the rain and mud. We got Marty, Freddie, Albert, Lance, and Larry Fishburne from the PBR and moving up to the Medivac tents that first day. When we lost the light, we rehearsed the interiors of the tents.

Just like in the morning, we had to walk back out through the mud
field to the roadway and then to be driven back to our rooms in Iba. We
ate in the rain, and some of us slept in the rain.

My leather belt disintegrated in my hands that night. Larry thought
it was from all the humidity and such. I became conscious that everything I had of leather was beginning to disintegrate from the dampness.
We never got dry.

At breakfast three crew members were comparing the rash that had
appeared on each of their feet. Dick White came by and said it was
known as the Vietnam rot. Enough of the crew saw the rashes and heard
Dick's comment that it started a major crew panic.

That morning when someone's boot got stuck in the mud and only
their foot came out, you could hear screams and curses. No one wanted
to put their uncovered foot down into that mud and get the Vietnam
rot!

But filming was great. The rain stopped about lunchtime, but we
went inside the tents and did the interiors, with special effects adding
some of their rain when the camera saw out the windows and doors.

We finished the interiors and started the exterior shots of our cast
walking back down to the PBR. Joe Lombardi and A. D. got their
pumps into the river and covered the whole area with their rain. It
looked great, and we filmed that way until we lost the light.

The outbreak of skin rashes on any surface that had touched the
mud spread throughout the company. We still had to walk across the
mud field, but without the rain the mud was not as treacherous. When
a crew member's boot was stuck, there was nothing that could be done.
He couldn't reach down his hand to try and pull up the boot, and he
couldn't just stand in the mud field balanced on one foot like a
flamingo. He had to step into the mud with his stocking foot, and he
knew that within hours he would have the same rash as his crewmates.

The final day of the Medivac scenes there was no natural rain, so we
relied on Joe and A. D.'s rain all day. We were all getting drenched with
it, but we only turned it on during the shots, so it wasn't as bad as the
previous days. In the middle of the morning, Nancy's script disintegrated and fell into the mud. For a script supervisor, her script was like
her child. All of her notes and drawings for the editors were on those
pages. Everyone realized how much that meant to her. She stood there

sobbing. Francis and Vittorio went to her. The whole company stopped. I felt the reason we were so affected was that we had all reached our breaking point, but Nancy had gone beyond that point and broken down. It could have been any of us, but it was Nancy.

That afternoon just after lunch, Dick White in the Jet Ranger brought three producers out to the set: Gray Frederickson, Fred Roos, and Mona Skager. They were very careful not to get muddy as they walked on a plank sidewalk we had built. All of us were standing in the mud watching the three producers walk and giggle along the plank walkway across the field of mud as they tried to stay clean. They were dressed in Manila's finest, and we were covered with mud. I knew who threw the first one, but soon there were a lot of objects landing in the mud near the walkway and splattering the three producers with mud. The three producers stood balanced on the planks and looked at all of us standing knee-deep in the river mud. No one said a word. There wasn't any laughter from the crew or angry glances from the producers. A moment passed, and the producers walked on to Francis, and the crew went on with their work.

Much later I got everyone ready for the final shot, started the special-effects rain pouring down on all of us, and rolled the camera. Francis called "Action" and when the scene was through, he yelled "Cut!" We all knew that our filming in the mud and rain was over. Most would be returning to the States or Italy. The construction crews would rebuild, and we'd all be back to finishing *Apocalypse Now* soon, hopefully in four or five weeks.

The bunnies were carried over the mud fields for the last time. The rest of us trudged through because we knew we had weeks to get over a bit of rash. My leather wristwatch band disintegrated on the trek out. I would buy a new one and a new leather belt when I got back to the States. I figured to be home within a week at the latest.

That night the Dragon Lady actually threw a bit of a party for us. Everyone was so excited to be going back to the States, Italy, or at least Manila. Larry and I packed for our chopper trip back to the Olongapo Hotel the next morning, where company vehicles would take us to a plane for our flight to Manila and civilization. All of us were tired from the rain, wind, and mud. We slept in horribly damp conditions and ate less-than-adequate food. All that was about to end. We were very excited.

The next morning Dick White's Jet Ranger shuttled us to the Olongapo Hotel in groups of four or five. Leon was there waiting for us. He had two big trucks for our luggage and a bus and cars for the ride to the U.S. Navy's airport at Subic Bay. Leon had begged the naval base, and they had finally consented to letting our chartered plane land and take off from their airfield. Things were definitely looking better.

The hotel bar did a lot of business that day, as we all waited for the last of our cast and crew to get shuttled to the hotel. Finally, with shouts and screams, we all entered the bus and cars for the trip to Subic. The trucks with our luggage had gone on before us. It was like a bus full of kids coming home from camp, with laughter, singing, and shouting all the way to the Subic gate.

The bus came to a stop, and I saw both our luggage trucks halted at the gate to the Subic airfield. Leon had gotten out of a car and was in a heated discussion with the guards. I looked out at the gigantic airfield, and I saw our chartered airliner parked about a half mile away with government vehicles around it.

Leon came fuming back toward the bus, and I got out to meet him. "Leon, what's up?" I asked.

"This is as far as we go," Leon said. "They gave us permission to land and take off, but we can't drive a vehicle onto the airfield! We have to carry everything to the plane!"

I looked out at the acres upon acres of vacant concrete. There were no other planes in sight except for our old four-propeller cargo plane. Leon was fuming. More people started to get off the bus and come toward us. I started toward the guards.

"Jer! Forget it!" Leon shouted at me.

There were two or three guards with the guardhouse and about four others with two government vehicles that were obviously placed to block any access to the airfield. I walked up toward the guards, but before I could speak one of the guards said, "You're not driving on this airfield, and that plane isn't moving any closer. You want to get on that plane, you hike it out there."

"What's going on here?" I asked.

"Look, *Apocalypse Now*, you want to get on the plane? Walk!" the guard said.

"Can we at least drive the luggage trucks up to the plane, and we'll walk?" I asked. "We've been through the typhoon."

"No vehicle is driving through this gate or on that runway," he answered.

"What harm can it do to . . . ," I began.

"You don't like it, leave!" he said.

I looked at the naval guards. Our chartered airplane stood out on the runway. Naval vehicles were at the gate and all around the plane, and we couldn't even drive our luggage trucks to the plane. I walked back to Leon and the crowd that had gotten off the bus.

"Looks like we have to walk. I'm sorry," I said. "Let's unload the luggage trucks." The cast and crew looked at Leon and me, at the guards, and out at the airplane a half mile away. It was just more typhoon, more mud and rain, more the Dragon Lady blue plate special, more sleeping in dank rooms and eating rain-swept food.

We all did it. We walked back and forth to our plane, past the guards sitting in their vehicles and watching us. We walked and carried all the luggage out to our plane and loaded it.

The charter pilots and Leon were concerned with all the luggage and people we expected to get on the plane. It was an old charter plane straight out of the jungles of Burma or Thailand.

"Got a lot of weight," the pilots said.

"Can you make it?" Leon asked.

"Hope so," was the answer.

Leon and I looked at one another. Now what? "Hope so" was not exactly a major vote of confidence.

We joined everyone inside, and the doors were closed. The two pilots came through the plane, checking on all the baggage and passengers. I looked at them, but when I caught their eye, they gave me no reason for optimism. Finally, they stood outside the cockpit area and looked at all the people and luggage. Leon and I approached them.

"What do you think?" Leon asked.

"Let's give it a try," came the reply.

I exchanged another look with Leon, and we went to our seats as the plane started up its four propellers with engine coughing and blue-white smoke belching from them. That caught the eye of some of our passengers.

Slowly the plane began to move down the runway, trying to get up speed. The engines where whining and smoking, the plane's body was creaking and groaning, and we were all very aware of the sounds.

"Get me to Manila!" someone screamed. That seemed to break the tension, and a lot of us just laughed in our anxiety.

Then the plane slowed down and began to turn back. One of the pilots came out to address us. "We didn't quite get 'er that time. Too much weight in front. Next try, some of you move toward the rear when she gets a goin',' " he said.

Larry Franco was out of his seat and ran to the back of the plane along with Terry, Nat, Josh, and some others. I looked at Leon. "Oh, baby," I thought, "after getting through the typhoon and all we'd been through, please don't let me die on the Subic runway!"

The plane had turned back and started its engines on full. The engines whined and smoked, the body creaked and groaned, and then the plane started down the runway. The crew was cheering as more went back toward the rear of the plane. The plane gained some speed, when suddenly the second pilot stuck his head into the passenger section and screamed, "More to the rear!"

Eight more of us rushed toward the rear of the plane. It was then that I noticed all three of the Playboy Bunnies were on their knees in the aisle praying. One bunny was shouting her prayers!

The plane gained speed, gained some more speed, and with little runway to spare, rose and flew low over Subic. Our passengers cheered and yelled, cried and screamed, and some continued praying. I wondered how long it had been since three Playboy Bunnies prayed together.

Slowly our plane gained altitude, and the second pilot poked his head out. "Was close, but she made 'er!" he shouted back, all smiles. We didn't gain a lot of altitude, but we got enough to get us to Manila. Leon had room arrangements for Larry and me at the Philippine Village Hotel right next to the airport.

Larry and I left Leon at the airport with the promise that we'd see him at the office the next morning, and we got a taxi for the short trip to our hotel. Manila looked so fantastic after the jungle of Baler and the water and mud of Iba and Olongapo. I didn't notice much damage from Typhoon Ruby at the Manila airport or on the ride to the hotel. The air smelled good, smelled like civilization, smelled as if I was going home soon!

We checked into the Philippine Village Hotel and arranged to meet in the hotel bar in a couple of hours. My room was wonderful. I had a huge bed, table and two chairs, dresser, closet, nice bath with a tub and shower. I took a long hot shower and scrubbed the mud and dirt off me; it felt so good. I would be home in less than a week! Maybe three days!

I selected the clothes I would wear that night and changes for the next day, then I called the hotel to wash everything else I had. I'd go home with clean clothes. I felt so good; clean at last, clean at last! I checked the view out my window; I looked out on the whole Manila Airport! Planes were coming and going all the time. In a few days I'd be on one back to Chris and Tim in West Los Angeles! Dad was coming home!

I went down to the hotel bar a bit early, and when I passed through the lobby I saw most of our crew huddled around the travel agents and airline offices. What great times these were. The crew had worked hard in horrible conditions. Now they were free for at least six weeks, and they were making the most of it. Australia and New Zealand were popular locations. Some of the more adventurous were going to India and Katmandu. The Italians were going back to their beloved Roma. Europe and Japan were popular. Those who just wanted to rest picked Bali. They were going to have a great time! Maybe a few years ago I would have been at the travel counter with them, but for me it was to be with my family in West Los Angeles. That's the place I wanted to go.

The whole bar was filled with crew members. Some were departing today! These folks didn't waste any time. Larry entered, and we laughed at the excitement within the crew. Our plan was to see Leon at the office in the morning and fly out that afternoon or early evening.

"Guess what, Jer?" Larry asked all smiles. "There's no McDonald's in Manila!" He laughed and nearly fell out of his chair.

"You'll be at McDonald's in Thousand Oaks in a day. What do you care?" I said, and we laughed at our great good fortune.

The next morning Larry and I met early and took a taxi to the *Apocalypse Now* production office in Makati, where I had met Gray Frederickson on my first day in the Philippines.

The offices were humming with cast and crew trying to get their travel money or airline arrangements. Leon was up to his elbows in calls and anxious crew members wanting to get out of Manila and all wondering if they were on salary during the shutdown and when the movie might start up again. Finally Leon had a break, and he motioned for Larry and me to come in.

"This is a madhouse!" Leon said, but he loved it. "Have you ever seen anything like this!"

"They're busting loose!" Larry said. "Party time!"

"For you! Oh, by the way, Larry, call your grandmother. Seems she has the International Red Cross looking for you!" Leon said, as we all laughed. We were feeling so good.

"Where are you going?" I asked. I knew nothing about Leon's family.

"I'm here maybe a week more. Then L.A., I've got to see family, you know?" he said. "Couple of weeks and I'll be back."

"Larry, got your ticket here. You leave this afternoon!" Leon said.

Larry was crazed. "This afternoon! Wow! Man!" Larry shouted.

"Not only that, kiddo. Francis is keeping you on full salary!" Leon added. "Nice, huh?"

Larry was as happy as I've ever seen a human; he was going home to L.A. and he'd stay on full salary. What a deal! I wondered what was going to happen to me. I looked back and forth between Larry and Leon; they were still enjoying Larry's good fortune. I could wait.

"Jer," Leon began, "Francis wants to talk with you. I'll let you know when. Just stay at the hotel and enjoy yourself. If there's anything, I'll let you know." He saw my face fall. "Hey, don't worry. You'll be outa here in a day or two!" he added.

"Wants to talk?" I asked.

"Yeah. That's all he said," Leon added, "Don't worry. You'll be in L.A. before you know it."

We stuck around the office for a bit, then got a ride back to the hotel. I asked our driver if he knew where I could buy a carton a Marlboro cigarettes; they weren't sold legally in the Philippines. I had been getting them from Allan Levine, our prop man, but he'd gone back to the States. On the way to the hotel, our driver stopped on a side street. Soon a man came to the car and leaned in the window. Our driver looked at me and nodded toward the man. I got the idea and asked to buy a carton of Marlboros. The man quoted the price, and I gave him the cash. In a couple of minutes a young boy brought a paper bag to the car with my carton of cigarettes inside. It was my first experience with the Philippine black market.

When we arrived at the hotel, Larry went up to pack. I looked around the lobby. Almost everyone was gone. Talk about a mad exodus; the entire cast and crew had left for destinations unknown. I wondered what Francis wanted to talk about.

Larry phoned my room and told me that he was going to leave for the airport a bit early. I could see it out my window. I understood that he was eager to be back home. So was I. My time was coming, maybe in a day or two. I met Larry in the lobby and helped him carry his luggage to the taxi. I saw Anjo, the taxi driver who picked me up that first day in Manila. He smiled and I waved. Seemed like a year ago that we first met.

Larry got in his cab, and I told him I'd call him as soon as I got to L.A. He laughed, "Full salary! Oh, man!" I smiled, and he laughed until the taxi pulled out. I stood outside the hotel and watched until his taxi was out of sight. Then I went back inside the hotel and entered the bar. No one was there. I ate in my room that night. Read the Milius script again, and fell asleep late. The next day I called Leon, but he had no word from Francis. He told me he would call as soon as he heard anything. I hung up and watched the planes coming and going from the airport. Soon I would be on one.

The next afternoon about two, I got a call from Leon. He sounded worried. "Jer, we just got a call from a hospital in Sydney. Two of our crew are in the hospital down there. They've lost a lot of weight."

"What's wrong with them?" I asked.

"They don't know," Leon went on. "They called to ask if we knew anything."

"What could it be?" I asked. "Maybe something they ate down there," I suggested.

"Maybe," Leon said, "but I also got a call from a hospital in Tokyo."

"Tokyo!" I said.

"Same thing. They have one of our crew members in the hospital. Dropping weight. They don't know why," Leon said.

My first thought was that maybe the boys had partied a bit too much, but that wouldn't cause them to drop weight. "You want me to come into the office, Leon?" I asked.

"No, don't worry. It's probably nothing," Leon said, and we hung up.

The following morning my hotel room phone rang at seven; it was Leon. "Jer! I got six more calls from hospitals in Hong Kong, Moscow, Los Angeles, and New York City!" Leon was beside himself. "You'd better get over here right away. Francis was checked into Makati Medical Center last evening! His weight's dropping!"

"Why? What's happened? Francis was fine a couple of days ago!" I said.

"Everyone was fine! Now we're getting calls from hospitals all over the world that our crew members are dropping weight, a lot of it and fast, and they don't know why!" Leon was in near panic.

I arrived at the production office, and Leon was very emotionally upset. The calls continued to come in from hospitals everywhere. We didn't know what to tell them. Six members of the Italian crew had dropped an average of twenty-five pounds! The hospital in Rome had been on the phone twice that morning. The hospital in Bali was transferring two of our crew to Singapore on a special plane with an intensive care facility. Los Angeles and New York City were calling nearly every hour. Nancy, our script supervisor, was in serious condition in New York, as was Josh Weiner and Nat Boxer. I looked through Leon's hospital notes, but there was nothing on Larry Franco.

I couldn't imagine what was happening. Then Leon called to me, "Jer, get a car right away. Francis wants to see you. He's in the Makati Medical Center! Someone will be waiting for you." A driver came running, and I followed him outside to his car. In minutes I was entering the medical center, one of the best medical facilities in Southeast Asia.

A man in a doctor's coat met me. He was obviously watching for me and escorted me to the elevator, then up to the top floor. When we got out, I followed him down a corridor that looked as if it might be part of one of the world's best hotels. He came to a door, knocked, and we entered.

The room could have been the Presidential Suite at any hotel in the world. There were beautiful drapes, a living room with carved wood furniture, cabinets with gorgeous china, and then there was the bedroom where Francis lay in one bed with IVs running into his arms. He looked as if he had lost thirty pounds in three days! I had left him in Iba after filming the final day at Medivac, and here he was in the medical center looking so emaciated. Why? What caused all this? Francis had his doctors and a nurse in the room. Ellie, his wife, was resting in the other bed. I had met her briefly in Baler.

Francis, with the IVs sticking out of his arms and his skin hanging from him, asked how I was.

"Francis, I'm fine," I said. "What happened?" I couldn't imagine the change in a human being in only three days.

"I'm going to be fine, Jerry. Have you heard about our crew?" Francis asked. "They're in hospitals all over the world."

"I can't believe it," I said. "What could have happened?" I asked.

He introduced me to the doctors. "I think we might know," Francis said. "Remember when the rain stopped in Iba?"

"Of course," I answered.

"Remember that we pumped the river water into the sprinklers to make rain?" Francis asked again.

"Yes," I said.

"Well, there's a chance that with the typhoon and the flooding, that the river was polluted, very polluted. Probably with every disease in Southeast Asia," Francis continued. "And we rained down the polluted river water on all of our cast and crew."

I was struck dumb. I didn't know what to say or think.

"The medical center is going to be taking all the calls from the hospitals. Everyone is going to be all right, but it's frightening. I lost twenty pounds in like two days!" Francis said.

"Thirty-two hospitals have called either the medical center or your office," one of the doctors volunteered.

"I'm going to go back to California as soon as I can," Francis said, and I could tell Ellie was pleased.

I nodded, "Yeah, I can't believe all this has happened."

"How are you feeling?" Francis asked.

"I'm fine. I'm fine, Francis," I answered. "If it had been the river water, Francis, I was in as much of it as anyone. Maybe more."

"I know. And you're feeling fine," Francis said. "I can't understand it either."

I stood and looked at Francis and then at Ellie. I was about to excuse myself and go back to Leon at the office.

"Jerry, I'm going to go back to the States. I have to," Francis started. "I want you to stay here and watch over the reconstruction and everything."

I felt faint. Did he say he wanted me to stay here? In the Philippines?

"I imagine you wanted to go back to see your family. I really need you to stay here."

"Stay here?" I asked, as I fought for breath.

"Dean tells me six to eight weeks of construction and we'll be filming again," Francis said.

"Six to eight weeks?" I stammered. "I thought I'd be here only six weeks."

"Jer, figure construction, six to eight. Then at the very most eight to ten weeks of filming after that and we'll be through. Maybe the end of October, who can tell?" Francis added.

"No one could have foreseen this," Ellie said.

"I know, but . . . the end of October." I tried to regain my strength.

"Maybe your family could come and visit you here? Gray tells me you get round-trip airline tickets," Francis suggested. Ellie stared at me.

"Right, I do," I said.

"I need you to stay," Francis said. "I have to have someone here all the time. There's too much going on. The sets, the PBRs, the housing, the caterer!"

"Could your family visit you?" Ellie asked.

"Yes, I think so," I said. I could only realize that I was going to be here until at least October! Maybe longer.

It turned out to be a lot longer. Nearly fifty percent of our crew would never make it back to the Philippines because of weight loss and exhaustion. Francis and I couldn't have guessed then how long the filming would eventually last. Those of us that stayed on to complete Apocalypse Now *undertook a journey that challenged our very essence as filmmakers. As the weeks and months went by, we fought collective wars against the elements of filming in a jungle in Southeast Asia and personal wars against our individual demons of loneliness, fatigue, and depression.*

"You'll stay?" Francis asked.

"OK. Sure. I'll stay," I said, but I felt lost. Somehow I left their medical suite and got back to the Philippine Village Hotel and up to my room.

I spent the next few hours watching the planes taking off from the Manila airport. My immediate problem was not with Francis, or *Apocalypse Now*, or typhoons and mud, but with my two boys. Chris and Tim were nearly out of school for the summer, and it looked as if I wouldn't be back home until they were back in school again. I tried to remember what I did during my summer vacation when I was six years old. My mom and dad had taken me camping up at the Twin Bridges Camp Ground outside Crivitz, Wisconsin. I fished from the bank or with my dad in our row boat. During the afternoons when the fish didn't bite, I pitched to my dad or we just played catch. Tim was only two and a half, but that's about when my dad began to teach me how to fish and catch a baseball. I spent the next few hours making travel arrangements for my wife, Chris, and Tim to come to Manila.

The next day I met Dick White at the airport. He had the Jet Ranger ready for us to fly over our locations to get some idea of the destruction from Typhoon Ruby. We took off and headed southeast from Manila toward Pagsanjan. I sat next to Dick as he brought the helicopter around and headed us out. There were two tall brick smokestacks to the southeast of the airport. When I first noticed them they seemed to be no more than a couple of yards apart. Dick continued to fly directly at them. The closer we flew, the more certain I became that the chopper could not fit between those smokestacks. It was obvious Dick intended to fly between them. When we finally reached the stacks, I screamed and ducked away from the side of the helicopter as we just fit between them. Dick White thought it was a fun game, and he did it to me every time we flew south out of Manila.

All of our sets along the South China Sea had been demolished during Typhoon Ruby. The Playboy Bunny Show set was just twisted metal and broken wood. Our two PBRs were junk even before the typhoon got to them. Pete Cooper was assigned to go to Thailand and get the two best PBRs he could find. We decided to rebuild all sets in the area around the town of Pagsanjan, where we were constructing a Cambodian temple complex as the set for Col. Kurtz's compound. Pagsanjan was a small town near Santa Cruz, about two hours southeast of Manila by car. It was a small resort town known for a boat trip that tourists could take from the Rapids Hotel up the Pagsanjan River to a series of beautiful rapids. Our production strategy was to move the entire cast and crew to Pagsanjan, get them settled in the best housing, and shoot all of the rest of *Apocalypse Now* without ever having to re-locate them again.

The insurance policy paid for nearly all the costs to rebuild our sets, get new PBRs, and relocate the film company, so in a lot of ways Ty-phoon Ruby saved Francis and *Apocalypse Now*.

David Salven, a second Hollywood production manager, was brought to Manila to help Leon Chooluck and to modernize the com-pany's housing and living conditions for the rest of the film. We took over the Rapids Hotel and the Tropical Hotel in Pagsanjan. Dave ren-ovated all the rooms with air-conditioning and water purifiers. A new caterer was hired from Hong Kong, and a complete modern catering kitchen and food refrigeration storage system was installed at the Tropical Hotel. In addition, more than sixty private homes were leased by the company and renovated with air-conditioning, window screen-ing, and a pure water system.

Each morning I would take a taxi from my hotel near the airport, along the main thoroughfare all the way into the *Apocalypse Now* office.

One morning I noticed that masses of civilians and soldiers were painting and repairing all the homes and businesses along the main route
from the airport into the center of Manila. All week long the painting
continued, with hundreds of workers.

I saw Anjo when I walked out the front of the hotel the next
morning. I signaled to him and got in his taxi even though he wasn't the
next cab in line. The painting was bothering me.

When he turned onto the main route into the center of Manila, I
pointed out to him that the businesses and homes were all being
painted.

"Anjo, what's happening?" I asked. "Look at all the painting!"

"Yes, very nice," he said, and then laughed as he jostled his taxi for
better and better position on the crowded road.

"Why? What's happening? Why paint everything at once?" I asked.

Anjo was enjoying my questions. He laughed and looked at me in
the rearview mirror. Finally he missed a stoplight, and we came to a
stop.

I didn't understand what was so funny to Anjo.

Instead of continuing straight ahead, Anjo made a sharp left turn
and then another left turn, and we were heading back toward my hotel,
but traveling on a side street.

"Don't worry. You won't be late," he said. "I want to show you
something."

He pulled his taxi to the side, and we both walked back to the main
thoroughfare.

"See?" Anjo said, as he pointed at the buildings fronting the main
route. "The World Bank Conference is coming to Manila in a week,"
he said. "President Marcos wants to show that our country is pros-
perous, so he is painting the homes and businesses along the route the
ministers will be taking from the airport to the center of Manila." Anjo
looked at me again and laughed. "Do you see?"

I saw that the buildings were all repaired and freshly painted in
bright colors, but only the fronts were painted, only what you could see
from a passing car. The sides and back were left unpainted and unre-
paired.

We got back in his taxi and rode the rest of the way to the office in
silence. I was trying to understand, and Anjo wasn't laughing anymore.

When my family arrived in Manila, we played baseball and swam in
the pool at the Philippine Village Hotel. At night the boys would chase

the hundreds of small frogs that inhabited the gardens around the hotel's pool. It's amazing that after having been away from each other for months, we were instantly back together again as though we had never been apart. Children are like that. Adults aren't; I had already learned that.

After a week in Manila, we moved to the Rapids Hotel in Pagsanjan and settled in for the remainder of their stay. The hotel was built with white plaster walls and dark tiled floors. The doors and beams were all rough-hewn native woods. The gardens were filled with lush tropical plants and palm and coconut trees. The dining room was built around a courtyard that contained a large swimming pool.

Francis and Elly and their three children, Gio, Roman, and Sofia, returned from California and lived in a leased home in Pagsanjan. They would all come over on Sundays to use the Rapids Hotel's pool and stay for the Filipino folk dancing presented by the Pagsanjan Women's Club every Sunday afternoon. Francis and Elly joined in cheering as Sofia, Chris, and Tim danced the Filipino rod dance. The kids would jump in rhythm to the music, avoiding two six-foot-long rods that two adults moved to the music. Seeing Francis as just another laughing parent enjoying his children somehow made me feel so good. Maybe we weren't so different after all.

Tim was still in diapers, and I was running low on his Pampers. They couldn't be bought in the Philippines, not even on the black market. I called Larry Franco in Los Angeles and had him bring two cases of Pampers with him when he flew back to Manila. He got the Pampers through Filipino customs by declaring that the diapers were camera lens cleaners.

Chris and Tim adapted surprisingly well to Pagsanjan. The boys lived on grilled cheese sandwiches and fried banana chips at the Rapids Hotel. They would search the halls hunting for geckos, Philippine lizards. We played baseball in the hotel garden bordering the Pagsanjan River. Our companion was a monkey chained to a cage hung from a tree. He would shriek and run on his chain as my boys got excited with our ball game. After dinner they would take bits of banana and grapes out to him, and he would eat out of their hands. We fished off the hotel's balcony; didn't catch much, but had lots of fun. I didn't remember catching much at the Twin Bridges Camp Ground either.

"Jerry!" Dick White shouted to me as he crossed the hotel parking lot in Pagsanjan on a beautiful Sunday morning. We still had about two weeks of preproduction left after the typhoon before we would start shooting again.

"Hey, Dick!" I said.

"You and Chris want to go for a little ride this morning? I'm taking Eva Gardos up to the Banaue Rice Terraces, then coming back. She's going up to talk with the Ifugaos. Should be back by 3 P.M. easy."

Tim and my wife were visiting with a family for the day, so it was only Chris and me. I knew Chris, my six-year-old, would love the helicopter trip.

"Yeah, great, Dick. I'll get Chris," I said, and went into the hotel.

About ten minutes later Chris and I joined Dick and Eva in the chopper, and we took off from the side of the Rapids Hotel and headed north. The view was fantastic! Dick took us over the Kurtz compound set, and then turned north for the Ifugaos' land.

Chris was excited and having a wonderful time. It was really a great way for Chris and me to spend a Sunday. We'd have some time together without Tim and get to see a bit of the Philippines. Just Chris and his Pops.

Dick took us north along the Pacific coast and then headed inland to avoid Manila. As we flew on, the clouds began to build up in the north, but we weren't going to be staying that long.

The Banaue Rice Terraces have been dug out of the sides of the mountains over hundreds of years. They're an engineering marvel, and I'm sure they're one of the eight wonders of the world. There was a large parking lot and store on a plateau about halfway up the mountain, and Dick set the chopper down.

Eva got out, took her bag, and set out on foot to trek up the mountain and make contact with the Ifugaos. She would stay with them and arrange transportation to bring them down to Pagsanjan to be the natives in the Kurtz compound. Eva was one brave young woman. Years later she became a film editor on many films, including *Mask*, *Barfly*, and *Things To Do in Denver When You're Dead*.

Dick, Chris, and I got a bite to eat at the store, but with the storm clouds moving in, Dick thought it best that we get back up as soon as possible. When we got back into the chopper, Chris snuggled next to me against the chill, and with the rhythm of the ship, he soon fell asleep.

The storm clouds were gathering, so Dick decided to take a shortcut and fly over a mountain ridge and drop down into Baguio instead of going around. He looked for the lowest spot in the mountain range and headed for it. He would skim the sides of the mountain all the way to the top, then just drop the chopper over to the other side. As we reached the top of the mountain, there was a small building there with a tall radio antenna. As Dick brought the helicopter over the rise and up toward the house, the chopper was thrown by the crosswinds toward the antenna and its guide cables. Dick's attention was on avoiding the cables, and he didn't see the front of the house.

As Dick maneuvered and turned the ship to avoid the cables, out of the house came eight armed militia with automatic weapons pointed up at our helicopter! I hung on to Chris and waited for their fire, but Dick was shifting and maneuvering the chopper to miss the cables, and his action froze the soldiers until Dick brought the ship over the top of the house and down the far side of the mountain. Dick never saw the soldiers, and because of his maneuvers, they never fired. Chris slept through the whole thing. I was very thankful. The storm clouds were buffeting the chopper, but Dick was holding it against the side winds and getting us along.

Fighting against the wind and storm had used more fuel than Dick had anticipated. He was following a small highway, hoping to reach a remote military airfield to refuel. Chris had awakened and was enjoying the flight. Suddenly every light on the interior of the helicopter started to blink and flash! Dick got real excited and the chopper started to rotate. We had run out of fuel, and we were headed down!

"Nothing to worry about!" Dick shouted, as the chopper turned and began to descend. I grabbed Chris and hung on. Dick landed the rotating helicopter on the small highway about fifty yards from an automobile gas station.

We got out of the chopper. Chris was amazingly calm. Dick was the total leader. I was the crazed parent.

"Jerry, Chris, get on the other side, and we'll push her to that gas station," Dick said. "Don't worry about a thing."

There I was with my six-year-old son somewhere in northern Luzon pushing a helicopter down a highway.

"Dick, did anything like this happen to you in Vietnam?" I asked, as I pushed the chopper.

"All the time. It's nothing. Keep her on the road, Jer." he said.

By the time we got to the gas station, the owner, his wife, and their two young children were outside and waiting for us. Chris assumed that attitude of many six-year-olds: Doesn't everyone push helicopters to gas stations?

Dick and the station owner talked, and they filled the helicopter with automobile gas.

"Dick, is this going to work?" I asked. "That gasoline is for cars!"

"Works, don't worry," he said. "Works every time."

I remembered Pete Cooper's putting helicopter fuel into the diesel tank of the PBR in Baler. I wished I had a couple five-gallon tanks of that helicopter fuel now.

"Used to do this a lot in 'Nam!" Dick exclaimed. "Always running out!"

Dick paid for the gas, got some directions, and the whole family helped push our chopper onto the highway. They all stood far back as we got back into the helicopter and Dick started the engine. The lights were still on, but not blinking and flashing as violently. After warming it up, Dick got the chopper up and moved us down the highway at a height of about a six-story building as he looked for the military airfield.

After about ten miles Dick wasn't sure where we were, so he gestured that he was going to put down and get directions. He landed on the highway alongside some workers in their rice paddies. The farmers helped with directions, the same as if we had been a motorist seeking help.

"Dick, did this ever happen in Vietnam?" I asked. "Putting down to ask directions?"

"Hell, yes it did! Lotsa times!" Dick answered. "Always got confused."

We thanked the farmers, got back into the chopper and made our way toward the airfield.

A strange helicopter was not very welcome at the military airfield, and Dick had to do a lot of explaining before they'd consider giving us fuel to get back to Pagsanjan. After Dick had told all his best Vietnam stories to the militia and after we had gotten our fuel, we thanked them and were on our way.

I wanted to call the production office to let them know we'd be a little late and to check on Tim, but there weren't any phones at the airfield.

"Jer, don't worry. There's an empty lot next to my house in Baguio. I'll drop down there, and we can use my phone," Dick said.

That's what we did. Right in the middle of the city of Baguio, Dick landed the chopper on a vacant lot. He got out of the helicopter as though it were a Ford station wagon, and we walked to his home. Chris played around our helicopter with the children in Dick's neighborhood. I phoned my wife and Tim and had Larry Franco make sure no one else was worried about us. We'd be back soon. It had just been another day on *Apocalypse Now*, and a Sunday at that.

• • •

My wife and I knew the love between us had gone years ago. We were there for the children and little else. When she and the boys got on the plane to return to the States, the loneliness and depression within every filmmaker took hold of me. In Wisconsin families stayed together. Fathers didn't go to the Philippines for months of filming in a jungle. That only happened in a war, a real war. The line way down at the bottom of the page was simply, I didn't have to be in the Philippines making *Apocalypse Now*, but I chose to do it. And my family chose to live in West Los Angeles.

As the years passed, Chris, Tim, and I continued to share the memories of the Pagsanjan monkey, our baseball games, and the frogs at the Philippine Village Hotel during our summer of *Apocalypse Now*. We each learned to cherish our times together and to let our separations be the price we each paid for my decision to spend my life making motion pictures. We never pretended that we could make up for the lost time.

Many of our original crew members didn't make it back when we resumed shooting *Apocalypse Now* after the typhoon. Nancy, our script supervisor who saw her shooting script disintegrate in the rain on the Medivac set, and Josh Weiner, our stillman who ran into the river with a camera platform to get us out of Baler, stayed in New York. For them the illnesses, the demands of the jungle, the stamina needed to endure the stifling heat and heavy humidity were all too much. Ray Quiroz replaced Nancy as our script supervisor. The Italian camera, grip, and electric crews all came back, but we had a new prop department headed by Doug Madison and Tommy Shaw, Jr.

The Saigon Hotel Room Scene

After our crew reassembled, we began our post-typhoon filming in the Saigon Hotel Room set where Willard was waiting for his next assignment. The city of Santa Cruz, about twenty miles northwest of Pagsanjan, was chosen to be our Saigon 1968 location. The camera was up in the second floor of the hotel, looking down through venetian blinds onto the town square. The building was really not a hotel at all, but a Santa Cruz government office building. It was the view out of the window and the room's ceiling fan that got it selected as Willard's

Saigon hotel room. Larry Franco and I had the streets filled with extras and vehicles. The art department had placed a Holiday Inn marquee in the back of one truck. We had fifty extras on bicycles, a hundred U.S. servicemen, and two hundred Vietnamese. We were ready. Larry stayed on the street, while I was at the camera in the hotel room.

It was horribly hot and humid on the set. There was no air-conditioning, little ventilation, and no relief from the heavy weight you feel by just being in the tropics. Most of us were standing in the set or hallway waiting for the lighting crew to finish. Vittorio was taking a long time to get the set lit to his satisfaction. It was the first interior shooting we had done, and Vittorio wanted it to be perfect.

The hotel room was decorated with a large bed, a dresser, and a self-standing full-length mirror. There was a bathroom opposite the windows. A large ceiling fan circulated, throwing slowly moving shadows over the room. Originally the scene was to have had a young Vietnamese girl in the bed, and we did film much of the morning with her, but in the afternoon we used only Marty.

The afternoon shots were designed to allow Marty freedom to move around the set. Francis had planned for a lot of improvisation during the scene. Marty was free to go anywhere within the set. There wasn't a safe place for any of us to stand that wouldn't be in the camera's view. Francis was sitting up on top of a cabinet looking down on all of us. I tried to stay behind Enrico and the camera.

I don't think anyone actually knew what was going to happen in the scene. Francis wanted to see Willard come out of Marty, for Marty to reveal the assassin inside himself. It was all vague, and a bit mysterious to me, but it was my job to help Francis get the piece of film he needed, so there I was, a sweating body on the second floor in Santa Cruz. I had a walkie-talkie to Larry to cue the extras when we began filming. I thought I was ready for anything, but I wasn't.

I don't know if it was because it was Marty's birthday or because of the introspective nature of the scene, but Marty began to drink red wine. Francis warned me that he had encouraged Marty to have the wine. It had been my experience that alcohol, actors, and trying to film a movie never seemed to work well together.

We rolled take after take, but the scene was uncharted water. I didn't know what to look for. I'm not sure Francis knew what he wanted. What would Marty do? No one knew. Was there a Willard to come out of Martin Sheen, the altar boy of Hollywood?

Late in the afternoon, the intensity of Marty's work as an actor, plus the wine, plus the searching probes from Francis began to bring elements of Marty Sheen to the foreground that had never been revealed.

Francis was throwing suggestions to Marty during the scene, trying to get Marty to release whatever was inside him. He talked to Marty about Willard's background of murder and terror, about the dark feeling we all harbor, about our repression of those feelings and what would happen if the dark feelings came out. I'd never seen a director work as intensely as Francis did with Marty; I felt as if Francis was pulling Marty inside out.

Marty began groaning, then sobbing. At times he intoned sounds as though it were part of a primal chant, then suddenly a single tone erupted from deep inside of him like a warning note or distress signal. He threatened and cursed Francis; his eyes became filled with hate. Then he became a child, whimpering and sobbing, and suddenly he was a primping, vain prima donna. He seemed to be doing a ballet, and then a karate move, and a ballet move again. We rolled the cameras as continuously as we could. Vittorio, Enrico and the whole crew sensed we were filming something unique that afternoon. Marty seemed to be going through self-revealing levels of a barbaric nature deep within himself. I watched as Francis continued to spew motivation and subtext to Marty, taking him through the suggestions of murder, of torture, of rank barbarism.

At the beginning of one take, Marty stumbled toward the full-length mirror in the set. He recovered, but he had mistaken his opening position, and when he did his karate move toward the mirror he hit it. The mirror shattered and Marty was cut. Francis leaped forward, and we were all ready to cut the camera, when Marty screamed and continued with the scene. He wiped his face with his bleeding hand. The blood stained his face. He looked at his image in the broken mirror. Then he stared at his own bloody hand and a deep primal tone came out of him. As he wiped his face with his own blood again, he began to move to some internal rhythm, and we saw the vain assassin of men begin to emerge from deep within Marty. He appeared to be beyond himself, as though in a spell, perhaps in shock, maybe caused by the alcohol and exhaustion, or perhaps by seeing his own blood. Marty posed and postured, then ritually attacked toward the camera. He moved, and it was as if we were watching a barbaric cult dance of a most lethal warrior. Marty's inner assassin was captured on film.

I watched Francis and the crew as Marty's experience unfolded before us. Francis watched in wide-eyed wonder, as did most of us.

Vittorio worked with Enrico and the camera crew, moving the dolly, suggesting pans, and shading the light. The Italian crew was transfixed by Marty's behavior. It was as though they were watching an event in nature, like an erupting volcano. I was terrified for Marty. That the dark being we'd seen coexisted deep within the gentle Martin Sheen, shocked me. I felt at fault for what had occurred. When I saw Marty cut himself on the mirror, should I have stopped the scene? Should we have pushed and prodded Marty to the extent we did for a performance in a motion picture? The wine, the exhaustion, the probes, was it all necessary? Did the end justify the means?

Days later I approached Marty about what he felt and what he remembered from filming the Saigon Hotel scene and told him how guilty I felt about it all. He just laughed at me and said that he remembered everything, absolutely everything. That every moment was pure acting and nothing else. There was no spell, no period of shock, nothing but an actor doing his craft.

Maybe and maybe not. I don't know. I do know *Apocalypse Now* found its assassin in that Saigon hotel room.

Our production offices at the Rapids Hotel were across the parking lot from the hotel's entrance. Leon Chooluck's and Dave Salven's offices were in front, and then the accountants came next. Way in the back was a small office for Fred Roos, the longtime casting director for Francis and one of his producers. Fred Roos was always impeccably dressed in fashionable casual attire. He looked like a country club member lost in the jungles of the Philippines.

One afternoon about the time we were to film the Saigon Hotel set, Fred saw me in the hotel's parking lot and asked if he could have a word with me in his office. I thought he wanted to know when the actors for the Do Lung Bridge set needed to be in Pagsanjan, so I followed him up to his office. He settled into his desk chair and motioned for me to have a seat. I did, and he just looked at me. I thought I should wait for him to speak first, so I waited him out.

"Jerry, you've done some acting, haven't you?" Fred asked, still looking at me.

"A little, why?" I asked. I wasn't proud of my acting, but I had done a few television shows between the time I got out of Northwestern University in 1961 and the time I got into the Directors Guild Training Program in 1967.

"Turn to the Briefing scene, please," Fred said, as he handed me a script. I paged through the beginning of the script. There was the Opening, then the Saigon Hotel, then . . . the Briefing scene. "Got it," I said.

"I'll read the General and the Colonel, you read the Civilian," Fred said.

I remembered the Briefing scene. I felt it would never be in the movie. All of that dialogue could be covered with voice-over as we saw the PBR go up the Nung River. It's the beginning of the movie! No one was going to want to have a scene in some kind of room when you could show the PBR going up the Nung River with miles of jungle around it!

"The General, the Colonel, and the Civilian are in an office in Nha Trang. The Civilian could be CIA or maybe from the Pentagon, or even the White House. A helicopter brings Willard from Saigon and he enters. OK?" Fred Roos was totally professional. He carefully set the scene for my audition.

I nodded that I understood. I liked Fred. I was sorry I threw the rock that splattered him with mud at the Medivac set, but it was the luck of the splash. I actually was trying for Gray Frederickson. No one knew who threw it, and I didn't think this was the time to confess or apologize.

Fred read the other actors' lines, and when it was my cue, I said my one line, "Terminate with extreme prejudice." That was it. No big deal. I felt the scene wouldn't be in the movie anyway.

"Good, Jerry." Fred said. "Would you mind doing the part of the Civilian for us?"

It had been fun so far, talking and reading with Fred Roos, but I was an assistant director. I hadn't acted since I did a one-line bit on *Gomer Pyle*, the old Jim Nabors series, and that was ten years ago.

"Fred, I'm the AD," I said.

"Couldn't Larry take over just for those two days?" Fred asked. "All the shooting is inside an office, a house trailer, at the Tropical Hotel." Fred raised his arms slightly from the top of his desk, tilted his head to one side, and mimed "OK" with his face and eyes.

Fred Roos was one of the nicest people on *Apocalypse Now*, plus I had splattered him with mud, even if it was a bit by accident.

"Sure, I'll be happy to," I said. "Larry'll do great."

The Briefing Scene

The set for the Briefing scene was a house trailer that was parked at the Tropical Hotel in Pagsanjan. We only did the interior part of the scene there. The exterior portion, where Martin Sheen walked up to and entered the house trailer, was done later.

As soon as the crew realized that I was an actor that day and not their assistant director, they began their teasing and taunting. Vittorio could not quite grasp the concept that yesterday I was the assistant director and today I was an actor.

Larry was doing fine as the assistant director. There were only four of us in the scene: Martin Sheen, G. D. Spradlin, who was playing the General, and then the young actor playing the Colonel, and me. I had never seen the young actor before, but I did recognize G. D. Spradlin from a lot of movies. The young actor stayed to himself and was very quiet; he seemed very tense, probably scared out of his mind to be working on a big movie.

All four of us were in the set, just standing around while Francis talked with Vittorio. I thought I should say something to the young actor, maybe make him feel more comfortable.

"Hey, how ya doing?" I said, as calmly as I could. I was a bit nervous that morning, even though I only had one line of dialogue.

"Good. You?" the young actor asked.

He was uptight. I thought they must have gotten him from Manila or maybe from the military base. Fred Roos probably wanted to save transportation money and had hired a local. Like Fred did with me. I didn't cost them a round-trip ticket or a hotel room; I was already here and in the hotel. Probably was something similar with the young actor. I thought I'd introduce myself; get him to talk, loosen him up.

"I'm Jerry Ziesmer. I'm usually the assistant director, but today they stuck me in the scene," I volunteered.

He smiled and then coughed. "I just came in yesterday."

"Where from?" I asked. I was just trying to lighten him up.

"I've been filming in England and North Africa," he mentioned calmly, and cleared his throat.

Well, at least he's an actor, I thought. "What have you done?" I asked.

"Star Wars," he said.

"Didn't see it," I said.

"Be out next year," he added, and coughed.

I had never heard of it, but it didn't sound very interesting. "Oh, yeah? Anyone in it? Who's directing it?" I asked.

"George Lucas," he answered. "Did *American Graffiti?*"

"Yeah, I liked that," I said. "That was great. You got a good part in *Star Wars?*" I asked.

"It's OK, you know," and he cleared his throat again. "Oh," he said, and he stuck out his hand and introduced himself. I shook his hand. I had never heard of him. I made a note to watch for *Star Wars* because I thought George Lucas was an up-and-coming director. I forgot what the young actor said his name was; it'd be on our call sheet. There were so many actors in *Apocalypse Now* that I couldn't remember them all.

Francis and Vittorio kept talking about the lighting or something. Larry was right there listening to them and glancing at me once in a while and pointing at me and smiling his ear-to-ear smile. I couldn't believe that the company had flown the General and the Colonel in to Manila and put them up in hotels all for this nothing scene.

I walked over to the bar area of the set and looked over the props. Doug Madison, our new prop man, had put out some postcards and pens on the bar, so I started to write a couple of postcards to Tim and Chris.

"That's what I want!" Francis shouted and it brought me back from my writing. "That's it, Jerry. You've made a nest over at the bar, writing. Good!" Francis went on talking to the actors. Francis thought I was acting or something, but I was just writing to my boys. OK, I could handle that.

Francis rehearsed and blocked the scene. Marty came in the door. The General and Colonel greeted him. The General called me over to the table to eat. We sat down. The young actor, forgot his name, started talking. G. D. Spradlin called me "Jerry" in the scene. Here I was with a one-line bit, and the actor used my real name for my character's name in the scene. I thought Larry Franco was going to die trying to hold back his laughter.

Marty was real nice to me. He did everything he could to help me. I just didn't want to embarrass myself. G. D. Spradlin was good, but that young actor kept coughing or clearing his throat or something. I hoped he didn't do that when we got to the filming. Maybe Francis would say something to him. It seemed like such a simple scene that I thought we might easily finish in one day instead of two. It was such a nothing scene that I hated to waste film production time on something that I was positive would be cut out of the movie. Why waste time filming something you'll never use?

After Francis was happy with the rehearsal, the actors got out of the set and Vittorio and his crew went to work. Larry had to tell me that I looked great, and Marty came over and said I was good. Now I *was* scared. I almost asked Marty to have a talk with the young actor, but I decided to let Francis deal with him. Thousands of actors in Hollywood, and Fred Roos hired one who coughed and cleared his throat all the time as if he had consumption. I hoped this guy had a trade he could fall back on.

As he did with every interior lighting job, Vittorio took forever. I had watched our dailies, the film from the previous day, and his lighting of the Saigon Hotel scene was fantastic. Maybe Vittorio took a long time, but you could use every frame in your movie and be proud of it.

Finally, just before lunch, Vittorio had the first shot lit for the Briefing scene. Larry got all the actors and Francis into the set, and I came along. The temperature inside the house trailer was in the high nineties. When Francis called "Action!" Marty came in the door and the General and the Colonel met him, said a few things, and moved toward the dining table. G. D. Spradlin called, "Jerry," and I got up from the bar and came over. I liked that G. D. was using my real name; I only wished Larry would stop laughing whenever G. D. said it.

I hadn't noticed Francis saying anything to what's-his-name, the Colonel. He was going to have lines in the next setup, and he hadn't stopped the damn clearing of his throat. I thought during the rehearsals that it was just a nervous inexperienced actor, but now I thought he was going to do that in the scene. Maybe I should mention something to Francis? He was pretty busy with Vittorio and all, maybe he hadn't noticed. Francis just let the young actor go and cough and clear his throat during the scene, even on his own close-up. I guessed that Francis knew he wouldn't use that part in the movie.

The next day the filming began with all of us around the dining table and the Colonel standing and telling about Kurtz in Cambodia. I couldn't miss the cue for my line; everyone turned toward me, I looked at them, and then said it. Once in a while I wasn't paying attention, so when there was a pause I would look up from my eating and if everyone was looking at me, I'd say my line as I offered Marty a cigarette.

I realized about halfway through the filming of the scene that I was wearing the wristwatch that Allan Levine, the pre-typhoon prop man, had given me when my leather watch band had disintegrated. I was afraid that someone would recognize the watch and Allan might get in trouble for having given it to me. No one seemed to notice it, so I just left the watch on.

I knew the camera was on me during the long dolly move. Francis and Vittorio were whispering, and then going for take after take. I felt

I must be doing something wrong. Marty must have sensed that I was getting a bit uptight.

"You're doing great, Jer. Getting tired of the beef?" he said.

I was eating on every take for the last two days. "It's OK," I answered.

"You think it's OK?" I asked. "The scene I mean?"

"It's fine. Don't worry," and Marty laughed. He was great, but I wasn't sure he was telling me the truth. I went up to Francis when he was alone.

"Francis? Everything OK?" I asked.

"Yeah, great," he said, "don't change a thing," and then scurried off like he was afraid to talk with me.

I went back to the bar and sat down. I was using H. R. Haldeman, the former Nixon aide, for my life model for the character of the Civilian. I started to think of all that had happened with the whole Nixon thing and what the talks with Nixon and Haldeman must have been like.

"Jerry!" Francis called. I was caught not paying attention, and all the others were already in the set. I got over into my chair, and we continued to film.

Vittorio and Enrico got into one of their friendly battles, and Vittorio was now behind the camera for a few shots. It seemed as if they were doing the close shots on me for hours! One line, and I must have said it a hundred times. "Terminate with extreme prejudice." "Terminate with extreme prejudice." "Terminate with extreme prejudice." I hoped I'd never hear that line again.

Francis and Vittorio were finally both happy with the scene, and Larry called a wrap. I was glad to be finished as an actor and to be back to the real world of being an assistant director. Everyone was saying something to G. D. Spradlin and the young actor. So I checked the call sheet for his name and said, "Hey, Harry!" He didn't respond, so I shouted louder, "Harry! Harrison Ford! See you around!"

Every Saturday we tried to wrap around 5:00 P.M. The cast and crew were so excited because each Saturday following shooting the company provided vans and buses to take us into Manila. We hurried to our hotel rooms in Pagsanjan, showered, then packed a change of clothes and ran out to the hotel parking area to get in one of the first vehicles for the weekend trip. You wanted to get into the first bus so you would be sure and get to Manila for dinner. The buses would drop you at one of the three main hotels in Manila on Saturday night and then pick you up Sunday afternoon at about 5:00 for the drive back to Pagsanjan.

The Manila weekends were like going to heaven for twenty pleasure-filled hours. Most of us would choose the same hotel and have the production office make reservations for us about four days ahead. I liked staying at the Philippine Village Hotel because I was familiar with it, and it had large comfortable rooms, two wonderful restaurants, a friendly bar, and a great swimming pool with cocktail service on Sunday afternoon.

The bus ride would begin with shouts and singing like everyone was going to camp, but about a half hour out, most of us would be dozing off. When the bus stopped at the first of the three hotels, we were all up and energized again. Manila, here we come!

Dinner plans—who, where, when—were made on the bus. As soon as I got to the Philippine Village Hotel, I went right up to my room, to turn up the air-conditioning as cold as it could go. I freshened up as quickly as I could, and then took the elevator down to the bar to wait for everyone who was going to the Japanese restaurant or the dining room right in the hotel.

Larry Franco and three or four of us would hold court in the bar, throwing down San Miguels and reliving the week's filming. The bar's musicians were always great. The Philippines exports musicians all around the Pacific Basin and Southeast Asia. Larry enjoyed their rock and roll and talking with them after their set.

As soon as enough of us were in attendance, we moved to the dining room and began the order of steaks rare or medium, something like baked potatoes with sour cream and chives, mushrooms, green vegetables, and desserts. The dining room was set with beautiful china, crystal, and silverware. They had real tablecloths and linen napkins. The waiters were dressed in evening wear. Oh, it felt so good! There was ice in the water glasses, and I actually saw a sidewalk outside the hotel, something that doesn't exist around Pagsanjan.

The room was so wonderfully cold when I got up to it. It smelled crisp and clean. I fell asleep in a big comfortable hotel bed with a firm mattress. I hadn't seen a gecko. This was civilization. In the morning I called Tim and Chris long distance, and we actually talked and could hear each other. They hadn't been gone long, but I missed them so.

I got down to the Sunday brunch and stuffed myself on real shrimp, crab, actual lobster, pears, strawberries, plums, real butter, soft scrambled eggs, pork sausages, biscuits, strawberry jelly, bacon, ham, rye bread, and all the other things we didn't get during the week. When I could hardly move, I slowly made my way back to my room.

I tried to relax and read an actual newspaper that told of world events, sports, the arts, and even a bit of politics. I began to feel human. At about 2:00 I got into my swimming suit and headed down to the hotel pool.

The waiter from the dining room last night saw me and brought a San Miguel and a bowl of garlic peanuts. I thanked him and laid out in the sun on a chaise lounge. How far was I from Pagsanjan? A long way. I heard Larry's laughter, and then he dove into the pool. Soon the others with him were in the pool, too. My moment of reflection was gone, and I was swimming and yelling with the rest of them.

About 4:30 the last of us left the pool and got back to our rooms for a final shower with dependable hot water. I packed my bag, checked the room, looked out at the view of all the planes leaving Manila, then took the elevator down to the lobby.

The bus was there, and some tumbled aboard bragging of this dinner or that salad. The weekend's purchases were shown and admired. While others cradled their purchases of Thai sticks, opium, and every drug in Southeast Asia, I thought that if the bus had ever crashed and burned, that whole section of the Philippines would have been stoned for a week.

On some bus rides back to Pagsanjan, the cast and crew druggies were stacked in the seats like so much limp luggage. It was a miracle to me that they would be on the set and ready to work in a little more than twelve hours.

Some of the younger guys hooted and laughed at their conquests as they waved nylon bras and panties taken during their weekend revelries at the illegal clubs and special private parties given for the cast and crew of *Apocalypse Now*.

Far back in the bus was a quiet man in his late sixties, looking totally out of place. He sat alone and held his jacket about him, concealing all that he wore underneath. Every weekend he rode to Manila and back; he always looked the same and never spoke. The rest of the crew guessed about him, but I didn't want to know.

Everyone relaxed and dozed off for the trip back into *Apocalypse Now*.

Village I Scene

I felt the purpose of the Village I scene was to establish the incongruities in the U.S. military action during the Vietnam War and to introduce

Lieutenant Colonel Kilgore. In our story, after the Briefing scene, Willard met the crew on the PBR, and they set out to rendezvous with the First Air Cavalry Squadron of the Ninth Air Mobile Unit, commanded by Lieutenant Colonel Kilgore, portrayed by Robert Duvall.

The Village I set was located on Lake Caliraya, a large lake and river complex about twelve miles outside Pagsanjan. We used various areas of the Lake Caliraya waterways for our river locations. The rebuilt Playboy Bunny Show and the French Plantation sets were located in the Lake Caliraya area. The Do Lung Bridge and Colonel Kurtz's Compound were our only sets on the Pagsanjan River.

For an assistant director, Village I was as demanding as the Village II scene on the beach in Baler. We had Hueys, ships and boats of all kinds, our new PBR, hundreds of Vietnamese extras and soldiers, and the fires and explosions of an attack by Lieutenant Colonel Kilgore and his airborne unit.

I was happy to have Robert Duvall back, but we had three new actors working in Village I as a TV news team: Francis, Vittorio, and Dean Tavoularis. Vittorio played the role of a news cameraman. Dean was the sound man. Francis was the TV news director who waved and shouted, "Keep moving! Don't look in the camera! Keep moving!" as Martin Sheen, Sam Bottoms, and Larry Fishburne passed by. If Francis, Vittorio, and Dean were not enough, Mary Ellen Mark, our new still photographer, got into wardrobe and was also in our film as a press photographer snapping shots of Robert Duvall during the scene.

I wasn't so bothered by all of our new actors, but Enrico, our camera operator, had a hard time adjusting to Vittorio and Francis being in his shot, and when Mary Ellen moved through his frame as she snapped photos of the action, Enrico had enough. He could no longer tell the performers from the crew. It took both Vittorio and Francis to calm him down.

In the scene, Martin Sheen was the first off the PBR, followed by Sam and Larry Fishburne. Albert and Freddie stayed with the PBR. Marty Sheen's oldest boy, Emilio, who kept the family name of Estevez, worked as an extra.

Francis and Vittorio had designed a long dolly shot from the water's edge all the way to first seeing Robert Duvall as Kilgore. It was a wonderful shot, but since our director, cameraman, and production designer were also in the shot, they couldn't watch what was happening. I felt it was a bit like an arrow shot into flight without the feathers to guide it.

We rehearsed and carefully planned the walk of Marty and the cast; we added all our extras and arriving attack boats, Kilgore's Hueys mopping up, the special effects, and the smoke. Larry Franco and I were doing pretty well until Francis called me over for a private chat.

"How does it look?" Francis asked quietly.

"It looks great! The whole background is attacking Hueys and boats! You got the wounded Vietnamese and captured Viet Cong! You got Willard and the cast coming through! It's great!" I answered Francis.

"No, I know that," Francis continued. "I mean Vittorio, Dean, and me; how do we look?"

I wanted to tell Francis what he told me after the napalm scene in Baler, "If they're looking at that we're in trouble," but I gave him a thoughtful look and said, "It looks real, Francis. You three are perfect."

What we wanted to depict were the incongruities within the Vietnam War. The military would destroy whole villages, burning and killing suspected Viet Cong, but at the same time they would carefully explain to the remaining citizens their options for various social welfare programs. Lieutenant Colonel Kilgore led a brutal attack on to Village I, killing and maiming many of the citizens, but at the same time he carefully and gently escorted the newly widowed and orphaned onto military vehicles headed for relocation camps.

Lieutenant Colonel Kilgore was the egotistical military commander. When we first see Robert Duvall in the scene, he is placing his squadron's playing cards, death cards, on the bodies of the dead Viet Cong and North Vietnamese as he rated each kill. The purpose was to tell the enemy which army squadron was responsible for the kills. Like so many of the military oddities in *Apocalypse Now*, the death cards action was based on actual practices by some of the commanders during the Vietnam War.

The whole concept of Village I was to meet Kilgore and to see the frivolity that was a part of the Vietnam War. What Francis wanted in the background was the ugliness of the Vietnam War, while Robert Duvall would depict the frivolous interests and habits of some of the war's commanders. In the middle of the hellish naturalism of the blood and gore of the battle, Kilgore was honoring a brave enemy soldier by letting him drink from his personal canteen. When Kilgore was told that Lance Johnson, the famous surfer, was there, he withdrew his canteen from the wounded soldier and walked away to talk with Lance.

We spread the horrors of war across the scene. Larry Franco and I set up wounded and maimed prisoners, with blood and gore everywhere.

Our makeup and wardrobe departments used gallons of blood. Special effects had huge fires belching smoke. We used Dick White's Huey pilots to dive and dip their helicopters into the camera's frame to offer the threat of further rocket attacks. Smoke grenades were giving Vittorio the colors he wanted for his cinematic vision.

Kilgore was told that where Lance and the PBR crew wanted to be taken was also one of the best surfing beaches in that area of Vietnam—unfortunately it was Charlie's beach. That was all the egotistical Kilgore needed to hear. That night he had planned a special steak barbecue, but tomorrow they would surf that beach!

The Village I scene ended with a Catholic priest serving mass to soldiers during the battle and a Huey lifting a cow over the bombed-out remains of a church. The flying cow was a borrowed image from Fellini's *La Dolce Vita* where he had a crucifix lifted over a similar church.

After filming for month after month, we became like the characters in a Fellini film: The insanity of man was all around us—the barbarism of war, its highs and manic excesses, then its depression and loneliness. Over time, we all became a part of it, slowly swirling down into a massive black hole.

The Playboy Bunny Show

In our script, following the Village II and Tiger scenes, the crew of the PBR came upon the sounds of rock and roll and the bright stage lights of a nighttime USO show at the Hau Phat Supply Depot along the Nung River.

On our first night of shooting, we filmed the PBR approaching the supply depot and the USO stage with the glare of concert lights and the noise of the show's sound check. While our PBR crew arranged to get more diesel fuel, the supply sergeant gave them press tickets to the Playboy Bunny Show that would be presented later that night.

Francis was using a houseboat as his sanctuary during the Hau Phat portion of our filming schedule. He would spend his free time working on Marlon Brando's scenes and the ending for our film. When we changed our shots of the approaching PBR, we often had to move his houseboat so it wouldn't be in the picture.

"Jerry, we must move Francis!" It was Vittorio. "His houseboat is in my shot."

"OK, Vittorio," I said. I hated to move the houseboat because it took so long. I wished I could dock it somewhere out of all possible shots, but there was no place for it.

I knocked on the door of the houseboat. "Francis?" I said.

"Come in!" was his shouted response.

He was rewriting the scenes at the Kurtz compound. "Francis, we've got to move you. The houseboat's in the shot."

He hated to be moved because it interrupted his writing, and everything had to be put away and secured. It took at least an hour to get the houseboat packed up and moving, then we had to re-dock it and tie it off again. I saw Francis's mind working on the problem.

"We got motorcycles. We got refrigerators. We got televisions! All standing around at the Hau Phat Supply Depot! Why couldn't they have a houseboat?" Francis asked me.

I stared at Francis for just a beat. I knew he had to work on Brando's scenes. An assistant director has to make a thousand decisions every day. Some are big, some are small, some are serious, some are silly. *A houseboat on the Nung River during the Vietnam War?* I thought to myself. Not likely, but maybe Vittorio could do something to keep the light off it.

"Right, Francis. Why not? You don't have to move. I'll let you know when we're ready to film," I said, and hurried back to Vittorio.

Vittorio was working with Enrico at the camera. It was a nice wide shot from the water showing the whole Hau Phat Supply Depot with Francis's houseboat full in the shot.

"Vittorio?" I approached carefully. I waited until Enrico moved away. "How're you doing?"

"Jerry, is the houseboat moving?" he asked, as he studied the shot through the camera lens.

"Vittorio?" I began. "They had houseboats in Vietnam." I just floated it to him.

He jerked his eye from the camera and stared at me, then he began laughing.

"No, Jerry, for sure not!" he laughed. "No houseboats in Vietnam! For sure," and he laughed again.

I had caught him in a good mood, and I was very thankful.

"Vittorio, do you think we could miss seeing the houseboat?" I asked.

Vittorio nearly collapsed in laughter. "Miss it? It's so big! Right there!" he said, as he pointed to Francis's houseboat in the dead center of our shot.

I followed Vittorio's look, evaluating his reasoning, perhaps measuring the distance in centimeters.

"Can you take the light off it?" I asked as my second line of defense.

"Francis doesn't want to move the houseboat?" Vittorio asked, still in good cheer.

"Right. Can you do something?" I said, and smiled for all I was worth.

Vittorio had never made a joke in my presence. We had worked together for months, and he had never kidded or even teased with anyone.

"OK, Jerry," Vittorio began, "I'll put an elephant in front of it!" Vittorio doubled up with laughter at his own joke. Vittorio had told his first joke, and he thought it was sensational. He called over Enrico and Alfredo and retold his joke in Italian. It went over better in Italian than it did in English. Francis's houseboat stayed in the shot.

For our second night of filming, we had arranged for four thousand extras to be bused to our location. We tried to hire as many actual off-duty U.S. servicemen as we could, but there was no cooperation from the U.S. military. We ended up busing most of our extras from Manila and Olongapo. At that time in the Philippines, President Marcos had declared martial law and had put a strict curfew into effect that didn't allow motorized vehicles on the roads outside of Manila between midnight and 5:00 A.M. We would bus all of our extras to our location during the day, film all night, and then bus them back after the curfew was lifted at 5:00.

My shooting plan was to film toward our audience of four thousand GIs, getting their reactions to the Bunny Show first, then at the end of the night I would get the landing of the bunny helicopter with Bill Graham introducing the three bunnies. Last of all, we would get the chopper's final takeoff. I wanted to finish with our four thousand extras as early as possible in case they got tired and left or just went to sleep somewhere.

Like so many scenes in making a motion picture, this was a "one-night deal." There would be no other chance to get all elements together again—the three Playboy Bunnies, Bill Graham, and the four thousand extras.

Leon Chooluck had told me that the caterer would be ready to feed the four thousand extras and all the crew at 9:00 P.M. There was no way that we could change that time, 9:00 was it! The caterer was stretched to his limit as it was, with four thousand meals. We had to feed at 9:00.

Tom Cruise and Suzanne. TC's last day, *Jerry Maguire*, 1996.

Cuba Gooding, Jr., and Suzanne. *Jerry Maguire*, 1996.

Suzanne and me at Rufus
King Senior Prom, 1957.

Ethel Waters. *The Member of
the Wedding*, Me as Greek
god Barney, Milwaukee,
1957.

Jerry Ziesmer

Height: 5'10"
Weight: 160
Hair: Brown
Unions: SAG, AFTRA, AEA

ALL MAJOR TV SERIES including . . .
  "THE LIEUTENANT" & Pilot.
  "GOING MY WAY" & Pilot.
  "SAM BENEDICT" & Pilot.
  "ELEVENTH HOUR"
  "MY THREE SONS"
  "RED SKELTON HOUR"

WALT DISNEY FEATURE "A TIGER WALKS"
BROADWAY . . . "INHERIT THE WIND"
SEVEN YEARS OF SUMMER STOCK.
NORTHWESTERN UNIVERSITY
UCLA

AUTHOR OF "STAN LAUREL: THE LITTLE
  ONE", a study of comedy.

My acting resume in 1963.

Top of Mount Hood. *Lost Horizon*, 1970. Shel Schrager, Ross Hunter, and me.

The Wrath of God. Laluz, Mexico, 1972.

My special day. *The Way We Were* with Sydney Pollack, Barbra Streisand, and Robert Redford, 1972.

With John Huston on *Annie*, New York City, 1981.

Me and Eric Stoltz,
Some Kind of Wonderful,
1986.

Our family at Disneyland.

Tim, Jillian,
and Chris.

Suzanne with her students Shane and Becky.

Suzanne with Mel Gibson.

Suzanne with Sissy Spacek.

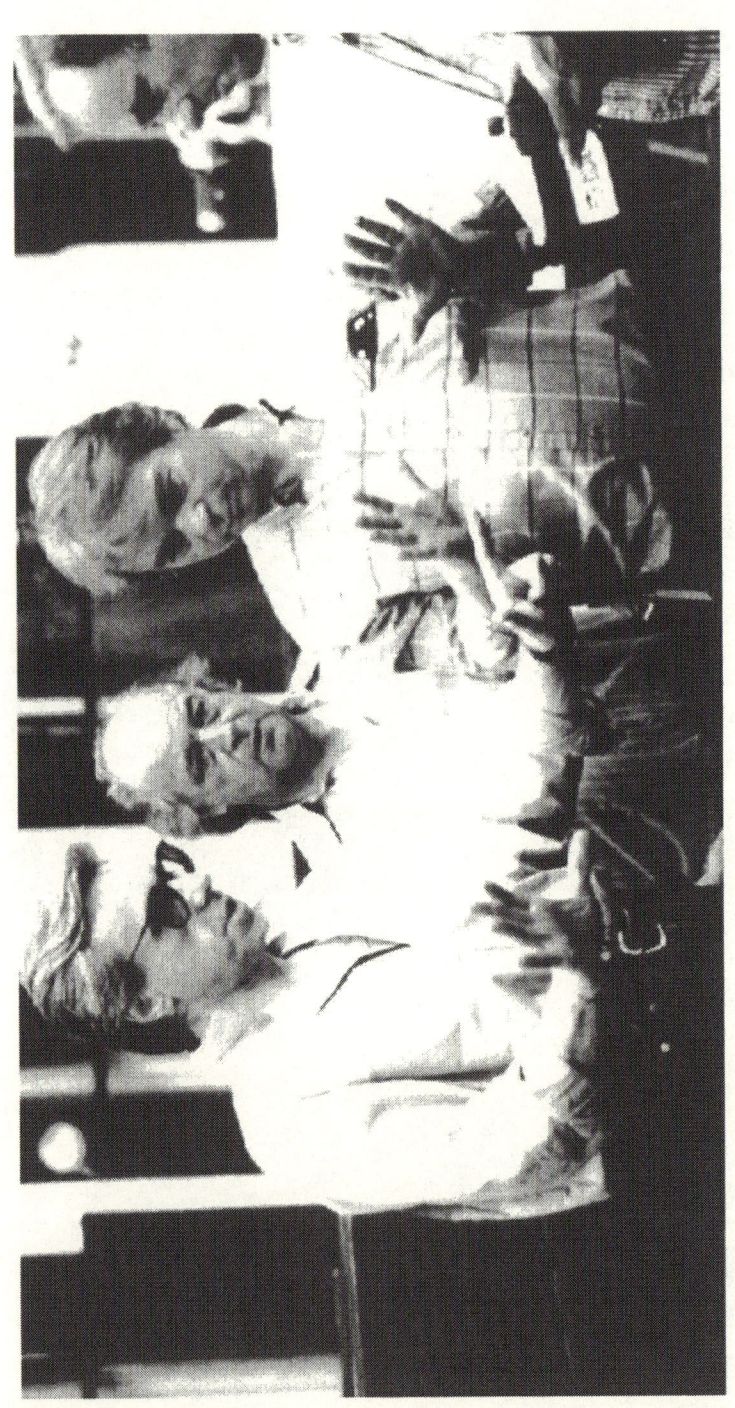

Me with Peter Bogdanovich, *Illegally Yours*, 1987.

Me with Alan Rudolph on *Love at Large*, 1989.

Being directed by Cameron. *Say Anything . . . ,* 1988.

Nancy and Cameron with Suzanne.

Suzanne with Bridget Fonda.

Matt Dillon with Jillian.

Me with Richard Pryor, *Jo Jo Dancer*, 1985.

Chris, Suzanne, and Campbell Scott.

Me and Cameron, *Singles*, 1991.

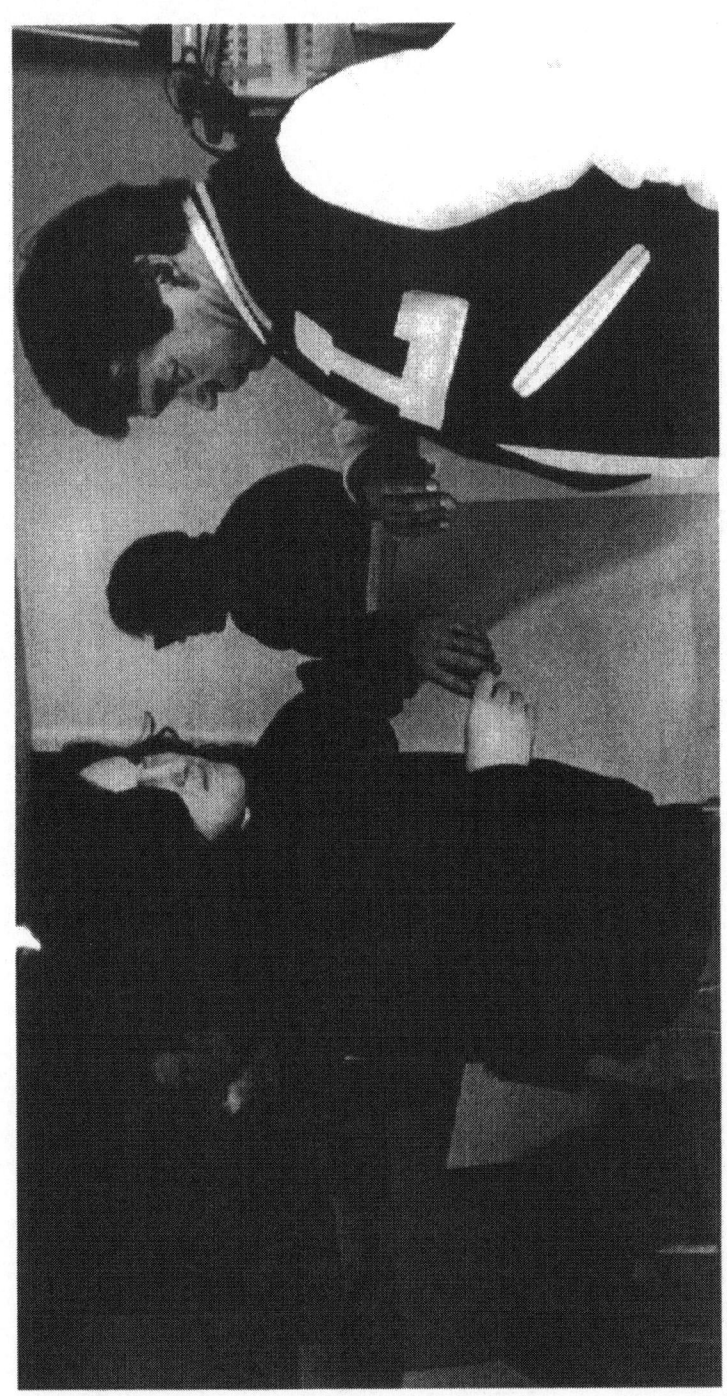

Me and Cameron, *Singles*, 1991.

We couldn't begin filming before the sun went down, but as soon as it was dark enough for Vittorio to film, we began with the close shots of the cast, with a few extras getting seated in the stands before all four thousand GIs were ready.

Francis and Vittorio took a little longer to get all the tight shots than I had expected. I began fearing the 9:00 dinner deadline. I hoped that maybe we'd be able to finish the wider shots of the crowd faster than I had anticipated. During the shots on the extras, I was standing behind the camera, yelling and waving at them to get them to react as if the Playboy Bunny Show were really there. Neither Francis nor I wanted to use the actual bunnies for the off-camera work. They would get worn out and would ruin their hair and makeup. It was a bit after 9:00, and we weren't halfway through with the GIs' reactions.

"Jerry!" Leon came up to me. "Can you break for dinner? We're all ready to feed the four thousand GIs."

"Give me a little bit, Leon," I answered. "I'm still filming with all the extras. As soon as I'm through, I'll send them to dinner."

Leon went back to the caterer, and I stayed with Vittorio and Francis and tried to get things moving as fast as I could. I jumped and waved and shouted off-camera to get the extras motivated. I knew if I didn't finish the crowd reactions before dinner, I would never finish the whole arrival of the bunnies, their show, and their exit before it got light at about 5:00 A.M. My assistant-director stomach was beginning to spin.

Larry and I tried to send the crew that were not needed to get some food and then get right back to the shooting. We were able to feed the actors, but none of the crew was able to sit down and eat a meal. At best the crew stood with a handful of food and ate and worked at the same time. The four thousand extras were in every shot and couldn't leave to eat.

We kept filming, and Leon kept coming back every fifteen minutes to plead with me to break for dinner. I couldn't; I still had more shots to do with the four thousand GIs.

At 11:00 Leon and the caterer came running up to me just as we were doing another shot.

"Don't break for dinner!" Leon was shouting. "The food is ruined!" The caterer was beside himself. Four thousand dinners ruined! He would put out all the edible food that was left on tables and let the people eat what they could. Leon led the caterer away.

I not only had the problem of four thousand extras getting very hungry and having little food to feed them, but they were also getting very tired of screaming and yelling at my antics. The extras needed something much more stimulating or we wouldn't get the excitement in the crowd that Francis needed. Along came Larry Franco.

Larry came up to me between shots. He had been back at the dressing rooms getting the Bunny Show performers ready and seeing to the caterer. I was exhausted. I had been jumping and yelling during every take. I had gotten the extras to this point, but we needed something more, and I didn't know what to do.

"How ya doin', Jer?" Larry asked, as I stood there slumped and drained.

"Larry, I've had it," I mumbled.

"What ya need?" he asked.

"Larry, we got to goose up the extras! We got to get them crazed! We got to . . ."

He interrupted me, "No problem, Jer. I'll dance. Don't worry," Larry said, and he moved out toward the center of the stage behind the cameras and started to limber up.

Larry Franco was going to dance? The *Apocalypse Now* Christmas troll with his big potbelly and full red beard? This was going to excite four thousand GIs? I looked at Larry standing behind the camera; he looked confident. What choice did I have? He grinned at me and put his arms up into the air, signifying that he was ready.

As soon as Francis and Vittorio were set, I started the cameras and cued the rock music. Francis called "Action!" Suddenly the four thousand GIs started to scream and yell and go crazy! They were applauding and shouting down toward the stage. Some stood and waved their shirts, some threw their arms to heaven and let out primeval screams of pure pleasure. It was with great trepidation that I took my eyes off the scene in front of the cameras and looked at Larry behind the cameras.

Larry Franco was born for this moment on this night. He gyrated and danced. He ran from side to side and did leaps to the music. He took off his shirt and waved it over his head. He was a wild man! The four thousand GIs loved it, and they went insane.

Eventually we had to cut the shot, and everyone in the cast and crew applauded Larry Franco! He was fantastic! I couldn't believe it. This was a side of Larry I had never seen, the rock-and-roll performer!

We continued to film shot after shot, with Larry doing his dancing off-camera. However, with each succeeding shot, the four thousand extras got less and less enthused with Larry's performance. Something new had to be added.

Francis and I told Larry that this next shot was the critical climax.

This was the shot where the GIs had got to get into a frenzy and leap out of the stands toward the USO stage. What could he do?

"Larry, one more time! Big! This has to be big!" I urged him on to his greatest effort.

"Don't worry, Jer! This is going to be big!" he assured me, as he took deep breaths and looked around the stage. He threw both his arms into the air!

I got the extras and crew ready, and we rolled the cameras. Before Francis could get "Action!" out of his mouth, the stands erupted! The whole spectator section of the set was vibrating from the jumping and stomping of the four thousand extras. We stared at the teeming mass of out-of-control GIs screaming, ready to tear past the cameras and onto the stage. I took my eyes from the four thousand and looked behind the cameras.

Larry Franco had found a partner! One of the Playboy Bunnies had heard all the screaming and excitement, and she had left her dressing room and had just arrived on the stage. Larry saw her, and right before we rolled the cameras, he took her hand and led this unsuspecting Playmate out to the center of the stage. When the rock music began, Larry gyrated around the totally amazed Playmate. As the four thousand GIs got into it, Larry and the Playboy Bunny became inspired. They began a dance that would bring blushes to Madonna. The GIs looked upon their dance as the hottest human activity ever seen in Southeast Asia. Larry and the bunny circled one another like a bull and a matador. They shook. They crawled toward each other. They throbbed. They inspired each other to greater and greater heights. They rolled around the stage. They rattled at each other. They knelt on the stage and pulsated with the music. There is no question in my mind that the four thousand screaming GIs who were there that night can still see in their dreams Larry's dance with that Playboy Bunny. The soldiers erupted out of their seats and charged past the cameras and onto the stage. The most amazing thing and greatest compliment to Larry and the Playmate was that none of the four thousand GIs ever complained about not getting dinner that night.

The crew was preparing the next shot. Alfredo and the grips were setting a dolly shot as Vittorio gave them marks. Luciano was next to Vittorio to get his lighting suggestions. I checked over the extras; the soldiers looked great. They were in good spirits. Suddenly I heard Francis calling me.

"Jerry! Over here!" He was yelling.

I looked in the direction of his voice, and I saw him kneeling on the stage floor and looking up at one of the Playmates, Colleen Camp, dressed in an Indian costume, sitting on a high stool. Francis had his viewfinder and was doing contortions to get a very low shot of Colleen against the night sky.

I walked over to Francis, since he was by then lying on the stage floor.

"What is it, Francis?" I asked. I tried to imagine what he was looking at.

"Jerry, I want to get a quick shot of Colleen!" he said. "Won't take long. Can we get it?" Francis asked, still setting the shot with his viewfinder.

We were really pressed for time that night, but what can you say? "Francis, what exactly do you have in mind?" I asked. I knelt down and looked up at Colleen dressed in her Indian suit.

"Get Vittorio! I want to get a shot of Colleen singing *God Bless America!*" Francis exclaimed.

I went numb. A Playboy Bunny singing *God Bless America?* I tried to make sense of it all. How could this fit into our movie?

"Get Vittorio!" Francis continued.

"Vittorio!" I shouted. "Got a shot over here!"

Vittorio, Alfredo, and Luciano all turned and looked at me and at Francis, now on his back staring up at Colleen on the high stool. They came at once.

"Yes, Francis?" Vittorio said.

"Vittorio! Look at this! Can we get this quickly?" Francis asked.

"Sure, Francis, there is no problem," Vittorio answered. That was always his answer to Francis.

I got Nat Boxer, our boom man, ready to record. "A song," was Nat's only comment, and it wasn't a question but a statement.

Luciano and Vittorio lit the Playmate Indian maiden as quickly as they could.

Francis was rehearsing with Colleen. He wanted a very melancholy rendition of *God Bless America* from her.

Vittorio was totally confused by the singing. None of the Italian crew understood what was happening. Nat Boxer had worked many films with Francis, so he accepted moments like this much better than the rest of us.

Finally we were ready. Francis talked to Colleen one last time, and we filmed her melancholy rendition of *God Bless America* sung a cappella.

I stood next to Francis during the shot and glanced at him. He smiled at me and held up his hand as if to say, "Just wait a minute." When the song came to an end, Francis yelled "Cut! Print!" All of the crew went back to preparing the next shot.

"Jerry," Francis called to me.

I walked over to him. He was grinning.

"Look, you never know what's going to work until you get into the editing room," he said. "I like to shoot everything! *Everything!* An eight-hour movie! Then I edit out all the bad, and what's left is the good. That's what's the movie. Only what's left, the good stuff!"

I smiled at him, but I had no patience tonight, and I'm sure my face showed it. Francis broke into his big laughter. He rocked back and forth, pushed his glasses back up to the bridge of his nose, bent over and roared again. His hands were out from his sides like he was doing a clumsy chicken dance. He turned away still laughing, and when he looked my way again, he pointed at me and roared with new laughter.

I loved working with Francis; I really did.

It was after 3:00 A.M. when we turned the cameras around and began filming away from the audience and toward the Playboy Bunny Show. Bill Graham, the rock-and-roll impresario, was leaving the Philippines that morning whether or not we had completed the scene. When Typhoon Ruby hit Olongapo, he had gone five days without making a phone call, and he wasn't going to chance that ever happening again. Two of our three Playboy Bunnies had also suffered through the typhoon with us, and they had reservations on the same plane as Bill Graham.

We had two hours to finish shooting the scene before the sun came up. Larry still had the GIs excited, so their off-camera work would be fine. Our shots began with Dick White landing the bunny helicopter on the USO stage and Bill Graham running out and introducing the three Playboy Bunnies. We would then reset all the cameras to capture each of the bunnies as they did their individual dances. Finally we would pull all the cameras back and the GIs would rush the stage, Bill Graham and the bunnies would scamper into the helicopter, and it would take off with Terry Leonard hanging down from the chopper's skid. End of scene.

Francis and Vittorio were doing all they could to move the filming along. Dick White put the chopper right on its mark, and the introductions of the bunnies worked great. Each bunny's individual dance was memorable, largely because of the off-camera GIs who were still excited from Larry's dance five hours ago.

We were filming toward the east, and just before 5:00 we began to see the hints of blue in the eastern sky. Dawn was minutes away, and we hadn't completed the scene. We had no exit!

The only thing to do was to pull all the cameras back, call action, and whatever happened would be the end of the scene. Francis talked to all the performers and the actors.

"Look! We've got one shot at this. The sun is coming up! No matter what happens just get in the helicopter! Dick, as soon as everyone's on board take it up! I've got to have an ending! Just fly off!" Francis loved the excitement and the pressure, but the whole scene was at stake.

Vittorio looked into the eastern sky and shouted that we had to film now! As soon as the dawn sky becomes blue, he couldn't make the shots look like night.

I saw the bunnies were on their marks, Bill Graham was ready and had his smoke grenades, Dick White was ready in the chopper and it was started. Larry Franco had the GIs ready and had selected the ones to jump to the stage and charge the Playmates.

"Jerry! Now! We have to go now!" Vittorio was shouting.

I went over to Terry Leonard. "Terry, are you OK?"

"Just go!" Terry said, "I'm all right." He grabbed onto the chopper's skid, checked his rigging. "I'm going to give Francis an ending he'll never forget!"

Vittorio was beside himself. I knew I had to roll the cameras. It was our last and only chance.

"Roll!" I shouted, and all the cameras began.

Francis yelled, "Action!"

Larry cued the GIs and the scene began. The GIs rushed the stage. Bill Graham lit the smoke grenades. He and the bunnies dashed into their chopper, and Dick White started it up. Terry Leonard hung onto the skid as the chopper flew higher. Terry was still hanging onto the skid! He hadn't jumped! Suddenly Francis, Vittorio, our crew, and four thousand GIs cheered the perfect ending to our scene when Terry Leonard, still clinging to the chopper's skid, dropped his pants to his ankles and mooned everyone, then fell safely to the lake far below as the bunny helicopter disappeared into the last moments of the night.

It's hard filming at night. We'd stop shooting just before dawn. If we wrapped before 5:00 A.M. and wanted to drive back to the hotel, we needed a government escort to lead us because of the curfew imposed by martial law. The local police and militia were always with us because of our weapons and walkie-talkies. If we had anything that the guerrillas could use, the militia kept it locked and guarded.

Our vans and buses would drive down the highway in the morning light. The early risers would be on their bicycles peddling to work or in front of their nipa huts getting their charcoal lit for the morning. The locals were used to us arriving back at the Rapids Hotel at about the time their children were getting up and ready for school. I often thought of Tim and Chris as the van pulled into the hotel parking area. I wondered how they looked when they first got up and plodded down the hall, what they would eat for breakfast. I laughed to myself at what might be finished first, this movie or my sons' childhood. I knew I was missing so much. And Marlon Brando wasn't here yet.

The hotel waiters greeted us as we came in. The lobby floors were clean and polished, and we would come in with our mud-caked shoes and boots. Most of us went straight to our rooms, but there was a group who sat down at a table near the pool and had breakfast each morning. Some of the crew had adapted to the eggs and toast, but I stuck to my grilled cheese sandwich with fried banana chips no matter what time of the day it was.

Once back in the hotel room, it was hard to get a sound sleep with the morning sounds on the streets and in the corridors of the hotel. We filmed while they slept, now they were up and working while we tried to sleep. I usually could sleep until about 3:00 P.M., when the kids came running down the streets after school. That did it for me. I missed my boys so much.

I showered and got dressed, walked down to the dining room, and found some crew around a table near the pool. I joined them, checked on the geckos climbing the walls, and ordered a grilled cheese sandwich with fried banana chips. Just about time for another night of filming.

The Do Lung Bridge Scene

The Do Lung Bridge location was about five miles downriver from the town of Pagsanjan. There had been a concrete bridge across the Pagsanjan River, but during the Japanese occupation of that portion of Luzon during World War II, the bridge was bombed and had never been rebuilt.

In our script, the Do Lung Bridge was the last army outpost on the Nung River. No one knew what lay upriver. There was only Cambodia and, somewhere, Col. Kurtz. Our PBR crew approached the Do Lung Bridge, which was destroyed each day by the Viet Cong and rebuilt every night by the U.S. Army.

Dean Tavoularis had made use of the existing portions of the bombed-out bridge and had John La Sandra, our construction coordinator, build bamboo structures over the river to simulate the nightly bridge reconstruction efforts. The special effects crew had prepared fires, smoke, and underwater explosions. Terry Leonard had stuntmen doing high falls from the top of the bridge. Strings of lights were hung on the bridge to give illumination to the scene. When I stood on the PBR and looked upriver, the Do Lung Bridge looked like the entrance to hell itself, a huge mouth with fire and smoke around it and, on the shore, decadent carnival lighting with long strings of bulbs. I thought of the entrance to a neglected and decaying Pinocchio's Pleasure Island.

Vittorio had two huge lighting barges built with massive candle-power. The barges were very useful, but we had a shot straight down the river and both barges were in the picture. Vittorio was stuck; he needed those lighting barges. I looked for Vittorio, and I saw him talking with Francis and Dean; they finished their discussion and hurried toward me.

"Jerry, they had lighting barges in Vietnam!" he said.

I took a deep breath. "Francis," I began.

"They had lighting barges! How else could they see to build the bridge at night!" Francis declared, as Dean smiled and nodded his approval.

"Jerry!" Vittorio was shouting, "I'm ready. Let's shoot!"

Most of Vittorio's lighting was done from high towers where Luciano, his gaffer, had set the large arc lights that would act as army searchlights.

As the PBR approached the bridge, soldiers tried to get aboard to escape the area. Francis's son Gio was one of the extras guarding the river. A messenger from Nha Trang delivered a packet to Willard then hurried off saying that Do Lung Bridge was "the asshole of the world." Willard and Lance, who had dropped acid, got off the PBR to find the commanding officer. As Willard and Lance moved along the riverbank and into the trenches, Vittorio did his lighting magic.

While Enrico was operating the camera during the scene, Vittorio would have a walkie-talkie to his men in the towers operating the searchlights. Vittorio ran behind the camera and jumped over the trenches during every shot, as he gave his lighting cues for each light. I felt he was the conductor, playing a symphony of light and shadow over the scene. The most bewildering thing for me was that someone would dare to conceive of such an original plan to illuminate a scene and then have a crew with the faith and dedication to follow his directions. Vittorio's lighting technique for the Do Lung Bridge scene was a new experience for me. He used shadows more than he used illumination. I felt his lighting did more than help tell the story—it was a character in the story as well.

On one of the nights at Do Lung Bridge there was an electrical storm with thunder and lightning. We were filming on the PBR as it finally pulled away from the bridge and headed upriver toward Cambodia. I was standing with Vittorio when he noticed that there seemed to be a pattern to the lightning and thunder. He wanted to have a bolt of lightning on the horizon while the PBR motored up river. I saw this *want* grow within Vittorio until it became a *need*. We now *needed* to have a bolt of lightning on the horizon as the PBR pulled away from the bridge.

Unfortunately the thunder and lightning seemed to stop just as we had the cast in the PBR and we were all ready to film.

"Jerry, excuse me," Vittorio whispered to me. "Could we wait just a few minutes, please? For the lightning to come back?"

I stared at him. An assistant director's job is to move the company along, to complete the day's work, and to use each moment to best get the director's vision onto the movie screen. I looked for Francis; he was talking to the actors.

"How long, Vittorio?" I asked in a whisper.

"Until the lightning comes back," Vittorio answered, and laughed. "There are two thunders and lightning in the east and then surely our lightning comes."

It was silly. We're filming nights in the Philippines with hundreds of crew members, hundreds of extras, and we're waiting for the lightning to come back? Or was that really what Vittorio and I were doing? I watched Vittorio smiling and pantomiming to his crew that he was waiting for lightning. It was as if he and I were bad boys and couldn't let Francis and the cast know what we were up to. It was a game. It was our conspiracy.

There was a sudden clap of thunder and Vittorio looked at me and smiled, pantomiming that he was sure we could begin soon. Francis and the actors were still chatting. Vittorio and I laughed quietly at the back of the PBR as we waited.

"What's going on?" Francis called to me. He had stopped talking with the cast and had noticed the crew standing around and saw Vittorio and me laughing together.

I hurried to Francis and took him to one side.

"Francis, we'll be ready in a couple of minutes," I said.

"What's happening?" he asked.

I glanced back at Vittorio, who was suddenly studying his light meter.

"We're waiting for lightning," I said, and looked at Francis. I tried never to lie to a director. He didn't flinch. He looked at me, glanced at Vittorio, nodded, and went back to the actors and started chatting again.

I went to Vittorio, but he talked before I had a chance.

"What did Francis say?" Vittorio whispered, as he still held out his light meter.

I felt we were like two kids in school talking about our teacher.

"I told him we were waiting for lightning. It's fine," I said.

We both laughed quietly, then watched Francis with the actors. We waited a few more minutes, but it was getting late. We decided to get a few takes without the thunder and lightning, then maybe we'd get lucky.

The shots were good, but we did it over and over. Either Enrico or Vittorio found something that could be improved. I was sure Francis suspected we were stalling, but he didn't say anything. We were turning the PBR around in the river getting ready to make another run upriver, when two claps of thunder broke and a bolt of lightning appeared in the east. Vittorio jumped into action. I yelled for Pete Cooper to get us back to our start mark as soon as he could. The PBR shot forward as the cast and Francis hung on and stared first at Pete and then at Vittorio and me as we shouted for everyone to get ready. Two more claps of thunder! The PBR made its turn and approached the start mark.

"This is about your lightning!" Francis shouted back at us, as he smiled.

"Yes, Francis! It will be wonderful!" Vittorio shouted back, then grinned at me.

"Get ready!" I shouted to the cast and crew. "Go, Pete! Roll camera!" Francis called "Action!" and the scene began.

Vittorio and all of his crew were looking toward the horizon for the bolt of lightning to magically appear.

Francis had to stop the scene because of an actor, but Pete kept the PBR headed upriver and Enrico kept the camera running. Francis called "Action!" again, and the actors restarted the scene. Suddenly, there was a loud clap of thunder and a bolt of lightning on the horizon. When the take was over, the crew cheered, Vittorio and I laughed together, and Enrico told Francis that the last shot was perfect! The best one!

"Yeah, yeah, I saw the lightning! Can we go home now?" Francis asked.

I don't know why it was me. It was never explained so I understood it, but every fifty days the movie company had to send me out of the Philippines. I didn't mind it; in fact, I looked forward to it. Leon would give me a round-trip airline ticket to Hong Kong and a fully paid reservation for one night at any hotel I wanted. After shooting on Saturday, a driver would take me from the hotel in Pagsanjan to the Manila International Airport. I'd get on a plane, and in a bit over two hours I'd get off in Hong Kong and take a taxi to my hotel.

That night I'd walk to the San Francisco Steak House across the street from the Hyatt Hotel in Kowloon, have a real steak dinner with a baked potato, and walk back.

Most Sunday mornings I'd walk down to the Peninsula Hotel, have coffee, and then spend a few hours on the Star Ferry, riding across the harbor from Kowloon to Hong Kong and back. I'd finally get off in Hong Kong and take a taxi to the Repulse Bay Hotel for their Sunday brunch. There'd be a long table of gourmet delicacies with a beautiful ice sculpture in the center. I'd sit at a table overlooking Repulse Bay, and for one hour my only care in the world was for the slowly melting ice sculpture.

On a couple of Sundays I took the hydrofoil from Kowloon to Macao on the Chinese mainland and wandered around that ancient Portuguese territory. There's something very soothing for me when I'm among antiquities. In one old building, I lost myself for nearly an hour as I gazed at an ancient mural depicting the career of Marco Polo. On my walk back to the dock, I stopped at a gambling casino and watched the ancient Chinese games of chance. When I finally left Macao, the Red Chinese patrol boats made a game of racing with the hydrofoil back to Hong Kong.

About the middle of the afternoon, I'd arrive back at my hotel, pack, and take a taxi to the airport for my flight back to Manila. A

*company driver picked me up outside the customs gate and drove me
to Pagsanjan.*

    I felt revived. I felt I had been to Shangri-La.

    *I never learned who decided that I had to be the one to leave the
country, but whoever you were—thank you.*

The French Plantation Sequence

In the movie, when the PBR and our crew left Do Lung Bridge, they
encountered a firefight and Mr. Clean was killed. The PBR escaped and
traveled farther up the Nung River until it entered a dense fog.

    The PBR crew couldn't see to navigate. They heard voices in the fog
and followed the sound until they came upon a French plantation
owner, his son, and ten armed guards at a smoldering outpost. The
plantation owner, played by Christian Marquand, invited them to his
rubber plantation a short distance up the river. There they could bury
Mr. Clean and make the necessary repairs to the PBR.

    The French Plantation set consisted of a large wooden dock along
the river with dockside buildings to process the plantation's raw rubber
and prepare it for transfer to markets. The rubber-processing equipment, cauldrons, tools, and the raw rubber had been shipped to our set
on Lake Caliraya from a rubber plantation in Bali.

    Leading from the dock was a long, suspended wooden walk bridge
that led up to the French Plantation's main house. To the left as you
walked up the bridge were gardens of tropical plants and the family
cemetery. That was where Mr. Clean was to be buried.

    The main house consisted of a large living room and sitting area, a
formal dining room, kitchen, various side rooms, and the bedrooms.
This sprawling plantation home was constructed to look as if it had
been built in the early 1900s. It was well appointed with French furniture and antiques from the 1800s, as though it had all been in the
same family for more than one hundred years.

    The first time I saw the French Plantation set, Dick White and I flew
over in the Jet Ranger shortly after the typhoon. The dock and the
rubber-processing buildings had been severely damaged and had to be
rebuilt. I noted at the time the large size of the house. It stretched from
the hanging walkways up the hill toward the only road in that area of
Luzon.

The next time I saw the French Plantation, we had added more construction and had actually built across the only road, closing down motorized traffic in that section of Luzon.

We began our filming at the French Plantation with the PBR approaching the long, wooden dock and the rubber-processing buildings. Joe Lombardi and A. D. Flowers had asked me to film the entrance as early in the morning as I could, so that their special-effects fog would stay on the cool water.

The plantation owner, his son, and the armed guards greeted our crew from the dock. After the PBR was tied down, the body of Mr. Clean was carried to the house.

The next scene we filmed was the burial of Mr. Clean in the plantation's cemetery. Chief oversaw the military ceremony and, at the end, handed the folded American flag to Willard.

That evening the French family gave a dinner for the PBR crew. The food was designed and the preparation supervised by a French gourmet chef brought in from Hong Kong. The serving was done by Vietnamese waiters from a French restaurant in Manila. A complete gourmet kitchen was part of the French Plantation set, and the chefs cooked the food as we filmed. The dinner was served with such grace and tradition. We had a wonderful adviser who supervised everything we did with the food and wine. It was a totally new world for me; the only French food Larry and I knew were the fries at McDonald's.

After dinner, Martin Sheen and the plantation owner's daughter, played by Aurore Clément, were the only people left in the dining room. She had lost her husband and son in the war. A tender scene between Marty and Aurore followed in which they smoked opium and attempted to have the opiate ease their pain. She looked and saw herself and her way of life on the edge of extinction, while Willard knew he had to travel farther upriver before he could view himself.

Vittorio lit the ensuing love scene with soft candlelight shown through the gauze netting that hung down from the sides of her large bed. I looked on it as a romantic fairy tale, as though it were possible to fall in love with someone from a different time.

• • •

The final scene in the French Plantation sequence was the early morning departure of the PBR with its remaining crew. Mr. Clean had been buried in the plantation's family cemetery. The boat moved away from the plantation dock and started back upriver into the dense fog.

One afternoon during our shooting at the French Plantation, Francis was sitting in a chair admiring all of the furnishings in the living room of the main house. He looked at the fine furniture, the antiques, the old family photographs, the needlework; every inch of set was decorated.

I was standing in the doorway to the main dining room, so I could be near Vittorio as he continued to light the dinner scene and I could still talk with Francis.

"Jerry, look at this stuff," Francis said, as he picked up a tiny silver box and looked at the bottom. "It's made in France! Look at it!"

He was intrigued by the intricate care and detail of the set decoration. It was like a museum.

"Look, Jerry!" Francis said, as he held up an old framed photograph to me.

I took it from him and looked at a couple of old folks on a street.

"Hotel DeVille! Look!" he exclaimed. "It's amazing!"

The couple was standing in front of a building, but I didn't see a hotel sign.

"Is all of this unbelievable?" he asked.

"It's pretty great," I said. I'm not an antique type of guy, but it looked right for the movie.

At that moment Bob Nelson, the set decorator, entered the room with a tiny silver dish and added it to a side table. He had received an Oscar for *The Godfather*.

"Bob!" Francis said. "This is unbelievable! Everything is great!"

Bob smiled and mumbled something, but Francis went on.

"All of these things! It's great!" Francis added.

"Thank you, Francis," Bob said. "It's been quite a job. I'm glad you like it." He looked around the living room with real pride in his accomplishment.

"What does it cost to get all of this here?" Francis asked, as he looked around the room again. "I mean all of it!"

Bob answered proudly, "Well, Francis, about $75,000 actually."

"Is that all? Jerry, all of this set dressing, all of it! It only cost $75,000! That's cheap!" Francis said.

"Oh, no, Francis," Bob added. "The $75,000 is *to get it here*! That's what I thought you asked. That's the cost of freight only! You know, from Paris to Manila!"

Francis was stunned.

"The cost for all this? I don't know, Francis," Bob continued. "I don't think anyone does."

Francis had a difficult time with the French Plantation scenes. We rehearsed the actors around the dining table, and we did take after take. Nothing seemed to work for him. Vittorio's lighting was somber; you could only see the faces around the table. Francis had said he wanted the people to be like ghosts from the past. The dialogue was to tell the history of the French in Vietnam from the mid-sixties back to the turn of the century—what they brought to Vietnam from France, how they imported the rubber trees from Brazil, how they created their plantations over sixty, seventy years, the culture and politics they brought to Vietnam, the food and the style they introduced into French Indochina.

While we filmed at the French Plantation, I became conscious of our character as filmmakers. We extended a set until it crossed the only road. We brought props and set dressing all the way from Paris to the Philippines. We used vintage French wines in the scenes. We hired local help and named them Red, Blue, Green. We had 600 local laborers building the Kurtz compound set. We served crew lunches for 550. Though Francis assured me he would use no extras at the French Plantation, I had 30 people hidden a quarter mile down the road. I felt I had to protect myself. What if Francis changed his mind? We had all gone a bit insane.

All of us worked to please Francis Ford Coppola, the world's most respected film director. If he asked for a hundred explosions, we prepared five hundred. During the rehearsals for the Village II battle scenes, two hundred extras fired their weapons because no one told Francis about the cost. If no Hueys were coming that day, Francis wasn't told because no one wanted to upset him. If he mentioned he wanted a corned beef and pastrami sandwich on his birthday, hundreds of pounds of each were flown in from Nate and Al's Deli Restaurant in Beverly Hills to the beach in Baler, where most of it rotted in the Philippine sun.

• • •

One day Francis and I were sitting outside the set at the French Plantation. We were sitting alone in the garden area where Mr. Clean's burial scene had been played. The crew was inside the house preparing the next shot.

Francis was dealing with a lot of pressures—personal, financial, and creative; there was no ending for the script. I talked to Francis about my weekend visit to Hong Kong and how much I enjoyed it. I told him about the hotel, the restaurants, the food, and my wandering around Macao. I mentioned to Francis that perhaps a weekend flight to Hong Kong might help him unwind as it had me.

He stared at me. For a second I thought he was angry, but he wasn't.

"Jerry, you've got to understand that I can't do that," he said.

"Why, Francis? You think you can't be gone for a day?" I asked.

"No, I think I could be gone for a week, but I can't do what you do," he continued.

I didn't understand. I looked at him for a long time.

"Why, Francis?" I asked.

"Because you can walk into the Peninsula Hotel in Hong Kong and get a room; all I'd be shown is the Ghengis Khan Suite! You walk to some steak restaurant, but I'd have to eat with the hotel president in their special dining room!" he explained.

I listened to him and tried to understand.

"Jerry, I had a perfectly good office in San Francisco. The art department wanted to redecorate it for me while I was away. I didn't need anything done to that office! How much do you think that cost me?" he asked.

I didn't answer.

"It cost me, me personally, Francis Coppola, $450,000, which I don't have!" He said. "I didn't need anything done to that office; I liked that office!"

I just sat there and listened. I couldn't relate to those amounts. My whole house had cost $35,000.

"I have an office building in San Francisco. They asked if they could paint the top. Do you know what they're doing? Patina! Like on a cup or something. They're putting patina on the whole top of the building! What do you think that's going to cost?"

I listened to Francis, but we were all at fault—every one of us, me included, and Francis, too. First of all, there were far too many of us in the Philippines making the movie, and probably far too many in his building in San Francisco, too. No one knew what everyone did because we were afraid to ask. We each wanted to please Francis so somehow we would become a part of his "immortality." To please him we felt we could never tell him, "No," and in order not to do that, we all bought more, hired more, rented more. We got the bigger, the newer, the best, and more of each until we became so overweight as a film company that we could barely function.

We all became self-indulgent and spent far too much money doing it. There was no one willing to say to us, "Stop! No more! You can't have that!" Even if there had been such a person, it wouldn't have done any good. We would've all run to Francis.

One day I was crossing the hotel parking lot in Pagsanjan on my way to our production offices, and Francis stopped me. He was holding a yellow tablet in his hand, and he had made notes on perhaps four or five pages.

"Jerry, do you know what this is?" he asked me.

I said that I didn't.

"It's a million dollars! I'm getting a million dollars for editing the two *Godfathers* together for TV!" he continued, as he held up his yellow pad. "And here are all my notes! One million dollars!"

"That's great, Francis," I said.

"And you know what I'm going to do with it?" He added, "I'm going to put it right back into *Apocalypse Now*, isn't that crazy?"

Maybe it was and maybe it wasn't. We all supported Francis as an artist. We just didn't know when or how to stop, and neither did he.

I was sitting at one of the caterer's long tables. We still had a few minutes of lunchtime left before we had to get back to work. Everyone else was leaving. I liked that. I worked closely around people every minute of the day; I liked some alone time.

Francis came in late, got some ice cream in a plastic dish, and sat down across from me.

"Steven Spielberg, Billy Friedken, and I are each doing a picture right now. Three pictures. Only one's going to be a success. Only one!" Francis said, as he ate his ice cream.

I just watched him.

"Spielberg's getting ready to do Close Encounters, *a science fiction piece. Freidken's doing an action/adventure thing,* Sorcerer, *in Honduras or somewhere. I'm doing* Apocalypse Now *about the Vietnam*

War. Which one's going to be a success?" Francis asked as he continued to eat. "Which one?"

Two years later I would work with Steven Spielberg on Close Encounters of the Third Kind.

"Apocalypse, Francis," I answered.
"What makes you say that?"
"Because it's universal," I replied.
"It's universal shit!" Francis said, as he continued eating his ice cream.

I just sat and watched him as he concentrated on the ice cream in his dish.

"You know why that little bear is in the center of all the Apocalypse Now *T-shirts?" he asked.*

"No," I said. It was a picture of a stuffed toy bear.

"Well, when I was a little kid, if I ate all my cereal I got to see that little bear on the bottom of my dish," Francis answered. "I got to see that little bear, and I got fat from eating all my cereal."

Francis finished his ice cream and looked around the empty catering tent.

"When are we back from lunch?" he asked, as he got up, put his empty dish in the trash, and started to walk back toward the set.

"We're back," I said, as I hurried to keep pace.

As the PBR left the French Plantation, it reentered the fog and continued its trip up the Nung River. It was as if the PBR were passing back into time. On the shore were hints of older civilizations—some huts, a ritual marking place, some rough-hewn canoes, and native voices imitating the calls of animals. We saw natives run into the jungle as the boat passed, then the PBR was attacked. It wasn't a firefight; it was an attack of arrows and spears.

All of us on the crew enjoyed the attack scene because we got to throw arrows at the cast. Before each take, we each would get a couple of handfuls of arrows, then during the take we would throw or lob the arrows at the cast. Freddie Forrest was a favorite target; even Francis threw arrows; Fred jumped the best.

The ending of the arrow attack was the killing of Chief (Albert Hall) by a spear. Mr. Clean died in a firefight, and the Chief was killed by a spear. Though Mr. Clean was buried at the French Plantation, the Chief was given a burial by Lance. He just held the Chief in the river and then caressed him and gently pushed him out into the current. Albert held his breath as long as he could and just floated away.

I was sorry to see Albert Hall complete his scenes in the film and go back to the States. He was always pleasant, professional, and he added so much of himself to the film. He brought dignity and integrity to the role of Chief.

If I ever saw that Albert Hall was in the cast of a film, I knew that film was going to be important. Because if the film wasn't meaningful, Albert wouldn't have done it. If you string Albert Hall's films together, *Malcolm X*, *Get on the Bus*, and *Beloved*, you get a pretty good picture of our culture for better or worse. Maybe that's all making films is about, reflecting our culture for better or worse.

The PBR left the body of the Chief buried in the water and moved upriver toward Cambodia and Colonel Kurtz. Chef (Freddie Forrest) was now the boat's pilot. Lance (Sam Bottoms) was at the stern and Willard (Marty Sheen) watched the jungle as they cautiously moved farther up the Nung River.

Apocalypse Now: Part Three

Marlon Brando was waiting at his home in Tahiti. We all felt that the success of *Apocalypse Now* depended on Francis directing Marlon to give us a world-shaking ending for our movie, an ending that might earn *Apocalypse Now* a nomination for a Nobel Peace Prize. That's how I felt.

We looked toward those members of the crew that had been with Francis and Marlon on *The Godfather.* They were confident that Francis and Marlon would work their cinematic magic once again. While Francis rewrote the ending of the script and the days counted down for Marlon's arrival, we filmed our PBR working its way upriver toward the Kurtz compound—Marlon Brando and the ending of *Apocalypse Now.* We were all on a collision course, but we didn't know it yet.

The PBR, with Willard watching from the port side, Chef piloting, and Lance at the stern, came around a bend in the Nung River and discovered a line of sixty bancas with 120 Montagnards blocking their path.

There were two Filipino boatmen in each banca, and they were covered in white makeup, with darker gray and black lines of Montagnard design on their faces and bodies. Francis had seen photos of such a line of boatmen from a ceremony in Borneo. He wanted the PBR's entrance to the Kurtz compound to be like a birth. The boatmen and their bancas only moved when the PBR pushed through them and entered the world of Col. Kurtz, and Marlon Brando.

The company had gone all over Luzon looking for boatmen and had brought them to Pagsanjan and housed them, fed them, and rehearsed them for this climactic entrance. It took six hours to put makeup on all of the boatmen. We used actual paint sprayers filled with white makeup to do their bodies, but all of the Montagnard makeup to their faces and bodies had to be done by hand.

Finally, all the boatmen were ready, in their bancas, and all in line. I was riding on the top of the PBR. I had my walkie-talkie to Larry and my bullhorn to communicate with the boatmen. We had pulled the PBR up to the line of the bancas as Vittorio continued to work. He had told me he had at least another ten or fifteen minutes before we could pull the PBR back to its start mark and begin to film.

Jerry Endler, a wonderful old special effects man, radioed to me and asked if it was all right if they set off an underwater charge about a hundred yards up river opposite the main temple. They wanted to test the size of the charge. I checked with Vittorio and he wasn't ready, so I told Endler to go ahead.

I was looking over all the boatmen in their makeup and all ready to film, when the underwater charge went off. To my horror, all 120 of the boatmen dove into the water and began to swim toward the underwater charge. All of the makeup we had put on the boatmen for the last six hours was instantly washed off. I sat there stunned as the boatmen began to gather the dead fish to sell in the local market.

I couldn't look at Francis, but Vittorio pointed at the boatmen and then called up to me, "Jerry, no. For sure not, Jerry."

Marty gave me one of his dry comments, "It's their first movie, Jer." Then he chuckled as he walked to the bow.

Larry called on the walkie-talkie, "Jer, what the hell happened? They shouldn't be in the water, right? Right, Jer?"

"That's right, Larry."

We finished the day getting some close shots on Marty, Freddie, and Sam for all of their reactions. We wouldn't be filming with the boatmen until they had all their makeup on again, sometime the next day.

That next morning the boatmen were lined up like cars at an auto plant ready to be painted, as the makeup people again sprayed them white. Farther along the assembly line, they got their faces and bodies lined. Larry seemed to be right on top of it all. He had about forty of the bancas and boatmen already out on the river.

Vittorio and the camera crew were down at the dock in front of the temple's festival area getting all their camera equipment onto the PBR. Nat Boxer was already on board with his mixing panel and boom mike.

Francis came down with the cast. Pete Cooper was revving the PBR's diesel engine. I checked with Larry on the walkie-talkie. He said the other boatmen would be in their place before the PBR was, so I got on board and took the PBR out.

Once again the PBR with Marty, Freddie, and Sam was in position, with the sixty bancas and 120 boatmen blocking the river. This time I made sure not to let anyone set off an underwater explosion.

When the shot began, the PBR moved slowly into the line of bancas and Montagnards, made its way gently through them, and headed upriver before turning toward the Kurtz compound on the north side of the Pagsanjan River. The people on the PBR gave me a friendly smile and some polite applause when the first take was over and none of the boatmen were swimming in the water.

I was one of the earlier crew members down to the hotel dining room each morning for coffee. The dining room was next to the swimming pool, and every morning about four or five of the hotel workers would be pulling deck chairs out of the pool. Tommy Shaw, Jr., one of the young prop men, would get a few drinks in him at night, and he'd throw all the deck chairs into the pool. Each morning the hotel workers would bring them out and set them back up. There weren't any bad feelings on either side. It was just another ritual on *Apocalypse Now*.

A group of the crew was gathered around the door to the projection room the company had built off the hotel lobby. Leon had posted the big news of the morning: United Artists was flying in film of each week's National Football League highlights. Didn't take much to get the crew excited in Pagsanjan.

We used the projection room to watch the dailies of our previous days' filming. On *Apocalypse Now* it took nine days from the day we filmed for the flight to the lab in Rome, the testing and eventual developing and processing, and then the trip back to Pagsanjan. Vittorio shot test footage of each camera setup, which the lab in Rome tested before they developed our picture footage.

When a batch of dailies came back from Rome, the next weekend the cast and crew would crowd into the projection room to view their collective work. We all were so proud of what little contribution we each had made toward the work of Francis and Vittorio. We felt part of something greater—it was a victory over ourselves.

• • •

In the morning there'd be vehicles outside the projection room in the hotel parking lot to take us to the set. They'd take us west about ten miles to our Kurtz compound road. The company had built a road south from the highway about a half mile to the base camp for the equipment at the edge of the compound. Kelly, who replaced the Dragon Lady as our new caterer, had all his tents and tables and chairs to the west; to the south, near the river and dock, was the main temple that housed the set for Col. Kurtz's living quarters; to the east were the wide temple grounds for the festivals.

Dean Tavoularis had designed the whole temple complex along the lines of the Angkor Wat temple in northwest Cambodia. Dean not only had the main temple building for Kurtz and the secondary temple, but farther east more temple ruins and giant Buddha heads spread for nearly a half mile. Every angle of the Kurtz compound could be filmed—360 degrees, over a half mile long and a half mile wide.

John La Sandra, the construction head, had hired six hundred laborers to build the temples similar to the way they had originally been built. The workers made three hundred pound blocks of adobe mud and fit those blocks together to construct the walls and floor of the temples. It was a gigantic undertaking in terms of manhours and materials, but when you stood next to one of their temples, it was real and not cardboard.

Away from the river and on the north side of the wide festival area was housing for the Ifugaos, which the art department had also designed as part of the temple set. Eva Gardos, a young production assistant, was responsible for bringing the Ifugaos to Pagsanjan. I remembered the Sunday when Dick White, Chris, and I first dropped her off at the Banaue Rice Terraces. She had hired about two hundred Ifugaos to portray the Montagnard natives who followed Col. Kurtz. The company bused them down to Pagsanjan from their mountainous Ifugao lands in the northern section of Luzon.

The next day we filmed the approach of the PBR to the dock. The camera was still on the boat, shooting over our crew out toward the temples, the dock, the Ifugaos, and Dennis Hopper.

Immediately to the west of the dock was a small island, less than twenty feet in diameter, that we called Monkey Island. The set dressers had bought thirty "nonswimming" monkeys, and they had prepared

little homes and perches for them on their island. The set dressers put
the thirty monkeys in cages and took them by boat out to the island and
released them. But before the set dressers could get back to their boat,
the thirty monkeys attacked them. They bit, scratched, and chased the
set dressers around the tiny island. The monkeys screamed and swung
on their perches as they grabbed at the set dressers, who were huddled
together on the river side of the island. When the monkeys had enough
of that, they all calmly walked into the river, swam to the shore, and
disappeared into the jungle. I'd occasionally see one sitting on top of the
temple, but never on Monkey Island.

Next to Monkey Island, Terry Leonard had one of his native stuntmen hanging from a tree and dangling over the water as he pretended
to be dead. That particular area was in a lot of our shots because it was
next to our docked PBR, and that poor stuntman would have to hang
from the tree for hours at a time while we filmed.

About ten feet from the hanging stuntman and five feet from the
river's shore, there were flames of fire coming directly out of the water.
The special effects department had been asked by the art department to
place a gas jet under the water and to light the escaping gas so the flame
looked as if it came out of the river. I stood on the dock and looked at
that flame and tried to imagine every possible scenario, but I could
think of no rational reason for a flame coming out of the water. Dean
Tavoularis came on the dock to check the dressing on the PBR. Vittorio
and his crew were positioning the camera for another approach shot to
the temple.

"Dean?" I called to him. I always liked him and respected him as an
artist, and he never embarrassed me if I asked him a question that wasn't
too bright.

"Yes, Jerry," Dean answered in his quiet voice.

I motioned for him to come to where I was standing on the dock
closest to Monkey Island.

"Dean, look at that flame," I said.

"What about it?" he said, and smiled. "Is something wrong?" He
smiled again.

"Well, where's it come from? I mean it's coming out of water, Dean,"
I said quietly.

"I don't know. Maybe there's a plane down there," Dean said, and
smiled. Obviously he was not bothered by a flame coming out of
water.

"Look out there," he continued, as he pointed out across the river. "There's fire coming out of the water there, too. It's there—*just because.*" Dean smiled, and was perfectly content without any rational reason for the flames.

"Jerry! Dean! What is it?" Vittorio could smell we were having one of those "art" discussions.

"It's nothing, Vittorio. Jerry just wanted to know how the flames could be coming out of the river. That's all," Dean answered.

Vittorio got off the PBR and hurried over to us. "Jerry, what is wrong with the fire? I like the fire!"

I had wanted just a quiet word with Dean, but now Vittorio was involved and the other Italians were all watching.

"No, Vittorio," Dean tried to explain. "Jerry just asked about the fire."

I looked around, and the work on the PBR had stopped. The Italians and the rest of the crew were either listening to us from the dock or from the front of the PBR.

"What is it, Jer?" Marty Sheen said, as he walked toward us. He had just come down from his dressing room and had seen Vittorio, Dean, and me talking. Marty could talk "art" with the best of them.

"Martin," Vittorio began (he always called him Martin and not Marty), "Jerry doesn't believe the fire in the water."

"No, Vittorio," I began. "I just wanted to know how could it be?"

"I don't really know, Jerry," Dean said quietly. "I just like it. *Just because.*" He smiled at all of us.

"I like it, too," said Vittorio. "I don't care where it comes from, Jerry."

Had I opened a can of worms! Now I just wanted everyone to get back to work.

"Maybe there's something down there?" Marty offered.

At that moment Francis came down the steps at the dock.

"What's going on, guys?" Francis asked.

Vittorio was about to answer, but Dean beat him out, "Francis, we were just looking at the flame in the water and . . ."

"Yeah, Dean, it's a bit much don't you think? Can you turn it down a bit or something? I mean where's it coming from? You like it, Dean?" Then he turned toward Vittorio. "How we doing on the shot? You going to be ready soon?" Francis asked, and he moved to the PBR.

Dean smiled, but he never did turn down his "just because" flame. I watched for it in the movie, and Dean was right. The flames coming out of the water added an other-worldly, mysterious, unnatural properties to the surroundings. I learned once again that I should let artists be free of my assistant director's rational world, *just because.*

Larry and I began to place the Ifugaos on the steps and the landing of the dock for the PBR approach shot. It was the biggest shot from the water, and it would establish the whole look of the Kurtz compound. We carefully placed the younger Ifugaos on top of the walls and statues. We put the tribal leaders in the center of the dock, along with many of the children. There were three little girls about three or four years old, whom we all called "The Three Sisters," because they were always together. They would walk around holding hands or with their arms around one another's shoulders. Everyone was in love with them from the first day.

Very few of the Ifugaos spoke English, but communication was seldom a problem. They were very attentive and tried hard to please; I just loved working with them. When I knew the tribal leader better, I told him how wonderful everyone was. He thanked me and smiled and said that they had left the good ones in the villages; all of these folks were the incorrigible ones!

The Ifugaos have never been conquered. The Japanese during World War II were unable to control them, and the Philippine government has a mutual understanding with them. Eva told me that it wasn't too many years ago that the Ifugaos were still headhunters.

Wherever Larry and I placed the Ifugaos in the scene, they seemed to make it their own. The Three Sisters were placed on the dock for the approach shot, and the set dressers had put some bullet casings on the ground. The three little girls began to play with the items of destruction, making them into families, huts, and friends. From the very first day of shooting, I believed that the Ifugaos were the Montagnards that followed Kurtz and that they understood the movie *Apocalypse Now* a lot better than I did.

The approach shot began with a tableau of the Kurtz compound, with all of the Montagnards watching the PBR as it came closer. Dennis Hopper, who played the American freelance photographer, would come running through the Ifugaos and call to the PBR. Chef wanted the Montagnards to go away before he docked. He was scared of them because they had killed Chief with a spear. Dennis told him to hit the PBR's siren. That was their cue. When the Ifugaos heard the siren they all ran off. We did the scene with them running off time after time; they never got tired, never complained, and always came back to their start marks.

My room at the Rapids Hotel wasn't large, but it was comfortable. I had a bed, dresser, a nice closet, and a small table and chair. All the rooms on the second-floor hall were the same size.

During the Kurtz compound shooting, my next-door neighbor was Dennis Hopper and the Baroness. Dennis was the same wild, crazy creature he played in our film, but the Baroness was ghostly white and always dressed; she could easily have been from a movie about Transylvania. It was about 2:00 in the morning. Everyone was asleep, and most certainly me. Suddenly, from Dennis's room came the sounds of his screaming, then the sounds of running, then the sounds of pistol shots!

I leapt out of my bed, keeping low in case the bullets would come through the wall. The screams were definitely from Dennis Hopper, and the low-toned shouts were definitely from the Baroness. I heard their door open, and then Dennis was pounding on my door, screaming that she was going to kill him. As I opened my door I instinctively ducked; Dennis was shaking, but the Baroness had not left their room. Some more of the crew came cautiously down the hall.

"Dennis, my God, are you OK?" I said.

"I'm going to be all right. It's OK, yes, I'm OK. She just gets like that sometimes, doesn't last long," Dennis said. He left my door, said something to the gathering crew, then knocked and went cautiously back into his room. I didn't hear another sound from them for the rest of the night.

The next morning Dennis and the Baroness seemed the same as always. However, the rest of us treated the Baroness with newfound respect, and none of the crew sat next to her in the van or at lunch ever again.

After the PBR docked, Willard and Chef walked with Dennis toward the temple to the west, which contained the rooms of Col. Kurtz. Along the path leading to the temple were the bodies of Viet Cong and North Vietnamese regulars who had been killed by Col. Kurtz and his Montagnards. Chef could take no more, and he returned to the PBR.

On the plateau in front of the temple steps, we had dug pits for extras to sit in, so that only their heads showed above the ground. It appeared that their heads had been cut off and were lying on the ground.

One of the heads belonged to Tony Dettman, a longtime friend of Ellie and Francis and the one who first introduced them to each other. Between takes we would give the heads cold drinks to keep them comfortable in their pits. Because of the set dressing around their necks to camouflage the pit they were sitting in, the heads couldn't move for hours while we filmed.

On the right-hand portion of the path on the way up to the temple was a shallow hole, in which Dean had placed real cadavers. Most of us couldn't believe it! The crew protested, and the cadavers were gone the next day.

As Willard and Dennis continued to walk toward the temple, they saw Captain Colby, played by Scott Glenn. Colby had been sent before Willard to kill Col. Kurtz but had joined his forces instead.

Our American actors, who played the U.S. servicemen with Kurtz, went out on jungle maneuvers at night with our military advisers to get the "feel" of being a Green Beret in the jungles of Vietnam. Charlie Robinson and Scott Glenn would go off on patrols into the jungles, searching all night for the Viet Cong. It was wild stuff. They lived in huts and ate roots and leaves. Our military advisers put them through the experiences of being commandos in Vietnam and Cambodia. It may have been the late-night maneuvers or just his natural talent, but Scott Glenn created a frightening character in Captain Colby. He had a lot more to do during our filming than was seen in the final cut version of *Apocalypse Now* that was shown in the theatres.

During the walk up to the temple, Francis had his hands full with Dennis Hopper. We spent one day with Francis just rehearsing with Dennis. Part of the problem was that Dennis didn't know his lines, but the basic problem was the struggle between actor and director. Dennis challenged Francis on every point of the script, the scene, his motivation, and personal aspects of their lives. At the end of the day, Francis was very frustrated.

The next morning Francis called me over to him and handed me a number of 3 × 5 index cards.

"Jerry, look. I need your help. Dennis is driving me nuts. I couldn't sleep," Francis began.

I looked at the cards. He had typed a series of signals I was to give him as to how I felt the scene was going or what he should do.

"What is this, Francis?" I asked.

"Look, I'm going crazy. I want you to signal to me what you think I should do. To help me, see? Look, pull your right ear if I should stay with the same shot and go again. If I should change the setup, you wipe your forehead, see?" he explained.

I looked down at the cards. I had never had hand signals with a director before, but this was *Apocalypse Now* and this was Francis Coppola. Somehow it all made sense. We used the signals for all the scenes with Dennis Hopper.

We got all the Ifugaos and the heads ready, and we began to film with Marty and Dennis. Just like the day before, Dennis challenged everything Francis wanted. Every time Francis would look at me I'd pull my right ear or wipe my forehead, or scratch my head or give whatever sign I thought would help Francis. Nothing helped. It got to be late in the afternoon of our second day on the first shot of Dennis and Marty walking up the path.

Finally Francis had it. He threw down his cap and shouted at Dennis.

"I've let you do it your way for two days! Just once! Once! Do the scene the way I want it!"

We all stood there. Francis would get frustrated and depressed, and sometimes angry, but very rarely did he ever shout. When he did the whole company tightened up and became very quiet. Even the Ifugaos were aware of the tension.

When the director and an actor go at it, all the assistant director can do is stand back and give the director all the silent support he can. When the battle is over it's the assistant director who's going to be talking with both the actor and the director to get the next shot going.

When the point of crisis was reached between Francis and Dennis, it was Dennis who chuckled and then backed down and finally did the scene the way Francis had always wanted him to do it.

One Sunday night I was riding in the company bus with Dennis Hopper. We were all returning to Pagsanjan from a weekend in Manila. He was alone; the Baroness had left the country that weekend.

In the Philippines they don't celebrate Halloween, but they do celebrate the Day of the Dead. One day a year the families meet and go to the cemeteries for a celebration. They bring food as if it were a picnic, and they spend the whole day and the night at the gravesites. At night the whole cemetery is lit by candlelight as people eat, drink, gamble, sing, dance, and have a good time. It was a very festive sight.

When we passed the first cemetery on our way back to Pagsanjan, Dennis was very interested and took note of the activities.

When we passed the second cemetery, Dennis was straining to see everything.

"Look! Wow! Hey, what's happening there? Can you see that?" Dennis said.

When we passed the third cemetery, Dennis was in the aisle of the bus.

"Slow down! Man, look at that! Slower, man! Hey, can you see that? Slower!"

When we passed the fourth cemetery, Dennis had discovered that I was on the bus and had the authority to get the bus driver to stop.

"Jer! Oh, man! Look at all that! Oh, Jer! Please, just stop for a minute, five minutes! Oh! Please, man, please!"

The rest of the crew on the bus knew Dennis like I did. If we had let him off, we wouldn't have gotten him back on the bus until Wednesday.

"No way, Dennis. We're not stopping," I said.

"Jerry, please!" Dennis was in the aisle in pain as the bus rolled past the cemetery. "I'll be good, man! I will! You can come with me! Oh!!!! Man, Look at that! See out there! Please stop! Please, Jer!"

The next cemetery was bewitching in the candlelight, with the dancing figures, the music, and the laughter. Dennis was sitting back in his seat.

"We're not stopping! I know that! But you assholes will regret it for the rest of your lives!" Dennis shouted.

I wish now I had stopped the bus, hung onto Dennis's arm, and walked through the roadside cemetery during the Day of the Dead with him. It would've been an exciting adventure, but I didn't, and Dennis was right. I'll regret it for the rest of my life.

We filmed Willard entering Kurtz's rooms and looking through his books and papers. He came upon *The Golden Bough* and a book of William Blake's poetry. Willard noted the photographs of Kurtz's wife and son and that his uniform was neatly hung up and ready to be worn. It was the first time in our filming that we had shot inside Kurtz's rooms. Of course, we didn't see Col. Kurtz because Marlon Brando wasn't there, not quite yet. I couldn't wait.

Marlon Brando was at his home in Tahiti and communicated with Francis by letter or cable. There were discussions as to the script, the sets, the set dressing, and Marlon's hair. Should his hair be long or short? Should it be in a ponytail or a crew cut? Should he have feathers and bones tied in his hair? The questions and discussions on Marlon's hair didn't end until he stepped off the plane in Manila. He had shaved his head; he was totally bald.

The first time I saw Marlon Brando I was surprised that I was taller than he. He must have been about five feet ten inches or less, but his weight! He was very overweight. I thought of him from *Streetcar Named Desire* and *On the Waterfront*. I remembered him as the tough rebel, but the short, overweight figure I saw in front of me wasn't that image. He seemed contented and satisfied, all the anger and rebellion had gone. There didn't seem to be any threat or danger about him.

The Sunday prior to Marlon's first day of work, he gave a large party, and everyone was invited—cast, crew, and the Ifugaos. The entertainers and the food were brought from Manila. There were long banquet tables spread with all the delicacies of the Philippines. Marlon hosted the party on the shores of Lake Caliraya; he was staying at a resort there.

I thought how gracious Marlon was to have a party for the entire film company. It was a wonderful afternoon, and everyone had a great time relaxing out at the lake and eating all the gourmet foods. The Ifugaos enjoyed the entertainment and music, but they were all sick the next day from eating the gourmet foods.

I had given Marlon Brando an 8:00 call to arrive on the set for his first day of shooting. When he hadn't arrived by 10:00, I got worried. We had a car and driver standing by at his resort. Should I send a second car and driver? Francis assured me that Marlon was probably just a little nervous on his first day. I accepted that; Francis had worked with him on *The Godfather* and knew him.

Finally, Marlon's car arrived on the set. He got out and walked directly to his houseboat. He opened the door, entered, and closed the door. Larry and I looked at one another. We'd never worked with Marlon Brando; maybe this was how it's supposed to be.

I looked over at Francis for some guidance. He was sitting on one of the large fallen trees on the edge of the base camp. An assistant director is supposed to get the company moving, doing something. I walked over to Francis and sat down. We both looked down at Marlon's houseboat.

"Let's let him get settled a bit," Francis said.

I looked around at the hundreds of crew members, cast, extras, and the two hundred Ifugaos. I looked at the masses of film equipment.

"OK. Let me know, Francis. I'm right here," I said, and I continued to sit on the fallen tree. I watched Larry move cautiously toward us.

"What are we doing?" Larry asked.

Neither Francis nor I said a word. We just looked down and glanced occasionally at his houseboat, and we waited.

Larry looked at the two of us, and he sat down, too.

Finally Francis said, "I guess I'll go down to the houseboat and talk with him."

Larry and I just nodded, but we didn't move. We didn't know what else to do. We had nothing to tell the crew or other actors. We just sat on the log and watched Francis enter the houseboat.

Three hours later I called lunch. We all went through Kelly's catering line. We sent two lunches down to the houseboat. Larry and I went back to sitting on the fallen log and glanced occasionally at his houseboat.

Vittorio wandered by. He had worked with Marlon on *Last Tango in Paris*.

"Vittorio," I called to him. "Was Marlon like this on *Last Tango?*" I asked, as I nodded toward his houseboat.

"Yes," Vittorio answered, smiled, and walked off.

Larry and I just stared at one another. What had we gotten ourselves into now?

The door of the houseboat opened slowly. Francis came out and motioned for me. Everyone in the cast and crew tensed up. I walked down to Francis.

"Jer, call a wrap. Send everyone back to the hotels. We can't film today," Francis said.

"Francis?" I began.

"We can't film. Maybe tomorrow," Francis said, and he reentered the houseboat and closed the door.

I walked up to Larry as the cast and crew gathered around.

"Guys, that's a wrap! Same time tomorrow. Thank you all," I said.

Everyone was full of questions and ideas.

"What's happening, Jer?" Larry asked. "What're we going to do?"

"It'll be OK, Larry." I answered, but the warning lights had begun to go off in my head.

In Marlon's contract we had him for fifteen days of work over a three-week span. That was all. No extra days. The first of the fifteen days was already gone, and he hadn't come out of his houseboat.

The second day Larry and I were back sitting on the fallen tree and waiting for Marlon's car to arrive. According to Francis, yesterday Marlon had questioned everything about the scenes, and his character. Francis had worked most of the night on rewriting the scenes, and he was waiting down at the houseboat to show them to Brando.

The cast, crew, all of the extras, and the Ifugaos got ready in all their makeup and wardrobe. Then we all just waited.

Marlon's car finally arrived, and he got out, waved his greeting, and headed down to his houseboat. He and Francis entered, and we didn't see them for five hours. The younger members of the crew got out the Frisbees. Others sat in groups talking. Some went for walks in the jungle near the compound. A few cleaned their film equipment. A couple told old movie stories. Two propmen went fishing off the dock.

Larry and I sat on the log and talked. I really missed Ziggy. One of the painters who came over after the typhoon had actually painted the yellow brick road on *The Wizard of Oz*. He said he remembered Ziggy playing the Captain of the Flying Monkeys.

Larry told me about his son, Matt, and how he missed seeing him play baseball in the kid league out in Thousand Oaks. (By 1997 Matt Franco played infield for the New York Mets and was one of the top pinch hitters in the major leagues.)

I told Larry about Chris in Group Two at Westland School. All the parents were supposed to help clean and paint the school on Family Work Day. I missed doing that.

I called lunch at 1:00 P.M. There was no word from the houseboat. While we were eating, I saw Marlon and Francis leave the houseboat and walk through the festival area of the temple complex. They walked slowly and were talking. Francis was trying to explain something, while Marlon kept slowly walking forward.

About an hour later Francis called to me. They wanted Marty to join them. Larry got Marty from his dressing room. He had been waiting for a day and a half. Now Francis, Marlon, and Marty walked slowly, stopped, talked, and walked some more.

Vittorio came up to me and pointed at the sun. The light wasn't good any longer for shooting outside. I nodded.

Francis, Marlon, and Marty were sitting in their cast chairs outside the main temple and talking. I made my way toward Francis just to let him know that we should dismiss the crew. The three of them could stay and talk all they wanted.

"Francis, excuse me, we've lost the light. Why don't I send the crew? I'll keep props and wardrobe here in case you want to talk with them."

Francis faced the loss of the second day. "OK, Jer," he said. We exchanged a look that said "What can we do?"

"Can you get me my script, please," Francis asked. "I left it in Marlon's houseboat."

"Sure. I'll be right back," I said, and I started toward the river.

I came to Marlon's houseboat and knocked. There wasn't a sound, so I pushed the door open a bit. "Hello!" I said. I entered and found Francis's script on a chair. When I turned to leave, I noticed all of the books on the dinette table. They were about the Vietnam War, the philosophy of war, and the history of U.S. diplomacy. There were also the poems of T. S. Elliot that Francis had mentioned in the script. I saw at least thirty books in all. So much for the notion that Marlon Brando didn't do research for a film. No wonder he and Francis had a lot to talk about.

I brought the script back to Francis. The shadows were getting long. We had used up our second day with Marlon Brando and still hadn't filmed one frame. My stomach was turning; I could only imagine what was happening to Francis.

The third day began like the first two, with Marlon arriving late and going directly into his houseboat. Later Francis, Marty, and Marlon sat outside the temple and talked all morning.

At lunch Marlon had something he had brought from the resort to eat on the houseboat. Marty joined Kelly's catering line. Francis sat on the fallen log. He looked as depressed as I'd ever seen him on the film. I knew he had been up most of two nights trying to get the scenes written so Marlon would accept them. We only had twelve days remaining with Marlon, and we still had to film the whole ending of the movie. Vittorio and I joined Francis.

"I don't know what to tell you. He's not ready!" Francis began. "What do you want me to do?"

"Francis, maybe we could prepare just one scene," Vittorio began.

"I don't have even one scene! I have nothing," Francis answered. "There's not one scene he accepts. None!"

I didn't know what to suggest. Francis and Marlon had to pull this off like they did with *The Godfather*. It was up to the two of them.

"Francis," Vittorio began, "maybe I can light Kurtz's room just for a test. Maybe we can film Marlon, just for a test, this afternoon?"

"Do you know what Marlon said to me? He wants his character to be hidden in the shadows so we can't see him! Every scene! Then he wants another actor to do his lines!" Francis explained. "I asked him if we aren't going to see him or hear him, why is he here at all? He said he wondered, too."

"Let's at least get the set lit and try to do a test," I offered.

"Go ahead," Francis said. "I don't know what to do. I might shoot myself."

"Oh, no! Francis," Vittorio laughed. "We'll do a test. You'll see."

Vittorio went into the temple with Alfredo and Luciano. Larry sent me the stand-ins for Marty and for Marlon. Vittorio started to light the test. At least the company was working on something. Everyone was feeling better.

Marlon had his own stand-in who traveled with him on every film. I had worked with that same stand-in on *Hello, Dolly!* and *The Way We Were*. Stand-ins are supposed to be the same size and coloring of the person for whom they are standing in, but Marie Squire was the stand-in for both Barbra Streisand and Marlon Brando. At least Marie was the same size and coloring as Barbra, but she didn't look at all like Marlon. Marie Squire was, however, married to Marlon's makeup man, who worked with Marlon on every one of his films, too.

It was late on Marlon's third day with us. Vittorio completed his lighting for the test shots. We all hoped that if we got Marlon and Francis working together in front of the camera, something would begin to happen. Marlon fought coming to the set; he didn't feel ready. Francis, Marty, and Marlon had rehearsed a scene where Willard and Kurtz are sitting in his rooms. It was the first time Kurtz and Willard talked together. Francis had to beg Marlon to just come into the set.

"Marlon, look, it's a test! We're not going to use any of this. It's just to see how it all looks," Francis assured him.

"Certainly, Marlon. A test only," Vittorio added.

Marlon was no fool, but I think he knew the time had come. He lay back in the bed on the set. Marty sat in the room, his hands were bound. There was no light on Marlon until he sat up in his bed and leaned forward. Marlon would stay in the darkness and then slowly lean just a portion of his face into the light. I felt it was another birth, getting Marlon born into the movie. Slowly Marlon began to speak, he used a wash basin, and became more comfortable with the scene. He talked about a gardenia plantation along the Ohio River he had floated by on a raft when he was young. Marlon began with his own Midwestern life and slowly moved into the character of Kurtz.

First we filmed the wide master shot with both Marty's back and Marlon facing the camera. When Francis was happy with that, we moved in and did all of Marlon's close-ups. Marlon worked the light and shadow, moving his face into and out of the light.

Marlon was on film, and he began to show us the very beginnings of Kurtz. I was just happy to be filming at last. We had waited most of three days. Even though Marty was totally off-camera for all of Marlon's close-ups, he was still there and giving total performances on every take. What was most shocking to me was that Marlon took pieces of note paper, numbered them, and then wrote very short line reminders on them. He then placed these numbered notes just off-camera so he could read them while we were filming. He put some notes on the camera, on Enrico, on the floor, and on Marty. When the scene began Marlon would glance about, searching for note #1. When he found it he would read the message and then say his line. When it was his cue to speak again, Marlon would search for note #2, read it, and then speak. Marty would not only be acting for Marlon off-camera, but he also had notes on his chest and forehead. When it was Marty's turn to be on camera and Marlon's turn to be the off-camera actor, Marlon gathered his things, said good night, and went home.

I was shocked at Marlon's leaving. I hadn't experienced one actor not staying to help the on-camera actor; it just wasn't done, not in a major scene. Francis was mystified by Marlon's departure. Neither Francis nor Vittorio had recalled Marlon doing that on *The Godfather* nor on *Last Tango in Paris*.

"Hey, guys, come on! It's no big thing," Marty said. "Let's do it. I'll be fine, really."

We had all sat around for nearly three days waiting for Marlon, and he left before the only other actor in the scene finished his close-ups! I wanted to wrap for the day and shoot Marty's close-ups with Marlon off-camera tomorrow, but Marty insisted on filming it that day. As always, Marty's performance was excellent, but we'll never know what having Brando off-camera would have added.

I believe Marlon left that day because he wasn't satisfied with his own performance. He was embarrassed that after making the company wait for three days, he couldn't perform up to his own high standards.

I became very curious about some of Marlon's acting techniques. Placing the numbered notes around the set and on the other actors was one, and later in the shooting schedule I asked him about it. We were between setups. He was standing by himself, just outside the temple. Vittorio and the crew were busy inside lighting. Marlon and I had become friends largely because I had worked with Marie Squire on other films, and she had given him a good report about me. Also, Marlon was just naturally kinder to the lower-level film workers than to the producers and studio executives.

"Marlon, can I ask you something?" I began.

"What?" he asked, and looked at me, but his voice was kind. I knew I could go ahead.

"You know the scenes. You study all of it. Why do you number the notes and write your lines and things on them?" I asked.

"Do you know what you're going to say next?" he asked me.

"No, but . . ." I began.

"OK, I don't want to either," he explained.

"So you get your cue, and then look around for the next numbered note?" I continued.

"Yeah. You think of what you're going to say, right? You look, think, look, then speak. Right?" he said.

"You mean, in the cab scene in On the Waterfront, *you had numbered notes all over the cab in the scene with Rod Steiger? I could've been a contender. You had numbered notes?" I asked.*

"Right," he said, and smiled. "I did. Damn right I did," he laughed.

"Let me ask you something else?" I began.

"What?" he asked. I knew he was enjoying our talk.

"When you just talk. You know, just talk? You don't mumble. OK?" I began.

"Yeah," he smiled.

"So why do you mumble when you're acting?" I asked.

He looked at me, and smiled. I knew there had to be a reason. He
had a perfectly clear speaking voice.
   "Because I want to have the last performance," he said.
   "What do you mean?" I asked.
   "We film a scene. Master. Close-up. Close-up. OK?" he asked.
   "Right," I agreed.
   "When the scene is all cut together, in the movie and all finished,
I come in and loop my lines any way I want. I have the final per-
formance before it goes into the theatres," he said. "If I see something
and want to change my performance, I can. No one else can, but I
can. I have the final performance." Marlon looked at me, smiled, and
moved away. The acting lesson was over.

After Willard entered Kurtz's rooms and saw his books and the photographs of his family, he left the temple without ever seeing Kurtz. As
Willard walked back toward the PBR, the Montagnards captured and
dragged him through the rain and mud.

Marty was such a popular person to the Ifugaos, that I couldn't get
them to roughly grab him and turn him upside down and forcefully
drag him through the mud. They loved Marty more than anyone else
in the company because he took time to be with them. Whenever he
wasn't filming, Marty would be sitting off somewhere and the Ifugaos
would be around him. They'd do their best at English, and Marty'd
communicate as best he could with gestures and facial expressions.
Marty was very interested in the Ifugao beadwork, sewing, and jewelry
making. He had either bought or traded for a brightly colored bag with
a long shoulder strap that they had made. He carried his script in that
bag for the rest of the picture.

Francis was getting a bit frustrated that the Ifugaos wouldn't grab
Marty and really pull him through the mud, so finally we had to get
Marty to talk to them. Even then they were too gentle. Later in the film
we would use the Ifugaos' love for Marty to help tell our story, but they
would never treat him roughly or with disrespect.

We were all huddled against the side of the cliff next to the smaller
temple. The noon rain was falling. It would only last for a few
minutes. Most of us didn't even bother to seek shelter. We'd just stand
out in it and let the warm rain pour gently down.
   I heard some talk and then cheers as information was passed along

the line of the cliff huggers. "Hey! Did you hear? Carter's been elected
president!"

I smiled at Larry; we'd guessed the right candidate on Black Sunday.

One late afternoon about 4:00 we arrived at the Kurtz compound location to film at night. The scene was Marty tied to a stake and Marlon
seeing him and walking off. That was it; that's all that was in the script.

I got out of the van at the base camp and greeted everyone. I saw that
Larry was getting all of the Ifugaos ready, because they'd be dancing in
the background of the scene. I got a cup of coffee from Kelly's catering
and looked around for the crew. Vittorio and his electricians were
already at work placing and rigging lights for the night shots. Vittorio
was lighting the scene by using the Montagnards' fires as his source. I
walked into the festival area where Marty would be tied; the set dressing
had the Ifugao fires and their festival materials. Special effects had their
rain standing by. It looked to me as if the company was working
smoothly and we'd be ready to film as soon as it got dark.

Suddenly I heard a shriek, "No! Not Chef! Not Chef!" and Fred
Forrest came running up from the direction of the docked PBR with
Francis in pursuit.

"He's not dying, God damn it! He's not dying!" Fred was shouting
and sobbing as he ran.

"Wait a minute, Fred!" Francis was imploring.

"Get away from me, Francis!" Fred threatened. "Chef is not going to
die, God damn it!"

"Fred, you don't understand," Francis said, trying to calm Fred down.

"You asshole! You asshole!" Fred screamed at Francis. "You're all
assholes!"

Fred was beside himself. His closest friend in the world, Chef, the
character he was playing in our film, was going to be killed. No one had
told him. It wasn't in any script that I knew about. The idea just up and
happened. Freddie fell sobbing near the temple with Francis continuing
to talk with him. What could Francis say? Freddie loved Chef, more
than a brother, maybe more than himself.

While Francis was comforting Freddie, our makeup department,
who had secretly spent all day making Chef's head, brought it to the set
for Francis and Vittorio to look at. Freddie took one look at the Chef's
head they were carrying, and he went into hysterics. We had to restrain
him, get him into a car, and take him off the location.

That night we filmed Willard covered with mud as he sat tied to a stake in the rain while the Montagnards danced in the firelight. Suddenly we saw the face of Kurtz painted with the green-and-black camouflage colors as he leaned down, looked at Willard, and then moved away. Willard relaxed for a moment, and then something was dropped in his lap. Willard looked down and screamed; it was the head of Chef.

Even though Freddie wasn't around to watch the scene, he still hasn't forgiven any of us who were there the night his beloved Chef died.

We went back inside Kurtz's rooms and picked up additional shots of the first discussion between Kurtz and Willard, the test scene we had done on Marlon's first day in front of the camera. Besides spreading his numbered note cards around the set, Marlon had also recorded various motivational dialogues on tape. Marlon's plan was to have an earpiece in one ear when he began a monologue. Then, when he felt the need, he would turn the tape recorder on and listen to some of his recorded material. When he'd heard enough, he would turn off the recorder and continue with his monologue. I had never seen nor heard of that acting technique, but with Marlon Brando you never knew what might be sensational. He was a proven artist; everything was worth a try.

Marlon was sitting in the hallway of Kurtz's room with the earpiece in his right ear, which was turned away from the camera. Vittorio had two cameras next to one another in the hallway. When the first was about to run out of film, he would turn on the second camera, which would run while the first camera was reloaded. No one in the world knew how long Marlon would continue his monologue about war, peace, diplomacy, leadership, honor, beauty, truth, and whatever else he had recorded on his tape.

Vittorio was excited and had all of his crew primed and ready. Francis looked at me as if to say "You never can tell." I was thrilled to be working with Marlon Brando, and if he wanted to try playing recorded motivation during his monologue, I was for it.

Everyone got ready. I asked Marlon if he was set. He was sitting in the hallway, and he checked his ear plug and made sure he could reach behind himself to start and stop the tape recorder. Marlon wanted to control everything connected with the tape.

I finally felt everyone was ready, and I rolled the camera. Francis called "Action." Marlon began his monologue. He talked of midwestern America. He talked of Kurtz's early career in the military. Then he reached behind himself to turn on the tape recorder.

"Where the hell is it?" Marlon shouted. "I got it! Wait! Louder!"

"You have the volume," Nat Boxer offered.

"I know that! God!" Marlon said, with his hand stretched behind himself.

He listened for about fifteen seconds. "OK, stop!" Marlon exclaimed.

"Marlon, you have to stop the tape," Francis offered.

"I know that! I'm not talking to you!" Marlon said, and then he relaxed back into his Kurtz position on the floor. He began to talk of honor, of the power in politics and government, and of his military command.

Behind the cameras Vittorio had ordered the second camera to turn on and the first camera to be reloaded. Marlon was going strong, and we were going to film every bit of his monologue no matter how long it took.

The camera crew kept reloading the two cameras. Marlon kept talking about truth, beauty, justice, and just about everything else. I began to wonder how much he had recorded on his motivational tape.

Forty-five minutes later, Marlon turned away from the camera. "That's the end of the tape!" he said. "I can't say anything else!"

Francis cut the camera, and we all looked around at each other. No one knew if we had just witnessed one of the great performances in an illustrious career or a nice experiment that didn't quite work.

Vittorio's camera crew had reloaded the camera five times during the scene. Nat Boxer had held the boom mike over his head for forty-five minutes. He was one of our most dedicated filmmakers, but even Nat was thoroughly exhausted after Francis finally cut the cameras.

But Vittorio was always Vittorio. "We go again, Francis?" Vittorio asked.

One Sunday afternoon on Lake Caliraya, Martin and Janet Sheen invited about seven guests, including Marlon Brando, to their home for a pasta dinner. All of the guests arrived, drinks were served, and happy conversation began. In the kitchen the water was boiling, the pasta was being cooked; the sauce was already prepared. When the pasta was cooked, it was placed in a large bowl and the sauce was poured over the top, to set for fifteen minutes to allow the sauce to permeate. Another drink was served and the conversation continued, but one guest was missing. Where was Marlon? When Marty and Janet went to investigate a noise in the kitchen, they found Marlon

had eaten the whole bowl of pasta that had been intended as dinner
for nine people!

Marlon smiled at us—he dared to be inexplicably extraordinary.
The rest of us waited for Marty and Janet to cook another pasta
dinner.

Francis didn't really know what to do with Marlon. We didn't have
any scenes that he accepted. It was decided to create a number of improvisational scenes with Marty and Marlon and see what would
happen.

There's great security for an assistant director in having a script with
a beginning, a middle, and an end. We had no ending. We had an
exciting story of Willard's journey upriver, but we had nothing after
he got to see Kurtz. I knew Francis was also concerned; I was over-
whelmed.

One day after lunch, while the crew was preparing the next shot, I
sat next to Francis on the fallen log between the base camp and the
festival area. I felt I had to express my feelings to Francis about the
script, especially the ending.

"How we doing?" Francis asked.

"We'll be ready in another forty minutes," I answered. "Vittorio's
still lighting."

Francis looked tired and worn down. The whole shooting sequence
with Marlon had been very hard on him.

"Francis, I'm really scared about this whole sequence," I said.

"I know. I am, too," he said.

"I don't know what happens after Marty gets here, you know?"

"What can I do? Marty'll kill Kurtz somehow. I don't know," Francis
commented.

"We have to have an ending," I said.

Francis looked at me. "We'll film a bunch of improvs until Marlon
has to go, then we'll kill Kurtz somehow, and that's the end."

We both stared down toward Marlon's houseboat.

"Don't worry. I'll fix it in the editing room. I always do," Francis
added.

Larry hung around Brando's houseboat so that when we were ready
for him, he would know right where Marlon was. I didn't want to waste
a minute of the eight days remaining.

"OK, Larry. Bring Marlon. We're ready," I radioed down to him.

Larry walked to the houseboat and knocked. There was no answer. Larry opened the door, shouted inside, and then looked in the houseboat for Brando. He wasn't there.

"Jer, Marlon's not in his houseboat," Larry radioed.

"Where is he?" I asked.

"I saw him go in. I sat right outside his houseboat. He couldn't have walked past me!" Larry answered.

"Looking for someone?" a voice on the walkie-talkie said.

"Who is this?" Larry asked.

"Stay off the walkie-talkie!" I snapped. "Larry, what do you mean he couldn't have gotten by you? Look around!"

"I am!" Larry answered.

"You're cold. Very cold!" a voice on the walkie-talkie said.

"Who is this?" Larry asked.

"Stop screwing around!" I said. "We can't find Marlon. Larry look up at the caterers."

"Colder, colder!" the voice said.

"Who is this?" Larry asked again.

"Keep off the walkie-talkie!" I said. "Larry, get everyone spread out and find Marlon!"

"He's not at the caterers," the voice said.

"Who is this?" Larry asked. "Marlon, is that you?"

"Who wants to know?" the voice asked.

"Marlon, we're ready at the camera, OK?" I said.

"Come and find me." It was Marlon's voice this time.

"Where the hell are you?" I asked.

"Now, now don't be crabby," Marlon said.

"Marlon, give me a hint?" Larry asked, as he got into the game.

Marlon had gotten hold of a walkie-talkie, slipped off the side of his houseboat into the river, and made his way to the riverbank without Larry seeing him. He had gone into the temple and was looking out at us through one of the doorways. He kept us running around playing "hot" and "cold" until Larry and I sat down and just quit his silly game.

"I'm ready you know, Jerry," Vittorio said.

"I know, Vittorio. It's Marlon. He's playing games with us. I don't know where he is," I replied.

"Marlon? He's right there," Vittorio said, and there was Marlon waving from the temple.

"Looking for me, guys?" Marlon said, as he made his way down toward us.

"There he is," Francis said, as he pointed at Marlon.

"Jerry, whenever you need me, I'm either in my houseboat or in the temple," Marlon said, as he handed me the walkie-talkie and walked past us to the camera. "That way you'll never have to look for me."

I just watched Marlon and wondered if he had been the same on *Streetcar Named Desire*. I bet he was.

Every day that Marlon worked, his makeup man was there, along with the makeup man's wife Marie, whom Marlon had in his contract as his stand-in. Every day the makeup man stood near Marlon with his makeup case and a water spray bottle.

We were between setups, so I approached both Marlon and his makeup man and asked them about Marlon's makeup.

"Marlon, do you wear makeup for Kurtz?" I asked.

"Yeah, very light," Marlon answered.

I stared at his face, and then looked to his makeup man and Marie. "Really? I can't see any," I said.

"No?" Marlon asked. Then he reached over, took the water bottle, and sprayed me full in the face.

"See it now?" he asked, as all three enjoyed Marlon's prank.

Marie, her husband, and Marlon laughed and pointed at me, hugged me, and laughed some more.

Marlon lives on Mulholland Drive east of the San Diego freeway, and I live about six miles away on Mulholland west of the freeway. Over the years I've occasionally seen Marlon trimming the bushes at his front gate. Then I think back to that day in the Philippines more than twenty years ago when I had water running down my face and three laughing pranksters hugging me.

We filmed Willard taken by the Montagnards and put into a bamboo cage that was only big enough for him to stand. Francis had Marlon do two improvisational scenes with Marty in the bamboo cage.

The first was a scene where Marlon came upon Marty in the cage and issued orders to the Ifugaos in French. That was a challenge. It was hard enough to get the Ifugaos to react to English, but now Brando and Francis wanted a scene in French. The justification was that the French had been in Vietnam and Cambodia for a hundred years and had worked with the Montagnards. The theory was that the Montagnards could understand French. Hearing Marlon Brando speak French to our

Ifugaos as he gestured for them to move prisoners was too much. I felt we were getting desperate.

The second scene was with Marlon talking to Marty while he was in the bamboo cage. This scene was also improvisation, but it had been well rehearsed, and there were actual lines of dialogue.

It was getting close to time for lunch. The lunch break is important for an assistant director, because there is a financial penalty if you work the cast and crew into their "meal penalty," which begins six hours after their first call in the day. Most of our cast and crew started at 7:00, so our meal penalty began at 1:00.

We had a shot of Marlon as he talked to Marty, who was inside the cage. I was rushing and pushing everyone so I could get the shot before the 1:00 meal penalty. Everyone was moving except Marlon. As soon as he realized what I was trying to accomplish, he got a ballpoint pen and began to slowly, so slowly, write his lines on the bamboo poles that made up Marty's cage.

"Marlon, come on. Let's go," I urged him.

"Just a minute, Jer," he answered, as he slowly, slowly wrote out his lines on the poles.

"Marlon, let me help you," I said. He had two pages of dialogue.

"No, can't. Won't work, Jer," Marlon said, as he *s-l-o-w-l-y* wrote and it got closer to the meal penalty.

"Please, Marlon, let's go!" I said. Everyone else was waiting as he printed each of his lines.

"Going as fast as I can, Jer," he answered.

I had had it. Marlon was just stalling to either get the whole company into meal penalty or just to drive me insane.

"OK, That's lunch!" I shouted. "Lunch everybody!"

Everyone immediately took off for Kelly's catering lines.

"Jer," Marlon said, "why'd you do that? I was just about ready." He laughed as he moved off toward his houseboat.

The last prank Marlon pulled involved the help of his longtime secretary. One day she began to circulate catalogues throughout the cast and crew of all kinds of electrical items, jewelry, anything that could be bought in Hong Kong. She told us that Marlon wanted to buy presents for all of the cast and crew—Marlon's thank-you gifts. She'd like everyone to look through the catalogues and select what they wanted and write the item with a brief description next to their name. When

Marlon finished shooting, he would take the list and go to Hong Kong, purchase the gifts, return, and pass them out at a special party he would give.

All of the cast and crew were going through the catalogues to find exactly what they wanted. Everyone thanked Marlon and told him how generous he was, how much they enjoyed working with him, etc., etc., etc.

It did look good. The presents were several hundred dollars each. Marlon's secretary was a sane and reliable person, and she was organizing all the gifts. It seemed sound. I had moments when I thought it might be real, but for the most part I didn't believe it; I never signed up for one of Marlon's thank-you gifts.

After everyone else had signed up for a gift, Marlon sent the list to Francis and his producers, asking them for $39,000 to buy all the gifts. Of course, Francis and the producers refused Marlon's request for $39,000, and that was the end of Marlon's thank-you gifts.

Dennis Hopper also visited Willard while he was in his bamboo cage. Dennis gave Marty a cigarette and disappeared as the Montagnards came back. They picked up Marty in the bamboo cage and began to carry it through the temple's festival area. Other Montagnards poked him with sticks and spears, and one of the priests moved a ceremonial knife back and forth across Marty's eyes. That time the Ifugaos were frightening.

Next Willard was placed in a small metal hut, a sweatbox, exhausted from his ordeal. The metal door swung open, and it was Kurtz with twenty children. He had come to read the news magazines to Willard.

Marlon read from *Time* magazine about the Vietnam War and the role of the United States in the war—and at the same time gave directions to the twenty Ifugao children, who couldn't understand a word of English.

"Hey! Don't stand in front me of me! Get back here," Marlon would say to a four-year-old Ifugao child.

Then Marlon would be reading again. Soon a child would wander.

"Get back over here! Where you going? See that camera? Stay back!" Marlon would direct the children, but they had no idea what he was talking about.

The close-ups on Marlon from inside the metal hut were left until Brando's last day on our movie. Francis filmed with Marlon until, after lunch, there was one shot left—his close-up as he came to the hut and looked in at Willard.

Dick White had landed the Jet Ranger in the base camp area. I knew Francis was eager to get away to Hong Kong for the weekend and to celebrate finishing with Marlon Brando.

Vittorio had the camera inside the metal hut. He was ready, so I radioed to Larry to bring Marlon to the set for his last shot.

"Jerry," Francis said, and he motioned for me to come over to him.

"What is it, Francis?" I asked. I thought maybe Francis was going to have some warm celebration for Marlon after his last shot in the picture.

"I'm leaving for Hong Kong. I'll see you Monday. Get these last close-ups of Marlon," Francis said, and he walked to the waiting Jet Ranger.

As Marlon walked onto the set, the Jet Ranger took off and headed north toward Manila and Francis's flight to Hong Kong.

I was numb. What had Francis said to me? Get Marlon's close-ups?

"Jerry! Who was that?" Marlon called, as he walked to the metal hut and watched the departing helicopter.

There are moments of utter fear in an assistant director's career, and this was definitely one of mine.

"That was Francis," I answered.

"Francis?" Marlon said, and stared at me. "Where's he going?"

"To Hong Kong," I said. "Let's get this last shot, OK?" I asked as calmly as I could. There I was, asking one of the greatest film actors of all time to let me, an assistant director, "direct" him in his final close-up. "Ready when you are, Marlon."

Marlon looked in the direction of the departing Jet Ranger and then back at me. My heart stopped. Vittorio was peering out from the metal hut. All the crew was watching. We waited.

"Please, Marlon, I've got to get your close-up," I said. "Help me."

He shook his head slowly from side to side as he looked down at the ground.

"OK, Jer. Let's get it," Marlon said.

We all moved quickly and filmed as efficiently as possible. We had one last setup to do and we'd be through. Vittorio, Enrico, and I were huddled around the camera getting the final shot ready, when the metal door was slammed shut and locked from the outside.

It could only have been Marlon. We laughed and continued, but soon into the cracks and slits of the metal hut Marlon began to pump the old "bee's smoke" that used to be used by special effects crews to simulate smoke on sets. Bee's smoke has a horrible odor and causes eye and throat discomfort. We continued to work because we thought Marlon would stop pumping the bee's smoke. He didn't.

Soon we were all coughing, crying, and shouting to get out. Marlon just kept pumping the smoke into the hut. When we were actually banging on the sides and begging to be released, Marlon unlocked the door. We stumbled and crawled out, coughing, gagging, and fighting for air. Marlon laughed and yelled, "You pissant! You pissant!"

There are two main delis along Ventura Boulevard west of Coldwater Canyon in the San Fernando Valley. The one I like is on the corner of Petit and Ventura, Jerry's Famous Deli; the one Marlon frequents is on Van Nuys and Ventura, Solley's Deli. If I require the services of Solley's, I look through the window for Marlon before I enter. If he's there, I get back in my car and drive on.

When Francis returned, we filmed an involved sequence with Marty, Dennis, and Scott Glenn that was eventually cut out of the movie. After Willard was given medical attention, he was released by Kurtz and allowed to wander around the temple compound. Willard walked in the festival area of the compound and came upon many Viet Cong and North Vietnam Army prisoners who had been tortured and killed by Kurtz.

While Willard was examining the prisoners, Dennis came up to him and said that Kurtz was going to kill him because he took his picture. Dennis was going to escape from the compound as soon as he could.

As Dennis and Willard were talking, Captain Colby approached and killed Dennis with a shotgun. Willard killed Colby and as he was dying, he told Willard to kill Kurtz. Willard then escaped into the jungle.

I thought that Freddie was upset when Chef was killed, but Dennis couldn't stand being present when his character of the freelance photographer was to be killed. We filmed all the dialogue with Dennis and got him into position, but we waited until he had left the location before we put in the life-size replica of Dennis and showed Scott Glenn shooting him with a shotgun.

One day I arrived at the Kurtz compound and noticed that the Ifugaos had a new pet, a dog. All of them were loving the dog and caring for it. They bathed it and fed it. The dog was happy and wagged his tail. After the weekend, when I returned to the compound, and looked for the Ifugaos' new pet. The dog didn't seem to be anywhere. Finally I asked some of the Ifugaos about their dog. They smiled and rubbed their stomach; they had eaten it.

When I asked the Ifugao mayor to explain how they could kill and eat the dog they had loved and cared for, he told me that for five days the dog is given every pleasure. After the five days, the mayor said, "They must die so we can live." It seemed horribly cruel to me until I realized that in our culture the cattle and fowl we use for food aren't even given five days of pleasure before they are killed so that we can live.

The Ifugaos were a most interesting people. One weekend they invited us to come back to the compound on Sunday afternoon for one of their festivals. The male leaders of the Ifugaos had been chanting inside one of their houses since Saturday night. In the early afternoon on Sunday, they came out and began their rhythmic dancing and the ritual killing of the festival animals. The priest directed the killing of the chickens and pigs and read the fortunes of the Ifugao nation by looking at the bile of the animals. During this activity, the members of the tribe kept time to the beat of the drummers as the dancers moved in large circles throughout the crowd. The dancers looked like huge birds, with their arms spread out as they moved slowly to the steady beat of the drummers.

All of us who were there that afternoon were taken with the dignity of the activities. The killing of the animals wasn't done in anger or haste, but was done with dignity and precision. It was obviously a religious happening rather than a simple killing. There was a beauty to the production. It was more a ballet than a contest of survival. The overall focus of the festival was on life and hope for the future, rather than on the death of the animals.

Francis decided to use the festival of the Ifugaos, the ritual killing of the buffalo, in symbolic juxtaposition with Willard's killing of Kurtz, as though Kurtz were the sacrificial water buffalo who must be killed so we can live.

The communication between Dean Tavoularis and Francis was usually clear and complete; they had done so many movies together. Francis dreamed, and Dean built the sets to house those dreams. However, when it came to the set for Willard to sneak back into the Kurtz compound to kill Kurtz, something went wrong.

We arrived out at the compound late in the afternoon because we

would be filming all night. Larry had all the Ifugaos dressed and ready
to begin the ceremony that would eventually lead to the killing of the
water buffalo. On the north side of the Ifugaos' living area was a huge
mound, a hill, easily thirty feet high, which Dean had built and covered
with jungle growth. It was wonderful what he had accomplished,
seemingly in one day, but Francis seemed a bit confused by it all.

"Dean, I don't get it," Francis said, staring at the hill. "I'm sorry."

Dean explained quite simply, "This is where Willard comes into the
camp.

You wanted to see all of the dancing and the temple in the background," Dean added.

"Francis," Vittorio began, "maybe a crane shot of Marty coming over
the top? Could be nice, Francis."

I could see that Francis was totally thrown by the set Dean had presented to him.

"No, Vittorio," Francis said gently.

"What did you have in mind?" Dean asked, as he stared at the hill
and then at Francis.

"I didn't see a hill," Francis answered quietly.

"What did you see?" Dean asked, and we all leaned forward to hear
what Francis would say.

"Not a hill. A swamp or bog," Francis said, and looked at Dean, as
we all did.

"A bog?" Dean couldn't believe it. He smiled and chuckled as he
looked at the jungle hill over thirty feet tall that his crews had built in
twenty-four hours. "You would like a swamp?"

"Yes," Francis replied, "and it has to be right here because I want to
see the temple and the dancing as he comes up out of the water."

"Here?" Dean said, as he gestured to his hill. "You want a bog here?"

"A swamp. Yes," Francis answered.

I was weak. We were looking at a thirty-foot-high hill, and we had
to have a swamp!

"Dean," I asked, "how long do you think it will take you to put a
swamp here?" I was already trying to figure out what to shoot for two
or three days, maybe a week, while Dean got the work done.

"It'll be a swamp tomorrow afternoon," Dean said quietly, and
laughed politely.

"Dean, I'm sorry," Francis said. "How could this have happened?"

"I really don't know," Dean answered.

Both Dean and Francis laughed, and the rest of us did, too.

I thought of it as if Cezanne had misunderstood and had gotten two shades of blue paint and Van Gogh wanted one blue and one yellow. It was just a misunderstanding between artists. Somehow he'd get his yellow paint tomorrow.

The next afternoon I couldn't wait to get back out to the Kurtz compound and see the swamp. And there it was. The thirty-foot-high hill was gone, and in its place was the most wonderful Cambodian swamp! Dean Tavoularis and his one hundred workmen did miracles.

We filmed Marty submerged and then rising up out of the swamp, and we ran the film backward through the camera and had Marty start out of the swamp and lower himself back down into the water. Marty was game; he'd stay in that swamp all night for Francis and Vittorio.

We had to have a photo double for Marlon as Kurtz because he had gone back to Tahiti. Francis wanted to see the figure of Kurtz in the background as he stood in the temple doorways during parts of the festival. I began to look around our crew and extras for the right person to be the photo double.

The requirements were that he be tall and well muscled. Even though Marlon is quite short, for the long shots Francis wanted a tall figure. The second requirement was that whoever was selected had to shave his head. It wasn't easy to find big men. For the most part the Filipinos were medium height, as were the Vietnamese and the Ifugaos. I searched the company looking for the perfect photo double for Marlon Brando and found him—Pete Cooper!

Pete jumped at the job. He got himself suited up in black robes like Marlon wore, and he put on some elevated boots to add a couple of more inches to his height, shaved his head, and became Kurtz in all the long shots. I wish I could've heard all of the tales he told back in his Olongapo bar about playing Marlon Brando in our movie.

When Marty came out of the swamp, he saw Pete Cooper as Kurtz way up in the temple. Marty made his way along the festival area as he slowly got closer to the temple and his chance to kill Kurtz.

We filmed Marty killing a number of guards, but the one killing no one could get out of their mind, and Francis couldn't watch, was when Marty used a trick spear that appeared to go through one of the Three Sisters and then into a guard who was holding the little girl as a shield in front of himself. Everyone still loved the Three Sisters. I thought that the three little girls reminded all of us of back home. We were so far away.

Finally the night arrived when the Ifugaos were going to do the festival that included the ritual killing of a water buffalo. We were going to film their festival just as they did it. My big concern was that our cast and crew would object to the killing.

For days before, the Ifugaos washed, fed, and loved the water buffalo just as they had done with the dog. They led the water buffalo through their area at the compound, and everyone petted it, but tonight was the night.

When the final portion of the festival was about to begin, the killing of the water buffalo, I was standing next to Francis.

"Francis, I think I'll announce to everyone what's about to happen and those who want to leave can, you know?" I said.

"Look behind you," Francis said.

When I looked there was a solid wall of cast and crew with their cameras ready to capture the climax of the Ifugao festival. No one had left, nor did they want to leave. They were hyped and ready.

"Say anything to you?" Francis smiled.

I nodded. The Ifugaos were killing as part of a ritual, but barbarism has its place within every human animal. We are the only animal with a blood lust, who takes joy in killing for no other reason than to kill. That night our crew snapped their own photos.

I stood next to Francis and stared at the festival with its dancing and chanting, the playing of crude musical instruments, and the rhythmic clapping of the Ifugaos. I watched as the living water buffalo was brought forward by two ropes around its neck. I looked at the animal, alive with fear, hope, bewilderment. I watched as it was held immobile by the two stretched ropes. Death was close by.

On Apocalypse Now *I first encountered the dark side of the human soul, and that enlightenment has stayed deep within me ever since. I've learned to recognize my own dark side and to accept it as a part of me.*

Often during my life I've returned in my mind's eye to the Ifugao festival and our killing of Col. Kurtz, where I first stared across the abyss of Death. Marlon, Francis, and I labored in making sense out of the final scene of Apocalypse Now: What does it mean to cross the abyss of Death? *Presently, in each of our lives, we'd learn that eternal truth through the death of our own children.*

The killing of the water buffalo and the assassination of Kurtz brought out both revulsion and fascination among the cast and crew. They were apparently appalled by each killing, but they took personal photographs of every moment.

The actual killing of the water buffalo was done with one strategic blow to its spinal column. What happened next in the festival was the butchering of the animal and the giving of the various parts to individuals and families. The music and dancing continued, but when a piece of the water buffalo was given out, those receiving it went into a frenzy as they got their portion and ran screaming into the jungle. I felt as if I were watching a large number of sharks gone crazy by the feeding on blood and flesh. I couldn't accept that the Ifugaos I saw running and screaming as they carried raw flesh into the jungle were the same quiet, gentle people I had known for months. In a matter of ten minutes the whole carcass of the water buffalo had been cut apart and given out to the Ifugaos. Where the dancers and water buffalo had been was now empty of all people. The festival was over. The water buffalo was totally gone, and so were the Ifugaos.

Willard's killing of Kurtz was done stylistically similar to the Ifugaos killing of the water buffalo. Willard entered the temple and searched for Kurtz. He found him in his rooms, and Willard struck once with his long blade. Kurtz fell back, and Willard continued to swing the blade as though he were cutting Kurtz into pieces. In the movie version, Francis intercut the Ifugao ritual killing with Willard's killing of Kurtz.

I can still see big Pete Cooper in the long shots, dressed like Marlon and wearing his high elevated boots, falling through the temple hallways as Marty takes swings at him with his big blade.

After Kurtz and the water buffalo were dead, Marty left the temple and walked through all of the Ifugaos who were crowded along the path from the temple to the PBR. We filmed the scene very late in our shooting schedule. It was one of the very last things the Ifugaos did. When I explained the scene to them, I used their natural affection for Marty as their attitude when they watched Willard leave; it worked.

I had loved working with the Ifugaos, and when they were through in the movie, they presented me with a carved mahogany figure of an Ifugao dancer.

The principal photography on *Apocalypse Now* came to halt on December 18, 1976, just in time to be back home for Christmas. I had promised my wife and boys that I'd be home for Christmas, and I kept my promise.

We all said our good-byes on the shore of Lake Caliraya one night, after filming the scene of Robert Duvall sitting at a campfire and strumming his guitar for his helicopter troops. We all laughed and hugged one another. All of the pain of the typhoon and Iba was put aside. All of the illnesses within the cast and crew were forgotten. The heat and humidity, the dirt and sand, the long hours for months and months, all the exhaustion and worry seemed to fade away. What remained was the sense of accomplishment; we had climbed a most difficult mountain, and now we were near its peak.

Francis and I stood on the beach and looked at each other for a long time. We had come so far since I first climbed up the ladder to his hut on the sands at Baler. I had come for six weeks and stayed more than eight months. I was a different person. We looked out at the water, then Francis turned to me.

"Thank you. You contributed," was all Francis said. We put our arms around each other and walked back away from the beach toward the rest of the crew.

I was glad it was night; I was crying like a baby.

It was over. The filming had ended, but the journey had barely begun.

Straight Time

After *Apocalypse Now*, Larry Franco and I teamed up with Ziggy again and took the assistant directing jobs on *Straight Time*, the directing debut for Dustin Hoffman. I felt he was one of our most exciting actors, and I didn't want to miss the chance to be his assistant director.

I thought Larry Franco, Ziggy, and I would be an assistant directing team forever, but it all ended in a slum apartment hallway four months later.

We prepared *Straight Time* for months with Tim Zinnemann from *The Great White Hope* as a producer. We looked over the Los Angeles locations for the film. We made trip after trip to Folsom Prison to scout each scene we would shoot there. Stephen Grimes, the production designer from *The Way We Were*, had built two complete homes on sound stages for the film. Dustin Hoffman had rehearsed the cast for weeks in the actual sets. I felt it was the best-prepared movie I had ever done.

Finally we were going to begin filming. The company moved up to central California, near Folsom Prison. The first shot on our first day of shooting would be a quick, wide establishing shot of the prison, and then we'd move inside the prison walls for the rest of our filming.

We had scouted the wide establishing shot many times. In fact, we had taken measurements and lens sizes, and we had the exact position for the camera marked on the roadway outside the prison. There was no activity in the shot, no actors or vehicles, just a wide shot of the prison.

I rode out to Folsom that first morning with Dustin Hoffman, and when we got to the prison, I walked him to the spot he had selected for the first shot. I had him check the shot with Owen Roizman, our cameraman. The position, height, lens size, everything was to Dustin's liking.

I urged Dustin to get the wide establishing shot as quickly as he could so we could move inside the prison and get to our day's work. Dustin agreed and understood the plan.

As soon as the crew was ready to shoot, I got Dustin and brought him to the camera. He looked through the lens and stepped back.

"Owen, could we move the camera a little to the left, please?" Dustin asked.

The crew had to reset the camera and the flags to shield the lens from the morning sun, but it was soon ready. I brought Dustin to the camera. He looked through the lens and again stepped back.

"Owen, do you think it would be better more to the right?" Dustin asked.

We moved the camera to the right.

We moved the camera higher.

We moved the camera lower.

I brought Dustin to look through the lens once again.

"Owen, do you think we should have a little fog in the shot?" Dustin asked.

Owen and I looked at each other. Fog? No one had talked about fog. We all scrambled, and the special effects men were able to give Dustin fog. He looked through the lens again.

"Owen, do you think rain would be better than fog?" Dustin asked.

The special effects crew ran around, and we got hoses from the prison, and finally we were able to show Dustin rain for the wide establishing shot. Dustin looked through the lens again.

"Owen, should we have a car drive through the shot?" Dustin asked.

I got a car, and I got some extras, but before I could get Dustin to check the shot, it was time for lunch. We had not filmed one foot of film the whole morning.

After lunch Dustin decided against the car, extras, and rain, but he would like to try a high shot. No mention had been made of a high shot, so we didn't have a crane.

The grip crew built a platform and lifted the camera onto it. When I brought Dustin to check the shot, he wanted the camera higher, so we took the camera off the platform and put it on top of one of our trucks.

When Dustin checked the shot from the top of the truck, he felt that maybe the high shot was wrong. Could he try a low shot with the camera right on the road?

At about 4:00, Dustin, Tim, Owen, Larry, and I had a talk and decided that it was probably best if we packed it in for today and went back to the motel. We had not filmed one shot.

That evening Dustin called us into his motel room to inform us that as producer he had fired himself as director, that the company would be traveling back to Los Angeles, and a new director would be hired.

Eventually, Ulu Grosbard was hired to direct *Straight Time*. I stayed on the film during his preparation period and for the first few weeks of shooting, but I had taken the movie to be Dustin Hoffman's assistant director on the first film he directed. When that was no longer possible, I wanted to move on. I asked Tim to take me off the film because I had the perfect assistant director to replace me.

We were filming in the slum apartment building where Dustin's character lived after he was released from prison. The camera was down the hallway and everyone was working to get the next shot ready.

I walked down the hall and stopped behind Larry. Ziggy was standing right next to him. I tapped Larry on the shoulder, and they both turned toward me.

"You've got it, Larry. I'm out of here. Ziggy, stay right next to him," I said.

Before either of them could say or do anything, I turned and walked back down the hallway, leaving my favorite assistant director and Ziggy standing at the camera behind me.

Ziggy and I would do many more movies over the years, but sadly, even though we've remained friends for more than twenty years, it was the last day Larry Franco and I ever worked together.

Right outside the gates, each studio had two restaurants that catered to the studio trade. Each noon you could find the executives, crew, office workers, and the actors crowded into one of the restaurants.

M-G-M had the Retake Room, along Washington Boulevard, and The Back Stage, south of the studio on Culver Boulevard. The Burbank Studios had El Chiquito and The River Bottom, both on Barham Boulevard, just west of the main gate. At Paramount Studios the two restaurants were Nicodell's, on Melrose Avenue, and a smaller place, Oblath's, right outside the main gate on Marathon.

It was 1978, almost two years after I had finished Black Sunday, *that John Frankenheimer and Bob Rosen asked me to come into their offices at Paramount and talk about doing their next picture, a science fiction piece called* Prophecy.

I entered their offices, and there was something about the two of them that told me something wasn't right. They laughed and giggled and seemed too anxious for me to read their script.

Rather than sit in their offices for the hour or so that it would take me to read Prophecy, *I told them I'd be at Oblath's and that I'd come back as soon as I had finished it. I entered Oblath's got myself comfortable, and began to read. I couldn't get the feeling out of my head that I was being put on. That this was all some kind of a joke on me.*

As I read the script, I became convinced that Prophecy *was not the script of their next picture, but was actually the worst script they could find. I became convinced that they asked me to read it as a big joke on me.*

I decided to put the joke on them. I went back to John Frankenheimer's office and told them that Prophecy *was the worst script I had ever read and that they were the biggest fools in the world for thinking about doing that script. I went on and on. When I finished my tirade, I waited for their laughter and the acknowledgment that they hadn't fooled me.*

When they didn't speak, I looked at their ashen faces and realized that I had made a very big mistake. Prophecy *was their next picture.*

They did it without me.

Sylvester Stallone and *Rocky II*

It was the summer of 1978. I drove past the Thalberg Building at M-G-M Studios and headed for the guard at the East Gate. He saw my red-and-white Mazda approach and motioned for me to hurry up to him.

"Hi, star. He's waiting for you in his office. Production building. United Artists. Park against the wall," Ken Hollywood said, and he ducked back into his guard shack.

I parked and walked back to him.

"Jerry, he's waiting for you. They've called twice. I'll catch you later." Ken brushed me off and went back to shuffling papers.

I walked west down the studio's Main Street. I'd been asked to interview for the first assistant director job for another movie star who was going to direct his first film. I had the memory of my experience with Dustin Hoffman in my mind as I walked around the old yellow wooden M-G-M production building and entered from the Washington Boulevard side.

"He's waiting for you, Jerry. Right down the hall," the production secretary said. "The third door's his office."

"Thanks. Got anything good coming up?" I asked. Maybe they had something else more interesting.

"He's waiting. Go right in, OK?" She said, and busied herself at her desk.

I walked down the hall and pushed open the third door. His secretary looked up at me.

"I'm Jerry Ziesmer, and I've got a . . . ," I began.

"Just a minute," she said, and moved quickly to the inner office door. "He's here."

"Yo, Jer! Come in!" he shouted.

I entered, and there was Sylvester Stallone, Rocky himself.

He was dressed in black slacks and coach's shoes. He was wearing an off-white T-shirt and one of those Rocky hats on his head. He was squeezing a rubber exercise ball.

His office was comfortable but not luxurious. It was functional, with dark leather chairs and a sofa, a walnut desk; it was serviceable at best. Stallone's office was not up to the quality of Sydney Pollack's or Mark Rydell's. If you'd compare it to John Frankenheimer's office, it was the difference between a garage sale and Tiffany's. For having last year's smash runaway top movie in *Rocky*, Sylvester Stallone didn't have much of an office to show for it, but he didn't seem to be bothered by it.

"Sit down, Jer. How ya doin'? You want something? Coffee or something?"

"I'm fine, thanks," I said, but I did sit down. I wanted to watch Mr. Stallone. I was already curious where Rocky stopped and Sylvester Stallone began.

"So what you think? What films you done? *Apocalypse*, right?" he asked.

I attempted to comment, but he went right on.

"I can't believe Francis didn't cast me. I cast his sister, you know?"

I wondered who Sylvester thought he could have played in *Apocalypse Now*. Col. Kilgore? No.

"Jer, you OK?" he asked.

I nodded that I was fine, as his secretary entered with a large vitamin drink for him.

"Sly, you're meeting Irving for lunch at noon. Don't forget," she said, and left.

He nodded as he bounced the exercise ball on his desk, the wall, and the floor.

"Gotta stay in shape, right, Jer?" he said, as he toasted me with his health drink.

"How's the script?" I thought I'd try to find out straightaway if *Rocky II* was its own film, or simply a *Rocky* rerun.

"Great, Jer! Great!" he answered, finishing the vitamin drink and bouncing the ball again.

"You like the script?" I asked. "It's different?"

"Totally different, you know? What you think? I wrote it, right?" He laughed and bounced the ball. His eyes beamed at me as a junior high kid's eyes will do when he's having a really good time.

"Where you going to film it?" I asked.

"Philadelphia for exteriors, here for interiors. All locations, no sets," Sly said. "Keep the budget down, you know?"

I couldn't shake the feeling that I was interviewing with Rocky and not Sylvester Stallone. It was a very strange interview, such a rapid-fire rhythm. I thought if he would stop bouncing the exercise ball, it would help.

"How long's the shooting schedule?" I asked. I always tried to find out the number of shooting days. It gave me some idea of what the studio thought of the project. The longer the shooting schedule, the bigger the budget, the more confidence they had that the film would be a success.

Suddenly the interview dropped from the fast tempo of the bouncing ball to two guys staring at one another.

Sly said slowly and quietly, "Forty-two days. What you think, Jer? *Forty-two days.*" He watched my eyes.

I felt he was concerned that he didn't have enough days, that he'd be over schedule, over budget, and under the studio's thumb, which meant he'd lose creative control. If that happened, the picture could be taken away from him and finished by another director. Finished also would be Stallone's career as a film director.

"I haven't read the script, Sly, but forty-two days is tight for a picture with a lot of action and. . . ." I stopped, not because Sly interrupted me, but because I saw some emotion was rising inside him.

"I get to direct, Jer. Don't you understand? If not now, when will I ever get to direct? But it's forty-two days. See? That's the deal." He stared at me. "What do you think, Jer? We can do it, right?"

As I stared at Sly, I believed for the first time that the man standing in front of me was more than a Rocky. He was a filmmaker trying to scratch a career out of Hollywood.

"The fight with the studio is always about the number of days, Sly, you know that," I said.

I stared back at a guy who two years ago was out in the cold. Couldn't get a job in Hollywood. Now he had a shot at directing his own movie.

"What do you think, Jer?" He asked again. "Can we do it?"

An assistant director gets to share the dreams and visions of the director; that's the special relationship you have. Sly certainly had visions and dreams, but in forty-two days?

I wasn't a beginning AD. It was ten years since my first day with Otto Preminger. I had nothing to prove. Why would I want to be saddled with a first-time director with a tight schedule, and one who's starring in the movie, too?

The forty-two-day schedule told me the smart money was betting against him. Betting that the lightning that hit *Rocky* wouldn't hit *Rocky II*. That Rocky was a fluke, a one in a million.

"What do you think, Jerry? Can we do this?"

If *Rocky II* was another hit, Sly could knock all Hollywood on their ear. If *Rocky II* was a flop, he could be out in the cold again.

"Jer! What do you think? Will you answer? You're worse than my mother!"

I'd be leaving my family again. This time I'd be in Philadelphia, and I didn't know for how long. Were the separations, the work, and the long hours going to be worth it?

None of those questions can be answered before you begin a picture. I learned that the hard way. No one knows how good or how meaningful the finished movie will be. But I knew from those first moments that the picture's director was someone who mattered. I believed in Sly, and I believed his film could make a difference, and that's all I ever wanted.

"I think you should go for it, Sly. Forty-two days. The whole thing. Let's go for it," I said.

Another journey began. I hoped I could contribute.

"Yo! Jer! Yeah, I knew you'd say that! Oh, Jer!" Sly was as excited as a school kid who's just been told by the coach that he's made the team.

"You've got a lot riding on this, Sly," I said quickly.

"Oh, Jer! You're right, man. You're right. You'll see. Forty-two days, we'll do it!"

Sly was one excited man.

"We're going to make this great film, Jer. The best boxing movie ever made! We're going to use slow motion so that when I get hit (he pushed his fist against his cheek to distort his face) you're going to see the sweat and blood fly off! And, Jer, the sound's gonna be distorted and. . . ."

I watched him as he moved around his office. I'd watch every boxing movie that was ever made, and I'd start with Ralph Nelson's *Requiem for a Heavyweight* with Anthony Quinn.

"I want to show boxing, real boxing," Sly was saying. "We'll train for weeks!"

I nodded, and he just kept moving.

"We'll be ready to do the real thing!"

He shadowboxed and did his fast footwork around the office.

"I'm in the gym now every day. I do my roadwork; I do the bags!"

I watched him dancing around in front of me.

"This is gonna be real! Listen, Jer, on how I want to do the boxing. We never stop except for the bell between rounds!"

I had to swallow to clear my throat. I needed a moment to think. I could hear the musical theme from *Rocky* playing as Sly went on with his shadowboxing and dreams for *Rocky II*.

"You gotta be with me, Jer! You gotta watch out for me. You got a copy of the script? You gotta start right away. We're going to make one of the best films ever! Do you love boxing? You do, don't you? I knew you did!"

There was no turning back for me; I was already with him, chasing his dream.

"Yo, Jer! We're going to do it!" He hugged me, handed me a copy of the script, and pushed me toward the production manager's office to sign my deal.

"This is a great day, Jer!" Sly shouted.

"Could I have the birth dates for you, your wife, and children, please?" Sly's secretary asked as I passed her desk.

I hadn't even signed my deal, and Sly's thinking about birthday cards?

I could still hear his cheering as I walked down the hall toward the production manager's office.

His office door was open. I knocked on the door frame to get his attention off the papers on his desk.

"I'm Jerry Ziesmer. I just met with Stallone, and he sent me in here," I began. "He said he wants to hire me as his first AD." I smiled at the small man crouched behind his desk as if he were hiding from the world.

"You met him?" he asked, as he stood up. "You met Sylvester Stallone?"

"Yes, just now. He seems great," I answered. The guy must have been deaf not to have heard Sly shouting.

"I don't have any money for you. Sly can't just go and hire people," he said, as he bent forward and twisted slightly from his waist.

I thought he might be having a stomach attack of some kind. Maybe he had ulcers.

"Are you OK?" I asked him.

"We've got a forty-two day schedule to do this picture. Forty-two days," he said. "That's all they'll give us. You know? That's it; the bottom line."

I looked at this production manager and realized that *Rocky II* was months away from filming, and already this guy seemed to be ill with stress and anxiety.

"I think we can make this happen," I said soothingly. *"In forty-two days."*

I hadn't even read the script, but I felt sorry for the guy and wanted to instill some confidence in him.

"This isn't *Apocalypse Now*, you know. With millions and millions of dollars. Hundreds of shooting days. This isn't that, you know!" he said, as he stared at me with anxious eyes opened wide in fear.

I wondered if the studio hospital was still over near the wardrobe department. This guy was wrapped tight.

"I know, but I think we can do Sly's film on time and for the price," I said as calmly as I could.

He put his knuckles in his mouth, and he actually began chewing on them. I hadn't seen anyone do that before. I'd seen Robert Evans, then the head of Paramount Studios during *Black Sunday*, put his whole index finger in the side of his mouth and move it violently up and down like an angry toothbrush, but he never chewed.

"Sly seems very motivated," I said, hoping this would lend a positive tone to our talk.

He continued to look down toward the floor with his fearful eyes as he gnawed on his knuckles.

"Sly mentioned that he'd like me to start right away, tomorrow," I said, and showed him the script he had given me.

The top of his head moved, but the lower part stayed chewing his knuckles.

"I only got you in for six weeks of prep," he said. His breath came in short gasps.

This guy was good, very good. I hadn't even realized that the cat-and-mouse game between assistant director and production manager had begun. He knew he had to hire me, but he wanted to get me for the fewest weeks and at the lowest possible salary. Never mind that we would be working together for months on *Rocky II*; at this time in our relationship, it was strictly cat and mouse and who's going to get the cheese.

"It's going to take a lot of prep. He's never directed before," I said, as I advanced toward the cheese.

"I know. I want you on the picture yesterday! Yesterday!" he said, and went to the knuckle biting again. He moved his cat's paw temptingly away from the cheese.

"Well?" I smiled, and I began to taste the cheddar. This was too easy.

"Look!" he shouted, and hit the papers he was studying, the budget for *Rocky II*. He lifted the papers so I could see the numbers. There was panic in his eyes.

"There's no money!" He sagged visually, but his cat's paw was above the cheese and ready.

If I wanted the cheese I had to come all the way out of the mouse hole and stand in the open.

"Jerry, I know what kind of money you get. Do you think I was born yesterday? If the studio knew this would be another *Rocky* there'd be no problem with your deal. Hell! I'd open the safe and you guys could scoop out the money!"

Nearly every picture it's the same way. Your own brother from the Directors Guild, the production manager, does anything he can to get you for less money. Anything.

"I'd love to have you on this, Jerry. You know how Sly feels about you. You're an important, big-picture guy. It'd make my life easier. I wish I could pay some of the difference out of my own pocket! I do!"

I looked at this whimpering person in front of me. I knew he had himself on the payroll for months and months, but he was begrudging me enough weeks to prepare the movie with a director who's never directed before. I could still smell the cheese.

"Look. It's not there," he said again, as he held the budget up to my eyes. "I'd love to have you. Sly would love to have you, but my hands are tied. We have no money. I'm sorry," he said, and fell back into his chair exhausted.

This production manager was a Hall of Famer. I'd have to take drastic action with this guy.

"I'm sorry, too. It would've been fun. Maybe next time," I said, as casually as I could, then I turned around to leave his office. I didn't hear a sound from him.

"I'll tell Sly on my way out that we can't make a deal," I continued, with my back to him as I stood in his door frame. There still was no sound from him, nothing. "See, ya."

Shit! I could never bluff! My whole life I never bluffed anyone.

"I'll take it," I mumbled and dropped my head. "The weeks and money you got in the budget, I'll take it."

"Great to have you on board," he said, and when I turned around to look at him he had a big cat's grin on his face.

He'd gotten the mouse, and he didn't lose the cheese.

Sly wanted me to do one thing before I began work on *Rocky II*. His secretary called and gave me a time and an address.

"Just take a meeting, Jer," Sly said. "It's nothing. Trust me."

I turned north off Sunset Boulevard onto Bellagio Drive and drove through the high-rent district of Bel Air. I turned west onto Chalon and started to look for the address among all the mansions.

When I found the address, it was a huge brick and leaded-glass mansion with black wrought iron gates and a gorgeous red brick driveway that by itself cost more than my whole home.

I drove cautiously through the gates and parked in the driveway; I hoped my Mazda wouldn't drip any oil. The gardener must have just finished, because all the plants and bricks were still wet. I wondered who could afford a house like this. Certainly not Stallone; he'd only done one hit movie. Whoever lived here was into the really big bucks.

There were two imposing, heavy wooden doors. I looked for the doorbell, but I couldn't find any. I was looking behind the potted trees on each side of the doorway, when she opened the door.

"Won't you come in, Jerry? You're very prompt. Are you always so prompt?" she asked, as she smiled and held the door open, inviting me in.

She was a tall, beautiful woman with long dark hair. She was dressed in a silver one-piece dress that clung to each of her many charms. She could have been a high-fashion model from any magazine she chose, or she could have been a. . . . I froze.

I couldn't stop staring at her, and I couldn't move. I held up the paper with the address on it, but I couldn't speak. What had Sly done to me, and why? I wanted to run.

"It's all right, Jerry. Won't you come in?" she said, as she guided me through the doorway and into the foyer of the mansion. The foyer was like in a hunting lodge of a baron's castle in Scotland.

She walked in front of me and said over her shoulder, "Would you like something to drink, Jerry? It might make you more comfortable."

Comfortable for what? When I didn't answer, she looked back and I shook my head no.

Who was she? She never introduced herself. Why had Sly sent me here?

We continued walking down a hallway and entered a large library. There were shelves of books across three of the four walls; the fourth had leaded windows that looked out on a pastoral scene. On the floor were pedestals with various globes on them. Not simply one for the earth, but many globes—for the moon, various other planets, and what seemed to be for star constellations. The whole ceiling was a picture of the heavens, with the planets, moons, galaxies, and other star systems painted in gold on black background.

Between the bookshelves on the wall opposite the windows was a large wall hanging of planets, moons, and spheres, with various numbers and signs running on the vertical and horizontal edges.

In nearly the center of the room were two dark leather chairs, placed on either side of a carved wooden table. On the table were charts of planets, pages of mathematical calculations, and what looked like geometric drawings of circles and intersecting lines and angles with notations of degrees and various other numbers and symbols.

She gestured for me to be seated at the table. I smiled and cautiously sat down. As she sat down, she moved her chair closer to my left side. I was cold. I stared at the room and at her as she sorted through the various charts of planets and organized the papers into four groups.

I felt I was in the house of a witch, a modern-day witch! What had Sylvester Stallone done to me? I was a Presbyterian!

She placed a large astrological chart on top of the small table and began to show me the positions of all the planets at the exact moment of my birth. I stared down at the notations on the chart.

"How did you know I was born in Milwaukee at 6:17 A.M. on May 31, 1939?" I knew I had given my birthday to Sly's secretary; I remembered that, but how did she get my birth place and time?

"Don't be so nervous, Jerry," she said slowly and calmly, as she unfolded more charts. "There are many ways, aren't there? You should know that."

I stared at her and the bizarre library.

"Trust me, Jerry. Sylvester does," she said, and smiled. "You're going to have a good time here, I promise."

I couldn't relax. I couldn't smile; I was terrified.

"How are your two children?" she asked, as she studied my charts and theirs. "Especially the Capricorn, January 11, early evening, Los Angeles?"

I wanted to bolt for the door, get in my car, and never see Sylvester Stallone again. It was one thing to be strapped with a first-time director with a forty-two day shooting schedule, but it's another for him to send me to a witch, and in the center of Bel Air?

"I want to know where you got all those times and places," I challenged. Chris was eight years old and Tim was only four; they didn't have driver licenses or draft cards. I was trying to piece it all together.

She ignored my question with a smile and a tiny laugh.

"Your sign and Sly's sign are very interesting together. You are sure you were born in the morning, aren't you?" she asked, as she had her slide rule working on my chart, Sly's, my children's, and my wife's.

"Yes, it was in the morning." I barely got it out. "My mother told me it was in the morning."

"Can I get you something, Jerry? Something to help you relax? It will make it all easier for you."

"No, I'm fine," I said as I watched her making notations, and measuring angles with a trisquare and a compass.

"You see here," she said, as she pointed to a convergence of lines and angles. "You and Sly should be very good for one another. I wouldn't have thought it at first, but you are very compatible!"

I looked down at the symbols, lines, and angles and then up at her. I didn't want to know anything else. I wanted to go home.

"Don't be so concerned about your little Capricorn, he'll be fine, though you will have some difficulties with his strong personality. Tim?" she asked.

"Yes, Tim, little sports guy," I managed to get out.

"I know," she answered, as she studied his chart.

She knew?

"Christopher, the Taurus, your writer, is much more complex. Perhaps some other time," she said, and smiled at me. "You will come back to see me again, won't you?"

"Oh, yes," I lied.

"When are you planning to begin filming?" she asked, as she continued to study the charts.

"The middle of September," I answered.

She got to work with the slide rule again. I watched her carefully.

"After the twenty-fifth would be better, a lot better. Yes, after the twenty-fifth," she said.

I nodded my head and looked around for my way out.

"That wasn't too bad, was it?" she said, as she stood up and smiled at me.

We walked together as we left the library and started down the hallway.

"Your chart was so interesting. I had to ask Sly to have you stop by. I hope you don't mind?"

"No, it was fine. I had a wonderful time," I said, and kept going for the front door. I was still confused and frightened.

Who was she, and whose house was this? She never told me her name. You can't afford a Bel Air mansion by doing astrology charts—or can you?

"I just want to make the best picture we can," I said, as we reached the door.

"Of course you do, Jerry, but promise to begin after the twenty-fifth," she said, as she opened the door and I stepped outside. "You will remember, won't you?"

I nodded and stammered as she smiled and closed the door.

We began filming *Rocky II* just after the twenty-fifth. It was Sly's suggestion, not mine, but I totally agreed with him. Why take any chances with the witch of Bel Air?

The weeks of preproduction for an assistant director are taken up with scheduling the shooting of the movie day by day. Under normal preproduction conditions, I'd be in an office breaking down the script into its various sets and locations and laying out a shooting schedule that I felt the director, cast, and crew could achieve.

When I had my schedule, I'd meet with the director, and we'd sit in some quiet, private room, and I'd go through the schedule with him day by day. We'd discuss each scene: how many shots he had, how difficult the scene would be for the actors, and any fears he might have. I'd listen and try to rearrange the schedule until the director was happy. When our meeting was over, he should be comfortable with the schedule and I should feel that the cast and crew can meet his expectations.

With Sydney Pollack and Mark Rydell the meetings were held in their offices. All calls were held, and they told their secretaries that they didn't want to be disturbed.

Brian De Palma and Steven Spielberg studied each day's scenes and discussed how many shots they would need for every day's work. It took hours of thoughtful concentration.

John Frankenheimer suggested a French restaurant near Paramount or perhaps a cruise up the coast on his fishing boat, but we decided on his office, and the two of us spent two hours going over the *Black Sunday* schedule, day by day.

For *Annie*, I met with John Huston at the Beverly Hills Hotel, and we sat in his suite and talked through the schedule until we were both happy with each day's work on the entire film.

It wasn't that kind of quiet, thoughtful meeting on *Rocky II*.

The M-G-M gym was a serious-looking place, with weights, pulleys, benches, mats, heavy and light bags, and a boxing ring. It was the only place I could get time with Sly to go over the shooting schedule.

I was standing with my production board in my hands ready to go over the film's schedule while Sly lay prone on the floor as a trainer beat on his stomach with both hands, causing loud thumps as the trainer's hands hit his stomach, and then louder yells from Sly.

Thus began the shooting schedule meeting with my director.

"Sly, on the first day of shooting, we begin with . . ."

THUMP! THUMP! THUMP!

"AAAAHHHH!!!!!!!!!!" Sly yelled.

"Sly, we begin with the scene where you . . ."

THUMP! THUMP! THUMP!

"AAAAHHHH!!!!!!"

". . . where you first enter the hospital from . . ."

THUMP! THUMP! THUMP!

"AAAAHHHH!!!!!"

". . . after the first fight and . . ."

I got through the first five days of the schedule.

Sly moved to the heavy bag.

"The sixth (BAM, BAM!) day, Sly, is (BAM, BAM!) your wedding. (BAM, BAM!) We're at the church (BAM, BAM, BAM!) and you (BAM! BAM-BAM, BAM!) get married and (BAM! BAM!) kiss Adrian, then (BAM! BAM, BAM!) Joe Spinelli talks to you about (BAM! BAM, BAM!) condominiums, and . . . (BAM! BAM-BAM, BAM!).

Sly went to the small speed bag, and I continued with the twelfth day of the shooting schedule.

"Sly, the next (bum-bum-bum-bum-bum-bum-bum-bum) into your (bum-bum-bum-bum-bum-bum-bum-bum) you place her (bum-bum-bum-bum-bum-bum-bum-bum). Next day you arrive (bum-bum-bum-bum-bum-bum) and then . . ."

I was halfway through the schedule when Sly grabbed a jump rope and began hopping as the rope "wopped" the floor.

"This is the twenty-third day, Sly, and (wop) we (wop) at (wop) home (wop) you (wop) up (wop) your (wop) with (wop) and (wop)."

I tried talking faster to get more words in between the revolutions of the jump rope.

"Sly, I (wop) think you (wop) listen to (wop)."

Sly began to increase the tempo of the rope.

"On (wop-wop) first (wop-wop) film (wop-wop) . . ."

I got through the thirty-third day of the schedule with only nine days to go when Sly threw the jump rope away and got into the boxing ring. He was dancing around the ring, throwing punches at an imaginary foe as he grunted after each punch.

"Sly, so on the thirty-fourth (AAHHH! UH!) shooting. We are (AAAHH! UH!) Spectrum where (UH! AAAHHH! AAHH!). What is best (UH! AAAHH! UHHH!)."

I was running around the outside of the ring to stay near Sly, but he continued to dance and throw punches inside the ring.

"Apollo will be (AAHH! UHH!) so you'll (UUUHHH! AAAHH!)."

I finished the whole forty-two-day shooting schedule. I was out of breath from running around the outside of the ring.

"Well . . . Sly . . . how did . . . you . . . like it?" I asked, as I held the production board to my chest and gasped for breath.

"Seems good to me, Jer. I trust you, ya know. Gotta do my road work now. You wanna run along?" Sly asked, as he got out of the ring and ran out of the gym with his trainers following him.

"I'll catch you later!" I shouted, as I collapsed on the ring apron with the official, director-approved shooting schedule for *Rocky II*.

The most important event during preproduction for the crew is to have the director take them on the location scout. For *Rocky II* this meant taking the key members of the crew to Philadelphia to finalize the choice of each location we'd be filming.

We all flew into Philadelphia from Los Angeles and checked into our hotel. Each person was told to be in front of the hotel at 7:30 the next morning, "having had breakfast." That meant if you wanted to eat breakfast, you did it prior to the leaving time.

In the morning, everyone, including Sly, was outside the hotel at 7:30 and we drove in our van toward our first location. Sly and the crew looked over the site, made their notes, then got back in the van. We started toward our second location when Sly asked if we could stop and get something to eat. It was 8:15.

The crew looked at me, but we all assumed that Sly had forgotten that we were to have breakfast prior to beginning our scout, so we stopped at a restaurant, and Sly had a full breakfast while the rest of us had coffee. When Sly was finished, we once more got into our van and headed for more sites.

We saw another two locations, but then at 10:00 Sly asked if we could stop at a restaurant to get a little something. Everyone turned toward me, but I assumed that Sly only wanted a cup of coffee and we'd be quickly on our way.

He ate another full breakfast.

We returned to our van and saw another two locations by noon, when Sly asked if we could now stop for lunch. The crew was beside themselves. In the last four and one-half hours we'd stopped twice for breakfast and once for lunch.

I felt I had to talk to Sly, because at this rate we'd be here for weeks.

"Sly, look . . . we've thirty-some locations to scout in Philly. We can't stop to eat every two hours." I tried to be as diplomatic as I could. "We have to do something."

Sly listened very attentively to what I said. Then he chose his words carefully and very slowly explained to me, "Jer, looking at these locations makes my brain very tired. I have to eat to keep all my parts going."

Sly had a knack for finding his friends and associates in the strangest ways. Sly first saw one of his employees (who also appeared in a bit role in the movie) one night outside his home in Los Angeles. When Sly drove up to his house, the young man dashed from the bushes to Sly's car, stared at Sly, then ran away. Sly was startled, but the man didn't return, so he put the encounter out of his mind.

About six weeks later Sly was in New York at a hotel, and he ordered room service. The waiter who wheeled the room service cart into Sly's suite was the same person who had run up to his car six weeks earlier in Los Angeles. Sly hired him on the spot, as much to know what he was doing as for his services.

Another of Sly's people he found asleep in an abandoned car in New York City; he became a Sly confidant and also played a small role in *Rocky II*.

The third he found literally hanging around; the person would hang from any overhead rafter or door frame. He was trying to stretch his spine to gain another half inch so he would meet the minimum height qualifications to be a Los Angeles policeman. He also played a small role in our film. I remet this gentleman years later, but he was then employed by Rosanne Barr.

I liked to film on locations around Los Angeles because you got to see new areas of the city, but the location for the interior of Rocky's apartment where he brought his new bride, Talia Shire, was in the center of the worst scuzzy slum in downtown Los Angeles. Ziggy didn't even want to enter the building.

All of us on the crew were standing on a filthy staircase, preparing the shot of Rocky carrying Adrian into his apartment after their wedding. We filmed the exterior of the building in Philadelphia, where Sly carried Talia down the street, past Sly's brother Frank, who was singing with his group on the street corner.

Our scene was the interior apartment building, where Rocky carried Adrian up the stairs and opened the door to his apartment. He greeted his dog, Butkus. Then he placed Adrian on the bed; the love scene followed. We filmed Sly as he carried Adrian up the stairs and opened his apartment door.

"Cut." Now we placed the camera inside his apartment and prepared to get a shot of Sly as he carried Talia inside and saw his pet dog, Butkus. Seemed simple.

We were ready to film from inside his apartment, the apartment door was closed, and Sly was holding Talia in the hallway. For some reason Sly decided to change the action of the scene.

"Hey, Butkus!" Sly yelled through the closed door, "Jump up on the bed, then when I come in you get off the bed and go to the dresser! Can you hear me?"

"Sly, let's work this out with Butkus," I suggested. "Why waste film?"

"Just roll the camera, Jer. Butkus, you hear me?" Sly was holding Talia behind the closed door. "Get on the bed, Butkus! Then get off the bed when I come in, OK?"

The crew were looking at one another.

"Roll," I shouted.

"Here I come, Butkus. Be ready," Sly yelled.

Butkus jumped on the bed and laid down as Sly turned the doorknob and they entered his apartment. When Sly with Talia in his arms reached the center of the tiny apartment, Butkus turned to look at them, then hopped down off the bed, and went to the dresser and laid down. Sly placed Talia down on the bed.

It was all a perfectly timed piece of action.

"Cut." We were applauding, falling over ourselves. How could that happen? How could an untrained dog take directions through a closed door and time the scene perfectly?

Sly realized we were all excited about Butkus and his performance.

"Hey, Butkus!" Sly hugged him. "You're the greatest!"

• • •

Sly loved that dog, and when it came time to fly to Philadelphia, Butkus flew with Sly in the first class cabin of our commercial jet. Butkus in the first class section raised a few eyebrows from the other passengers, but they settled down when they realized that Rocky was sitting in the next seat.

I first met Brent Musburger, the sports announcer, at Northwestern University, and we've remained friends over the years, largely because Musburger has four season tickets to the Los Angeles Dodger games, aisle 109, row D, seats 1 through 4. They are sensational seats. Suzanne, the kids, and I have enjoyed going to the Dodger games and sharing Brent's tickets for as long as I can remember, so when Sly wanted a sports announcer to appear in *Rocky II*, I naturally suggested Musburger. Brent had been doing sportscasting for years, and he was very good. Though I had only seen him a few times since college, the Dodger ticket connection was strong. Sly went with my suggestion, and Brent was hired.

We were filming Apollo Creed's training headquarters down at the old Ambassador Hotel in Los Angeles, and as an added piece of work for the day, we had set up a simple background and a desk for Musburger to give a sportscast about the big fight between Rocky and Apollo.

Nothing had been written in the script as to what Musburger should say, so when Sly gave Brent directions, he really left all the dialogue up to Brent.

"Look, Sly," Musburger said, "if you'll just give me the date of the month, and the day of the week, I'll be fine."

"OK. AAhhh, give me, let's see. The fight is Thanksgiving, so give me August 25," Sly said.

Brent nodded, "August 25, a Friday."

The cameras rolled and Sly called action.

Brent Musburger totally made up a sportscast, with baseball games, scores, events, plays, batting averages, errors, the whole thing. Then he continued into off-season rumors and trades in the National Hockey League and the NBA. When Sly didn't yell cut, Brent went into the pre-season games coming up in the National Football League, Olympic hopefuls, softball scores in the NCAA, and on and on, doing his Musburger Special Edition of the day's sports news.

Finally Sly yelled "Cut!" and the set exploded in applause for the ability of Musburger to make up the news.

"Give me July 13! A Thursday!" Sly yelled.

Musburger went through another sportscast for Sly.

"I want an April 14! Monday!" Sly shouted, as he doubled up with laughter at Brent, who was enjoying the challenge.

I believe Stallone and Musburger would still be doing bogus sportscasts if the camera hadn't run out of film. Even now when I watch Brent do a sportscast, I have to ask myself if it's really news or a Musburger Special Edition.

That same day someone walked into our set, stole one of the big heavy bags that we had hanging in Apollo's training quarters, and walked out without anyone noticing him.

Sly went wild and was running around looking for the person who had stolen the bag.

"Sly! Sly!" I yelled at him. "We've got other bags, don't worry!"

I couldn't understand why Stallone was searching so frantically.

"I don't want the bag!" Sly screamed back at me. "I want to put whoever took it in the movie!"

If we had a role in the film that was still not cast, and we were getting close to filming that scene, I would make Sly aware of it.

"Sly, who you casting as the real-estate salesman?" I asked. "It's getting close."

"Don't worry, Jer. You trust me on this like I trust you, OK?"

The scene in question was Sly and Talia being shown a home by the real-estate agent and deciding to buy it. The interior house was filmed in Los Angeles, but the exterior of the house where Talia, Sly, and the real-estate agent drive up in Rocky's car was filmed later in Philadelphia.

On the morning that we were scheduled to film the real-estate agent scene in Los Angeles, Sly was bursting with anticipation.

"Jer, come here," Sly beckoned, "I want you to try on this suit."

"Why, Sly? Why do you want me to try on that suit?"

"Because you're playing the real-estate agent! You surprised, Jer?"

Talia quickly added, "Just take these business cards and put them everywhere. That's what real-estate people do."

She handed me a stack of fifty business cards.

"You surprised, Jer?"

"Sly, look . . ."

"Get into your suit; we got to fix your hair." Sly was so happy, like getting Daddy to wear a funny hat.

I put on the suit, resolved to go through this "joke" for Sly's benefit. "Daddy will wear the funny hat, but let's just make this movie" was my whole motivation.

I came back to Sly with the suit on, and he sat me down in a makeup chair and directed the hairdresser how to make me look "real-estate man-ish"; he finally took the comb and brush himself. He was having such a good time, I had to go along with him.

I drew from the patience I learned from having been a junior high school teacher.

"Jer, you, me, Talia drive up in Philadelphia in my new car with Butkus and then . . ."

"What? Butkus?"

"Yo, with Butkus. He's in the backseat with you. Now . . ."

"Wait, Sly. There's no Butkus in this scene. Look at the script. You wrote it. There's no Butkus in the backseat."

"Come on, Jer. Don't you like Butkus?" Sly was beside himself because not only did he have Daddy wearing a funny suit with a funny hairstyle, but he also had me cramped into the backseat with Butkus for the exterior shot in Philadelphia.

I just surrendered. Sly wanted me to look silly and be licked by Butkus for his picture, I did it. He was happy. The picture was getting made.

Both Talia and Sly directed me in the scene. Talia would not let up that I had to use all those business cards, and Sly wanted me to stomp my foot on the floor and then slap the stairs to show the great construction of the house.

"Jer, listen, you want to show him how strong the house is. Got it? Rocky is a fighter, ya know? Strong, get it?"

"OK, Sly, I'll do it."

"Just put these business cards everywhere. That's all they do," Talia kept insisting.

I did kick the floor when I said that the house had hardwood floors, and I hit the wall when I mentioned the copper plumbing, but I never used Talia's business cards.

Sly had his makeup person and Talia had hers. I had both Talia and Sly fixing my makeup, my hair, my coat, telling me how to read my lines, and doing everything they could to help me. All of which made me more nervous, more self-conscious, and more wanting to be just the assistant director behind the camera yelling "Roll 'em."

After each take, my two directors tried to help me. First Sly gave me his notes: "Jer, just show him the house, ya know? Hardwood floors, get it? Copper plumbing?" Sly again thumped the floor with his foot and whacked the walls with his hands.

Talia took me to the most private portion of the set and whispered to me, "Do what you want to do. Don't listen to him. Do it your way." She gave me a knowing look and nod as though I had just been given the secret of life.

Finally I did a take that was acceptable to both my directors.

Sly gave me the "Yo, Jer, way to go!"

From Talia I got the index finger pointed from her nose directly toward me, and she raised eyebrows along with an "I told you so" expression in her eyes.

When we moved to Philadelphia, one of the first scenes we filmed was Sly, Talia, and the real-estate salesman arriving outside Rocky's house. Sly and Talia were in the front seat, and I was cramped into the tiny backseat of Rocky's Trans Am with Butkus all over me.

Sly was enjoying this more than the interior scene.

"Yo, Jer, make sure Butkus doesn't get out of the car. Just push him back."

Sly knew I was uncomfortable with the big dog, and he had me pushing Butkus.

The car came forward in the shot and stopped with a bump. Sly and Talia were out of the car, and I was struggling with Butkus.

Finally, on the fourth take, I got Butkus to stay in the car.

"Good boy, Butkus. Way to go!" Sly said to Butkus. "Nice shot, huh, Jer?"

Once in awhile an opportunity would arise for a lowly assistant director to get back at a superstar, and one day Mr. Stallone got his. We filmed all of the interior hospital room scenes in the Queen of Angels Hospital in Los Angeles. While we were filming Rocky in a hospital bed following his first fight with Apollo Creed, it was time for lunch. I called a half-hour lunch, and all of us rushed to the elevators that would take us down to the first floor to our caterer.

The elevator was very full, and as I looked around to see who was riding with me, I noticed that Sly was in this elevator. He had jumped out of the hospital bed and did not wait to put on his normal shoes but was wearing the thin-soled hospital slippers. Sly is not a tall person; in fact, he is on the short side. His normal shoes do give him a bit of a lift.

As the crowded elevator descended I pantomimed to everyone in the elevator except Sly to stand on their tiptoes, which would add another inch or two to their height. When everyone was as tall as they could be, I began: "How tall are you? You look like you're 6'1" or 6'2" tall."

It took a split second for the film crew to catch on, and soon everyone in the elevator was discussing their height.

Sly glanced up at us and then just stared straight ahead. When the elevator door opened, he rushed out.

After lunch, Sly was one of the first back up in his hospital room set. He was storming around, "You are not 6'2"! Who do you think you're kidding? There's no one over 6' on this crew!"

There was another opportunity for payback on *Rocky II*, and it was most unexpected. The interior boxing gym that we used for our filming was the Main Street Gym in downtown Los Angeles. We had hired a lot of local boxers to work as extras, and we hired a few professionals to be the featured boxers. Sly had filmed *Rocky*, and he had done a lot of training for our film, so he knew his way around the gym and the boxing ring. Against the local boxers, Sly really did look good.

One day we were filming down at the gym, and Roberto Duran, the legendary boxer, came to work with us. Immediately Sly wanted to spar with him. I had a quick talk with Mr. Duran to be sure that he understood not to hurt Sly in any way and to make him look good.

Roberto and Sly danced and sparred around the ring as we filmed them as part of Rocky's training. Between takes Sly told me that he was doing pretty good boxing with the great Roberto Duran and felt he could outfight him in the next take.

I couldn't resist; so I went over to Roberto and told him what Sly had said. He laughed and said Sly was a good fighter—for an actor.

I nodded and suggested quietly to Roberto that perhaps one relatively mild body punch during the next take would be acceptable.

Roberto nodded at me, all smiles.

I rolled the camera, and Sly came steaming out of his corner.

Roberto spun him gently and then hit Sly with a kidney punch. That was the end of that take, as Sly staggered and groaned around the ring like a wounded water buffalo.

I never said a word and neither did Roberto Duran.

The pet store where Adrian worked was located in Philadelphia. We were filming at night, doing the scene where Adrian was all alone in the store moving heavy barrels of pet food. While she was moving the heavy barrels, Adrian was to feel a sharp pain, supposedly from the baby she was carrying.

No matter how many times Talia did the scene, Sly was unhappy with her performance. He talked with her, and he rehearsed the acting, but Talia could not give the reaction Sly was looking to get.

We did take after take, until during one shot Talia actually dropped the heavy barrel on her toes and screamed in pain.

"That's it!" Sly shouted. "Now you're getting it. Finally a real reaction! Let's do that again."

"I dropped it on my foot!" Talia screamed in pain.

"Do the same thing again. It was great! Just turn more toward the camera," Sly directed, as Talia lay on the floor crumpled in pain. And she did take after take.

Sly sustained a training injury, which meant we had to film the final fight later in Los Angeles. The largest and most difficult filming we had to do in Philadelphia was Rocky's training run from his house, through Philadelphia, and then up the avenue and steps to the state capitol building. This run not only brings out the final training feat for Rocky, but it also is the force for the *Rocky* theme music. Besides the final fight with Apollo, Rocky's final training run was the most important event in this movie, just as it was in the first *Rocky*.

When Rocky left his home and began his run, there were only a few neighborhood youths that ran with him. Then as he ran throughout Philadelphia, more and more joined his ranks until, when he ran up the avenue and steps to the capitol, there were literally thousands of people running with Sly. When Rocky reached the top of the steps, he danced around and was joined by hundreds of his followers, all dancing and cheering for Rocky.

The running scenes throughout Philadelphia were relatively simple as we added fifty or one hundred extras to run with Sly at each new location. Finally, we were to film the final run up the avenue and steps to the capitol. A Sunday was chosen so there would be less traffic and minimum public inconvenience. Extras to run for us had come from all over the Philadelphia area to be in the scene with Rocky. The purpose of the scene in the movie was to show that Rocky was the best-conditioned athlete in Philadelphia, who could run farther and faster than anyone else. We got the ten thousand runners lined up behind Sly. It was a long run up the avenue, then up the steps. Sly wanted to do this run only once, and I didn't blame him.

It took two hours to line up everyone and to remind them not to pass Sly; they must run behind him. That was the whole point of our scene; Rocky was the best. Finally we were ready. I got all the cameras set, and I cued Sly and the runners.

Everything was perfect. Sly was running great. The runners were back behind him and looking great. They ran up the avenue and then the steps. Suddenly, as Sly got to the top, a lone runner darted out from the side and danced on the top of the stairs. It looked like the runner had beaten Sly up to the top. Sly was devastated as he saw the runner. The shot was ruined.

There was no way to stop the ten thousand other runners coming behind. They continued to run and came up the steps dancing and joyful. Sly was beside himself. We all knew that there was nothing else to do, but to get all ten thousand people back down the avenue to their start marks and do the run again. Sly had run flat out; he only expected to do the run once.

He was in his motor home, exhausted and waiting for me. After getting all the runners to understand what had happened and why we had to do the shot again, I walked to Sly's motor home. He would expect an explanation from me, and that was my job.

"How you doing, Sly?"

"How you think I'm doin'? I ran my heart out!"

"I'm sorry. We have to do it again, Sly."

He looked at me. I stared back at him. There was nothing I could say. The wide-angle shots showed the runner waiting on the top of the steps; we had to do the shot again. I felt terrible about it, but Sly had to do the whole run again.

Sly nodded. "Let me know when you're ready, Jer."

I was so thankful Sly was in such wonderful physical condition.

The second take on Rocky's long run definitely showed a more focused Rocky; you could see the added determination on his face. Then when Rocky got to the top of the steps and no one else was there, you really believed in his happiness along with the joy of the other ten thousand runners who also had to make a second run.

• • •

My son Chris was eight years old when he flew to Philadelphia to spend Thanksgiving week with me on *Rocky II*. Tim was only four and stayed in Los Angeles with his mother.

It was a special treat for the two of us to be together for that week. I loved having him with me, and he loved being with his Pops, a name he called me all his life.

Chris appeared in a store scene with Sly and Talia when they bought a watch and then in a baseball scene with Sly outside Rocky's new home, and he was in the big run up the steps of the capitol.

On Sunday we drove through the Amish country and spent the afternoon in Washington, D.C., visiting all the sites. We ate hamburgers for lunch across from the Watergate Building and talked about Nixon and burglaries and topics that interested an eight-year-old. We were just a dad and a son spending Thanksgiving together. He was only with me seven days, but the memories haven't faded.

Paradise Alley, Sly's second starring film, opened in his hometown of Philadelphia while we were there filming *Rocky II*. The movie did very little business, even though the crowds to watch us film *Rocky II* were enormous.

Why would a couple thousand people stand out in the cold to watch Sly film *Rocky II*, but so few people would go to the theatres to see him in *Paradise Alley*?

I always felt that the crowds watching us film came out to see Rocky, not Sylvester Stallone. Rocky was the celebrity; Sylvester Stallone wasn't. I felt it took Sly's creation of Rambo to finally make him, and not Rocky, the celebrity.

We filmed the exterior locations in Philadelphia in bright, clear fall weather. According to the script, the big fight was to be held on Thanksgiving Day, and since that was the last event in the movie, everything in the film occurred before Thanksgiving.

One morning I was awakened by a phone call of total panic. I looked out of my hotel room window and Philadelphia was covered with SNOW!!!!! There was no snow in the movie! We'd filmed scenes of Rocky leaving his house to go to the big fight; there was no snow!!!!! Panic ruled.

What could we do?

The transportation captain was with his trucks, trying to find someplace off the busy streets of Philadelphia where he could park our armada of trucks and Sly's motor home.

We had planned on filming a simple little scene of Sly and Talia walking through the tiny park near the Liberty Bell, but now there was snow everywhere. The blizzard would match nothing we had filmed.

The Philadelphia traffic was a disaster, with cars stuck everywhere. Our transportation captain had put our fleet of trucks, dressing rooms, and trailers in the only open spot he could find that morning—the Philadelphia Zoo.

I got out of the van at the zoo and looked at the Hollywood crazies who were in either total panic or else in some kind of euphoric glee as they played in the snow.

"Where are Talia and Sly?" I asked.

"Sly is in his motor home, and Talia's playing in the snow," someone volunteered.

The snow was more than a foot deep and still falling. There was no way those trucks were going to leave the zoo that day. My head was spinning as I trudged through the snow in my tennis shoes to Sly's motor home.

I knocked and entered in the midst of my Assistant Director Hell, having a whole company with actors and crew and not being able to shoot. Somehow, somewhere, someone back at the studio will make all this my fault.

"Sly . . ."

"Yo, Jer, you see the snow?"

"Sly, look, I don't . . ."

"Pretty, right?"

"Sly, you don't understand. We . . ."

"You OK, Jer? You want anything?"

"Sly, don't you understand? We have a whole film crew outside in the snow, and we can't shoot anything! Do you know what that costs? Don't you realize what a disaster this is? Do you know what the studio will say about this? They will kill us! We can't film!!!!"

"Jer, it's gonna be all right. Don't worry."

"Sly, this is your second film. Trust me. Losing a whole day will kill our budget, our schedule, the studio will eat us alive. We can't film because of the goddamn snow!!! They'll kill us!"

"No they won't, Jer. We'll do the Proposal scene."

"What? There's no Proposal scene, Sly. What are you talking about?"

"You want us to film, right, Jer? What's outside there? Where are we?"

"The zoo, Sly. We're at the Philadelphia Zoo! There's a goddamn tiger out there in a foot of snow and a blizzard happening!!!!"

"Get Talia. I'll propose to her in front of the tiger. It's right after the first fight, so it's winter. Catch you later, Jer. Hey! You got a pen or something? I wanna write this down, ya know."

There are moments in life where you go from drowning in the depths of despair to suddenly riding the crest of the most perfect wave you have ever seen. That morning at the Philadelphia Zoo was one of my moments. Sylvester Stallone instantaneously put me on the top of the wave and at the same time gave us all one of the best scenes in *Rocky II*.

While we were filming the wide shot that included Talia, Sly, and the tiger, none of the crew could get the tiger to look at Sly and Talia.

"Don't worry, Jer. Hey, Tiger! When we walk over here . . . I'll say, 'Hey, Tiger!' You turn to us. OK?"

There wasn't a doubt in my mind. "Ready when you are, Sly."

"Roll it."

"Action."

The talk, the proposal, the walk, and the tiger turned right on Sly's cue as though it was a finely trained actor, like a Butkus.

The next day we also filmed in the snow. Sly came up with a short scene where two theatrical agents attempted to get Rocky to sign a contract to represent him to do commercials as he was leaving the hospital after the first fight.

That was it for our filming in Philadelphia. The sudden blizzard made filming in snow-covered Philadelphia impossible for our story, so we headed back to sunny Hollywood and the big fight.

The whole movie of *Rocky II* came down to the audience's enjoyment of the final fight between Rocky and Apollo Creed. Unless the excitement of our film's fight topped the first *Rocky*, all was lost. Everything, from Sly's achievement as a first-time director to the financial success of *Rocky II*, depended on the film audiences' excitement on viewing our fight. Certainly Sylvester Stallone's directing career was on the line.

Sly and Carl Weathers had worked for weeks on Sly's detailed choreography for the fight, but because of Sly's injury we had to delay filming the fight for nearly eight weeks. I was concerned that Sly and Carl had lost their edge because of having to concentrate on their acting scenes for the last eight weeks instead of first filming the fight, when all of their training and the choreography was fresh in their minds.

Tom Wright was the illustrator on *Rocky II*. He would draw suggestions for camera positions and specific shots for Sly's consideration. Tom and I watched a lot of fight films to try and determine which camera angles best showed the drama of boxing. We would then bring our suggestions to Sly for his comments. We studied staged boxing for films as well as films of actual boxing matches.

From the very beginning, Sly wanted to depict the feeling of boxing in *Rocky II*, not only great camera angles, but also what the fighters actually felt during the fight. Sly wanted to use various speeds of slow motion along with sound distortion to give the movie's viewers the feeling of what a fighter experiences when he is boxing.

Sly wanted to have the audience experience what a knock-down punch does to a boxer's vision and hearing. He wanted to use exaggerated makeup and excessive moisture on the actors to heighten the illusion of the effect of a punch to a boxer. Sly wanted to see the excessive moisture and blood *rain* off of the fighter who took a hard punch. He wanted to film his boxers in backlight to intensify the spray of liquids whenever a punch was landed to their head.

For mainline Hollywood filmmaking, Sly was breaking new ground. Of course movies had done slow motion to show boxers in action, but they had never done it from the subjective point of view of a boxer, had never used slow motion along with distorted sound to create the subjective experience of a boxer.

I felt that for Sylvester Stallone to direct his first film was in itself taking a big career chance, but then to use his camera and sound in a unique, impressionistic mode for the most critical scene in *Rocky II* seemed to me to be certain career suicide. I begged Sly, that if he insisted on his extensive use of slow motion, to also film all shots in normal speed; that way in editing he would always have the choice in case the slow motion didn't work.

Sly was right in his decision to use slow motion. His different filming techniques not only created the unique impressionistic style of the *Rocky II* fight, but also created one of the highest-grossing boxing films of all time.

It took six days to film the *Rocky II* fight, from the entrances through the finale. Sly and Carl were asked to do every knockdown until we got it right. The end result was one of the most exciting boxing sequences ever filmed and certainly the best ever filmed by a first-time director.

The day I first met Sly in his office, he told me he wanted to top the first *Rocky* fight, and he did it. Sly wrote, starred in, and directed one of the most successful sequels to any film Hollywood has ever made. He did this as a first time-director with a tight shooting schedule and a very limited budget.

The most amazing thing was that after all the hard work when the film was completed, there wasn't a member of the cast or crew who wouldn't have *killed* to work with Sylvester Stallone again, and most did.

Whenever I run into Sly I remind him that I believe it was a stroke of genius how he instantaneously created the Proposal scene during a blizzard at the Philadelphia Zoo and probably saved the picture.

He always says the same thing to me.

"Really, Jer? Really? You think so? Come on . . . I never knew you thought that, Jer . . . Yeah?"

Yeah, Sly. A memorable moment.

I arrived for work at the backlot of the Burbank Studios around 5:00 P.M., even though it really didn't get dark enough to film night until almost 8:00. I liked getting to a rehearsal early and then letting the crew work while it was still light and they could see. By the time the actors were through with their makeup and hair, the crew would have the set lit. It worked fine.

I got a cup of coffee and watched the rehearsal. It was 1985, and Richard Pryor was directing his first and only film. It was a simple scene we were doing, a café late at night, with four people sitting in a booth. We were using the backlot because Richard wanted to see cars driving by in the rain outside the café's windows. I hadn't ordered quite enough extras, so Suzanne and Ziggy were driving through the shot that night.

Richard finished his rehearsal. The crew began their work, and the actors scattered to their dressing rooms.

About fifteen minutes later, one of the older actors brought a metal folding chair and placed it about thirty feet away from the set. He sat down and put a stack of three hundred photographs of himself on his lap with a black marking pen on top. He sat still and waited. There wasn't anyone near him. I'm sure I was the only one who realized he was out there sitting all by himself.

I felt sorry for him. He had all those photographs of himself, and no one even knew he was there. He had been a big star in recordings when Suzanne and I were in high school, nearly thirty years ago. He had never done a movie. In all those years, Jo Jo Dancer *was his first film. I didn't think anyone remembered him or would care about some seventy-year-old crooner after all those years.*

A couple of people saw him sitting out there and walked over to him. He autographed his photo for them. They stayed to chat for a moment, but now more people were coming around him. He laughed and they laughed. Some more people came, and a few crew members left the set and stood in line for him to autograph a picture for them and their wives.

I continued to watch, and in less than thirty minutes all of his pictures were gone. He stood, promised to bring more pictures another night, folded up his metal chair, and Billy Eckstine wandered back toward the set, still a big star.

The Steven Spielberg Films

Close Encounters of the Third Kind

It was June 1996, and I was assisting Cameron Crowe in filming *Jerry Maguire* on one of the sound stages at Sony Studios in Culver City. We had less than a month of shooting remaining.

The crew gossip around the set that day was that Steven Spielberg was coming to the sound stage to visit Janusz Kaminski, our cameraman. Janusz had done *Schindler's List* with Steven, and they were going to do the *Jurassic Park* sequel, *The Lost World*, during the summer after *Jerry Maguire* had finished.

"Think you need to call in a pass for Steven Spielberg?" a crew member asked me, and then laughed at his own joke, as if Steven Spielberg needed a pass to get into any movie studio in the world! I smiled at the crew humor, but it wasn't always that way for Steven.

Twenty years earlier, in 1977, Columbia Studios hired me as Steven's assistant director to complete *Close Encounters of the Third Kind*. It would be the first of two films Steven and I would work on during the next two years. The second was Steven's only comedy, *1941*, with John Belushi and Dan Aykroyd.

The principal photography for *Close Encounters* had been completed during 1976, while I was in the Philippines with Francis Coppola on *Apocalypse Now*. After Steven looked at the cut footage for *Close Encounters*, he wanted to film some additional scenes. Columbia Studios was very nervous about the picture and about Steven Spielberg.

At this time in his career, Steven had one commercial success, *Jaws*.

Many people in Hollywood were pointing not at Steven for that film's success, but at Verna Fields, the film editor, who received an Academy Award for editing *Jaws*, while Steven wasn't even nominated for directing it. For mainstream Hollywood, Steven Spielberg was still an unproven commodity.

The first time I met Steven was at the Burbank Studios, outside the production offices for *Close Encounters*. William Fraker, the cameraman, his key crew, and I were all going to scout the California deserts with Steven. We were looking for the right location for a new scene in *Close Encounters*, the discovery of scores of formerly missing aircraft now mysteriously found intact on a Mexican desert.

When Steven came out of the production office dressed in Levi's, a sport shirt, tennis shoes, and a baseball cap, my first impression was that he was the guy in high school who belonged to the audio-video club, liked science and math, had only three good friends in the whole school, didn't speak up in any classes except chemistry, and never, ever dated.

Clark Paylow, the production manager, introduced all of us to Steven as we entered the studio van for our ride into the California desert. Steven sat in the passenger seat next to the driver. William Fraker and Clark Paylow sat in the next seat, while the crew and I filled up the van.

Steven had just turned thirty years old in December 1976, but he looked even younger. This was our leader? He reminded me of the kid who plugged in the sound system at the junior prom because he couldn't get a date. Columbia Studios was betting millions of dollars on his taste and judgment?

We were used to film directors being big men dressed like great white hunters, who smoked cigars and told stories from their filming days of twenty or thirty years ago. This wasn't Steven; he was very different. Steven was at least two inches shorter than I, and I'm barely 5'10". He was thin and had small features; I was sure he never hung out at the beach. He looked like he should have been in the sound department or accounting, but not the director of a multimillion dollar movie.

After the introductions and the morning pleasantries, Steven was all business. He focused into the task at hand, to find the desert location for his new scene. He spent most of the ride reading his script and then staring out the front window, deep in thought.

William Fraker was a tall, gray-haired gentleman who looked to me like a very happy Don Quixote. Bill was quite a sight going back and forth to the studio each day in his black VW Thing, that military-type car Volkswagen used to make. He sat up high in the driver's seat, with his long, white hair flowing behind him as he drove majestically down the Hollywood Freeway.

William Fraker was a good storyteller and I was always a good story listener. To pass the time getting to the desert, Bill began a story.

"Now, Jerry, I get home and before anything else," Bill began, "I go into my bar and get Pedro out of his cage. . . ."

"Bill," Steven said, "what I need is a flat desert area where we can put twenty planes in a circle, but I need a dawn shot, so we'll have to have a good eastern scenic look, you know, Bill?" Steven continued to stare out the van's front window.

"OK, Steven, we'll find it," Bill answered, and quickly returned to telling his story. "Pedro is a parrot I've had for fifteen years. Maybe longer. Anyway, I take him and put him on a perch I have for him on my bar, then I . . ."

"Bill, is it better to film sunset for sunrise? Do you get more time to film?" Steven turned around and asked Bill.

"Always better, Steven," Bill answered.

"Then I mix me a large container of margaritas, big mother jug full, each night. I get me seven peanuts from a jar and . . ."

Bill?" Steven asked. "We also need a good approach for Lacombe, but from another angle, you know? To bring Truffaut into the scene."

"OK, Steven, whatever you say," Bill said.

"I line up the seven peanuts in a row, and after each margarita I have . . ."

"What would be the best direction for Lacombe to arrive? Should Truffaut come from the north or where?" Steven asked.

"South, Steven. Good light all day."

Bill immediately went back to his story. "After each drink I give Pedro a peanut and a sip of a margarita."

"Bill, do you think we'll be able to find that?" Steven again.

"Yes, Steven."

Bill continued, "I keep drinking all night until the peanuts are gone and . . ."

"I hope so, Bill. This is a critical scene. It's early in the film, you know?" Steven said.

"Right, Steven."

Bill smiled at us, "And . . . Pedro falls off his perch!"

All of the crew, Bill, and I, and even the driver laughed and hollered as the van continued down the highway.

"Pedro falls off his perch!" Bill said again.

Steven never heard a word about Pedro or the peanuts or all of our laughter.

"I hope so, Bill. I hope so," Steven said anxiously, as he stared pensively out the front window and then back into his script. "I hope so."

It was a long trip from the studio up to the desert area of central California, and it was around lunchtime when we got to a small city just before the desert began. The crew started their mumbling about stopping for lunch.

It was Clark Paylow, the unit manager, who suggested to Steven that maybe it would be a good idea to get something to eat.

"Sure. Let's get something," Steven said. "Would McDonald's be OK?"

The crew looked around at Clark and me. It was almost a ritual in the movie business to stop at a good steak and beer restaurant for a location scout meal, stretch your legs for an hour, and then get back in the van well fortified for the rest of the trip.

Clark gestured behind Steven's back, "What can we do?" The crew reluctantly nodded their agreement, and we headed for a McDonald's up the street.

Just as our van was about to pull into the McDonald's parking lot, Steven spoke again.

"No, don't pull in here," Steven said as he pointed to the McDonald's drive-through lane. "Just pull to the take-out window. We'll get some Big Macs, fries, some Cokes to go and be on our way. Why waste time stopping to eat?"

Directors have different ideas about food. Steven Spielberg in those early years was a definite fast-food freak, as is Cameron Crowe today. Steven couldn't pass up a Burger King or a McDonald's, and Cameron does quite nicely on Pizza Hut and Taco Bell.

Mark Rydell was a deli guy, but specialized in Art's Deli on Ventura Boulevard in Studio City.

Francis Coppola was an all-Italian guy, with pizza from Damiano's on Fairfax Avenue across from Canter's Restaurant in West Hollywood.

John Frankenheimer was a four-star French restaurant man with flair.

> *Sydney Pollack liked his deli, too, and he could put a good dent into Italian, as could Brian De Palma.*
>
> *Marty Ritt couldn't stop eating "the little sausage things at the track."*
>
> *John Huston and Richard Pryor liked their Chinese food.*
>
> *Tom Cruise, the twenty-million-dollar-a-picture guy, liked his favorite pizza. Flown in from Roma? Paris? London? Chicago? New York? No, from a pizza-by-the-slice stand in West Los Angeles.*

A miracle happened when we arrived at the desert location. The quiet, shy kid from the high school audio-video club was nowhere to be seen. As soon as Steven stepped on the location there was no doubt that he was in charge.

"Over here!" Steven called, and hurried out into the desert. "Here! Look, Bill, we'll have the planes in a huge circle here."

All of us were coming across the desert as fast as we could.

"Where, Steven?" Bill Fraker said, as he panted up to Steven.

"Here's the circle. Planes all around. Noses pointing to the center. Right?" Steven continued.

"OK," Bill replied.

"Which way is north?" Steven asked briskly.

I had my assistant director's compass out.

"Over there, Steven," I said, as I pointed to our left.

"Truffaut comes from the south, right, Bill?" Steven asked, and started off in a near trot.

"Right, Steven," Bill called, and we were all running to catch up to our director.

"Jerry!" Steven called, as he continued striding across the desert.

"Here, Steven," I yelled, and I was sorry I was smoking two packs a day.

"We'll put the Mexican shack here. The road comes from the south; that's how Truffaut arrives. OK?"

"Great! Steven," I got out, as I had trouble catching my breath.

"This is good, Steven," Bill added, as he caught up to us.

"Trucks go over there," Steven said, as he pointed to the southwest. "I'll never see over there. Jerry, put the trucks . . ."

"I got it, Steven, trucks will be right there," I said, and wrote notes at the same time.

"What time is sunset?" Steven asked.

"About 7:00 when we film here," Bill answered.

"Right, Steven, we'll be here . . . ," I began.

"Good, we'll film sunset for dawn. Better!" Steven said, and strode off back toward our van. "The shack is facing east. That's perfect, Bill."

"Right, Steven!" we all answered together, as we hurried to keep up.

For the first time in our lives we watched Steven Spielberg in action. He was our leader, the decision maker, and the one with definitive answers to all our questions. Steven Spielberg at age thirty was the unchallenged director of our film.

Steven had a presence that assured us that he knew exactly what he wanted and why. His crew knew he'd stand by his decisions and would support us in our efforts to carry out his wishes.

Even on *Close Encounters*, if Steven asked you to do something, no one dared to stop you. Steven was a giant force that put all members of the crew in motion, and he was the only force that could stop them.

The short, thin kid from the audio-video club, who didn't have a date for the junior prom, was just starting to run the big show in Hollywood. I saw it happen as naturally and inevitably as the coming of tomorrow's dawn.

The first day we were to film out in the desert, I saw François Truffaut looking out at our armada of trucks, motor homes, trailers, vans, and cars. We had more than forty trucks. There were the production vans, the generators, the equipment trucks for the crew, and three trucks for the caterer. Most actors and Steven had a motor home; the other actors had trailers. It was a sea of motorized stock.

Truffaut motioned to me.

"Jerry, you have more trucks than I have people when I make a movie in France," he said, and smiled.

I nodded and wished I could be his assistant on one of his movies in France someday.

"We have four, maybe five trucks, no more. No dressing rooms. A caterer, but no kitchen in a truck," he smiled.

Truffaut had directed three of my all-time favorite films: *400 Blows, Shoot the Piano Player,* and *Jules and Jim.* I remembered seeing them while I was at Northwestern University.

I knew that the total budget for my three favorite Truffaut films was less than the transportation budget for our trucks on *Close Encounters.*

Truffaut was given to impersonating Bugs Bunny's friend, Elmer Fudd, but he did it in a slight French accent. "You kwazy wabbits," he said, smiling and continuing to look out at our trucks and hundreds of crew members.

● ● ●

When it was time for François Truffaut's first scene as an actor, I wondered how he would take direction from Steven. François had written and directed so many wonderful films for many years. Steven was a young director with one successful movie.

I knocked on François' dressing room door and then on Steven's. I told each that we were ready at the camera. I then hurried back so I wouldn't miss a thing. What would Steven's attitude be toward directing Truffaut? Would Truffaut take direction from the young American?

As was usual, Steven was the first one onto the set, but François was close behind. Whenever Steven came onto the set as the director ready to work with his actors, there was no doubt that Steven knew exactly what he wanted from the actors and the crew.

I watched as Truffaut came onto the set.

François didn't enter as a famous director. He came into the set as an insecure, questioning actor. He listened as Steven explained the scene to him.

Steven showed him the Mexican peasant with the burned face who was sitting on the wooden chair outside the desert building. François looked and studied the peasant and then nodded his understanding to Steven.

Steven showed François exactly where he wanted him to stand and how he wanted him to lean down and talk to the peasant. François studied Steven and kept nodding his constant approval and understanding.

There were two fine directors standing in front of me, but only one was directing that day—Steven. François was being a most attentive actor, trying to do his best for his director.

After each take, Steven would give François comments on his performance and on his positions in relationship to the seated peasant. François listened and followed each of Steven's directions.

Later in our shooting schedule, we were filming an outdoor warehouse set. In the script, the preparations were being made to outfit those who would be trying to make contact with the aliens arriving at the Devil's Punch Bowl.

We were using the back loading dock of the prop department at the studio. There was an office above, then a long stairs and walkway down to the loading dock and the parking lot beyond. The set dressers had piled cases and boxes of various supplies on the dock and in the parking area.

It must have been in the summer, because my two sons, Chris, seven and Tim, three, were at the studio with me. Ziggy had them watching from down below the loading dock in the parking area.

We had gotten a rehearsal, and the crew was working in the office set, when I glanced down and saw François Truffaut talking with Chris and Tim. The boys were on a large packing case, and François was leaning over the case as he talked with them. I was forty feet away and couldn't hear, but I could see the laughter coming from Ziggy and the boys and Truffaut.

When I got a break, I made my way down toward them. François was telling a story, and the boys were watching with wide-open eyes and smiles like only little boys can get. Suddenly I heard François.

"You kwazy wabbit," he said, and the boys erupted in laughter.

"You're the kwazy wabbit!" they shouted at him.

By the time I got up to them, Tim and Chris were begging their new friend for another story about "that kwazy wabbit." Truffaut and I exchanged smiles, and his next story began in hushed tones as the little boys' eyes grew round with each new wonder.

Ziggy leaned in to hear, but I clicked it all into my memory and headed back to Steven at the camera up in the office.

On our sound stage, the art department had built the front of the alien spaceship, including the door and the ramp used by the aliens to exit the ship. The majority of the aliens were children and little people, wardrobed and made up as the extraterrestrials.

The main alien was a mechanical puppet that was controlled by air sent through hoses that ran from a series of controlling levers fifteen feet across the set and up into the alien's body. The puppeteer would gently push or pull to make the alien move his body, head, face, etc. The technicians had worked months to master the movement of the main alien.

As soon as Steven saw the levers, he had to try them. Within an hour, Steven was controlling the alien for our filming. All that meant to Steven was another element of play within the greatest kid's game ever made, the motion picture set.

"OK, are we ready? Steven, set?" I asked, to try and get the company moving.

Steven was sitting on a metal folding chair in front of a wooden sawhorse with the levers attached to it and the air tubes running along the floor to the alien.

"Wait! Jerry, look. Watch the alien! Look!" Steven would get so excited as he made the alien bow, or wiggle, or appear to do a dance.

"Steven, we've got to go," I said.

"Wait! Look, Jer, look! Watch his body!" Steven was happily playing with the alien.

"Please, Steven, we've got to shoot this," I said, as I got the rest of the crew away from him and at their posts ready for the shot.

"Why? OK, OK," he said, as he gave the puppet one more hip movement like it was twirling a hula hoop.

Everyone laughed.

"OK, Jer. Here we go!" Steven said, and we went for a take.

When the shot was over, Steven would leave the controls and go to the video monitor to have it replayed for him.

"I was good! Did you see that?" he said, as he pointed to the main alien.

I whispered to Steven, "How were the actors?"

He laughed, amused at himself for only watching his work with the alien.

"Let me see that shot again!" he called to the video assist technician. "Were they OK?" he asked quietly as the videotape was rewound.

François Truffaut would rarely come back to watch the monitor. All of the mechanics and video gadgets were not his way of making films.

I talked to him about whether he would ever direct a movie like *Close Encounters*. I meant a movie with a lot of special effects, a big mechanical movie with aliens and spaceships.

He smiled and shook his head.

"In my movies there's a man," he said, as he pointed to himself, "and everyone he meets is an alien. They come out of doors, taxis, and around corners."

He looked at me, and I nodded.

"Those are my movies," he smiled. "Our scene today with the hand signals? It's the same thing I do, but without spaceships."

François laughed, then smiled, and he widened his eyes and nodded his head to assure me that all he said was true.

The filming with the aliens was great fun for everyone, and I was glad to be a part of it. We were getting marvelous shots, but our shooting days were slipping by, and we were going over schedule and way over budget. No one at the studio seemed to care, and if they did they never told us on the set.

The situation was very similar to what occurred in the Philippines with Francis. Everyone from the studio knew we were going over budget and over schedule, but no one wanted to do battle with either Francis or Steven. It was more comfortable to leave them alone and pray for another *Godfather* or *Jaws*.

Steven's *Jaws* had enriched Universal Studios, and *Close Encounters* saved Columbia Studios from bankruptcy. The two studios happily backed Steven's next film.

1941

I wasn't available when Steven began *1941* because I was filming *Rocky II*. When I finished with Sly, I began to work around our new home, which had an additional bedroom and a full playroom. My wife was expecting our third child about the beginning of February. Medical science informed us it would be a girl.

Columbia Studios called me on the morning of my third day of doing home repairs and said that there was a problem on *1941*. Steven wanted me to take over the picture that night. I called Ziggy to be at the Burbank Studios by 7:00 P.M.

"Beau-tee-ful!" was all Ziggy said.

Steven was doing night shooting along the New York Street on the backlot. I turned off Riverside Drive and drove through the Hollywood Way Gate. I parked my Mazda in front of Sydney Pollack's old office from *The Way We Were*. It was easy to find a parking place; most of the studio had gone home to their families. I walked a block west, past the water tower to the backlot and New York Street, now made over into Hollywood Boulevard for *1941*.

It must have been before 7:00 because it was still light. As I got closer to the set, I could see the crew preparing for the night work. The electricians were setting their lamps and pulling cable. The grips were building a dolly track in the street.

There was a movie theatre on my right with *Dumbo* on the marquee. A big, twenty-foot-tall Santa Claus was attached to the corner building in front of me, and the USO entrance was to the right of it. It was quite a set, Christmastime in Los Angeles, 1941.

I'd told Ziggy to be here, but I didn't see him.

Suddenly, from my left, I heard someone talking to me like a vocal machine gun.

"You're Jerry Ziesmer. Hi, I'm Chris Soldo, your second AD. You OK? I got the extras on Stages 23 and 24, the stuntmen are on Stage 13 and in their dressing rooms, the crew is arriving, and they're setting up for a dolly shot, see?" he said.

As he talked, I looked at this person in front of me, Chris Soldo. He was younger than Larry Franco and a bit taller, but he had Larry's energy. He wore a New York Yankees cap. Chris was thin, wiry, with an intense face, but one that smiled easily. I really hadn't found any second assistant director that both Ziggy and I liked since Larry. I stared at this one; Chris Soldo was different.

"You OK?" Chris asked me, as he took his first breath.

"Chris, you're the only one I want to talk to, OK?" I said.

"Oh, OK?" He stared at me with wide, questioning eyes.

"I asked Ziggy Frohlich to be here," I said, as I looked around the street.

"He's with the extras on Stage 24," Chris said. "He told me to get out here and find you. What do you need?"

That told me Ziggy liked him.

"Get the actors ready. Tell me what's happening in the scene. Get me a script later."

"The shot is a lot of Christmas shoppers, and then the stunt guys run out of the USO, and a tank comes around the corner," Chris said.

"Where's Steven Spielberg?" I asked.

"Steven isn't here yet," he said, and stared at me.

"Chris, it's you and me and Ziggy, OK?" I asked.

"OK," he answered, and left to check on the actors.

"Thanks, Chris," I called after him.

I had a hunch that Ziggy and I had found a good one.

I knew Bill Fraker was the cameraman on *1941*; that would make my job easier and a lot more enjoyable. I couldn't wait to ask him about Pedro and his margaritas.

I was watching the crew and the activity, just easing into things, when I saw Steven walk onto the New York Street. I started toward him.

It had been six months since I'd worked with him, but he was dressed in the same fashion, Levi's, sport shirt, tennis shoes, and a baseball cap. When I saw a white paper bag in his hand, I knew it was the same Steven Spielberg.

"Jer! How are you?" he asked, as he opened the bag. "Want a Burger King?"

As we ate the burgers, I asked Steven what was happening in the shot.

"I'm not sure. It's crazy. Have you worked with John Belushi?" he asked me.

I nodded that I hadn't, as I swallowed the last of my Burger King.

"He and Dan Aykroyd are crazy!" Steven laughed. "No one knows what's going to happen next. They're out of their minds. Brilliant, but totally crazy! John Candy!" Steven laughed and tried to swallow at the same time.

I nodded as I watched Steven finish his burger.

"Should we try a rehearsal with all of the actors?" I suggested.

"OK. Good idea," Steven said, as he looked for a spot to throw the Burger King bag and wrappers. "You'll see, Jer. It's crazy!"

John Candy, Treat Williams, Mickey Rourke, and the rest of the tank crew walked onto the set for the rehearsal. Steven was there and Bill Fraker, but I didn't see Dan Aykroyd. I was about to radio to Chris Soldo to check for Aykroyd, when an authentic New York taxi drove down our Hollywood Boulevard and stopped in front of the USO. It was Dan Aykroyd driving and John Belushi riding with him.

It was quite an entrance for the two leading comics, as they got out of their cab and danced over to Steven and the rest of the cast, while everyone laughed.

I already felt that I was in for some rough times with those two, but when I learned that the New York taxi wasn't the property of the movie studio, but that Dan Aykroyd and John Belushi owned the taxi as well as a real New York ambulance and that's what they drove on the streets of Los Angeles, I knew I was in major trouble.

All of the crew and extras stood or sat on the street near the movie theatre. Terry Leonard had his stunt people watching from underneath the huge Santa Claus. That left the USO entrance and the street outside free for the rehearsal.

Everything started like a normal rehearsal.

"OK, look, Treat, you and Bobby have been in the USO," Steven began. "You're on the street by now."

Treat Williams and Bobby DiCicco moved to the center of the street near Steven.

"Where's the tank, Steven?" Belushi said, and squinted his eyes in a challenging, foreboding manner. He was straight out of his work on *Saturday Night Live.*

"We come around the corner, Steven?" Aykroyd asked, as he pointed to the right of the USO.

"Right," Steven answered.

"I'm driving?" Mickey Rourke asked.

"Right," Steven answered. "The tank begins back there and comes up to about here." Steven stood in the middle of the intersection, nearly straight out from the Santa Claus.

"It'd be funny if the tank hit something!" Belushi offered.

John Belushi wasn't even in the scene at that point. He didn't arrive until after the tank had left.

"What do you mean?" Steven quizzed, but he was intrigued.

"I could hit a pole!" Rourke suggested.

"The tank crushes a car!" Belushi yelled, and gestured with his whole body to simulate a monstrous tank crushing a car.

"What?" Steven laughed. "What about the driver of the car?"

I shot a look of desperation toward Steven.

"Steven," I began, "we can't crush a car with people inside of it."

"It's parked!" Aykroyd reasoned. "There's no people!"

"Right!" Steven joined in.

"The tank comes whipping around the corner, crushes a car . . . ," Belushi began.

"A parked car," Aykroyd adds, as though he also added sanity to the discussion.

"The tank stops here!" Steven continued.

"I come out of the top of the tank and machine gun the area!" Aykroyd added.

"You what?" Steven asked.

"Everyone hits the street, then I begin my speech!" Aykroyd continued.

"That's it!" Belushi said.

Steven was laughing, and the cast was excited.

As the assistant director I was in cardiac arrest. First of all, we didn't have any junk cars that we could just crush one after another, take after take after take. We could easily go through thirty cars. Second, the street was filled with people. The fast-moving tank hitting a car was dangerous, as was a machine gun shooting blanks. Third, we weren't prepared for the special effects of the machine-gun bullet hits.

"This is great!" Steven was elated. "Some of this is in the script!"

"Steven," I began.

"Jer, just call me when you're ready. Is this a great scene? It's crazy!" Steven said, and strode off with Belushi and Aykroyd. From their laughter I knew the creative process was still in first gear.

It wasn't thirty minutes later that Steven, Belushi, Aykroyd, John Candy, and Treat Williams walked quickly from the dressing room area back up to the set.

"Jer!" Steven called, as he held a sheet of paper.

I went to him, ready to explain that it would still be a while before the crew was ready for the entrance of the tank and all.

"What is it, Steven?" I asked.

"Here's a list of some of the special shots we want to get as part of this sequence," Steven said, as he held back his laughter.

"Just a few quick pops," Aykroyd added. "These won't take long."

"The first one," Belushi began, "is me as Marlon Brando, the Godfather, eating spaghetti in an Italian restaurant when a car drives through the front window."

I just stared at him.

"Right!" Aykroyd said. "Then there's one in a department store where an electric train runs into a Marine's face!"

"There's a fire engine with a ladder, see," John Candy began, "and an MP is hit by the ladder and lifted across the street."

I became numb. There was no Italian restaurant set. We didn't have a department store, nor an electric train. Where would we get a 1941 fire truck?

"Is this great!" Steven said, as a statement of fact.

Belushi was improving eating the spaghetti à la Brando as everyone joined in the laughter and fun.

After Dan Aykroyd and the tank left the front of the USO and headed toward the Santa Monica Pier, John Belushi's airplane flew over Hollywood Boulevard and crashed into the base of the huge Santa Claus on the building next to the USO. As Belushi staggered out of his airplane, the Santa Claus fell on him.

The flight of Belushi's plane down Hollywood Boulevard was done on a miniature street with a small airplane on wires, but the actual crash into the Santa Claus was done in full scale out on the Burbank Studios backlot.

The special effects crew had a full-size airplane with a dummy for

Belushi in the cockpit. They would shoot the plane off a catapult. The plane would be propelled like a rocket, starting about twelve feet in the air, bouncing in the street once, and crashing into the base of the Santa Claus. It was the final shot of the Belushi flying sequence, and we spent many nights out on the backlot redoing it until Steven got the plane crash exactly as he wanted it.

I always found Steven to be a very loyal director. When you were making your first movie with Steven, you couldn't imagine that he was a warm individual. He appeared to be cold, absorbed, centered on his film, with a pure case of tunnel vision. It took at least two pictures with Steven to learn his ways.

He hired many of the same crew members picture after picture, and he became very attached to them. To Steven they became more than associates or friends, they really became part of his family. Charlsie Bryant was such a crew member.

Steven first worked with Charlsie on *Jaws*, and after that experience he would have no script supervisor other than his Charlsie. She was in her late fifties when she did *Jaws* and *Close Encounters of the Third Kind* with Steven. Charlsie was overweight, with a round face and squat body. She had a soft voice and a twinkling Irish eye that we all enjoyed. Charlsie didn't often talk to Steven about his selection of shots, but on the few occasions that she did, Steven Spielberg listened attentively to her every word.

Charlsie and I first worked together on *Black Sunday*, so we had a running start to our relationship before I worked with her on *Close Encounters*. An assistant director and a script supervisor have to work closely together, and Charlsie and I did.

She knew that I had little talent for matching the background from the previous take, seeing that the extras and vehicles did the same thing. I knew that Charlsie had a bit of a glow and a slightly bigger smile every afternoon following lunch and that the glow and the smile got progressively brighter and wider as we came closer to the end of the day.

She hadn't been in good health at the end of *Close Encounters*, but we all thought that with a month off Charlsie would be fine. She wasn't. Before *1941* began filming, Charlsie died.

It was a difficult time for Steven. He had relied on Charlsie for her quiet style and film expertise. He also loved her like a member of his family.

Between setups on *1941*, when there would be a break in the conversation, Steven would point his index finger toward the top of the sound stage and say that Charlsie was there with us.

"She's with us. Can you feel her? She's here!" Steven would say and smile, but with a tear in his eye.

During the filming of *1941* Steven got some pretty big checks for *Jaws*. Those were the first sizable payments Steven had ever received. I didn't notice any immediate differences in his clothes or habits, but he did buy a new Cadillac. One day he drove it to the studio.

All of the cast and crew admired Steven's new car. He was very proud of it. After lunch the car was taken to have the windows tinted. Steven wanted them tinted as dark as possible—maybe a bit darker; Steven enjoyed pushing the envelope.

Before we wrapped that Friday afternoon, his Cadillac was brought back with the newly tinted windows. After shooting it was still light outside, and Steven got in his new car and drove to his friend's home for dinner.

When Steven left his friend's house and got back into his new car, Steven knew he had pushed the envelope a bit too far. He couldn't see to drive home.

Much of Hollywood's history deteriorates as sets and props weather and become lost forever because they are not stored properly. One day when we were filming *1941*, Steven walked out of our sound stage and looked across the studio street. There, sitting in an alley way, unprotected from the elements, was one of the Devil's Punch Bowl replicas used in *Close Encounters of the Third Kind*. As soon as Steven saw it, he went into action to have that replica protected and stored properly, even if that meant it had to be trucked to his home in Coldwater Canyon, and that was where it went.

On Friday nights when we were filming the miniature Hollywood Boulevard on Stage 16, for about the last two hours of our shooting week there would be a party. Wives and girlfriends would drive into the main gate of the studio, wave at the studio guard, and make their way to our sound stage. Many of the guests would be close friends and relatives or neighbors invited by the crew members to come to our sound stage on Friday nights to see our fabulous miniature set of Hollywood Boulevard, have some food and drink, and enjoy our last filming of the week.

Normally Steven kept a very closed set, but on Friday nights it was wide open. The stage was filled with people. Everyone and anyone could wave at the studio guard, drive onto the lot, and walk into our sound stage. No one had any trouble, but one person, Steven's lady, Amy Irving. For some mysterious reason, the studio guards wouldn't let her on the lot. I never learned why.

The first Friday that the studio guards wouldn't allow Amy to enter the studio was taken to be an accident. Studio guards were just doing their duty.

The second Friday that Amy couldn't get on the lot was looked upon as amusing.

The third Friday that Amy was refused entrance to the studio, Steven became furious.

"Ziesmer!" he shouted, as Amy had to call Steven from the studio gate for him to talk personally to the guard, "why won't the guards let Amy on the lot? Why?"

"Steven, I don't know." I tried to calm him down.

"Look at this stage! Everyone is here! Every wife, girlfriend they're all here," Steven said, as he pointed around the huge sound stage.

I followed his look and I took in the whole stage. He was right; it was crowded with over a hundred guests.

The waitresses from El Chiquito, the Mexican restaurant across Barham Boulevard from the studio, were all there. One of the grips had brought his son's Cub Scout pack. They just drove their van onto the lot, and the guards didn't even question them.

I saw Amy talking to Steven after she finally had gotten to our sound stage. She was not happy.

"Ziesmer!" Steven called to me.

I walked over to them, but I knew it wasn't going to be pleasant.

"Amy, this person," he pointed to the center of my chest, "is in charge of seeing that next Friday night you drive onto the studio, OK?" Steven asked, and looked at both of us.

I obediently nodded. I recognized a "hot one" when I heard it.

Occasionally as an assistant director I got involved in a director's private life, and getting Amy Irving onto the studio lot was one of those times.

Early one morning a tree fell and blocked Brian De Palma's driveway, and I was given the task of seeing to its immediate removal so someone could use the driveway as soon as possible.

> *Mel Gibson needed a Sears store in Tennessee opened at midnight on a Sunday because he had forgotten to buy toys, clothes, and beds for his children who were arriving from Australia in four hours.*
>
> *Peter Bogdanovich needed a specific brand of toothpicks in three hours to satisfy his uncontrollable habit of breaking and dropping hundreds of toothpicks on the set during the shooting day, and that brand was not sold east of the Mississippi River; we were in Florida.*

The Amy Irving adventure was solved, as many of my problems were, by Ziggy. He sat with the studio guard at the main gate of the Burbank Studios the following Friday night until Amy had driven onto the lot. He had done the same thing for Mickey Rooney's friends at M-G-M thirty-five years earlier. A friendly smile will get you onto a studio a lot faster than a demanding smirk.

On February 7, 1979, Jillian Erin Ziesmer was born. She was our daughter after Chris and Tim. Jillian was born very late at night, and I got to work a bit late that morning. We were filming at the Long Beach Airport.

Steven was all excited.

"What is it? Was it a girl?" Steven wanted to know.

We knew it would be a girl.

"Jillian Erin," I told him.

"Jillian! That's what I want to name a girl if I have one. Jillian," Steven said.

Steven cared. He sincerely listened to all the details of her birth like every other member of the crew. Family was always special for Steven.

Steven often got ideas to improve the film. That was the type of creative mind he had. It didn't come as a great surprise to me when Steven called me over to him one morning to explain an idea that had occurred to him the night before.

"Jerry, listen. This is great. Now just listen," Steven began.

I took a deep breath and nodded.

"Akyroyd's tank, after it leaves the USO and Santa Claus, OK?" Steven checked me.

I nodded, and I thought I was ready for most anything.

"The tank," Steven exclaimed, "crashes into a paint factory!"

Steven was laughing at the images in his head.

"There's paint everywhere! Paint! All colors!" Steven was laughing and trying to speak at the same time.

"Crashes through the whole paint factory!" Steven said again, trying to coax a laugh out of me.

I was panicked. We had filmed all of the miniatures of the tank at its final destination, the Santa Monica Pier, and the tank didn't have any paint on it. My head buzzed as I thought what would happen if Steven said he had to refilm all of those miniatures because he wanted paint on the tank. That would add weeks to our shooting schedule. I became weak.

"What's wrong? Don't you like the idea?" Steven questioned.

An assistant director's job is to aid the director in getting his vision onto the screen, but the tank through a paint factory was all new. It wasn't in the script. Steven had just thought it up one night.

"Steven," I began very cautiously, "the tank didn't have any paint on it for all the miniatures. Right? We can't refilm all that," I said, and watched his face.

"Oh, you're right," Steven said, but there was nothing in what he said or how he said it that told me Steven would forget the paint factory idea.

"It's a funny idea, but . . . ," I said.

Steven interrupted me, "Let me think about this, Jer."

"Steven, it would take weeks to refilm . . . ," I began.

"What're you crazy? I'm not shooting those miniatures again!" Steven said. "Let me think about this."

The next morning Steven called to me before he even got on the sound stage.

"Jer! Jerry!" he yelled.

I hurried over to him. It could be anything. I had to stay calm.

"Remember that paint factory?" Steven asked.

"Sure, Steven," I said.

"Well, it's in!" he yelled.

"But, Steven," I began.

"No, wait!" Steven exclaimed. "We crash the tank through a paint factory. Paint everywhere. All the colors. All over the tank, OK? No, wait!"

Steven was so excited. The crew was gathering around.

"There's paint all over the tank, right? We can't have paint on the tank because of the miniatures, right?"

I was nodding at every point.

"What's next to the paint factory?" Steven was beside himself.

"What?" I offered.

"A turpentine factory!" Steven cheered.

I stared at him. He was dancing with joy.

"The tank comes out of the paint factory full of paint! Crashes through the turpentine factory and all the paint is removed!" Steven explained. "Smashes out of the turpentine factory a clean tank! The miniatures work!"

I was so happy I had taught junior high school, because it prepared me for moments like that.

"It works! It works!" Steven yelled triumphantly.

As an assistant director you have to know when to concede defeat and regroup behind the director to accomplish whatever his new vision might be. The paint factory was one of those moments. Forget logic, reality, the script, the budget, and get behind the director and keep going forward. Especially if his name's Steven Spielberg.

One day during the filming of *1941*, Steven was on the sound stage with one of his friends.

"Jerry, come over here!" Steven called, all full of smiles and giggles.

I obediently walked over to them and waited.

"I want you to play the part of an airplane spotter in the movie, OK?" Steven asked.

I looked at the smiling two in front of me.

"What's wrong?" Steven smiled.

I could only remember Butkus and Stallone and the real-estate salesman in *Rocky II*.

"Come on. You'll like it," Steven encouraged. "What can happen?"

"What do I do?" I began cautiously.

Both Steven and his friend began at the same time.

"You see a plane and run in. . . ." They broke up in laughter.

Steven continued, "You see a plane and you run into the building and call on the phone. That's it." He grinned and teetered back and forth on his feet, as he did when he was having a very good time.

His friend was laughing, "You just run in and call! It's an air raid!"

I wondered to myself, *Who is his friend?*

"You'll be SAG! You'll get residuals for the rest of your life!" Steven added.

I looked at Steven, and I knew I had no choice.

"Ready when you are, Steven," I said.

The airplane spotter's set was up on a platform. There was an exterior section of a balcony about twenty feet long supposedly looking over Los Angeles. A door led to a civil defense office with phones and red lights and warning devices. The idea was that I had been stationed at a civil defense outpost as part of an early warning system in case of an air attack.

I came from the dressing room area in my airplane spotter's costume and walked onto the set. I had on an overcoat with a civil defense armband, a scarf, binoculars, a compass, a whistle, combat boots, the civil defense hard hat, a flashlight, and a book of civil defense procedures with a set of pencils.

I thought Steven was going to die laughing.

"That's perfect!" Steven yelled.

"You look great," his friend grinned.

For me it was just like being an actor for Stallone: do the part, let them laugh, get on with the movie.

The crew was enjoying it all. I was glad it was the last shot of the day. I knew it would take a while.

"OK. You know what you do?" Steven asked.

"I see a plane. I run into the office and call on the phone," I said, ready to get it all over with.

"But you're very excited!" the friend offered. "You're confused. This has never happened to you before!"

I stared at him and then at Spielberg.

I asked myself, *Who is directing?* I was about to say something to Steven.

"Let's just try a rehearsal," Steven suggested, and I got onto the platform.

"You're relaxed!" Steven shouted. "Just look for planes."

"Look through the binoculars!" his friend cried.

I stood on the outside balcony and looked off toward Hollywood.

"You see a plane!" Steven screamed. "Run!"

I ran.

"Stop!" the friend screamed. "Check the compass!"

I stopped and checked the compass.

"Run to the phone!" Steven screamed.

I ran.

"Stop!" the friend yelled. "Look through the binoculars!"

I stopped and looked through the binoculars.

"Run!" Steven screamed again.

I ran toward the office.

"Stop! Go back!" the friend shouted. "Make your notes!"

I stopped and got the paper and a pencil and began to write.

"Run into the office!" Spielberg screamed.

I ran into the office.

"Run back outside!" the other ordered.

I ran back outside onto the balcony.

"Stop! Stop!" Steven ordered. "OK, that's it! You got it!"

Everyone was laughing at my sporadic running, stopping, running. I was out of breath and ready to collapse. Having two screaming directors was doing me in.

"Jer, that's perfect!" Steven said.

I nodded as I caught my breath.

"I've got to go," Steven began, "but he'll be here, OK? Really! I have to go! You're doing fine, really."

I just looked at Steven, then at his grinning friend, and then back to Steven.

"What's wrong?" Steven laughed, and teetered heel-to-toe. "Look, you'll get residuals for the rest of your life!"

Everyone laughed as Steven left the studio.

I turned and faced Steven's friend. He had a big Hollywood shooting company to play with, and I was his only actor. How did Steven get me into this one?

We did take after take of me running and stopping, looking and running, phoning and running, compass, binoculars, paper, until I was near death.

Steven's friend seemed like a nice guy, but he had no idea how to direct. All he did was shout conflicting orders up at me. I thought he was probably one of Steven's longtime friends from college or high school, or maybe from his agent's office.

What a slave driver this guy was! Why couldn't Steven have left a real director? I was running all over the balcony and into the office, on the phone, up with the binoculars, up with the compass; what an asshole.

I did whatever Steven's friend directed me to do. I just wanted to finish the scene.

Why has Steven left, I thought. *His friend will never be a director,* I thought, *never.* I was exhausted. The guy had no idea how to direct, none.

At last Steven's friend felt he had the scene.

I called a wrap and we all went home. I hoped that'd be the last time
he'd ever direct.

My acting scene in *1941* never made it into the movie, but Steven
was true to his word. "You'll get residuals for the rest of your life!"
Steven told me, and I have.

I was wrong about Steven's friend who directed me that day on *1941*.
He not only went on to direct the three *Back to the Future* films, but for
directing *Forrest Gump*, an Oscar was awarded to my director for that
day, Robert Zemeckis.

On the *Jerry Maguire* set in the spring of 1996, I wasn't watching for
Steven to arrive, but I knew he'd be there soon. I'd just made an announcement around the camera, when I heard Steven.

"That voice!" Steven said.

Everyone turned, and there was Steven Spielberg walking across our
set to the camera.

"You've changed. Your voice hasn't," Steven said, and laughed.

His clothes hadn't changed much in the twenty years since we
finished *1941*. He still wore denim pants, a sport shirt, tennis shoes,
and a baseball cap. His hair and beard had a bit of gray in them, but I
checked his hands because he was enough of the old Steven to have had
a bag of Burger Kings in them.

"Hello, Jer. I couldn't miss that voice," Steven said, and laughed.

"Hi, Steven," I got out. It had been a long time. I wished I had
planned something to say.

"Twenty years since *1941*," Steven, said and looked at me.

I nodded, still trying to adjust to the memories.

"You know, *1941* set two records. Most shooting days, 175. And
most stuntmen called for any one day, 276," Steven said, and laughed.

He was still the film historian, wrapped up in details and bits of
knowledge.

I smiled at him as I tried to see if his wife's influence showed on him.
Suzanne and I knew Kate Capshaw briefly at Westland School when
Jillian attended there, and we also did a film with Kate, *Love at Large*,
directed by Alan Rudolph. Steven looked clean and pressed. Maybe the
blue colors matched a bit better.

Kate was the favorite of the crew. We filmed with her up in Bend,
Oregon, and she fit right in. She laughed and joked with all of us,
never needed any special treatment, and her performances were

always right on. Kate could be Hollywood, but she was the home-and-family girl, too.

"It made money, you know," Steven continued. "*1941* is in the black."
I smiled.
The crew began to gather round. Steven was a star, maybe the biggest.
My mind kept going back to my early experiences with Steven. Twenty years had passed, but he was basically the same. I bet he can still get himself wrapped up staring out the front windshield of a van looking for his next "Mexican desert." I wondered if he ever got to hear the story of Pedro and the peanuts.
Steven's eyes contained a bit of life's pain within them; that was different. The deaths of all the Charlsie Bryants in his life showed on Steven. We were both twenty years older now.
"Jillian!" Steven said, happy that he had remembered her name.
"Right," I answered, but my mind was back to Steven as he left that first scouting van in 1977, going across the desert with Bill Fraker and me running after him as he pointed out where all the planes for *Close Encounters* would go and asked which way was north.
"You remember Belushi?" Steven asked. "Remember the backlot with the plane crash? How many times did we do that?"
I nodded and smiled.
"Do you remember shooting the miniatures? Wait! Do you remember the paint factory? Do you?" and Steven laughed.
How could I forget? It was so much of my life.

What Ifs

Clark Paylow, the production manager from *Close Encounters*, called me in 1980 to come down to the Culver Studios and meet with a writer who had won an Oscar for a screenplay and had gone on to write another script that he wanted to direct himself.
I parked on the Culver lot and made my way over to their offices. Clark greeted me, and he brought me into the writer's office.
Our meeting was very cordial. I liked him at once, and I had the highest respect for Clark Paylow as a production manager. Though everything felt good about their project, I asked to read the script as a matter of course.
When I got back to my home, I began to read. In the first scene there

was an auto accident and a hand ran off down the road. I reread the first scene again and again.

I called their offices the next day, and told them that a movie with a hand running down the side of the road was not a film I wanted to do. Clark told me that the director would be upset, but I felt I had my standards and had to stick with them.

Sixteen years later, during the making of *Jerry Maguire*, Oliver Stone came onto the sound stage to visit Tom Cruise. They had done *Born on the Fourth of July* together. Oliver Stone had also done *Platoon* and had received an Oscar for each film.

I've admired Oliver Stone's films for his attack of social and political issues, the ensemble acting performances of his cast, and the completeness of all aspects of his productions.

I watched Tom Cruise and Oliver Stone crossing the sound stage twenty feet from me, and I wondered, *What if?*

What if I had been the assistant director in 1980 for Oliver Stone on his picture, *The Hand?*

It took Francis more than two years to edit Apocalypse Now. *It was released in August 1979. At the Directors Guild Award dinner honoring the films released that year, I was seated with my wife.*

I looked for Francis and Ellie, but I didn't see them. Of course, I hoped that Apocalypse Now *and Francis would win that year's DGA Award.*

We were enjoying Frank Capra, the famous director of Mr. Smith Goes to Washington *and* You Can't Take It with You, *as he introduced each of the nominated directors. Each director gave a very smart and meaningful thank-you speech and then returned to his table.*

Apocalypse Now *would be announced next. I searched the audience for Francis. He'd have a speech to deliver. I couldn't wait.*

"The final nomination," Frank Capra announced, "is for Apocalypse Now."

I was bursting with anticipation for Francis's speech. He could be so eloquent, so moving.

"And accepting the nomination for Francis Coppola is his assistant director, Jerry Ziesmer."

I don't remember rising and leaving the table. I don't remember walking up to the dais, but I do remember Mr. Capra.

"*Mr. Capra,*" *I uttered,* "*I'd no idea I was to give a speech. I don't know what to say.*" *I looked out toward the audience, frozen in fear.*

"*Don't worry, kid,*" *Frank Capra said.* "*say anything you want. No one listens to any of this. It all ends up on the cutting room floor.*"

I stared as Frank Capra left me, walked to the rear of the dais, enthusiastically applauded, and smiled back at me.

I've no idea what I said, but Mr. Capra was the best audience I'd ever had.

History of the World: Part I

It was 1980, and I was preparing a Mel Brooks film called *History of the World: Part I* at Francis's Zoetrope Studios in Hollywood. Francis was in his mogul period. He had bought a movie studio. I would see him walking around with a Panama hat on, looking like a Brazilian plantation owner.

Zoetrope Studios was a very nice lot. It was small, with only about six sound stages, but it was a studio and it belonged to Francis. He was also beginning the preproduction for *One from the Heart*, his first movie since *Apocalypse Now*. Though Francis and I talked about my doing *One from the Heart*, we both knew that *Apocalypse Now* had been *our* movie. There'd be no other.

For everyone at Zoetrope Studios, a big moment occurred each day at 10:00 A.M., when a car drove through the main gate and stopped near the front office building. The studio came to a standstill and watched. The driver would get out, open the rear door, and George Burns would walk slowly to his office. When he disappeared from view, the studio would go back to normal.

It must have been the spring vacation at school, because it was a work day and my ten-year-old son Chris was with me at the studio. We had gone on a tour of the sound stages and had seen all our sets. Most were still being constructed, but Chris seemed to enjoy them. We returned to my office, and I got some work done.

About noon Chris began to lose interest in my office and began looking around the halls at the movie posters and pictures. Lunch seemed like a good idea, so Chris and I walked through Zoetrope to the pedestrian gate on the east side of the studio. There was a little sandwich café right across the street, just perfect for a ten-year-old's lunch with his dad.

While we were eating our cheeseburgers and fries, I noticed Gio, Francis's fourteen-year-old son, sitting at a table with three of his friends. Gio had a whole order of takeout food boxes in front of him. I assumed Francis had sent him to pick up some lunches. I remembered Gio from a few Sunday afternoons at the Rapids Hotel in Pagsanjan and a night or two as an extra on the Do Lung Bridge sequence on *Apocalypse Now*. That had been four years before.

Chris was talking to me and had taken my attention. I didn't notice Gio again until he stood next to our table.

"I remember you from Pagsanjan," Gio said to me, "*Apocalypse Now*."

"Right. I'm Jerry Ziesmer. I was your dad's assistant director. This is my son, Chris. He was in Pagsanjan, too," I said.

Gio put the takeout boxes down on our table. He wasn't in a hurry.

"I know. I remember, the swimming pool," Gio smiled.

"Remember the monkey?" Chris asked. "On a chain?"

Gio thought about it.

"Out the back, yeah, I remember," Gio said. "You played ball."

I asked Gio to sit down, and he sat next to Chris. I hoped Francis wasn't anxious for the lunches.

"What are you doing?" Gio asked me.

"*History of the World*," I said. "Mel Brooks's comedy."

"You have that big set, Caesar's Palace, on the lot," Gio added.

I nodded.

"What are you doing?" Chris asked.

"Helping my dad. I get lunches and hang around," Gio answered.

"You want to be a director?" Chris asked.

"I think so," Gio answered.

"I want to be a writer," Chris said.

We all laughed a nice afternoon laugh. I looked at the two young boys in front of me. Maybe there would be a second Coppola-Ziesmer movie team, Gio as director and Chris as writer.

But it wasn't meant to be. Both Gio and Chris died in their twenties, long before their dreams had a chance to come true.

John Huston and *Annie*

It was January 1981, and I was driving in the morning traffic down Benedict Canyon Drive toward Sunset Boulevard. I turned east onto Sunset and then made a sharp left turn into the Beverly Hills Hotel. It was the same turn that Robert Redford had made when we filmed *The Way We Were*. Sydney Pollack and I had stood on the south side of Sunset Boulevard and watched as the early dawn light disappeared. That had been 1972, nine years earlier.

The Beverly Hills Hotel was a light pink stucco building with white wooden trim. Thick jungle vegetation on each side of its circular drive and around the front of the hotel hid it from the traffic of Sunset Boulevard. On the southeast corner of the hotel, right at Sunset Boulevard, was a large planting area that the hotel kept full of flowers the year around. The Beverly Hills Hotel was the favored place for visiting movie moguls, directors, and stars to stay.

"I'm Jerry Ziesmer," I said at the hotel desk. "Would you please tell John Huston that I'm here? I think he's expecting me."

My stomach was churning. John Huston was a legend. He had directed quality movies for more than thirty years. I wanted the job. I wanted to work as John Huston's assistant director on *Annie*.

"Suite 127. To your left," the clerk said.

I glanced at the entrance to the fabled Polo Lounge, the hotel's club area for breakfast and lunch. Producers, agents, and actors competed for the tables, to be seen and to make deals. It was the war room of Hollywood.

Twenty years before, when I had worked for the Beverly Hills post office, I picked up mail from the hotel's desk. I had been told that some of the waiters in the Polo Lounge made as much money selling their gossip about Hollywood stars as they made on their restaurant tips.

I walked down the hotel corridor, looking for suite 127 and wondering what great stories of Hollywood history occurred in the hallway, rooms, and suites I was passing. Howard Hughes lived there. Orson Welles, Spencer Tracy, and Errol Flynn all stayed there and at the same time. What an era it must have been, and John Huston was part of it all. I bet he had great stories.

The hall carpet was a simple maroon, as in a lot of hotels, but the wallpaper was a jungle-vegetation print. The wall lamps were bronze and dimly lit. It felt as if I were going back in time to Hollywood's Golden Age during the 1930s and 40s.

Suite 127. I knocked even though the door was slightly open.

"Come in!" the famous John Huston voice boomed out to me.

I heard more voices, and I eased the door open and entered. I didn't want to barge into a major production meeting or a script discussion. I needn't have worried.

John Huston was dressed in his pajamas, slippers, and a bathrobe. His hair was uncombed and he hadn't shaved. He was having orange juice from a room service cart, while two production executives from Columbia were eating their morning bagels and drinking coffee.

Ray Stark, the producer from *The Way We Were*, was holding court with one of his old war stories about filming with John Huston on *Reflections in a Golden Eye* with Elizabeth Taylor and Marlon Brando.

The suite wasn't much. I was very disappointed. It looked like a large bedroom; that was all. I wondered if all the suites were the same. Did Howard Hughes live in the same size suite?

"Jerry! Come in." One of the Columbia production men encouraged me to step further into the suite. "Have some coffee, a bagel?"

Ray Stark didn't stop with his story, but John Huston paused long enough to give me a glance and then went back to his orange juice and nodding at Ray's story. Whatever the story was, Ray was enjoying telling it a lot more than John Huston was enjoying listening to it. Ray had been an agent, and it often showed; he tended to oversell his stories. Ray was still my hero for the Thanksgiving turkeys he gave all of the cast and crew on *The Way We Were*.

I felt I was in the room with Hollywood history. John Huston had directed *The Maltese Falcon*, *The Treasure of the Sierra Madre*, *The African Queen*, *Moby Dick*, and more than thirty other movies over a fifty-year career as a writer, actor, and director. He had directed Humphrey

Bogart, Katharine Hepburn, Gregory Peck, Orson Welles, Clark Gable, Marilyn Monroe, and many, many others.

As soon as Ray said the punch line to his story and imitated the voice of Elizabeth Taylor one last time, the Columbia production people laughed and quickly introduced me at the same time.

"Ray, Mr. Huston, we want you to meet Jerry Ziesmer, a first assistant director," the executive began.

"I know Jerry," Ray said. "What picture was it?" he asked me.

"Is that a Dutch name or German?" John Huston asked me, as though he were a serious student of names.

Ray Stark didn't give me a chance to answer.

"*The Way We Were*, right?" Ray asked. "I knew it was with Barbra."

I looked around at Ray, John Huston, and the two production people. It was my first interview for a job where the director was dressed in pajamas, but it was my first interview with John Huston, too.

"Jerry, we're doing a film of *Annie*, the Broadway musical," a Columbia man began, as if no one knew. Everyone in Hollywood was talking about John Huston directing *Annie*.

"What musicals have you done? Hell, we don't do musicals anymore, do we?" Ray asked.

"Well, I did *Hello, Dolly!*" I said.

"With Barbra," Ray added. "I knew you'd worked with her." Ray continued with his stories.

I looked over at John Huston, and he smiled at the group and then nodded toward me as if to say that they're all crazy and we're not. I smiled back.

He drank again from his glass of orange juice, then winked at me.

"Ray!" John Huston said in his booming voice, as he then concentrated on buttering a piece of toast.

Everyone stopped and looked toward him.

"Yes, John," Ray answered politely.

"Jerry will do fine," John said. "He's hired!" He took a bite of his toast, and that was very obviously the end of that discussion.

I thought to myself, *So this is John Huston. A wink and then a right hook.*

Ray and the two Columbia production guys nodded, and Ray began another old war story, about *The Night of the Iguana* with Richard Burton acting and John Huston directing.

Gladys Hill, John's assistant, entered while Ray was telling his next story. She came to John with some mail on top, then a couple of reading magazines, and underneath was the *Daily Racing Form*. She was in her early sixties, but very much alive and interested in every minute of the day. I liked her from the first moment.

"Gladys, I want you to meet our first assistant director, Jerry Ziesmer," John said.

Ray went right on with his story, and the Columbia people were still laughing.

"Jerry, I want you to meet my longtime associate and friend, Gladys Hill," John continued, as though we three were the only ones in the suite.

"I'm happy to meet you," I got out.

"Jerry, nice meeting you," Gladys said, and continued with her work of caring for the writing and reading demands of Mr. John Huston.

"Do you know Tommy Shaw?" John asked me. "He was my assistant director for years. Many pictures. Not up to this one, though," John added.

"No. I've heard of him. His son, Tommy Junior, was on *Apocalypse Now* in the Philippines," I said. "Worked in props."

"Really?" John Huston said in his famous resonant voice, as though I had uttered the most interesting statement he had heard in months.

"At night, after a few drinks, he'd throw the hotel furniture into the swimming pool," I laughed.

"Tommy Senior did that a time or two," John added, and laughed. "In Mexico."

Ray went right on to the war stories of *Fat City*, another film he did with John Huston, a boxing movie starring Stacy Keach. The Columbia guys would have laughed at Ray's stories for another week. He was a big man at Columbia, probably the biggest.

"You've seen *Annie*?" John asked me privately. "The Broadway musical?"

"No, I haven't," I admitted.

"Neither have I, but I will," John laughed quietly. "Don't worry." Then he put his hands on the small of his back and tried to rearrange seventy-one years of rugged living back into place by stretching and straightening his frame.

Suddenly the others in the room erupted in laughter, and Ray repeated the punch line for John, who just smiled and nodded as he stretched his back.

John's right ear had a bit of cauliflower to it; he must have been a boxer at one time. His breathing was strained, but he had a gleam in his eye, and his words were sharp and quick.

I liked John Huston's spirit of devilment. When I was a teacher, I enjoyed that trait in my students. I knew he was "John Huston, Hollywood legend," but I also felt that he was "John Huston, mischievous little boy."

And I was right.

My first day as the assistant director to John Huston was on a sound stage at the Burbank Studios. We were doing a screen test with Albert Finney as Daddy Warbucks and a number of young girls who were trying out for the part of Annie.

The art department had given us a simple three-wall set for the test. There was a large window wall in the center and two walls with doors on each end.

The crew had a 7:00 A.M. call, and Albert Finney and the first Annie would be ready at 8:00. I had asked Mr. Huston to be on the set at 7:30 for rehearsal, but he hadn't arrived from his hotel and it was nearly 9:00.

The crew was just standing around, not knowing what to light. We needed John Huston to show us a rehearsal of the scene and where he wanted to place the camera.

I wanted the crew to begin their work so we'd be ready to shoot as early as possible. My problem was I didn't know where John Huston would place the camera.

Marshall Schlom had been John Huston's script supervisor on many of his films. I decided to seek his advice.

"Marshall, how do you think Mr. Huston will shoot the scene?" I asked.

"What do you mean?" Marshall answered.

"Well, where do you think he'll want to put the camera? If I knew that I could get the crew started to light the scene," I said.

"Jerry, where do you want him to put the camera?" Marshall asked.

"What do you mean?" I asked back.

John Huston was one of the most respected directors in Hollywood. Where do *I* want him to put the camera?

Marshall moved closer to me and lowered his voice, "Where do you want him to put the camera?"

I felt we were like two conspirators.

"Well, Daddy Warbucks is in the room and Annie enters, say from the camera left door, so . . . ," I began, and looked at Marshall.

"So?" Marshall whispered. "Where do you want him to put the camera?"

"OK, how about a fairly wide shot, put the camera in the room and just to the right of center, facing the door on camera left," I said.

Marshall lowered his voice even more, "Take his chair and put it right where you want the camera to be."

I stared at him.

"Jerry, take Mr. Huston's chair and put it where you want the camera to be, and have the crew light the set," Marshall said, and gave me an assuring nod.

John Huston was late. The crew was standing around. The actors were ready. I picked up John Huston's chair and placed it exactly where I felt the camera should be for the first shot.

"Fellas!" I announced to the crew, as I looked at Marshall for assurance, "The camera is right here, looking camera left toward the door. Annie enters, crosses to Daddy Warbucks at the desk. Let's light it, please."

I was scared. If that wasn't where John Huston wanted the camera it could have been my first and last day as his assistant director.

Marshall just nodded to me that everything was going to be all right.

About forty-five minutes later, John Huston and Gladys entered the sound stage. He was dressed like a great white hunter, exactly how every studio wardrobe department would have dressed a famous film director. He had tan slacks with a light-colored bush jacket, a tan shirt, and he was carrying his morning mail, magazines, and, underneath, the *Daily Racing Form*.

"Good morning! Good morning, all!" The John Huston voice bellowed to everyone on the sound stage.

I stood next to his chair.

Gladys saw me and his chair. The two of them moved toward me.

I was very nervous.

"Mr. Huston, good morning. Gladys," I said.

"Good morning, Jerry. Good morning," John said, as he settled into his chair. Gladys smiled and placed his bottle of water, reading material, and mints in the chair's pocket.

"Mr. Huston, ahhh," I began. "the scene is Annie entering and . . ."

"Entering, you say," John said, and stared at me, searching my face.

"Yes, well, she enters the room and Daddy Warbucks is already there," I continued.

"In the room?" John asked.

"Yes," I said. "The thing is, I mean," I tried to say.

"I see," John said, and stared at the set and then at me.

"Ahhh, Mr. Huston, where do you think you'll want to place the camera?" I asked.

John Huston looked slowly to his left, then slowly to his right.

"Well, right here, Jerry! Right where I'm sitting!" he said. "This is perfect!

For the rest of the filming on *Annie*, I always knew where the camera would be for the first shot of the day.

The preproduction period for *Annie* was done in New York City. John Huston, Ray Stark, the art directors, and I flew to the East Coast and checked into the Essex House on Central Park South.

My first priority was to scout a title sequence that John Huston wanted to do. His idea was to follow Sandy, Annie's dog, from lower Manhattan all the way to Annie's orphanage on 34th Street. It was to be a long montage of Sandy walking through New York City while the opening titles were shown. It was my first opportunity to show John Huston my production planning abilities as his assistant director.

Each morning a car for John, Gladys, and Ray Stark would follow our crew van to various locations around New York City. The location manager would show John a possible site for Sandy's walk, and if John seemed interested, I would take a snapshot of the location site. It would just be a wide shot of the area, showing the buildings and streets; often our scouting party would be in my snapshot as well. It didn't matter because the snapshots were just for my own reference.

After three weeks of scouting, I had forty snapshots showing each location John had selected. I got poster board and mounted the snapshots in the continuity of Sandy's walk from lower Manhattan all the way to 34th Street.

I was very proud of the thoroughness of my assistant director work for John, and I made an appointment to come to his suite at the hotel and show him the entire Sandy montage.

I proudly held the four poster boards under my arm as John opened his door.

"Well, good morning, Jerry. What have you there?" John said, as he graciously ushered me into his suite.

"Good morning, Mr. Huston," I said, as I struggled to place the poster boards with the forty photographs of Sandy's walk in their proper order on his sofa and two companion chairs.

John watched most attentively.

"Now," I began, "what we have here is the whole walk by Sandy through New York. Your whole title montage."

I glanced at him and smiled.

John studied the poster boards and my face.

I proceeded to go from each location site by pointing to the corresponding snapshot. When I finished, I turned and smiled at him.

"Jerry," he said slowly, "I don't know what in the world you're talking about."

I suddenly became very cold.

"Sandy's walk, Mr. Huston. Your opening title montage," I explained.

"Sandy walking through New York? A montage? That's silly," John said. "Wherever did you get such an idea?"

"We've been scouting all these locations for three weeks," I said, as I pointed at the poster boards and the photographs.

"Jerry, I've never done such a thing," he said.

I was panicked.

"Mr. Huston, look at the snapshots!" I begged. "You're even in some of them!"

I pointed at him in the pictures.

He came closer and bent down and stared at the photographs. After a few moments he rose and looked at me.

"Jerry, how did you do that?" he asked, totally mystified. "I was never there."

I've panicked very seldom in my life. Once when I was teaching, a boy named Allan set a girl's hair on fire in my class. The second time was that day in John Huston's suite at the Essex House.

I quickly excused myself, gathered up my poster boards, and left John's suite. I took the elevator down to the lobby and called Ray Stark on the house phone.

"Hello," Ray answered.

"Ray, it's Jerry. I just met with John Huston on the title sequence with Sandy? Well, he doesn't remember a thing about it," I panicked.

"Is that so?" Ray asked calmly.

"Ray, John's forgotten all about Sandy walking through New York! The whole montage! Everything!" I yelled into the phone.

"And?" Ray asked. "What seems to be the problem?"

"We scouted New York for three weeks! He's forgotten everything!" I repeated. "You've got to do something, Ray. We begin filming in a couple of weeks! You've got to get another director now!"

There was a long pause.

"Jerry," Ray began, "*Annie* is one of my last movies. I want to enjoy making it. When John Huston directs, I enjoy making my movies."

"But, Ray," I begged, "you don't understand!"

"No, Jerry, you don't understand. John Huston is directing *Annie*, and you're the assistant director who's going to see that he does, and I'm going to have a good time," Ray said, and hung up.

I looked around the lobby. The hotel desk clerks were staring at me. I put down the house phone, picked up my poster boards, and realized that *Annie* and John Huston were going to be my most unique assistant directing experience.

John Huston was not a well man. He had many ailments, including the early stages of emphysema. In his suite at the Essex House John had an oxygen bottle with a plastic tube and mask to help his breathing. I became accustomed to meeting with John in his suite to have discussions with him while he was attached to the oxygen bottle to help his breathing. However, I was not ready for a more radical treatment.

I hurried down the hall to John's suite, as I did almost every day. As I approached his door I thought for a moment that I detected the sweet aroma of marijuana smoke. I imagined that one of the room service waiters or bellhops had had a couple of hits in the hallway and had recently moved on. I knocked on John's door and waited.

When John Huston opened the door to his suite, the marijuana smoke cascaded out of his rooms and into the hall. I entered quickly, and he closed the door.

My eyes were wide in shock as I stared at John Huston in the midst of a cloud of marijuana smoke.

"Good morning, Jerry. How are you this morning?" John asked.

I was afraid to inhale. I tried to hold my breath.

"Fine. I'm fine. Thanks," I said.

I half expected Robert Mitchum to be present.

The marijuana smoke seemed to have no effect on John Huston. He walked back over to his sofa where he always sat. I moved cautiously to my customary chair and sat down.

Someone had placed two containers of smoldering marijuana, one on John's coffee table and the other on the end table next to where he sat on the sofa. I tried to take shallow breaths as seldom as I could. John noticed my spasmodic breathing.

"Jerry, does this smoke bother you?" John asked.

"Well, I . . ." It was very hard for me to talk because I didn't dare breath in.

"It's all medicinal, you know. The marijuana. It's to help my breathing," he said. "But I don't think it does a thing. Do you?"

I stared at John and at the amount of marijuana smoke in his suite. He had to have been breathing the smoke for at least an hour, maybe longer. It seemed to have no effect on him. He was totally sober.

"I think, John, the smoke might help if you breathed in deeper," I suggested. "Try to breath in and then hold the smoke inside for a bit."

I couldn't believe it. I was teaching John Huston how to get high from marijuana smoke!

"Jerry, I know how to smoke a reefer! It just doesn't work," John said, and he demonstrated to me his best breathing in and holding capabilities.

I was beginning to relax a bit. I nodded that I understood completely. I totally understood everything. I giggled and then laughed and looked again at John. He was staring at me.

"Jerry, I've been trying for two hours," he said sadly.

"Really?" I laughed.

"Well, what do we have to discuss today?" John asked, as he got down to business.

I fought to get myself back to the world.

"When the orphans go up Fifth Avenue looking for Daddy Warbuck's house, where would you like them to begin?" I asked.

I felt I had good control of myself.

"Well, at the beginning of Fifth Avenue," John said. "At Washington Square, of course."

John Huston sounded so much like John Huston that I started to laugh and couldn't stop.

The next time I looked up, John was bent over one of the smoldering marijuana burners and breathing as deeply as he could. It never worked.

About a week later I hurried to John's suite. He had called me to come to see him at once. He sounded very upset.

I knocked, and when he opened the door I realized John was in emotional pain.

"Jerry, a most unfortunate thing has happened," John said, as he returned to his sofa.

I sat in my chair and waited.

"Jerry, they found Gladys Hill this morning in her room. She died last night," he said.

The shock kept me quiet. I recalled the Messenger of Death from a festival field in the Philippines.

"She was found just lying in her bed," he continued. "The hotel people found her a couple of hours ago."

"I'm so sorry," I said.

"Yes, yes," John said very softly. "She's gone. Gladys is gone."

John looked much older and somehow smaller as he sat on his sofa and rocked forward and back. I stayed with him the rest of the day. I learned that sometimes being an assistant director means just to be there.

We became closer after Gladys's death. We shared some dinners in his room, and once I talked him into coming down to Eleanora's, an Italian restaurant a couple of doors south of the hotel.

Our dinners were unique. John had a very specialized diet of extremely bland foods, which he ate sparingly. The hotel would prepare his diet, and room service would deliver it. I'd get mine from Eleanora's and join him in his suite. His main interest during our meals was watching me eat and talking about the foods he had enjoyed years ago.

"And the food doesn't bother you, Jerry?" John would ask. "All that pasta!"

I'd twirl more pasta onto my fork, swirl it into the olive oil and garlic, catch an anchovy, and then joyously add it to my mouth.

"Eat steak, do you?" he'd ask.

I'd nod, with my mouth full of pasta.

"Lobster with butter?"

I'd smile and drink my wine or Heineken beer.

"Cold is it?" he'd ask about the beer.

"Yes," I'd offer.

"They have a wonderful stew in Ireland, you know."

I'd nod and catch more pasta with my fork.

"You should be dead. You know that, don't you?" John would say, as he watched my every move.

His dinner looked pretty bad. It was small portions, no sauces, and nothing interesting.

"If I ate what you do I'd die, right here. *John Huston dead from olive oil and garlic!*" John said, and laughed as he licked his lips. "Doesn't bother you, does it? Do you like ice cream?"

I'd nod and smile.

"You're Dutch, aren't you? They can eat anything."

I never saw him cheat on his diet, except for his daily mints. He took it all very seriously. It was one of the very few things he did take seriously.

The location for Daddy Warbucks' mansion was at Monmouth College in West Long Branch, New Jersey. It was a huge, grand mansion that showed off Daddy Warbucks' immense wealth. The entry hall was three stories high. There was an Olympic-size indoor swimming pool, a bowling alley, and interesting hallways and anterooms for Daddy Warbucks, Annie, and the servants to dance through.

Ziggy played the role of one of the servants and was a stand-in, too. *Annie* was a big picture, and Columbia Studios had brought Ziggy from Hollywood to help Chris Soldo and me. Ziggy should've saved a lot of money working on location, but Atlantic City and the gambling tables were a bit too close. Two things Ziggy could always hear were the rattle of the dice and the beating of the horses' hooves.

I had to have two chairs for John Huston. The first was where the camera would go, and the second was about thirty feet away, in front of his TV monitor.

When John arrived in the morning, his driver would deposit all of John's reading materials and the *Daily Racing Form*, water bottle, and mints in his second chair at the TV monitor. John would walk further onto the set and greet everyone in the mansion.

"Good morning, all!" John would say in his booming, resonant voice. "Good morning!"

He'd sit in his first chair, and the key members of the crew would gather around him as his extended morning greetings would continue.

"Marvelous morning, isn't it?" John would offer. "Do you know what I saw this morning? Well, I'm not certain, mind you, but what I believe I saw?"

From the exciting way John spoke, I imagined that he had seen a spaceship with Martians on his way to the mansion.

"I can't be totally certain, but I believe I saw a *Wilshire oriole!*" John exclaimed. "Just there in a tree! It was marvelous!" John said, with wide eyes still shocked by that morning's sighting.

After the crew recorded their amazement, there was a moment of silence, and I jumped in.

"John, this morning . . . ," I began.

"Jerry! Good morning!" John interrupted. "And how are you this morning?"

"Great," I said. "John, today we want to continue with Annie's first arrival at the mansion, OK?"

"Ahhh!" John vocalized, and smiled as he nodded in perfect harmony with me.

"Yes, so Annie and Warbucks, Grace and the servants are all continuing into the entryway," I continued.

"Of course, Jerry," John said, as if I'd said something as simple and obvious as reciting the ABCs or counting by twos.

"OK. So, John, why don't you watch a rehearsal and we'll get going?" I suggested.

"Why not? Why not, Jerry? Can you imagine? A *Wilshire oriole* this close to the Atlantic!" John exclaimed. "Good morning, Ziggy."

I got the dancers, servants, and cast all ready for the rehearsal, then looked over at John. He was sitting in his first chair watching everything. I'd gesture to him by either nodding my head or pointing my finger and saying "Ready when you are, John." He would call "Action!" and our rehearsal would begin.

It was no surprise that the camera for the first shot was placed right where John's first chair was, and as the crew went to work, John moved to his second chair by the TV monitor. I'd look over at John. He'd be reading a magazine, the newspaper, or the *Daily Racing Form* as he munched on his mints.

Occasionally, the crew and I would have a question for John that had to be answered before we could continue lighting the scene. Usually the cameraman and I would go to John at his TV monitor.

"John, excuse me," I'd begin.

"Yes, Jerry," John would say, as he put down his reading material.

"We need to know if you'd like to see out the windows or if we can just paper them and pour light through?" I asked, and waited.

"I see," John said gravely.

"We can't see too much," I continued. "That's supposed to be New York's Fifth Avenue out there. What do you want us to do?"

"Of course," John said, as he extended his right arm and shook his index finger toward the windows. "Of course! Of course!" Then John would smile at us and go back to his reading and mints.

The cameraman and I would glance at each other as we walked back to the camera, unsure of what had been agreed upon. We'd always go with our best judgment of what John wanted.

When we were ready to film, Chris Soldo would get all the performers ready and in place, while I saw to the crew. I'd glance at John to be sure he was watching before I would roll the camera. Rather than yell "Action" all the way from his monitor, John would just wave at me, or sometimes he'd just nod, and sometimes he'd just look into the monitor and wait for me to call "Action."

After the take I'd look at John, and most often he'd gesture for me to come to him at the monitor. He'd give me a piece of direction for the actors or for the crew. I'd hurry back to the camera and deliver John's direction, and we'd try the shot again.

Occasionally, between the time that I checked John to be sure he was watching his monitor and the time that the actors began their scene, something would distract Mr. Huston, and he would miss seeing the performance. He'd gesture that he wanted to talk with me, and I'd walk to him.

"Jerry, ahhh," John said, and pointed at his monitor.

"Yes, John," I answered diplomatically.

"What did you think of that one?" he said, and smiled at me as he searched my face.

"Let's go again," I suggested.

"You're right," John agreed, and nodded his head. "Of course," he said, as though I had told him the answer to a most puzzling riddle. "Of course!"

We filmed in Daddy Warbucks' mansion for weeks. Little changed in the management of the set. John would come in the morning to chair number one, then go to chair number two in front of the monitor and stay there the rest of the day. Though we all liked John Huston, we wondered if his directing style on *Annie* was the same as it had been on *The Treasure of the Sierra Madre* and *The African Queen*. One day we had our answer.

We were working on a shot of the dancers moving and leaping down a hallway. It was part of the scene in which Annie first sees Daddy Warbucks' mansion. The camera was on a crane, and the crane's arm rose as it moved down the hall with the action of the dancers. The shot was a bit complex, and it was taking the crew extra time to set up.

"Jerry!" John called to me.

I hurried over to him at his monitor.

"What is it, Jerry? What's taking so long?" he asked.

"Just setting up the shot, John. That's all," I answered. "Crane move with the dancers and all."

He grunted and reached for another magazine, and I went back to the camera.

About ten minutes later we still hadn't gotten the dancers' action and the crane move worked out, when I heard John's voice right behind me.

"What is it, boys?" John resonated.

The cameraman and operator started to explain their difficulty.

"Now, now, now!" John said, and gestured for them to step aside. He wanted to take a turn operating the camera. He hadn't done that during the whole picture. All of the crew and the dancers exchanged looks as John Huston at seventy-one sat himself down behind the camera on the crane.

"Take me back to one!" John bellowed.

The crane and the dancers went back to their start marks.

"All right now. You, front dancer, move back, away from the camera a foot! Good!" John began, as he looked through the camera. "I have to see your feet! You're dancing, aren't you?" John asked, and laughed. "My father always wanted to crowd the camera, too!" John laughed. "I never let him!" He laughed again.

Everyone smiled to think of John directing his father, Walter Huston. It was probably on *The Treasure of the Sierra Madre*.

"Lower on the arm!" John bellowed, and the camera grip lowered the crane arm that held John and the camera.

"If I'd had this contraption in Africa, we'd have saved three weeks! We stood, mind you *stood*, in the water! Damn cold! With the camera, lights, and everything while Kate and Bogie did those damn talk scenes! There were snakes, too! Lots of them."

The dancers and crew exchanged looks; that had to be *The African Queen*!

"Dancers! Back up one more foot. Good! Up on the crane arm, please!"

"Focus forward," John said. "Good. On the feet first, then ease through the dancer's body as you feel the crane arm rise. Got it?"

The camera assistant nodded as he marked his focus points.

All of the time John was positioning dancers, signaling to the crane grip to raise or lower him or to take him left or right.

"Good!" John yelled. "That's where you begin. Mark everything!"

The camera assistants and grips put tape at everyone's start position.

"Can't put marks in water, you know?" John bellowed, and then laughed. "Jerry, can't put marks in water." He laughed again.

"Right, John," I answered.

"*Moby Dick!* Had crew out in the water, neck deep with poles and a flag. They'd wave their flag when the boat would come abreast of them. Only way to get focus!" John laughed.

I was amazed at John's transformation. It was as if he'd shed thirty years. I looked around at the crew and dancers. They were enraptured with the Hollywood legend. I wished I could've been with him in Africa, the Mexican desert, the whaling ship of *Moby Dick*, and on all of his pictures.

"All right, let's try the move!" John said. "Jerry, you give action! Not yet!"

John had his body all bent over behind the camera to begin the shot. I didn't believe his seventy-one-year old frame could bend like that.

The crew were all at their positions and feeling the challenge of working with one of the masters.

"Ready, Jerry!" John said, as he bent over the low camera on the crane arm.

"Ready when you are, John. Action!" I said.

The dancers began their moves, the crane followed, and John Huston operated the camera, cued the crane moves, called the focus, and he was amazing. I'm sure it was the same on a river in Africa, on a sand dune in Mexico, and on a whaling ship in the high seas.

"That's it!" John said, when the take was over. "Maybe a bit faster on the move, I don't know. Feel it for yourself!"

"Now, boys," John said to the camera crew, "Begin on the dancers' feet. The move takes you to their knees. Let the first dancer's leap—his first leap, mind you—take you to the whole line of dancers, and then crane up to finish the shot!"

Everyone just stared at him and nodded in agreement, as I'm sure crews and actors had been doing on all of John Huston's films for forty years.

John smiled at all of us, moved slowly back to his second chair in front of the TV monitor, and went back to his reading and mints.

Even though I looked every day for the real John Huston of old from that day in the hallway with the dancers, John went back to sitting at the TV monitor, reading his magazines, and eating mints. One day in the middle of May, I thought perhaps things had changed.

"Jerry!" John called to me.

I hurried over to him as he sat in his chair at the TV monitor.

"Yes, John," I said.

"This Saturday, Jerry," John began, "what're we filming?"

"John, the whole finale. The orphans, Annie, everyone, the finale," I said.

"Good, good," John said.

"We're going to have elephants, a tiger, fire-eaters, high-wire act. It's the whole finale, John," I explained again as I sensed his interest.

"Yes, marvelous, Jerry. Just marvelous," John said. "For Saturday would you please get a large monitor for me? The biggest you can get!"

My prayers had been answered. The real John Huston of old from that day in the hallway was finally going to come back! He wanted a big monitor, the biggest!

"Yes, John, I'll get the biggest monitor we can get. I'll have it for you Saturday," I said, and went off to call the production managers.

When Saturday came we were filming in the garden area of Daddy Warbucks' mansion. It was a magnificent set and decorated for a child's party, with a circus motif and real animals and circus acts. All of the cast, circus performers, and extras were very excited, but none more than me. The real John Huston was back; he had ordered the biggest monitor we could get. I couldn't wait to watch him direct the finale of *Annie* and create his legendary cinematic magic.

John's second chair was set up in front of his old TV monitor. The first thing he asked me that morning was where his new monitor was. I was very excited.

The video truck drove up and unloaded a new monitor with a huge screen. I directed them to set it up right in front of John's chair.

"Oh, Jerry!" John said. "That's wonderful! That will do just fine."

I could see his excitement, and I hurried the technicians to get the new monitor hooked up.

"OK, John, I'll get your old monitor out of here . . . ," I began.

"No! Oh, don't do that, Jerry!" John interrupted.

He wants two monitors! I felt John was more interested and dedicated than even I had hoped for!

"All right, John, we'll put the old monitor on top of the new one," I said.

"Yes, that'll be fine, Jerry," he added.

"John, we're almost ready. We'll have to split the lead from the camera so you can get the image on both the monitors. It'll just be a minute," I said.

"That won't be necessary, Jerry. Leave the cable from the film camera in the old monitor," John said.

"But, John, what about the big, new monitor?" I asked.

"Just turn that to channel seven, Jerry. The Kentucky Derby starts in an hour, and I don't want to miss a thing!"

John Huston was one of the most gracious and warmest people I've ever met. It was no surprise that when Monmouth College asked him to substitute for their scheduled speaker at their graduation ceremonies with only two days' warning, he grandly accepted. Also, they were giving him an honorary degree.

"Jerry, it will be marvelous. The graduation. The cap and gown. I'll be wearing a cap and gown!" John said. He was very excited about the ceremony.

"What are you going to say, John?" I asked.

"What, Jerry?" He said.

"Your speech, John. At the graduation ceremony. What are you going to say?" I repeated. "You're to give the commencement address."

John Huston turned white! His breath stopped and then started in spurts; I considered calling for our company medic.

"Oh, my god!" John said. "Oh, my god!"

"John, are you OK?" I was shocked at his appearance.

"Get our scriptwriter, Carol Sobieski, to the set!" John said to me, with utter fear in his eyes. He hadn't considered that he would have to deliver a speech to the graduates.

Carol Sobieski was the screenwriter for *Annie*, and she was staying in West Long Branch with us.

For the next two days, John and Carol wrote and rewrote his commencement speech. I didn't hear the speech, but Honorary Doctor of Arts John Huston delivered it in full cap and gown, and his picture was on the front page of the West Long Branch daily newspaper.

One day at the mansion, John was sitting in his chair in front of his monitor, as he always was. Instead of reading his magazines, John was watching me, with a worried look on his face. Finally he called me over to him.

"Jerry, sit down," John began, as gravely as if he were a doctor at the bedside of a dying patient. "I must ask you something. Something personal. I hope you don't mind?"

"*Of course not,*" *I said, and I pulled up a chair and sat next to him. I looked into his face and waited.*

He patted my hand and appeared to be tearing.

"*Jerry, I'm so worried about you,*" *John began.*

Even though it was my fifteenth year as an assistant director, you're never ready for everything that the superstars or film legends will throw at you.

"*Why, John? I feel fine,*" *I assured him.*

"*Jerry, you mean a lot to me. You know that,*" *he said confidentially in his best doctor-patient bedside manner.*

I studied his face and prepared myself.

"*I hope that in our relationship you could tell me everything,*" *he continued.* "*Everything,*" *he said, as though he knew my darkest of dark secrets.*

"*John, I really feel fine,*" *I said, and then I thought he'd heard of my divorce proceedings and that was the cause for his behavior.*

"*I'm in the process of a divorce, John, but really that . . . ,*" *I began, but he interrupted me.*

"*No, no, Jerry! I'm sensing something much more severe,*" *he said.* "*Hell, I've been divorced three or four times! That's nothing!*"

I glanced back at the camera. The crew was working, Ziggy was standing in, and Chris Soldo was watching the set. I had time to sit with my personal medical specialist.

"*John, what is it you sense?*" *I asked. I thought I was ready for anything.*

Again, he patted my hand and looked sadly into my eyes.

"*I don't think you have any* vices," *John said gravely.*

You can't be ready for everything. Once in a while they'll rock you, and John Huston rocked me.

"*Vices, John?*"

"*Yes, I've been meaning to talk to you about this for some time,*" *he continued.*

"*I do have vices, John, let me assure you,*" *I answered, and smiled at him.*

"*Jerry, are you sure?*" *he asked, as gravely as if he were asking me if my heart beat steadily or not.*

"*Yes, John!*" *I assured him.* "*I drink beer, a little wine. I smoke nearly two packs a day. You know that,*" *I said.*

"*Yes, well, I just wanted to be sure,*" *he said, as he patted my hands again and breathed in a sigh of relief.*

As I moved back toward the camera, I glanced back, not at the

*foremost world authority on migrating Wilshire orioles, not on the
supreme scholar on family names and their geographic origins, but
today I saw the world-famous medical specialist of the terminally ill,
as he turned back toward his monitor, reached for a magazine, and
put another mint into his mouth.*

It was about a week later. We were still filming at Daddy Warbucks'
mansion. John was attempting to put together a deal for his next
picture. He had arranged for the financing to come from Germany, and
the German bankers had sent over to West Long Branch their representative, Karl, to receive the final script from John, and then to sign
the financial contracts. The problem was that John didn't have the final
script.

He would have the script within two weeks, three at the most, but
his scriptwriter had not finished, and there was no script to show Karl.
If Karl didn't receive the script, John knew the German financing for his
next movie was lost. John's problem was how to stall Karl to keep him
in West Long Branch for another two to three weeks.

The first few days John simply charmed Karl. He talked to him at his
monitor, introduced him to all of the actors and crew, and took him out
to dinner. That worked for nearly a week, but then Karl insisted on
seeing the final script or he was going back to Germany.

The next morning I arrived on the set, and after we had decided on
the first shot, John asked to talk to me privately. Karl was at John's
monitor, so the two of us sat in one of the anterooms in the mansion.

"Jerry," John began, "I've had the very worst time casting the role of
the Bolshevik, now you know that?" John stared at me for my comment.

I'd learned not to open my mouth too soon.

"You know, the bomber who throws the lighted bomb into Daddy
Warbucks' mansion?" John continued. "The Bolshevik."

"Yes, I know the part," I answered cautiously.

"Well, he has to have a European look to him, Jerry. Can't be an
American, you know that?" John said, and looked at me.

I stared at him with my mouth tightly closed.

"I can't find any actor to do the part! New York, Hollywood!" John
looked frustrated and anxious. "I've searched everywhere. It's only a
two-day part!"

I waited for John to continue.

"Have you seen Karl, the man from Germany? He'd be perfect!"
John smiled.

I nodded.

"Now, Jerry, I know he's not a U.S. citizen nor a member of SAG, but I want to cast him as the Bolshevik bomber! I simply must! Can you arrange that for me?" John asked, and smiled at me like my mother did to get me to eat my vegetables.

Because of the world-renowned stature of John Huston, it wasn't that difficult for Columbia Studios to get permission from the Screen Actors Guild and the two governments involved, and Karl was granted a special waiver to perform the two-day part for John Huston in *Annie*.

On the first day of his employment, Karl performed as the Bolshevik bomber, and he was quite good. Karl was tall and thin, with wild black hair, and a gaunt face. I agreed with John that he was the perfect Bolshevik bomber, and I congratulated him on his eye for casting.

It was at that point that John informed us that the two days that Karl had to work were not continuous, but separated by two and maybe three weeks. There was nothing to be done, but Karl would have to stay in West Long Branch longer than he had planned.

Though Karl strongly objected, he had no choice. With special arrangement from the United States Immigration Service, the German government, and the Screen Actors Guild, Karl was bound to complete the role of the Bolshevik bomber under a personal, ironclad contract to that world-renowned motion picture director, John Huston.

It was a pleasant June evening in Manhattan, a bit before midnight. The movie company had completed shooting in Daddy Warbucks' mansion and had moved back to New York and the Essex House. We were filming nights on the streets of New York City.

The crew was lighting the front of the New York Library on Fifth Avenue. The shot was of the orphans running north from Forty-second Street past the New York Library on their way to Daddy Warbucks' mansion to warn Annie. The police had blocked off both Fifth Avenue and Forty-second Street for our filming.

John was sitting in his chair at the monitor on the west side of Fifth Avenue, and I was seated next to him. When it took a long time to light a shot, I liked to spend my downtime chatting with John.

Suddenly, a large black limousine broke through the police barricade across Fifth Avenue, roared north past Forty-second Street, and headed toward our crew with its horn blaring.

Both John and I stared at the approaching limo as it made its noisy way down Fifth Avenue toward us. I got out of my chair, because I thought we might have a drunk driver who had run our police line. It was no such luck.

The limo swerved from the center of Fifth Avenue and headed to the west side where John and I were. The large car screeched to a stop, and the limo driver jumped out and doffed his chauffeur's cap. It was Dan Aykroyd. He opened the rear limo door and John Belushi exited. The two comics then began their dances and patter for the crew and our orphans.

They shook the electricians' ladders. They walked on the grips' dolly track. Dan sat behind the camera while John pushed him on the crab dolly. They shouted one-liners, sang songs, and screamed to our cast and crew. They ran over and hugged me as they threw one-liners from John Huston's movies at him: *"I don't have to show you no stinking badges!"* and the like.

Our crew and orphans were laughing with Aykroyd and Belushi and imitating their dance movements, when I looked at John Huston. He was totally mystified by the happening. He had no idea who Aykroyd and Belushi were; he had never seen them before, nor had he heard of them.

As fast as they'd arrived, they left. Aykroyd got Belushi back into the limo, then he got in the driver's seat and screeched and honked off down Fifth Avenue.

"Jerry," John motioned for me to lean close to him.

"Yes," I said.

"Are they friends of yours?" John asked.

"Well, yes," I answered.

"Jerry, you have the most unusual friends I have ever seen," he said.

After filming on Fifth Avenue, the *Annie* company returned to Hollywood to finish the film. There was a two-week period in our schedule for the orphans and the dancers to work with the choreographer, while the rest of the company was shut down.

John wanted to spend his two free weeks at Las Caletas, his home outside of Puerto Vallarta on the west coast of Mexico, and he invited me to come along. He insisted that it would be good for me. I was adjusting to being a recently divorced father, and I welcomed the chance to get away from Los Angeles and just think things out.

We flew from Los Angeles to Puerto Vallarta where Maricela, John's female companion, and his driver met us. We left the airport by car and drove for nearly a half hour. Finally we stopped at a thatched open-air bar on the shore of the Bay of Banderas outside of Puerto Vallarta. It was then I learned that John's home was unreachable by car and there were no phones. The only access was by water or a long trek on a footpath through the jungle. While we waited for a boat, John insisted that I have two cold Bohemia beers. He hungrily watched my every swallow.

"Are they cold, Jerry?" he asked. "They must be cold, you know."

"John, they're fine," I said.

"Ice is hard to come by down here. Ice, most important!" he said.

I nodded my agreement.

I tried not to smoke when I was with him because he would position himself down wind to catch the smoke, and I knew cigarette smoke was not good for him.

"You always smoke two cigarettes with each bottle of beer, Jerry. Did you know that?" John asked.

"I do? No, I didn't realize that," I said, as I became self-conscious about my vices in front of him.

"Yes, you do," John said, dreamily remembering the years of his own vices.

The boat was not much more than a canoe with an outboard motor. John, Maricela, and I got in with our luggage and the two cases of Bohemia that John had insisted on purchasing, and we headed west across the Bay of Banderas toward the Pacific Ocean and John's home.

It took more than forty minutes by boat, but we finally approached John's home. John pointed to a small, sandy beach and the three buildings set on two hills above. Near the water's shore were a table and chairs under a thatch-roofed shelter, just made for Mexican beer and sunsets. The boatman turned south and headed toward John's beach.

John had been the famous film director on the trip there, but as soon as he set his feet on the sandy beach, he became John Huston, the squire of his jungle outpost. At his compound John wore white pajamas and an old safari hat, and he went barefoot.

John's outpost was a compound consisting of three principal buildings: the main house where John stayed with Maricela, a second building that served as a dining room and visiting area, then a third building that was the guest quarters where I stayed.

John gave me a quick tour, pointing out where the refrigerators were,

all fully stocked with Bohemia beer. A carton of cigarettes was promi-
nently displayed in my room.

When he showed me his living quarters in the main house, I couldn't
help but notice his pet squirrel.

"Oh, yes, Jerry, he's a dandy! Panchito!" John said, as he opened the
squirrel's cage and took him out.

The pet squirrel was the most docile, loving little creature I had ever
seen. John let me hold him, and he just curled in my arms and let me
pet him and carry him through John's quarters.

After I commented on the tenderness of his pet squirrel, John told
me a story. It seems that his pet squirrel was warm and loving to
everyone John brought to his compound, except one person. When that
person took his turn holding the docile squirrel, the animal became fe-
rocious. It dug its teeth into the guest's arm and scratched with its claws
as it ripped and tore flesh up and down the man's arm.

"John, who was the person? Your guest?" I asked.

"Ray Stark!" John laughed, "I guess the squirrel knew a producer
when he saw one!" John laughed at his story, and I joined him.

Ray Stark and John Huston had a long relationship over many
movies. I know on *Annie* that John was still paying substantial sums on
his former estate in Ireland and that Ray Stark paid John a bonus
halfway through the picture to help him out financially.

That evening at sunset I was sitting in an outside bar area with the
thatched roof that John had near the beach. I was enjoying the quiet
and peace with a Bohemia and a cigarette when I looked up and there
was John Huston coming toward me from the main house with two
more bottles of beer.

"Jerry!" John called. "I thought you might need a fill up!"

I smiled and thanked him. We sat for a few moments and then John
began to tell me of a most unusual happening not twenty yards out into
the bay from where we were sitting.

"Jerry, you see that little jut-out? Well, just look out about another ten
yards," John began. "It was about five years ago, I was sitting up in the
main house looking out at about this time of evening. Suddenly the water
foamed and spewed! Then a giant manta ray! Jerry, it was huge! Maybe
ten feet across! Right out there," John said, and pointed out in the bay.

I looked out and then back to John's face; he obviously was reliving
one of the most traumatic happenings at his compound. John was very
excited and deep within his story.

"The water turned red! Red, Jerry! I continued to look at this giant manta ray swimming and thrashing in the water, when the cause of all came straight out of the water. A killer whale, Jerry! Right out there." John's eyes bugged with the memory.

I glanced back at the water to be sure the location was firmly in my mind.

"Blood mixed with water and foam as the two creatures tore at each other and turned and attacked again. Oh, Jerry, it was a sight!"

"What happened, John?" I asked.

"Finally the manta ray gave out and the remains of the huge creature washed up on the shore east of where we're sitting. The killer whale swam off, and it's the only one of its kind I've ever seen here," John said. "Just a chance meeting between two of the sea's greatest creatures."

The battle between the killer whale and the giant manta ray was a wonderful story, but it was Herman Melville who created it, in one of his fictionalized sea stories that he wrote a hundred years earlier. John Huston was just retelling it all as his own, which was something he was very good at doing.

One night John and I were in the dining room building at his compound. It was quite late at night, and we were siting at the wooden dining table. John was drinking his water, and I was having a cigarette and a Bohemia. It was the end of a very relaxing day. There was just the two of us. No one else was around.

I decided to take advantage of my time with the legendary John Huston, so I asked him a very important question.

"John, we're all alone here. No one can hear us. There's a question I'd like to ask you, and I'd appreciate your most honest answer."

"Of course, Jerry," John answered. "Anything."

"John, what is it that one should do to become a great film director?" I asked, and looked intently at the Hollywood legend in front of me.

He stared at me and then out at the moonlight on the bay. He looked again at me and then at the bottle of beer next to my glass. He began very slowly and quietly, as though it were the secret of the ages.

"Jerry, you've got to get the very best script you can get. From the very best screenwriter you can find," John began, from the very depths of his artistic soul.

I nodded and waited for him to continue.

"You've got to hire the very top production designer you can find. One that fits your story perfectly!" John continued.

I nodded.

"The cameraman must be imaginative and of the very highest quality available," John added.

I watched John as he again looked out at the bay.

"The costume designer must be an artist in his own right. Hire the very best, no matter what the cost, Jerry!"

I leaned toward John. I realized what I was hearing from the master was pure gold.

"Casting! Only the very top actors! In every part. Take your time and hire only the very best. They are costly, Jerry, but you must have the best!" John said.

I nodded and waited for John's next thought.

"All of the cast and crew must be dedicated to your story. Dedicated, Jerry!" John continued. He breathed heavily, looked out at the beach and moonlight, and seemed to be resting. I waited as long as I could.

"But, John," I said, "you! What do you as the director, what do you do?" I stared at his face.

"Jerry, you just try not to fuck it up!" John said.

It was the fall of 1981 when John Huston gave that advice to me on how to become a famous film director. It was nearly ten years later, in 1992, when I read about the advice another film director, Howard Hawks, gave to young film students. Howard Hawks said the exact words that John Huston had said to me that night on the Bay of Banderas, but Howard Hawks had said them twelve years earlier, in 1969. John was retelling and doing it well.

On my last night at his compound, John and I were sitting at the table under the thatched roof near the beach. We were chatting and looking out over the bay. The next day I was catching a late afternoon flight back to Los Angeles. Tim, my seven-year-old, was having a soccer game that Saturday, and because of my divorce, I felt I had to be there.

John looked at me for a long time before he spoke. I'm sure he saw a young man in pain.

"Jerry," he began slowly, as he moved the bottles and ashtray off the table, "I want you to put all the people that matter to you on this table-top. All of them."

I looked at him.

"I've had to do this often during my life, believe me," John said, and smiled.

I wasn't sure what he was asking.

"All right, you've got your parents, your children, and relatives. Who else?" John asked.

I mentioned Larry Franco, Ziggy, Russ Lunday from my North-western days, and Ray Cooper, a teaching buddy I had from John Adams Junior High School. There were a few others, and then I mentioned Suzanne.

"Put them all on the table!" John insisted. "Look at them all. All the people that have been important to you. In your whole life!"

I watched John's face. He was very intense.

"Draw out the one who can best help you now. No matter who it is, where they are, what they're doing, ask them to come back into your life and help you now," John said.

We sat there another hour and talked of films, politics, and religion. My religious faith bothered him. He told me that if he ever became a Christian, I should come back here and put a bullet through his head. I countered by promising not to pray for him. He smiled at that.

The next afternoon I took the boat back to Puerto Vallarta, then a plane back to Los Angeles. I saw Tim's soccer game that Saturday morning; it was important I was there. That afternoon I phoned Suzanne in Appleton, Wisconsin.

She was a fifth- and sixth-grade teacher at Huntley School. Her first husband had died; they'd never had any children. I was trying to make sense out of a life in the motion picture industry. I'd been divorced, and I had three children to raise. I needed help. Would she consider flying to Los Angeles for a visit?

John Huston's films were about men. He was the Ernest Hemingway of the film directors; he defined the masculine image through his films. When we began filming inside the orphanage, it wasn't Humphrey Bogart or Clark Gable that John was directing. It was twenty little girls between the ages of seven and twelve. He would've gladly traded for twenty Richard Burtons' whiskey bottles and all.

John Huston became the orphans' grandfather on the set. The little girls soon found his stash of mints, and John doled them out to them like a warm, loving grandpa would do. John could control the most difficult male stars, but the little girls seemed to be able to get around him.

"Jerry!" John called.

I looked over at John with the orphans all around him, all talking at once, and each eating a mint. I hurried over to him.

"Yes, John?" I asked.

"Well, we really must be getting on, Jerry," John said, indicating the twenty little distractions around him.

Chris Soldo and Ziggy got the little girls with the studio teacher when they could, and with their mothers when they couldn't. John kept moving his chair and monitor farther and farther from the set, but the little girls followed him.

We finished *Annie* the day before Thanksgiving. The orphans gave John drawings they had made and little gifts they had gotten him. I saw his eyes tear up, and I wondered if Richard Burton or Humphrey Bogart had given him an end-of-the-picture gift that had touched him as much.

Ray Stark told me he had enjoyed making *Annie* with John Huston. The day after *Annie* finished, he hired Chris Soldo, Ziggy, and me to begin work on *Blue Thunder*, an action movie he was producing.

"Just a little movie, Jerry. *Annie* was my last *big* picture!" Ray assured me, and smiled. Ray Stark was a piece of work.

John invited me to spend Thanksgiving back at his compound on the Bay of Banderas. He knew I'd be alone; joint custody dictated that I had my children for Thanksgiving on the even-numbered years, and that was 1981. I thanked him but said I'd be fine. I was busy preparing *Blue Thunder*, and Suzanne had said she'd come out to Los Angeles for a visit during her Christmas vacation. I wanted everything to be ready.

It was one of those warm and sunny Los Angeles days that sometimes happen close to Christmas. I had picked up my children for the first half of their Christmas vacation and was taking them to my home.

When we walked up the sidewalk, the front door opened.

"Suzanne, I want you to meet my children, Chris, Tim, and Jillian. Kids, I want you to meet Suzanne. She lives in Appleton, Wisconsin. We went to high school together."

Chris and Tim wanted to hear everything about Wisconsin, our high school, and what Dad was like way back then.

There was a pause in the questioning and Jillian turned to Suzanne and looked into her face. "Do you like us?" she asked. It was warm and lovely and as direct as any three-year-old could be.

> *"Very much. I like you all very much," she said, as she gave Jillian a firm Wisconsin hug.*

Years later John Huston was to appear at a news conference to publicize the importance of creative rights for film directors. I was waiting outside the Directors Guild building in hopes of having a moment with John.

I watched as a black limousine drove up and stopped. The driver got a wheelchair out of the back, and Maricela helped John out of the limo and into the wheelchair.

I was shocked at John's condition. He was so thin. An oxygen bottle was attached to the wheelchair, and tubes ran into a plastic mask that was attached over his nose. Maricela was making John comfortable, when he saw me. He stretched out his right hand, pointed his finger at me, and shook his arm just like he had done during the making of *Annie.* I hurried to him.

I asked about Panchito, his pet squirrel, as I helped Maricela push John's wheelchair into the building and across the lobby toward the reception area.

"How are Suzanne and your children?" John smiled, so sure of himself.

"We're fine, John. Just fine," I said, as I looked for the press conference.

He patted my hand. "I told you so," he said, as he smiled, winked, and held his tongue between his teeth and lips all at the same time. John Huston was the only one I've ever seen could do that.

An official of the Directors Guild came up, greeted John, and said the television networks were waiting for him. John gave him a nod that he was ready. He turned and winked at me, as he once again became John Huston, legendary Hollywood director, his favorite role and one he played so well.

Al Pacino and *Scarface*

The *Hello, Dolly!* Street was still there. I turned off Pico Boulevard into Twentieth Century Fox and drove past the entrance to Harmonia Gardens. It was the first week of March 1982, fifteen years since I worked with Chico Day on *Dolly!* The street was still there, but a lot had changed, including what I wanted for my career.

I still wanted to do the best pictures, but I also wanted to work alongside our best film directors, even if their pictures were not always the top pictures of the year. The man I was meeting had directed some of the most innovative films of our day. I was very anxious to work with him.

I went to a sound stage where some added shots for *Blow Out* were being done. Ray Hartwick, one of the production managers on *Annie*, had asked me to come down and meet Brian De Palma. They were planning on doing a little feature, all in Miami, with Al Pacino, a remake of *Scarface*. Both Ray and their cameraman, John Alonzo, had recommended me for the assistant director job.

Ray met me on the sound stage and took me outside to Brian De Palma's dressing room.

He knocked on the door. There was no response.

"Brian?" Ray called.

"Yeah? Come in!" Brian answered.

Brian De Palma was sitting on a couch in a very modest trailer for a director. He was dressed in a tan safari jacket, loose shirt, tennis shoes, not unlike the wardrobe of John Huston. He was very overweight. I don't know why I was shocked.

"Brian, I want you to meet Jerry Ziesmer," Ray said.

"Yeah, yeah," Brian answered, and looked impatiently at Ray as he ignored me.

390

"John Alonzo's done *Black Sunday* and *Blue Thunder* with Jerry, and I did *Annie . . . ,*" Ray began.

"Right!" Brian interrupted and looked at me for the first time.

"Jerry did *Apocalypse Now*," Ray continued.

"He didn't DO *Apocalypse Now*! OK, Ray?" Brian demanded. "He worked on it, OK?"

Ray stared at Brian, then glanced at me.

Brian wasn't in a good mood. I'd have walked away and forgotten Brian De Palma, but he was too good a film director to pass up.

"I enjoy your films, and I'd like to be your assistant," I said. I just put it out there.

Brian stared at me as if I were concealing some terrible lie.

"John Alonzo and I both think . . . ," Ray began again.

"All right! He's hired. OK?" Brian said to Ray, as though he were making a great concession.

Ray started to leave, and I did, too.

"Nice to meet you," I said.

"Yeah!" Brian answered. "See you in Miami."

Ray and I walked away from his trailer.

"He's just not having a good time with the re-shoots and added shots, Jerry," Ray said in an attempt to apologize.

I nodded. A lot of directors had their moments. Otto Preminger, Steven Spielberg, even Francis Coppola could be difficult sometimes. Maybe Brian De Palma was no different.

"The whole picture is being set up independently in Miami," Ray said. "We'll shoot the whole thing down there, eight weeks, May and June. Cuban extras, everything's there, so why not?"

I listened and thought about being away from Chris, Tim, and Jillian. Maybe they'd come to Miami for the Memorial Day weekend?

"I'm going down now to set it up. I'll send for you in a week, maybe two," Ray said. "All the prep's in Miami."

Probably five weeks of prep and eight weeks of shooting with Brian De Palma and Al Pacino. It'd be an experience, but it was exactly what I wanted, to work on an important picture with a top director.

"You're on salary beginning today. I know what you got on *Annie*, remember?" Ray said, and smiled. "OK?"

I nodded, and the deal was made.

"I'll call you. Don't worry. It'll be all right," Ray said.

• • •

That next week I expected to get Ray's call and to be on my way to
Miami.

"Jerry!" Ray phoned.

"Ray, how's it going?" I answered.

"Look, we're going to be delayed a bit. Don't worry; you're on
payroll, OK?" Ray said.

"Yeah, Ray. How long do you think?" I asked.

"I don't know. Pacino. You know. Could be another week or two,"
Ray said. "Relax and enjoy life!"

"Is there anything I can do for you here?" I felt guilty being on salary
and doing nothing.

"No, enjoy it. You'll be working hard enough later," Ray said.

Ray called each week for a month. It was always the same.

"Jerry, look, I'm sorry, but we're into another delay. Miami. Pacino.
You're getting your checks, right?" Ray asked.

"I am, Ray, but how long's it going to be? I mean I thought we'd be
through before my kids' school was out," I said.

"I'm sorry. Hey, what can I do?" Ray stated. "Delays!"

Suzanne was coming out in June after her school year ended. I had
custody of the kids for the first five weeks of the summer. It was all
planned. With the delays I'd be in Miami the whole month of June and
part of July.

"Jerry!" Ray called again.

"Ray, what's happening?" I was getting anxious.

"Universal Studios just bought the project. Everything's changing.
Looks like we'll be filming in Los Angeles, five day weeks. Big push
back! You're in the package deal; you'll get a check every week until we
start. Don't worry."

"Ray, how long?" I asked.

"At least a month, maybe two. Universal coming in has changed
everything. *Scarface* is a big picture now!" Ray said.

"Yeah, Ray, but I got custody of my kids from the last week in June
through July," I explained. "I've made plans."

"Don't worry! You won't be needed until at least August," Ray
assured me.

"August!" I said. I had been on salary since March and hadn't done a thing.

"Jerry, have a nice paid vacation with your kids," Ray said. "I'll see you at Universal Studios in August. It's going to be fine."

Two days after Ray had talked to me, Paramount Studios called.

"Jerry, we got a little film you're going to love!" the production executive began.

"I'm doing *Scarface*," I explained. "For Universal."

"Right, but they're not starting for months!" the executive said.

"Yeah, but they're paying me," I said.

"Five days a week? Monday through Friday?" he asked. "Right?"

"Yeah," I answered cautiously.

"That's why you'll love our film! We can only work Saturdays and Sundays. The whole picture is shot on six Saturdays and six Sundays!" he explained.

"You're kidding!" I said.

"The whole cast is every comedian you've ever heard of: Dan Aykroyd, John Candy, Gilda Radner, Cheech and Chong, everyone. They're all booked except during the day on the weekends. We film six Saturdays and Sundays, 9:00 A.M. to 5:00 P.M., so they can fly back to Vegas or wherever for their club dates at night." He chuckled at the absurdity of the film business.

"For six weeks you and the crew get paid for five days a week, but you only work Saturdays and Sundays. You interested or not?"

"I have my kids every other weekend," I said.

"Bring them to Paramount with you! The studio's closed. Who cares?" he said.

"It's a deal," I said.

I knew Ziggy'd love this one, and the kids would enjoy the filming and the backlot. Maybe they could be in the movie.

"What's the title?" I asked.

"*It Came from Hollywood,*" he said, and laughed. "Can you believe it?"

Dan Aykroyd came to work driving a tow truck onto Paramount during his weekend on *It Came from Hollywood*. John Candy had become a big star since *1941*. Cheech and Chong were crazy, and then there was Gilda Radner. She was alive and just a joy to be around. Gilda was everybody's favorite.

It Came from Hollywood was an enjoyable diversion for six weekends and financially rewarding, but it wasn't the reason I had left teaching. I wanted to work on *Scarface* with Brian De Palma and Al Pacino.

When I reported to Universal Studios in August, Brian was having readings with actors on a bare sound stage. He'd bring in actors to audition for the various parts in *Scarface*. Al Pacino was in New York, so Brian had a young actor read the part of Tony Montana, the Al Pacino role, in the scenes with the other actors. I had never seen the young actor before. He was so natural in the role. Obviously he wouldn't be playing the part of Tony Montana, but I hoped he'd be cast in some other role. He wasn't, but four years later he was nominated for an Academy Award as Best Actor for *Stand and Deliver*, Edward James Olmos.

Scarface was an Al Pacino property. Martin Bregman was hired as the producer, and Brian De Palma was hired as the director, but the power belonged to Al Pacino, and no one forgot it.

Al Pacino was shorter than average and conscious of his height, as were Sylvester Stallone and Dustin Hoffman. I felt he had a hard outer shell that protected a very vulnerable being inside. He had a large smile with gleaming eyes, but I found it was in place as a shield to defend himself rather than to welcome outsiders.

Al was a private person with a very small inner circle of friends and employees that cared for his every need. They drove him from where he was staying on Malibu Beach to the studio; they even had their hair cut by the hairstylist who was to cut Al's hair before the stylist touched Al, just so Al could see what his haircut would look like.

While Dustin Hoffman and Sylvester Stallone would stand and fight out in the open, Al Pacino lived on the perimeter of our world and stayed in the back rooms of his trailer and his producer's office to do his fighting from the safety of his inner circle.

Al had a very quick mind and quicker tongue. He was very adept at trading barbs and one-liners, but the fun lasted only as long as Al Pacino wanted it to last. It was like playing with a deadly cobra; he could strike you dead at any moment.

He wore a dark sport coat, jeans, dark shirt, dark sport shoes. He was very casual. There was no show of wealth or position in his clothes or car, yet you knew he was a king.

He challenged all of us with his presence. He was Al Pacino. Who would dare confront him? He had the power to terminate anyone on the picture at any time. Al Pacino was as unpredictable as a person as his characters were unpredictable on the screen. For me, that's what gave his acting such compelling interest; you never knew what his character was going to do next. We all knew we were making a good picture with a great actor, but we also existed in a world of fear and insecurity.

When we started *Scarface*, we were to finish in early December. Suzanne and I planned a December 18 wedding. I felt confident that we'd be finished filming by then. That would give us nearly two months free before we were to begin with Mark Rydell on *The River*, starring Mel Gibson and Sissy Spacek.

Suzanne and I did get married on December 18, but instead of being finished with *Scarface*, the film was months over schedule. Our start date with Mark Rydell for the end of February was in great jeopardy.

When you hire a talent like Al Pacino or Marlon Brando you know it's going to take longer to film because of their perfectionism. Marlon and Francis talked for three days on *Apocalypse* while the rest of the cast and crew waited. On *Scarface*, we waited for Al Pacino from the very beginning of the production.

Al Pacino was most particular with the casting, especially when it came to the part of Elvira, his love interest in the movie. Every young actress in Hollywood wanted the part. The role of Elvira opposite Al Pacino was a breakout role for any actress lucky enough to get cast. The search for the right Elvira went on for months.

It seemed that the choice had come down to four actresses, and we decided to screen test them all. The first two were very competent actresses as well as beautiful models, but not the Elvira to do battle with Al Pacino throughout *Scarface*. Elvira was a classic beauty, like a supermodel, but with a strong backbone. The third contender was the daughter of a famous movie star. She was the best actress of the three, but she towered over Al Pacino. I knew she wouldn't get cast. The fourth girl was late for her screen test. It was a screen test for the most sought-after role of the year and with Al Pacino, but she was still late.

She came onto the stage like a frightened butterfly, first flitting toward the makeup tables, then toward the set.

"Hey!" I yelled to her, "Are you . . ."

"Yes, oh, I'm sorry I'm late, you know," she said, and giggled and flitted away from me back toward the set.

I looked at that creature. Her hair was pulled over her face, she wore a man's shirt and loose slacks. She looked like a second baseman, with none of the classic beauty of Elvira. She moved like a tomboy with wings; Elvira was statuesque and controlled.

"She'll never get the part," I thought. "She's too thin, plain, giggly, and acts like a second baseman, not a supermodel."

"Look," I started at her again, "you're late. Please get outside to the makeup trailer. Your clothes are in your dressing room trailer. OK?" It wasn't a question as much as "Get your ass moving!" I hated wasting time testing people who had no chance of being cast.

"Yes, oh, great! Thanks," she giggled, and hurried off the sound stage.

Elvira never would have giggled.

It took about two hours, but when the second baseman came back on the set, she looked pretty good. It was amazing, but she was so thin and small that I couldn't imagine her standing up to the tirades of Al Pacino during their scenes. I was sure it took a stronger Elvira to compete with Al Pacino, an actress with inner strength, a backbone, not some emaciated ninety-pound weakling.

The first scene she did in the screen test was a simple talk scene. She could do that, but all the actresses could. It was the confrontation scene that they all failed. It's hard to confront someone with the stature of an Al Pacino and hold your own.

I got the crew ready. Al Pacino and the second baseman were set, and Brian was ready. I rolled the camera, and Brian called action. She came on like a pit bull, a gorgeous, supermodel, pit bull! She attacked Al, held her own in the exchanges, and was tantalizingly attractive, like a fine piece of sculptured crystal.

When Brian yelled "Cut!" there wasn't a doubt that the second baseman, Michelle Pfeiffer, was our Elvira.

I knew that Francis Coppola had tried to interest Al Pacino in the role of Willard in *Apocalypse Now*. Steve McQueen had been the first choice for Willard, but he was with Ali McGraw at the time and Robert Evans would not allow his and Ali's two children to be taken out of the country. When Ali and the children couldn't accompany him to the Philippines, Steve McQueen passed on *Apocalypse Now*, and eventually Martin Sheen played the role.

From what little Francis told me about directing Al Pacino as

Michael Corleone in *The Godfathers*, you had to do a lot of takes to convince Al Pacino that he had done the best he could. He always wanted to go "one more time, please."

The perfectionism of an Al Pacino or of a Barbra Streisand was artistically fulfilling, but as the saying goes, "Even Rembrandt stopped sometime." Both Al and Barbra stopped only when the director convinced them they had done their best. Sydney Pollack had the respect of Barbra Streisand on *The Way We Were*, but on *Scarface* Al Pacino hired the producers, the director, and the rest of us. No one had the power or respect that could get Al Pacino to stop shooting his scenes in *Scarface* until he wanted to stop. Sometimes Rembrandt took a long, long time before he stopped.

"No, Brian, no. I want to go again. Please, once again," Al would say.

"Why?" Brian would ask. "We've got the shot."

"I don't know. I'm not sure," Al said. "I want to go again."

We'd try the take again and again. There was nothing Brian or any of us could do.

The film crew on *Scarface* was very creative waiting for Al Pacino. When the delays stretched into hours each day, the crew began to create diversions to keep themselves entertained. It began with the card games, then progressed to chess and checkers. That grew into sports pools on every possible sporting event. From there it went into raffles. An object would be acquired, a television set for example, and the raffle tickets would be sold among the cast and crew. At the end of the day the lucky winner would be announced. A very popular betting pool was created on how many times the *F* word would be in the printed takes each day. Those kinds of activities amused the crew for a few weeks, but the delays and waiting increased, and so did their creativity.

John Alonzo, the cameraman, brought a ballet teacher to the sound stage each morning. It was John's idea to teach his camera crew how to gracefully hold and move with the camera. That grew into proper lifting and moving for the grips and electricians, then proper walking and posture, and finally the crew was walking around the sound stage with books on their heads as they practiced their posture and lifting positions.

At about that time the idea was conceived to have a funny hat contest. Each member of the crew spent the waiting time designing an outrageous hat, and on Friday we held the contest. Everyone was excited. Even the Universal Studios' publicity department took pictures of our crew as they paraded up and down the inside the set of Tony Montana's mansion, displaying their artistic creations. Everyone had a good time. There was nothing else to do, why not have a funny hat contest? The executives of the studio didn't see it that way.

The following week, when the studio newspaper was distributed around the offices and sound stages of Universal, the front page had a picture of the crew of *Scarface* modeling their funny hats for the studio photographer. That night a meeting was called in our producer's office to find out the cause of the delays on *Scarface*.

We all crowded into his office. The heads of all the crew departments were there. All of the production workers were there. The transportation department and the craft service departments were there. The producer finally asked how we could work more efficiently. How could we speed up the filming? We all looked at one another and smiled. The producer had invited everyone to the meeting to discuss how we could work faster, except one person, Al Pacino.

Pepe Serna was an actor I had known for years. I first met him in the early 1970s when I was doing the *Kung Fu* series, then I worked with him on *Movie of the Week* and on a feature in Mexico. On *Scarface* he played the role of Angel, one of Tony Montana's friends. Angel was the character who was dissected by a chain saw in a motel bathroom while Tony Montana was forced to watch. It was a memorable chain-saw cutting scene, but it was the actor, Pepe Serna, and not the scene that has stayed in my mind all these years.

Pepe and I had become friends over the years. I liked him for his humor and his perspective on racial issues. It seemed that Pepe grew up in Texas. He faced racial slurs most of his early life. When he reached his early teens, he could take it no longer. Instead of lashing out, he took a white T-shirt and wrote all of the racial insults he had ever been called onto the shirt. Then he put it on and wore it to his high school, work, and church.

It takes little thought to say a racial slur, but it takes much more if you have to read it, and look at the man at the same time.

During the time we filmed the Bolivia sequence and the exterior of Tony's mansion in Montecito near Santa Barbara, Al Pacino gave a large, expensive party for the cast and crew. A grand banquet room at a Montecito beach hotel was rented, and the whole party was catered with food, drink, and fine music. The banquet room was set with round tables with ten chairs per table. There were tablecloths and cloth napkins, silverware, china, crystal glasses, and real flowers on each table. Waiters served cocktails and wine from an open bar. The dinner was a sumptuous buffet, with chefs carving roast beef, ham, and turkey for each guest.

The cast and crew had invited their friends and families to come up from Los Angeles for the Saturday night of Al Pacino's party. People flocked into the party, laughing, eating, drinking, and glancing at their famous host.

Al Pacino sat with his female companion of the time, Kathleen Quinlan, at a table with his close friends and looked out at the crew and guests. They never danced. They never moved among the guests. People eventually formed a line at Al Pacino's table to thank him for the party. He smiled with gleaming eyes, nodded, and said something warm to each of them. All the guests were thrilled to see and talk with him. Al Pacino was a benevolent king.

I looked over the cast and crew enjoying themselves, but I couldn't find one of my best friends on the crew. Sydney Baldwin was the stillman on the movie. Suzanne and I had invited Sydney and his wife to a Dodger game during *Scarface*, and we all had a good time. I had hoped that the four of us could sit together at the party. He wasn't there, and it bothered me.

Monday morning out at the set, after the crew had begun preparing the first shot, I saw Sydney getting out of a late van with his stillman bags of cameras and film.

"Sydney," I asked, "why weren't you at Al's party?"

He looked at me, and I waited. He took a long time and stared directly into my eyes.

"Because I can't be bought so cheaply," he answered.

The memory of Stan Laurel's story of all the other guests scrambling for the precious gifts at the William Randolph Hearst parties came crashing back into my mind. Was that what all of us did Saturday night at the Al Pacino party? Scrambled for food, drink, a kind word from Al Pacino? Had I been bought, too?

I endured the tedious months with Al Pacino and Marlon Brando because eventually those actors gave us some of the greatest performances we have in film, and I wanted to be a small part of it. That's why I left teaching. It's why Ethel Waters continued to hang on to *The Member of the Wedding*. We all wanted to be a part of something good, something that would last.

Mel Gibson and *The River*

Suzanne had left teaching after sixteen years at Huntley School in Appleton, Wisconsin, to join me in a life of making movies and raising three children. Her first job on a motion picture company was as the teacher for the children employed on Mark Rydell's film *The River*. Shane and Becky Jo, who played Sissy Spacek's children in the film, were her primary students, but her most challenging pupil was Mel Gibson himself.

Suzanne had her classroom on the second floor of the farmhouse we had built for the movie in a cornfield outside of Kingsport, Tennessee. The classroom was air-conditioned and one of the most comfortable places on the location. Suzanne would take her flock of young actors and actresses up to the second floor and begin their studies that she'd received from their regular schoolteachers.

Seeking the comfort of the cool air on the second floor, Mel Gibson would climb the stairs and quietly take a seat in her classroom. Suzanne was pleased to have a movie star sit in her classroom, until the day Mel Gibson raised his hand to speak.

"Suzanne?" Mel asked, with his hand in the air.

She nodded in his direction, and he continued.

"You know, I only went to school until I was sixteen. And I think that was the biggest mistake I've made as an actor," Mel continued.

Suzanne beamed. What better motivation for her young actor-students than to have Mel Gibson, the star of their movie, talk about the values of education.

"That's right," Mel continued. "I never should've gone to school. Not one day. No actor should. It's best if you know nothing!"

I'm sure it wasn't the first time Mel Gibson had been asked to leave a schoolroom, but it was the first time Suzanne had told a movie star to "Go to the principal's office!"

Thanksgiving Day on *The River* changed me and my whole family. Chris, my oldest son, had come to live with us the day after Suzanne and I were married, and my first wife and I shared joint custody of Tim and Jillian.

We celebrated Thanksgiving dinner in Birmingham, Alabama, with the other families of filmmakers making *The River*. Chris and I had celebrated Thanksgiving together on *Rocky II*, but it was just the two of us in a restaurant in Washington, D.C. It was great, but it wasn't as a family. The Thanksgiving in Birmingham was the first time I was able to combine filmmaking on location with hands-on raising and enjoying a family.

Suzanne had to make a lot of trips between locations and Los Angeles. We had to have an exhaustive list of housekeepers, baby-sitters, drivers, and so on, as a huge safety net for our brood, but somehow it all worked.

I remembered how Marty Sheen and his wife Janet were able to combine filmmaking and raising a family, even on *Apocalypse Now* in the Philippines. It was all possible, you just had to have the right ingredients and the will to make it happen. Suzanne had the will, and she made it happen.

We began to schedule our films to shoot in Los Angeles during the school year (*Some Kind of Wonderful* and *Jo Jo Dancer*), and on locations during the summer vacations (*American Flyers* and *Short Circuit*). During all their summer vacations, our kids were in our "movie camp," and they loved it.

Peter Bogdanovich

In 1986 I was at Paramount Studios finishing the last few weeks of *Some Kind of Wonderful* with Eric Stoltz and Mary Stuart Masterson, when I got a call to meet with Peter Bogdanovich. He was to direct a picture called *Illegally Yours* starring Rob Lowe.

I wanted to work with Peter Bogdanovich because of three films he had done: *The Last Picture Show*, which that he did with the cameraman, Robert Surtees; his picture with Barbra Streisand and Ryan O'Neal, *What's Up, Doc?*; the sensitive film *Mask* with Eric Stoltz and Cher.

I drove over during a lunch break at Paramount and hurried to Peter Bogdanovich's office at the old Hollywood General Studio. The decor was rich, with dark maroon drapes and carpet, dark walnut furniture with leather, and deep comfortable chairs.

I couldn't help noticing all the red-bound books that filled every shelf of his bookcase. There must have been two hundred of them. I thought they were an encyclopedia or a matched set of research books. On closer examination I found that they were two hundred copies of the same book, Peter Bogdanovich's own book on John Ford!

Peter entered dressed in Hollywood-elite casual. He was well tailored, with immaculate shirt, slacks, and loafers. He had a courtier's elegance about him, as if he were from the court of Louis XIV, and always a bit of a smile that told you he was enjoying life.

When he didn't say anything, I decided to introduce myself.

"Hi, I'm Jerry Ziesmer," I said.

"I know. They told me," he said, as he sat at his desk and looked through some papers.

"You're doing *Illegally Yours?*" I asked.

"What?" he laughed.

"You're doing *Illegally Yours?*" I repeated. "Your next film, *Illegally Yours?*"

He laughed again and looked around his office as though he had misplaced something.

"Have you read the script?" he asked.

"No," I answered.

"I haven't either. Well, not hardly. It's terrible," he continued.

"It's terrible?" I was confused. Usually directors were excited about their script.

"It's one of the worst scripts you'll ever read. Really." He laughed again and continued to look for something on his desk.

"But aren't you going to direct it?" I asked.

"No one's going to direct that picture. No one," Peter said.

"But . . . ," I tried to figure out what he meant.

"You're hired, but we're never going to make *Illegally Yours.* Trust me," he laughed. "Don't even bother to read the script." Then he found a magazine on the desk and walked out of his office.

The production manager had my deal and contract all worked out for me.

"Just sign your contract, Jerry," he said. "It's all made out for you."

"But," I tried to fathom what was happening.

"You start today. Don't worry about coming in. Here's a script," he continued.

I signed to do *Illegally Yours* and left the studio a very confused assistant director.

Each day during my lunch break from *Some Kind of Wonderful,* I would drive over to the *Illegally Yours* offices. Peter assured me that *Illegally Yours* would never get made. No one would be stupid enough to put up the money to film that script. I should just enjoy myself before they folded the whole picture.

Believing what Peter had told me, I let it be known that I was available for another film. A day or two later I got a call from an independent producer who was preparing *The Principal* with Jim Belushi.

I went to his offices and met with him.

"We'd love to have you on this, Jerry," he said, "but you're doing *Illegally Yours* with Peter Bogdanovich."

"No," I explained, "that's just a weird deal. It's a terrible script, and no one is stupid enough to put up the money to film it. We're just on it for another week until everyone comes to their senses and folds the whole project," I said, and laughed.

He didn't laugh. He stared directly at me.

He spoke very slowly as he continued to stare at me, "I guaranteed the money to film *Illegally Yours* this morning. You start filming in six weeks."

I raced back to Peter's office.

"Peter! Did you hear?" I asked.

He was sitting at his desk, casually reading a magazine.

"No, what?" he asked in his supercasual, Louis XIV manner.

"The money's in place! We're shooting *Illegally Yours* in six weeks!" I exclaimed.

"Oh, my God!" Peter said, then giggled, "I'd better read the script."

Peter was not a good morning person. One day he arrived for filming, and when he got out of his car he looked around and began screaming for me.

I ran over to him.

"Peter, what is it?" I said.

He was beside himself.

"I can't film here! Look at all the trucks and cars!" he shouted.

I leaned in as close as I could to him so no one else could hear.

"Peter, you're in the *parking lot*; we're filming in the house down the street," I whispered.

"We are? Oh, good," he said, giggled, and moved off toward his trailer, snapping and dropping toothpicks as he went.

I only had worked with one member of the cast before, Colleen Camp. Twelve years ago she had been Larry Franco's dancing partner when we filmed the final night of the Playboy Bunny Show on *Apocalypse Now*. Who could forget?

Most directors keep their copy of the script in a canvas pocket on the side of their chair. That way their script is always close to them, and they can refer to it whenever they choose. Peter had a different concept.

A young man was designated as the script person. Whenever Peter wanted to see his script, he would call for him.

"*Script!*" Peter shouted.

The young man would come running to Peter with the script, open it and wait for Peter's next command.

"Turn!" Peter would say, and the script person would turn a page and wait.

"Back!" Peter would say, and the young man would turn a page back.

When Peter was through looking at the script, he simply walked away from the script person, leaving him holding the script. Marie Antoinette would have been proud of Peter.

Of course Peter and the cast were served breakfast when they arrived for work at 7:30, but then at 10:30 Peter had to have a midmorning snack and the cast did, too. Their midmorning snack consisted of a large fruit salad with mint sherbet for each of them.

There wasn't any problem serving fruit salads to Peter and the cast when we were in St. Augustine or near our caterer, but one day we were doing car shots way out in the country of northeast Florida. We had been towing a picture car with the four principals in it, and at 10:30 we were miles from anywhere.

"Time for snack," Peter informed me. "Where are our fruit salads?"

"Peter, we're in the middle of nowhere. Can't you wait another hour for your fruit salads?" I asked. "If we could film for another hour, we'd be back at our caterers."

"We could," Peter explained, "but no one's performance will be any good until we get our fruit salads. You know that, Jerry."

The cast looked at me. I looked at them, and then back at Peter.

We all sat on the edge of the road while a car and driver went to the nearest town in northeast Florida to get fruit salads with mint sherbet for Peter and his cast.

Rob Lowe and three girls were the cast in the car. Peter married one girl, the script person married another, and the third girl married Samuel Goldwyn, Jr.

Peter Bogdanovich had the reputation for not liking a lot of extras in his shots, and I had the reputation of working with large numbers of extras. We were filming in the spacious square in St. Augustine, Florida. I suggested to Peter that we would need a lot of extras to make the square look active. To my amazement he suggested a parade with marching bands, majorettes, and spectators lining the sidewalks. I immediately got to work auditioning marching bands and hundreds of extras to watch the parade.

On the day of shooting we had all the people ready for Peter. The marching bands were set, and the spectators lined the streets. The town square looked alive and active.

First Peter had me get rid of the marching bands and the majorettes.

Next he had me get rid of the spectators. Finally, when we filmed, we
had one man walking slowly through the town square.

Eventually we finished filming all of the scenes in the script, but
Peter wanted to keep shooting. Each day he would have new scenes for
us to do. Sometimes it was a romantic love scene on wet grass, or in a
tree, or walking in a sunlit field.

We filmed day after day, until one afternoon the crew called a
meeting. They gathered everyone together and took a vote. When the
votes were tabulated, the cameraman called me over.

"Jerry, we've voted to stop the movie. This is the last day. It's over,"
he said. "We're going home tomorrow. You'd better tell Peter."

I looked at the crew, and they all nodded their agreement. I turned
and looked toward Peter.

He was sitting thirty feet away watching everything. I slowly made
my way over to him. I had never heard of anything like this happening
in the history of Hollywood.

"What're they up to?" Peter asked, before I could speak.

"They've taken a vote, Peter," I began.

"And?" he asked.

"They've voted to stop the movie," I said.

"Can they do that?" he asked.

"They're leaving. They won't work any more," I added. "The crew is
going home."

It was one of the strangest moments in my career. A film crew had
taken a vote and had decided to end a picture. Surely it had to be a his-
toric moment.

Two days later Suzanne and I flew from Florida to Atlanta and were
changing planes for the flight back to Los Angeles. As I walked down
the concourse and found our connecting flight, I saw an old friend, Shel
Schrager, from the production department at Columbia Studios.

I greeted him and mentioned that Suzanne and I had just finished a
picture in Florida and were on our way home. Shel had been scouting
the possibilities of shooting a film outside Atlanta and was also headed
back to L.A.

"You won't believe what happened on our picture," I challenged. *"It's
a first!"*

"What?' he smiled.

"Have you ever heard of a crew voting to stop a picture?" I laughed, thinking that I had one of the all-time great Hollywood stories.

"Happened on one of my films once," Shel said.

I was startled.

"It did?" I exclaimed. "Who was the director?"

"Peter Bogdanovich," he answered. "Ever work with him?"

The First and Only Mutiny in the History of Hollywood

The film crew with Peter Bogdanovich had voted to *end* the filming after all the scenes had been filmed, but I'd never heard of a mutiny by a film crew happening in the middle of making a film, not until Suzanne and I were walking down a country road in the middle of Arizona, and the staff and crew of the picture were walking down the road with us. It was a film crew mutiny, and I was right in the middle of it.

The picture was different, right from the casting. Bruce Willis, Richard Pryor, Cher, and Robin Williams were all considered for a part in the movie—the same part! They were all considered to play the same part, and opposite an Academy Award–winning actor.

We began filming in New York City. Our Hollywood crew joined forces with the New York filmmakers, just like we had done on *Annie* and *The Way We Were*. We filmed in Grand Central Station and on the East Side of Manhattan. We ate corned beef and cheese cake at the Carnegie Deli and saw *Fences* on Broadway, starring James Earl Jones. The filming went smoothly, and we were enjoying the work.

The company moved from New York to Chicago, and we continued to film without incident. We stayed at the Westin Hotel on Michigan Avenue, ate pizza at Gino's East, and believed we were having a wonderful time and making a good film.

The first sign that something was wrong happened when we were filming at a little railroad station outside of Chicago in Indiana. The grips and electricians asked to meet with the cameraman and me during the lunch period.

The crew told us that they weren't being sent the supplies they had ordered from the studio in Hollywood. When the crew called to check on their requests, they were told no orders had been placed. The producer hadn't signed and forwarded the crew's orders for materials back to the studio.

I had known the producer for years. He wouldn't do that. The cameraman and I went to his dressing room trailer for a talk. He was arrogant, antagonistic, and largely incoherent. It was early afternoon. Substance and chemical abuse had become a part of Hollywood moviemaking. You tried to avoid it if you could, and to work around it if you couldn't.

I had known for years that the producer kept a bottle of vodka in the lower right-hand drawer of his desk. A lot of studio people kept a bottle. Everyone knew he drank, but he did his job. Saul Wurtzel, the production manager on *The Great White Hope*, began opening his lower desk drawer at 10:30 every morning. I never asked him a question after lunch.

The producer's antagonism and arrogance toward the crew continued when we moved to Arizona. Still no supplies or equipment ever came from the studio.

The crew called their unions, and I called the Directors Guild. To the Directors Guild's credit, an additional unit manager was sent to us in Arizona, but he was kept off the set and in the production office.

No one listened to us, and the materials and equipment never came. When safety as well as the quality of work became an issue, the crew called for another meeting.

On a Sunday night at our motel, the key members of the crew and staff met and agreed to issue an ultimatum to the producer and the director. If the reordered materials and equipment were not received by the end of filming on Saturday, the crew would leave the picture and return to Los Angeles. Copies of the ultimatum were sent to the studio and to all the Hollywood unions and guilds involved.

I communicated the ultimatum to the director, but he refused to speak with me on the subject. He wanted nothing to do with the controversy and told me to talk to his producer.

The producer listened to our ultimatum, but mocked us and our efforts. He told us that he was in charge of the movie, and would remain in charge as he had been on all his pictures. If we didn't like the way he was running the film, we could all leave.

On Friday night I put in a personal phone call to the highest executive I knew at the studio. I was explicit in my description of the problems within the company and the imminent danger of the staff and crew leaving the film that next day. He said he'd make a call to the producer and the director that night, but I never believed he took me seriously. I never heard a word that night from either the producer or the director.

The last shot on Saturday was from inside a diner on the side of a lonely Arizona country road. As soon as I called a wrap, the staff and crew began packing their gear like they did on any other day.

The producer watched from his dressing room trailer. I'm sure he believed that a mutiny would never take place, not on a big Hollywood movie, not in the middle of Arizona, fifty miles from anywhere. He was betting that the crew wouldn't walk away from their paychecks, that they'd take the abuse like they always did, look the other way, and keep on making the movie and getting their paychecks.

On that late Saturday afternoon in Arizona, something changed, and it could never go back the way it was. Maybe the pendulum of chemical and substance abuse in Hollywood had finally begun to swing back the other way, or maybe one Hollywood crew had enough and weren't going to take it anymore.

We all walked out to the road. Fifteen of our local Arizona extras had parked their cars across the road from the diner, and were waiting for us. They'd gotten our luggage and checked us out of our motel rooms. We got into their cars, and they drove us the fifty miles to the Phoenix airport and our flight back to Los Angeles.

The first film crew mutiny in the history of Hollywood had just taken place.

The Cameron Crowe Films

The Arizona road was still on my mind. I wasn't looking for another film just yet. Suzanne and I and the kids needed time at home. We all needed to play in the swimming pool, listen to some Thelonius Monk and Miles Davis, and just kick back. Hollywood could wait.

Eric Stoltz had become a friend ever since we did *Some Kind of Wonderful* with him in 1986. Sometimes he'd sit in our kitchen and talk acting with our son Chris or try to sell me something.

"I want you to talk to the guy, Ziesmer! That's all," Stoltz was saying to me. "Read the script. That's all. Cameron Crowe is a great guy."

I had never heard of him. The guy had written two films: *Fast Times at Ridgemont High* and *The Wild Life*, but he'd never directed.

Suzanne and I were having such a peaceful life that I wasn't anxious to go back to the studios.

"He's great. The guy's a great writer. Did you see *Fast Times?*"

I shook my head.

"Cameron Crowe is one of the nicest people you'll ever meet. Like me," Eric joked.

Suzanne laughed and glanced at me. When she did, I knew it was all over. Eric always had a way with women.

"OK, OK," I mumbled. "Have him call me."

About two days later, Suzanne handed me the phone and smiled.

"Hello?" It was Cameron Crowe. He sounded young. I didn't want to like him. I didn't need a first-time director at this stage of my career.

"Look," I interrupted, cutting right to the chase, "send me your script. I'll read it and we can talk."

410

• • •

His office was at Fox. It was more than twenty years since *Hello, Dolly!*, and the cobblestones and exterior of Harmonia Gardens were still there. I drove up the studio street past where Chris had been the newspaper boy in *Harry and Walter* and where James Earl Jones had entered a Chicago nightclub in *The Great White Hope*. The studio guard directed me to Cameron Crowe's office.

He was young, late twenties. Smiling, friendly, not Hollywood friendly but eager to please. His clothes were casual jeans, a T-shirt displaying a Seattle rock group, and tennis shoes. He had long hair and a big grin.

Cameron was so young. Francis and I were about the same age. Richard Pryor was a year younger, but all the other directors I had assisted were older than me. Cameron could have been my younger brother or my oldest son.

I didn't listen closely to what he was saying. I tried to get a sense of what he was about. I'd liked his script. I'd watched the videotapes of the two movies he had written. His characters were real people, suffering with the rest of us.

Our meeting that day reminded me of the first interview I had with Sydney Pollack on *The Way We Were*. Cameron's attitude was a lot like mine had been sixteen years ago. He deeply cared about his movie, and that was important to me. That's the reason I agreed to do *Say Anything . . . .*

I was excited. It wasn't the same excitement as when I was hired to do *The Way We Were* or *Apocalypse Now*, but that was a long time ago, when I was much younger. Then I looked for every movie I did to be a big, important picture. *Say Anything . . .* wasn't a big picture. It was a little picture with a first time-director, but there was a *maybe* floating around. Maybe this director and his movie would be special.

The story took place in Seattle, but it would be shot in Los Angeles, Cameron said. That was good for me and my family. It was harder to be away from the kids during the school year now that they were older.

I already knew what scenes of *Say Anything . . .* our kids could be in: the high school graduation and the kick-boxing class. Family's important, and it was the first question the kids asked whenever we took a new movie: "What scene are we in?"

Laszlo Kovacs from *Harry and Walter Go to New York* was the cameraman. He was a gentleman and probably one of the top ten cameramen in the world. Laszlo had done *Ghostbusters, What's Up, Doc?, Five Easy Pieces,* and *Easy Rider.* He had been trained as a cameraman in Hungary but left during the Hungarian Revolution. He knew big, he knew small. He'd done everything in film. I knew he'd be perfect for Cameron on his first movie.

Ray Quiroz was the script supervisor, and a good one. He was a meek and mild man. Ray had taken over as the script supervisor on *Apocalypse Now* after Typhoon Ruby. He had a dream during all those months in the jungle, to own and drive a formula-one race car. When we finished *Apocalypse Now*, that's what Ray did.

My preproduction meetings with Cameron were like none I've ever had with a director. He trusted me to make the scheduling decisions, but I had to provide him with all the time he needed to get the acting performances he wanted out of his actors.

We had a long rehearsal period before the film began shooting. John Cusack had to learn kick-boxing, and Cameron had to learn how to work with his actors.

There were the inevitable actor-vs.-director challenges. It was similar to a new teacher at the beginning of the school year, when the students challenged you to see how far they could push. Francis had his time with Marlon Brando, Brian De Palma with Al Pacino, Sydney Pollack with Barbra Streisand, and Cameron with John Cusack.

What I thought would be a liability, the writer directing, became Cameron's greatest strength on all his pictures, including *Jerry Maguire.* The actors respected Cameron's script, and the respect for the writer flowed into respecting Cameron as a director. It worked for him.

Cameron would rehearse with the actors in the set, next with only Laszlo, and finally with the whole crew watching. It was the same rehearsal procedure Sydney Pollack had used on *The Way We Were.* Once Cameron had finished with his actors, he went back to his dressing room and left Laszlo to design the shots for the scene. Some directors worked exactly like that. Francis left a lot up to Vittorio Storaro, and on *Jo Jo Dancer* Richard Pryor relied on John Alonzo to select the angles and shots for him.

That work procedure was successful if the cameraman and the director were in perfect sync. The director had to accept the choices made by the cameraman. Francis did, Richard Pryor did, and Cameron did *most* of the time.

When Cameron didn't accept the shot Laszlo had set up, you could read it all over his face. Laszlo and his crew had the experience to quickly adapt to Cameron's wishes. He may have been a first-time director, but he was *The Director*.

About six months after finishing *Say Anything . . .* , the studio called me to do a few days of added shots. They were quick, easy pieces the editor needed. It would only take a couple of days to film.

I called Ziggy and my two second assistant directors, Vicki Jackson LeMay and Bryan Denegal, who had been with me on *Say Anything . . .* , and before that, on *Midnight Run*, *Illegally Yours*, *Some Kind of Wonderful*, *Short Circuit*, *Jo Jo Dancer*, and *American Flyer*. I told them of the week's work.

When I went into the studio's production department, that old "race card" jumped out of the deck.

"Why don't you hire *white* assistant directors?"

"Something wrong with them?" another asked. "Just wondering."

I couldn't believe what I was hearing.

"Yours aren't doing the job for you, Jerry," the man continued.

"Their paperwork is poor. They're not helping you," another man added.

"We have a list of ADs we've used," one said. "Take your pick."

"It's only a week's work at best. Hire two off our list."

"Brian and Vicki are with me," I answered. "We're a team."

There was a pause in the proceedings.

"One of your producers told us if you want your team back, you'll have to go over to her office and beg."

Beg and Wisconsin have never gone well together.

I called Vicki to meet me at Rancho Park, across from the studio. She thought it was best for me to hire the other ADs for the added shots, and we'd all be together on the next film. But not to beg.

"Please, don't beg," Vicki said to me.

I could've called Cameron and started a war, but I never told him.

I left Vicki, and drove back on the studio to the *Say Anything . . .* bungalow.

As soon as I entered her office, she knew why I was there.

"They tell me you want your team," she said to me.

"That's right," I answered.

"And you're willing to beg, they said?"

"That's right."

"Well . . . ," she said, and waited.

"I'm begging to have Vicki and Bryan with me," I said.

She enjoyed the moment so much. She was so pleased with herself.

"Well, since you're *begging*," she intoned, and smiled at me, "I'll let you have them." She giggled and stared at me.

I smiled, politely nodded, and left her office.

I hadn't begged. I'd done the cruelest thing I could do to her: Without opening her eyes, I let her sink blindly into the paralysis of her own bigotry.

During the filming of *Illegally Yours* and *Say Anything . . .* , Vicki, Bryan, Suzanne, and I had planned our trip to Paris. A week before we were to leave, Bryan became ill and decided it was best for him to get treatment rather than to go to Paris.

His illnesses were far more serious than any of us thought. It'd be eight years before Bryan worked with us again, on *Jerry Maguire.*

It was the spring of 1988. Suzanne's feet were hurting her after a full day of walking around Paris with Vicki. She needed to rest a few hours before dinner, and I wanted to buy a gift for an old friend.

I walked out of the Latitudes St. Germain Hotel and made my way down Benoit to Boulevard St. Germain. I waited for the walk light and crossed south, heading past the drugstore to a small street that ran from Boulevard St. Germain to the northern edge of the Luxembourg Gardens.

There was a little shop on the east side of the street where I'd seen the perfect thing for him. I knew he'd love it.

I entered the shop, picked up his gift, paid the thirty francs, and hurried back across the Boulevard St. Germain.

I walked north on Bonaparte all the way to the Seine and west along the river to the bridge at the Place de la Concorde. After I crossed the bridge, I entered the Tuileries, a park between the Champs Elysees and the Seine.

I was looking for an area he had told me about. He had mentioned that there was a camel ride for the children near shade trees. He said that he liked to sit on a park bench and enjoyed watching the children playing.

Maybe it was the wrong time of year for the camel ride. I did find a park bench under some shade trees, and I saw a lot of children playing.

I carefully unwrapped my gift, and placed Bugs Bunny, that kwazy wabbit, on the bench, watching the children he loved. I just left it there. I couldn't ask him if it was the same park bench where he had sat; François Truffaut had died four years earlier.

Say Anything . . . was a fine movie, and Cameron Crowe had proven to all that he was special. I was anxious to work on his next film, but his next film was years away.

Singles

It was two years later that Cameron asked me to do his second movie, *Singles*. He had new producers, a new studio, and the film was to shoot in Seattle. To do *Singles* was a doubly hard decision for us. Suzanne and I had decided that our next film would be our last, and I wanted to end my career with something special.

Suzanne made a home for all of us in the Westin Hotel in Seattle. Chris was with us for all the months of filming; he worked as a production assistant. Tim visited on his school breaks from the New England Conservatory of Music in Boston. Jillian appeared in *Singles* and spent as much time with us in Seattle as she could. We were a family making a film on location. Maybe that was special enough.

We used Seattle's rock bands of the early '90s, Soundgarden, Pearl Jam, Alice in Chains, in the movie. The soundtrack was one of the most successful in the history of Hollywood, but the movie wasn't. *It wasn't one of the good ones,* as Robert Surtees would've said.

Singles was fresh in ideas and scope. It explored our age and showed us what we were. It was worth every day I spent on it, but I'd always

n to retire like Ted Williams, who'd hit a home run on his last at
bat. *Singles* wasn't a home run.

Suzanne and I did retire after *Singles*. It was time for us to live the
good life and to enjoy our home and children. And I returned to
something I had missed for thirty years, *teaching in the classroom.*

I taught a film production class for UCLA extension, The Craft of
the Assistant Director. Suzanne taught alongside me. We each had loved
teaching *and* cinema; our film production class combined the best of
both worlds for us. We turned away from Hollywood and toward mentoring our young film students.

Four years after *Singles* had finished filming, Cameron began to
e-mail me about a new script he'd been writing, *Jerry Maguire*. Simple,
easy film. All in Los Angeles. Would I be interested in reading it?

I thought about Ted Williams's last at bat and how good he must
have felt. About Michael Jordan going out with a championship. I
wanted a better exit for my career. Just one more—something *special* to
go out on. A final exit line. A home run. A last championship.

Tom Cruise

Bryan Denegal was watching the cast read through for me. He was the
most diplomatic assistant director I'd ever known. Everyone loved him,
from Whoopi Goldberg, to Robert DeNiro, to Kevin Costner.

Cameron was using a large room off the first-floor kitchen of the
Sydney Poitier Building at Sony Studios for the first read-through with
Tom Cruise. He'd just agreed and signed to do *Jerry Maguire*. Cameron's
little movie had suddenly taken on world-class proportions. The budget, which had been a respectful thirty-five million dollars, an average
budget for a Hollywood film, now shot to the middle sixties. All because of two words written on a piece of paper—*Tom Cruise.*

Who was Tom Cruise? Would he be similar to an Al Pacino, a
Marlon Brando, or a Barbra Streisand?

Whoosh! A charging figure with another behind it double-timed
through a doorway, down the hall, and into the rehearsal room. They
were a *blur.*

"Who was that?" I asked Bryan.

"That was Tom Cruise!" Bryan answered.

• • •

I walked into the room and looked carefully at our lead actor. He wore dark jeans and a white T-shirt. His hair was wet. He moved quickly around the room, introducing himself, while the second part of the blur, Michael Doven, listened and jotted notes.

"Hello, I'm Tom Cruise." It was a bit like introducing Christmas; he was internationally the biggest movie star, financially, in the history of cinema. His pictures brought in more money than the pictures of anyone else, *by far*. And with the soon-to-be released *Mission: Impossible*, his popularity and fortunes would grow even larger.

"Tom," Cameron called, "I want you to meet my assistant, Jerry Ziesmer."

Tom turned and moved quickly to Cameron's side.

"I'm Tom Cruise," he said, as he crunched my hand in a firm handshake while his eyes riveted into mine. He was *landing* his words. There was no doubt that he was *Tom Cruise*, and he made sure I'd never forget him. And I never will.

Marlon Brando mumbled a "Hi" when we met. Mel Gibson and Kevin Costner were coherent and friendly. I think Michele Pfeiffer was stoned. John Huston was the warm-hearted King Lear, and Laurence Fishburne was fourteen and the pure soul.

Tom Cruise? He was a force. He was energy. He was stronger and inwardly more powerful than any actor I'd ever met. Was it Tom Cruise, or was it "Tom Cruise, Megabucks superstar"? The answer came the next morning in about a thirty-pound package.

The next morning the "blurs" were not blurring. Tom Cruise walked peacefully through the doorway and down the hall carrying his young son. Michael Doven was walking behind him holding a stuffed toy.

Tom remembered each of our names as he introduced his three-year-old son to us. There was no doubt in my mind that was the Tom Cruise who would become Cameron's *Jerry Maguire*.

Every studio has them, and Columbia Studios was no exception. The "Suits." They're the executives who come down to *talk* if there's any problem with the shooting schedule or the budget. On *Jerry Maguire* we had the finest production executive in Hollywood, Gary Martin. We'd known each other for years. Whenever it was time for a talk, I always started with the geraniums.

Every day during lunch I watched our dailies at the Backstage Theatre, across the studio alley from the Poitier building. After the dailies, I would hurry down the alley to Main Street and Suzanne's production trailer. We always tried to share a few moments during lunch.

While I walked down the street, I checked John Milius, one of the writers on *Apocalypse Now*. He always sat on a white bench on the south side of Main Street as he surveyed the studio crowd. He had taken Steven Spielberg skeet shooting during *1941*; I'd have paid a lot of money to have seen that.

I smiled and nodded at John, when, out of the side of my eye, I caught the image of a large man eating an ice-cream cone. He was a *suit*, but I had first met him when he carried a hammer and was the construction coordinator on *Annie* in 1981.

I knew he had better places to munch his ice-cream cone; he was waiting for me. We had fallen a bit behind schedule. I was expecting a "suit" to come acalling.

"Gary!" I greeted him. "Those geraniums you gave me from the Finale set on *Annie*, they're still growing. What's it been? Sixteen years?" I glanced back at John Milius; he never missed a thing.

Gary took another bite of his ice cream.

"Nineteen eighty-one right? The summer?"

Gary nodded and ate his ice cream.

"You know Suzanne is right down there in our production trailer. I'd sure like to take her by your office and show her your wife's needlework. Suzanne does a bit with a needle, too."

Gary nodded and ate his ice cream.

"You still have the one your wife did of the Columbia logo on your wall? Lot of work in something like that. Different colors," I went on.

Gary kept eating his ice cream.

"Ever see Howard Pine?" Howard was an old Columbia executive when Gary first switched over to production, right after *Annie*.

Gary stopped eating for a moment.

"He's down in Arizona. Not so good. Really sad, Jer."

"I'm sorry to hear that," I said, and I was.

We stood together on the studio's Main Street for another few minutes without saying a word. Gary finished up his ice-cream cone, and I watched him and John Milius.

Finally, Gary took a little paper napkin and wiped his fingers.

"We've talked," Gary said to me, and checked my eyes to make sure I understood.

"Don't worry, Gary. Our film's fine. Nothing to worry about. I'd tell you if there was," I said.

He nodded, tossed his napkin into a trash bin, and walked back toward his office.

Gary Martin's a movie person who knows what you go through in making a movie, plus he's a studio executive. You can't hardly find those anymore.

Different actors prepare in different ways. Marlon Brando played a tape into his ear. Al Pacino sat in his dressing room and waited for the right moment to come to him. Dustin Hoffman gently nodded his head until he was ready. But Tom Cruise? He jumped rope.

"Give me a warning," Tom would say.

He was on the set. We'd rehearsed the scene. The crew was tweaking the last little bit, and Tom wanted his final warning.

I looked over the crew, signaled for them to be very quiet, then I gave Tom a nod signifying we were ready when he was.

Tom held his hand out, and Michael Doven placed a jump rope into his hand.

Womp . . . womp . . . womp . . . Tom's jump rope would hit the floor as Tom jumped faster and faster.

I watched his face, and when I thought he was about ready, I yelled, "Roll it!"

He'd throw down the jump rope and walk into the set, and Cameron would call "Action!" It worked for him; it worked for Cameron; it worked for *Jerry Maguire*.

Tom wasn't that different. When Robert DeNiro would be ready, he'd give me a "roll it" gesture with his hand, and I'd get things going.

James Earl Jones made it easy. He'd say "Ready," in his deep, resonant voice.

Dustin Hoffman and Al Pacino were already acting and in character as they got to their marks; I'd roll the camera as soon as they were in front of it.

With Marlon Brando, when he heard me roll the camera, he'd say, "What? Why'd you do that?"

"Are you ready, Marlon?" I'd ask quietly, not wanting to disturb his preparation.

"Yeah, I'm ready. Let's go," he'd say, then he'd give me his impish bad-boy smile.

Ziggy and I sat on an old concrete bench where we could look east down the whole length of Main Street at the old M-G-M Studios. I didn't want Jerry Maguire *to end without Ziggy being with me.*

Tom Lawrence, an old friend, had picked Ziggy up at his apartment, about three blocks north of the studio on Motor Avenue, and had driven him to our production trailer. Suzanne then walked with Ziggy and found me on our sound stage. It was lunchtime, and neither Ziggy nor I was hungry, so the two of us walked outside and sat down on the concrete bench.

Ziggy had been with me most of my career, and now he was eighty-six. We sat quietly together. I thought of how we met on The Way We Were, *of working together on* Annie *in New Jersey, of all our films over the last twenty-five years.*

Ziggy had other memories.

"Your sound stage, that's where Mickey filmed the Hardy Boys, *right there," Ziggy began. "We used to come back this way toward wardrobe, back down Main Street. That was 1937, or '36 I think," Ziggy added.*

I watched my friend's face, and I knew he was seeing himself and Mickey Rooney back then, running between the sound stages, shouting and laughing, and probably causing a lot of hell. That was more than sixty years ago.

"See there, that big sound stage? That's where we did Captains Courageous. *Good picture!" Ziggy looked and smiled, then turned back to me. "Do you remember it?"*

"Of course," I answered, but I was only remembering my Ziggy and our years of working together.

"Mickey hated working on that!" and Ziggy laughed, "I re- member!"

I laughed with my old friend, then I turned away. Ziggy had never seen me cry.

We traveled to Tempe, Arizona, to film the football game at the end of *Jerry Maguire*. The football game and the extras reminded me of being with Larry Franco on *Black Sunday*.

One of our production assistants was excited about working with the fourteen thousand extras on *Jerry Maguire*.

"What's the largest number of extras you've ever worked with?" he asked me.

I thought of Larry and me at the Super Bowl twenty years before. The *national anthem*.

"Eighty-six thousand," I answered casually, as I walked toward the far end zone.

Cameron had used me as an actor in *Say Anything* . . . and in *Singles*; my part in *Jerry Maguire* was at the final football game. He cast me as the trainer who gave aid to Cuba Gooding as he lay in the end zone at the end of the movie. "Can you feel your legs?" I asked. "Blink!"

The cast and crew enjoyed seeing me look into Cuba's face and ask him over and over, "Can you feel your legs?" I tried every line reading I could, hoping Cameron would find one he liked and I could get back to just being the assistant director. I must have tried too hard.

"Ziesmer, you're *pushing*!" Cuba said to me during one take. I was going to ask for a jump rope, but I wasn't sure how TC would take it.

We finished filming football in Tempe late on Saturday night. Suzanne and I took the early Sunday morning flight back to Los Angeles. It was April 28.

No one was in our home when we arrived. We got our suitcases inside, then checked the mail, and turned on our answering machine. The message played that's every parent's nightmare: *Your son, Christopher Ziesmer, is in the Intensive Care Unit at Century City Hospital. We suggest you* . . .

Suzanne and I walked toward his bed. Tubes, IVs, monitoring equipment crisscrossed his body. Chris looked like he had been caught in a web. I looked for injury, the result of an accident, broken bones, blood, wounds; there weren't any.

"What's wrong with him?" I asked the nurse.

A young doctor answered. "Your son took a number of sleeping pills, eighty-three," he said.

"Sleeping pills?" I fought my mind. "How could he take that many?"

"Your son attempted suicide last night."

I was in Death's abyss. I looked back at the Ifugao dancers, then I

*turned and stared as deeply into the abyss as I could. I saw nothing
as I inched forward.*

We had more than two months of filming left on *Jerry Maguire*. I had
heard a rumor that Steven Spielberg was coming to our stage the very
next day. To go to the studio each day was a blessing; to be at our home
and to *wonder* would've been so much harder.

I wasn't sure what depression was. Where did it come from? Chris
was placed in a rehabilitation facility in Tarzana, near our home. We
could visit him every weekend. Our education to understand the beast
that dwelt deep inside Chris began.

There was a family support group at the rehabilitation center
that met Saturday mornings for just the parents and family. Afterward
you could go outside to a concrete patio area and meet with the patients.

I sat with Chris at a small wooden table. I had brought his electric
razor, some deodorant, and a carton of cigarettes. After the pleasantries,
we sat in silence.

"Chris, I love you. I just don't understand. We all love you," I said,
searching for meaning in all that had happened.

It took a long time for him to speak.

"Dad, do you remember Yuri's class at Westland School, Group
Three?"

I nodded that I remembered. Group Three at Westland was the
second grade in most schools.

"You remember that outside Yuri's room there was a harbor made
out of concrete?"

I remembered. I had helped repair the harbor during a family work
day at the school.

"Well, Yuri got a whole lot of tadpoles, and we put them into the
harbor. We were supposed to watch them over the months as they
became frogs. First, some developed into frogs and got out of the
harbor, then more and more, until there was only one tadpole left."

We stared at each other. I could tell Chris was struggling to tell me
something. I couldn't seem to grasp it.

"One tadpole never became a frog, and I'm that tadpole."

*Suzanne and I sat in the pew for family. She held my hand and
squeezed compassion from her body into mine. Even with her
strength, my tears came, as I knew they would.*

> *We walked across the tiny cemetery past the crypts of Helen Hayes, Ross Hunter, and Marilyn Monroe to the new grave, with the fresh flowers and the ribbons still in place.*
>
> *I stood silently deep within the abyss and said a prayer for my son's soul and mine, one that I would repeat each day for the rest of my life.*

I could still hear the *Jerry Maguire* celebration as I walked down Main Street toward Suzanne's production trailer. The last of the crew and drivers hurried past me on their way to the second floor of the Poitier Building. The champagne would still be cold.

The old television wardrobe department was on my left; that's where I was wardrobed thirty-five years ago for the pilot of *The Lieutenant.*

I passed the M-G-M production building where we had our offices for *Rocky II.* That production manager from *Rocky II* lives right near where we do. We're friends.

Suzanne wasn't quite ready to go. A few more notes to be *sure* that all of the communication equipment was marked correctly to be returned the next day. She looked out at me. Usually I was anxious to leave the studio and go home. I didn't mind if she took her time that night. It was our last one.

The Premiere of *Jerry Maguire*

It was more than five months later—the middle of December 1996. Suzanne and I left our home and drove south on the San Diego Freeway toward the Village Theatre in Westwood. We were going to the premiere of *Jerry Maguire.*

Westwood was jammed with the press and movie fans. We couldn't find a parking place near the Village Theatre, so I drove south down Gayley to Kinross Avenue and found an underground parking garage.

We walked onto Gayley and saw the pizza stand that was Tom Cruise's choice for "Best Pizza." We went another block east and then walked back up Broxton Avenue.

I let go of Suzanne's hand as I walked to the curb in front of the Regent Theatre and stopped. That was where I'd stood twenty-five years ago with Robert Surtees after another premiere. I remembered how he'd tried to comfort me. He told me to drive to Carmel and stay a couple of days at the Blue Bird, and I did.

Robert Surtees had died in 1985.

I saw Suzanne watching me.

"The premiere of *Lost Horizon* was here at the Regent Theatre," I explained.

Suzanne was very good at understanding without having to speak.

I looked north, toward the lights for *Jerry Maguire*. I could hear the loudspeakers and cheers as another celebrity arrived. I took Suzanne's hand, and we walked toward the premiere of *Jerry Maguire*.

The lights, limos, and police lines were in front of the Village Theatre. A few thousand movie fans were behind the police barricades, and another two hundred studio people were loitering in front of the theatre.

Suzanne and I looked at the entrance to the theatre. It was carpeted with a thick maroon carpet. On each side of the carpet, brass pedestals held long maroon ropes that kept back the scores of fans and photographers. It was a frightening corridor, but it was the only way into the theatre.

We crossed Weyburn Avenue, showed our tickets, and quickly made our way along the carpet and into the crowded theatre.

Jonathon Lipnicki, the young boy in the movie, arrived just as we did. He wore a suit he'd gotten especially for that night. He had to show it off to Suzanne.

Alice, Cameron's mother, greeted us. She played one of the divorced women that talked in Dorothy's living room in the movie. Alice always thanked us for being so good to "her" boy.

We saw Cameron and Nancy. They hid their excitement well. We'd talk later. It was Cameron's night. I was glad Suzanne and I were a part of it.

Cast and crew members greeted us. Our *Jerry Maguire* production assistants talked about their new romances, new apartments, and the movies they were doing then.

Ziggy wouldn't be there. The hour was too late for him, and there were too many people.

An old friend from my Northwestern University years, Russ Lunday, sat next to me. In *Jerry Maguire* he played the doctor in the hockey player's hospital room at the beginning of the movie.

Tom Cruise and Nic had attended the premiere in New York City, three days earlier. They were in London doing a film with Stanley Kubrick. I wondered how Mr. Doven got along with Stanley Kubrick and his assistant directors.

The theatre lights dimmed a bit. Suddenly I got a chill all over. People hurried to their seats. There was an excitement in the theatre. My heart was thumping. I squeezed Suzanne's hand. I knew she cared as much as I did, and always had. It was more than just another film for us; *Jerry Maguire* was very special.

> *I couldn't help looking for our son Chris, wanting him to come walking down the aisle looking for his Pops. Suzanne had told me it could take years before I'd stop looking for him. I was still on my journey within the abyss, but every day was bringing me closer to the other side.*

I glanced at Cameron; he looked so happy and confident. Nancy was smiling. Suzanne was smiling. I was the basket case. I could feel the perspiration on my palms. Suzanne patted my hand.

"It's going to be OK," she whispered.

I nodded and squeezed her hand.

"You're always nervous," she smiled at me. "Every time."

"I am?"

"Remember our senior year in high school, the opening night of *The Member of the Wedding?*" she asked.

I remembered. They all meant so much to me.

The screen lit up and *Jerry Maguire* began. I glanced at Russ Lunday when the hospital room scene came on. He smiled and mouthed his lines as he watched his image on the screen. Suzanne and I exchanged a look and settled in to watching the film. We'd pretty well decided that the baggage scene at the airport and Tom's first scene at Dorothy's house were key scenes to judge the audience's reaction.

There was so much laughter around me, that I forgot to pay attention to those scenes. When the house lights came up at the end of

the movie, there was applause. Honest applause from a premiere audience that loved *Jerry Maguire*. They *loved* it! They *really* loved it!

I knew that somewhere Robert Surtees was happy for me and so was
Chico Day. Ethel Waters and Gene Kelly were laughing. John Huston
was shaking his right arm at me, grinning with his tongue between his
teeth. And Chris was happily learning all of the lines for *Jerry Maguire*,
just like he'd done for *Apocalypse Now*.

Suzanne's face told me everything: *Jerry Maguire* was a winner. A big,
big winner! A home run! I was so happy for us, for Cameron, for all
who'd worked on *Jerry Maguire*, and for all those who'd be seeing the
film in the years to come.

What makes a movie a winner? It's the same as for any art form. It's
when you remember it with terrific excitement, whether it's an *Apocalypse Now* or it's a *Jerry Maguire*.

I got another one! My last one. Just like Ted Williams and Michael
Jordan.

Index

About the Author

For three decades Jerry Ziesmer has been the assistant director for the major film directors and cinema artists of our age, including Francis Coppola and Marlon Brando on *Apocalypse Now*, Steven Spielberg with François Truffaut on *Close Encounters of the Third Kind*, Brian De Palma and Al Pacino on *Scarface*, Sydney Pollack with Robert Redford and Barbra Streisand on *The Way We Were*, and Cameron Crowe plus Tom Cruise on *Jerry Maguire*.

Mr. Ziesmer is a longtime member of the Academy of Motion Picture Arts and Sciences and the Directors Guild of America. He attended Northwestern University and did his graduate work at UCLA, where he wrote *Stan Laurel: The Little One*, a study of comedy film technique.

He and his wife, Suzanne, live in Los Angeles and are currently working for Steven Spielberg on another Cameron Crowe project. They also teach two film production classes each year for the UCLA Extension: The Craft of the Assistant Director and The Path of the AD, as well as mentoring serious film students and young professionals by e-mail at AC563@LAFN.ORG.